The Currents of War

The Currents of War

A New History of American-Japanese Relations, 1899–1941

Sidney Pash

University Press of Kentucky

Scholarly publisher for the Commonwealth,
serving Bellarmine University, Berea College, Centre College of Kentucky, Eastern Kentucky University, The Filson Historical Society, Georgetown College, Kentucky Historical Society, Kentucky State University, Morehead State University, Murray State University, Northern Kentucky University, Transylvania University, University of Kentucky, University of Louisville, and Western Kentucky University.

Editorial and Sales Offices: The University Press of Kentucky
663 South Limestone Street, Lexington, Kentucky 40508-4008
www.kentuckypress.com

Library of Congress Cataloging-in-Publication Data

Pash, Sidney.
The currents of war : a new history of American-Japanese relations, 1899-1941 / Sidney Pash.
pages cm. — (Studies in conflict, diplomacy, and peace)
Includes bibliographical references and index.
ISBN 978-0-8131-4423-8 (hardcover : acid-free paper) --
ISBN 978-0-8131-4425-2 (pdf) -- ISBN 978-0-8131-4424-5 (epub)
1. United States—Foreign relations—Japan. 2. Japan—Foreign relations—United States. 3. Pacific Area—Strategic aspects—History—20th century. 4. World War, 1939-1945—Causes. I. Title.
E183.8.J3P35 2014
327.7305209'04—dc23 2013041233

This book is printed on acid-free paper meeting the requirements of the American National Standard for Permanence in Paper for Printed Library Materials.

Manufactured in the United States of America.

Member of the Association of American University Presses

For
my mother
and father

A nation committed irrevocably to a course of action loses the power to exercise choice, to accept offers, to make conditions.

—Harry Dexter White (1941)

War contains so much folly, as well as wickedness, that much is to be hoped from the progress of reason; and if anything is to be hoped, every thing ought to be tried.

—James Madison (1792)

Contents

Preface xi

Introduction 1

1. The Foundations of Containment 13
2. The Rise and Fall of the Washington Conference System 49
3. Into the Abyss 85
4. Containment at High Tide 111
5. Sinners in the Hands of an Angry Department 143
6. The Revolutionary Summer 171
7. Rollback 193
8. All or Nothing 217

Conclusion 251

Acknowledgments 257

Notes 259

Bibliography 311

Index 333

Illustrations follow page 110

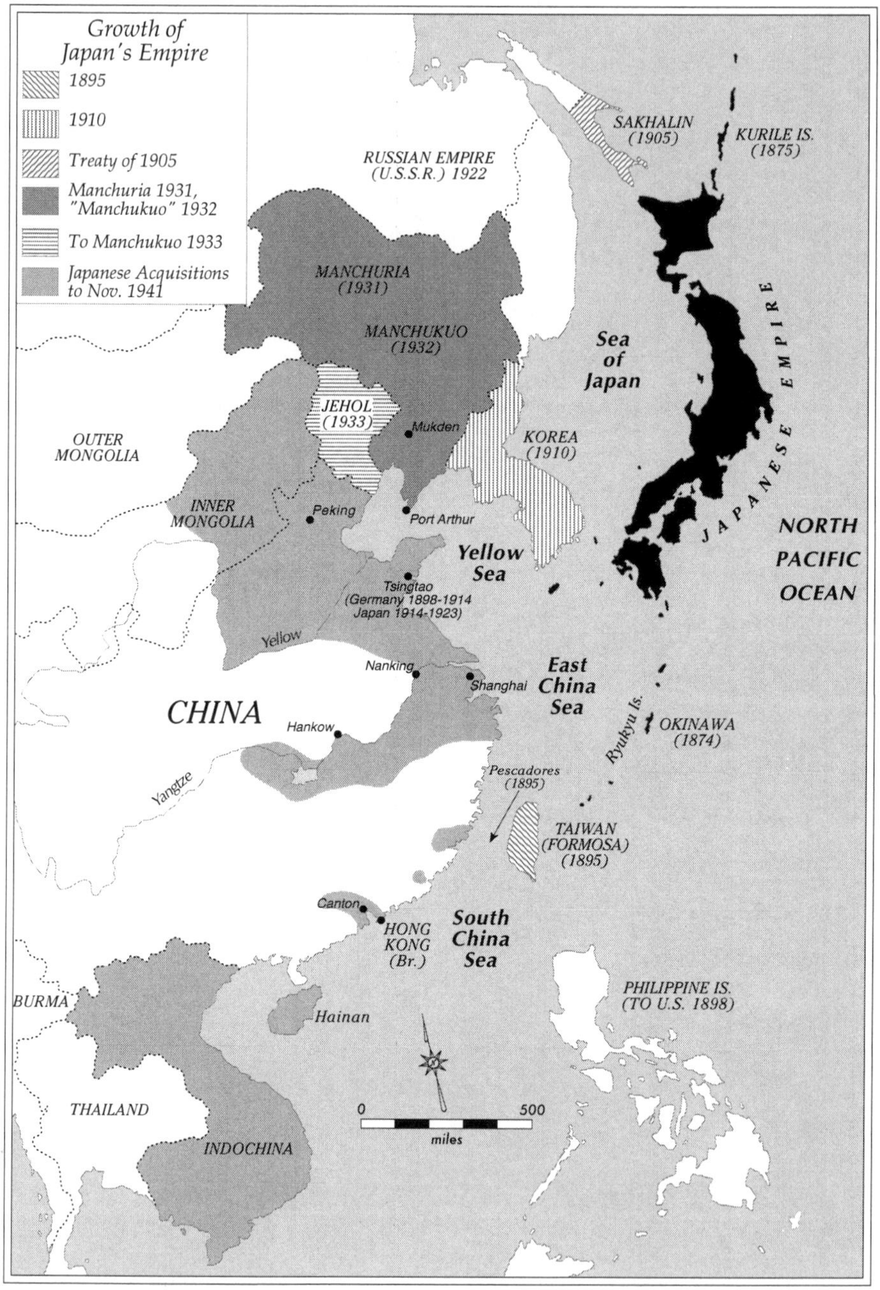

Map by Dick Gilbreath, University of Kentucky Cartography Lab.

Preface

Admiral Yamamoto knew that the Japanese Empire's future rested on the opening battle of the war. His task force had to sail undetected over a vast sea and destroy the enemy fleet in port. If Japan's opponent detected his ships or set a trap, all would be lost. A smashing victory in the war's early hours could lead to a negotiated settlement but not victory, for the enemy possessed a true two-ocean navy, and Japan's European ally had not proved that it could prevent the redeployment of this second, more powerful armada. Compared to its opponent, whose people numbered over 100 million and whose territory spanned a continent, Japan was a second-rate power.

The roots of the fast-approaching war stretched back to the last century and centered on competition over China. Japan's rival across the sea, driven by economic and security concerns, supported Chinese resistance to Japanese territorial and commercial expansion and in doing so made a fundamental solution to Sino-Japanese difficulties all but impossible. Successive cabinets attempted to reconcile competition over China and stabilize Japan's position on the Asian mainland, and, when these attempts failed, Tokyo sought a great-power alliance. While the prime minister, Taro Katsura, believed that an alliance would ease Japanese security concerns, make the empire's rivals more tractable, and pave the way for the fulfillment of Japanese ambitions in Asia, events soon proved him wrong.[1]

Japan's alliance with Europe's strongest power did nothing to deter its rival. Thousands of miles from Tokyo, at the edge of a great continent, in the capital named for its legendary leader, the empire's adversary pursued a complicated strategy designed to contain Japanese expansion. This policy was predicated in part on the belief that Japan would never wage a war it could not hope to win, and, while race no doubt played a part in this calculation, so too did numbers. Population, industry, wealth, and military power all weighed heavily against Japan. The empire did have a small advantage in that any conflict would take place near the home islands, but the enemy could easily offset this limited tactical edge with a redeployment of men and matériel to the Far East. Tokyo's rival was a continental power, yet with its great naval base standing astride Japan it projected military might to the very heart of the empire.

In the months leading up to war, Japan's rival celebrated the success of its strategy as desultory negotiations bought time for the deployment of tens of thousands of soldiers and scores of warships to Asia. Yet this policy may have been too successful, for in the final autumn of peace the conviction that Japan would never fight had spread to friend and foe alike, thus undercutting any impetus to reach a successful agreement. On the eve of war, both the British and the Russian ambassadors doubted that Japan would fight, and, given this conviction, how could a great power make concessions to a second-tier nation? Moreover, might Japan interpret an eleventh-hour compromise as a sign of weakness? The commander of the Pacific Fleet thought so and warned: "Concession to Japan will lead us to a more certain break."[2]

In Japan, meanwhile, the government at last cast the dice for war. Japan's last prewar prime minister, Katsura, a stubborn opponent of the coming conflict, maintained that the enemy gave the empire little choice. "There is no question," he argued, "but that . . . [our opponent's] aim was from the start to increase her military and naval forces and then reject Japan's demands." Given this policy, he noted, "if Japan does not now go to war and defend her threatened interests, she will eventually have to kowtow." The decision to wage war, however, could not mask fatalism akin to desperation. Another former prime minister and onetime general, Aritomo Yamagata—hardly a rarity for interwar Japan—neatly summarized his nation's position: "Although we cannot foretell victory or defeat, we must enter the battle confident of victory. If we should by any chance fail, it would be an immeasurable catastrophe." With no better option available, Japan's senior leaders opted to gamble all on a war that the country would not likely survive. One day after the imperial conference endorsed the cabinet's decision for war, Admiral Gonnohyoe Yamamoto, the navy minister, ordered Admiral Heihachiro Togo to attack the Pacific Fleet at Port Arthur.[3]

Russian containment had failed.

Japan's victory over Russia in the ensuing Russo-Japanese War fundamentally reshaped the Far Eastern strategic landscape as well as Japanese-American relations. Before 1904, Americans saw Japan as the Open Door's champion. By the end of 1905, Tokyo replaced St. Petersburg as the greatest threat to China, and for the next thirty-six years successive American administrations worked to safeguard the Open Door and contain Japanese expansion on the Asian mainland.

The Open Door, which supported commercial equality in China as well as China's territorial and administrative integrity, defined American foreign policy in the Far East for nearly half a century. Every president sought to guarantee equal access to the China market for American business, and, while military strategists differed as to the importance of the Open Door, preserving that country's territorial integrity remained a critical objective of US foreign policy.[4]

The architects of the American containment of Japan did not use the term *containment* to describe their policy of combating Japanese continental expansion. Nonetheless, beginning with one Roosevelt and ending with another, Washington protected the Open Door, though not always perfectly, by limiting the extension of Japanese control over China.[5]

Successive administrations built containment on four firm pillars, the first three of which President Theodore Roosevelt constructed between 1905 and 1908. Roosevelt broke ground on containment's first pillar, maintenance of the balance of power, in 1905 when he helped broker the Portsmouth Treaty, which ended the Russo-Japanese War. He recognized that a balance among the competing powers could exercise a restraining hand on further Japanese expansion, and, while Japanese power in Asia only increased over time in relation to that of Great Britain, France, Russia, and the United States, preventing Japan from gaining hegemony in Asia remained a consistent American goal. He erected a second pillar, military deterrence, when he sent the Great White Fleet to Japan on its 1907 world cruise. Coming at a time when a US-Japanese war seemed so likely that the president also ordered commanders in the Philippines to prepare for a Japanese attack, the fleet appeared to deter Japan and convinced Roosevelt that his decision produced "the most important service [he] rendered to peace." While this was not the last time that Washington used military deterrence, thereafter policymakers preferred to use a third pillar, diplomatic engagement. In May 1908, before the fleet had even returned home, Japan and America agreed to a five-year arbitration treaty. In November of that year, Secretary of State Elihu Root and Ambassador Kogoro Takahira forged a pivotal agreement that provided for American recognition of Japan's sphere in Manchuria in return for Tokyo's recognition of US control in the Philippines. The agreement also pledged both governments to respect the status quo in the Far East and work to support Chinese independence. Successive administrations used diplomacy to gain even more explicit Japanese support for the Open Door as well as for the League of Nations, naval disarmament, and the renunciation of war.[6]

President Woodrow Wilson built containment's last pillar, economic warfare, following America's entrance into the First World War. On August 2, 1917, the White House announced that the United States would export steel only under export license. This, coupled with Washington's earlier decision to rejoin the multinational banking consortium and challenge Japan's growing financial hold on China, led Tokyo to dispatch the Viscount Kikujiro Ishii to America to reiterate Japan's fidelity to the Open Door. Overall, these four pillars supported a remarkably successful policy that helped maintain American commercial, missionary, and political activity in China and prevented, especially after 1918, the strongest nation in Asia from imposing its will on China.[7]

Following the Far Eastern Crisis of 1931–1933, in which Japan seized Manchuria and created the puppet state of Manchukuo, policymakers modified the means and methods for containing Japan, yet the overall goal remained essentially unchanged. After 1933, containment sought to prevent Japan from expanding beyond Manchuria, and, following the start of the Second Sino-Japanese War in July 1937, the Franklin D. Roosevelt administration sought to limit Japanese gains in China proper. If American goals remained unchanged, Washington's methods for halting Japan changed considerably. First, while successive administrations had employed diplomatic engagement, the architects of containment now sought to restrain Japan by a deliberate policy of disengagement in which Washington refused to conclude any diplomatic agreements that might in some measure strengthen Japan or weaken China. Second, with China now united under Chiang Kai-shek and the Nationalist Party, senior officials worked to increase American economic and military aid in order to even the odds on the battlefield and bolster Chinese morale. Along with these new measures, the architects of American containment employed, on a scale previously unknown, traditional methods, including military deterrence and economic coercion.

While often unpopular among supporters of China as well as among interventionists who felt it did too little, isolationists who felt it did too much, and competing government agencies and turf-conscious officials, American containment succeeded beyond all expectations. By July 1940, Chinese armies had tied down the vast Japanese war machine for three years, which was no small feat given that as recently as 1931 Japan had driven China from Manchuria in a matter of months and set up the puppet state of Manchukuo the following year.

Even as America thwarted the Japanese war effort in China between 1937 and 1940, the prime objective of American containment had begun to undergo significant changes. For decades, American strategists worked to check Japanese expansion in China in order to support a long-range American foreign policy goal, the Open Door. After September 1940, however, *policymakers sought to contain Japan within China in order to secure a more important, more immediate, short-term goal, the weakening of the Axis Alliance.* If Japan remained mired in China, policymakers reasoned, it could threaten neither the Western democracies nor the Soviet Union. This change paralleled Hitler's threat to Europe and the growing German-Japanese rapprochement that culminated in Tokyo's decision to join the Axis Alliance in September 1940.

The following year, policymakers rightly celebrated the success of the new American containment policy. Tokyo did not follow up on its occupation of northern French Indochina and also refrained from violating Thai sovereignty. Nor, despite German triumphs in Europe, did Japan move against the East Indies, Malaya, or Singapore. Most importantly, Japan did not join its Axis partner's attack on the Soviet Union in June 1941. By confining the Japanese military within China, Washington had apparently secured its more important short-term objective, the weakening of the Axis Alliance.

Despite their continued success, American officials began to abandon their heretofore cautious and successful containment policy during the summer of 1941 in favor of a strategy that sought to secure *both an immediate imperative, the weakening of the Axis Alliance, and a fundamental long-term objective, the maintenance of the Open Door.* This shift in policy was not always clear, nor was it universally popular, especially among naval leaders and some State Department and Treasury officials. Unfortunately, their cautious voices increasingly were in the minority, especially after the German invasion of the Soviet Union convinced a growing number of policymakers that, as long as the Nazi-Soviet War continued, the United States could drastically increase economic sanctions against Japan with little risk of war. As the fighting in Russia dragged on into autumn without a decision and the Anglo-American strategic position improved worldwide, senior officials discarded containment and, in an effort to secure at once both short-term objectives and a long-term goal, worked to roll back Japanese gains in China and break the Axis Alliance. Tragically, this decision coincided with the final success of American containment. After a generation of effort, this patient American policy had brought about during the last half of 1941 a Japanese decision to reorient the empire's foreign policy in such a way that the attainment of both short-term goals and a long-term objective were within Washington's grasp.

Throughout the summer and fall of 1941, American officials, like their Russian counterparts some forty years earlier, conducted elaborate negotiations designed to buy time but never bear fruit. In Japan, meanwhile, the government of Hideki Tojo grew convinced that additional negotiations were useless and would only further play into American hands. Mirroring the fatalism of an earlier generation, Japan for the second time chose to wage a war that most senior statesmen did not believe the empire would survive.

The Currents of War is an attempt to tell two stories at once. One is the interesting story of a critical chapter in the history of Japanese-American relations that ended at Pearl Harbor. The other story is the far more important examination of why American officials abandoned their successful containment policy in favor of a strategy that brought on the Pacific War, a conflict that sowed the seeds of instability in Asia for a generation and led to American military involvement in both Korea and Vietnam.[8]

This study does not try to uncover a Roosevelt administration plot to deliberately bring the United States into World War II. Many postwar writers and historians have labored to construct a compelling narrative that connects the White House to the agonizing image of the Pacific Fleet, smashed and burning at anchor in Pearl Harbor. That the president sought to ensure England's survival and bring America into the war goes without saying. That Japan's attack on Pearl Harbor and Germany's prompt declaration of war on the United States served these ends is a given. But the argument that the president and his advisers deliberately brought about the Japanese attack remains spurious. While there is little to celebrate in the run-up to war with Japan, there is no need to twist a series of mistakes into a conspiracy.

Where possible, this study attempts to tell the Japanese side of the story, but those wishing a fuller account should examine any number of excellent works, including James William Morley's multivolume translation of *Taiheiyo senso e no michi* (Japan's Road to the Pacific War) or Michael Barnhart's single-volume *Japan and the World since 1868.* Prewar Anglo-American diplomacy and the coming of the Pacific War, meanwhile, can best be understood by reading volume 1 of Warren F. Kimball's *Churchill and Roosevelt: The Complete Correspondence* or Anthony Best's *Britain, Japan, and Pearl Harbor: Avoiding War in East Asia, 1936–1941.*[9]

Race, religion, and economics also played a role in shaping American-Japanese relations, and the reader interested primarily in these issues should consult John Dower's *War without Mercy: Race and Power in the Pacific War,* James Reed's *The Missionary Mind and American East Asian Policy, 1911–1915,* or William Appleman Williams's *The Tragedy of American Diplomacy.*[10]

The story that follows is primarily an American one, based largely on American sources and records and the papers of the Americans who influenced, made, and carried out the policy that protected the Open Door and eventually led to Pearl Harbor. What follows, then, is in some respects an old-fashioned diplomatic history that focuses on the hopes and fears of elites, primarily Americans. A focus on policymakers and their policies long ago fell out of style among historians, but, especially when studying the history of American foreign relations, I have become convinced, we forget the old ways at our peril.

Introduction

Commodore Matthew Perry was not a superstitious man. If he were, he would not have decided to follow the course to Edo Bay charted by earlier, failed US expeditions to Japan. Since 1790, some two dozen American vessels and countless others from Europe had visited the secluded islands. The Japanese, however, had turned away all expeditions because they threatened the shogun's self-imposed policy of isolation. During the fifteenth and sixteenth centuries, the islands' great feudal landed families, the daimyo, had waged a brutal and protracted civil war for control of the nation before Nobunaga Oda all but unified the country in 1580. Several factors contributed to Oda's success, foremost among them the skillful use of Western technology, which allowed him to impose his will on the other, less fortunate families. Oda was murdered, however, before he could cement his control over the country, so for another decade the great families vied to rule Japan. Finally, with its victory in the epoch-making battle of Sekigahara in October 1600, the Tokugawa clan began its 268-year reign. Determined to isolate Japan from the outside world and deny the other powerful feudal families access to the kind of Western technology that had proved so vital to men like Oda, the Tokugawa instituted a strict policy of isolation. Perry had come to Japan to tear down this wall of seclusion.[1]

Perry's first glimpse of the shore revealed little owing to the typically dense July haze, but he believed that he knew what awaited him. The Japanese would resist him as they had the USS *Morrison* in 1837 when that vessel arrived in the islands carrying shipwrecked Japanese sailors. More recently, the Japanese had defied the US Asiatic Squadron, and a Japanese sailor knocked its commander, Commodore James Biddle, to the deck during an altercation. Despite this disheartening résumé of failure, President Millard Fillmore had decided to send Perry on yet another mission, this one to open Japan to American commerce and to arrange for a permanent diplomatic presence.[2]

Perry felt certain that he had devised a successful strategy for dealing with the sure-to-be-truculent Japanese. The key to success, he believed, lay in the story of an 1849 expedition sent to Kyushu, the southernmost of the Japanese main islands, which succeeded in securing the release of seventeen stranded seamen. Japanese authorities had attempted to drive the vessel, the USS *Preble,* from the harbor by marshaling nearby forces. However, when the expedition's leader, Commodore James Glynn, explained "with the rough bluntness of a sailor . . . that they must immediately give up the men, or means would be found to compel them to do so," the sailors were quickly released. The Japanese apparently respected force. Perry thought that the 1849 incident provided a reliable blueprint, and he determined to build on Glynn's strategy and employ both the threat of force as well as "lavish pomp and ceremony."[3]

Soon after arriving in Edo Bay on July 8, 1853, Perry had occasion to test his strategy. As the fog lifted, Mount Fuji became visible, and Perry ordered his crew to make all the usual preparations for "meeting an enemy." He then summoned his captains to his flagship, the USS *Susquehanna,* for a last-minute briefing, after which his four vessels, half a world away from the nearest home port, dropped anchor. The small American flotilla received warning shots from shore and was virtually surrounded by Japanese ships but made no attempt to leave. When a Japanese boat drew alongside the *Susquehanna* in an effort to question the commodore, Perry refused and instead sent an ominous message to the nearby ships that surrounded his small fleet. "If all the boats were not away in fifteen minutes," he warned the Japanese, "he would not be responsible for the consequences." His stick worked, and the offending ships departed. While the commodore had managed to stare down the Japanese, he realized that neither the carrot nor the stick would force the Japanese government to abandon immediately the most effective policy yet devised for controlling its main rivals. Giving up sailors was one thing. Giving up a 250-year-old isolation policy was quite another, and, with supplies dwindling, Perry departed. He warned Japanese authorities, however, that, when he returned the following year, he expected to have his demands met.[4]

The following February, when he returned to Edo Bay, Perry got his answer from a somewhat more cooperative Japanese government. The shogun's senior advisers and the other great families had reached the consensus that resistance was futile and that playing for time—giving in to the Americans slowly and gradually while modernizing the nation—was the best option. Consequently, with the March 1854 Treaty of Kanagawa, the Japanese government agreed to open two ports and receive an American diplomat. Four years later, additional ports were opened, and, as feared, the Tokugawa shogun's days grew numbered.[5]

While it is impossible clearly to define an American view of Japan in the 1850s, it is apparent that in 1853 the US-Japanese relationship was adversarial. Perry sailed into Edo Bay with a specific goal, and the Tokugawa stood in his way. The Americans who came in 1853 also had a predominately negative view of the Japanese and expected to find a people who mistreated American sailors and abhorred Christianity. These were negative qualities indeed, especially to Perry and his four boatloads of Christian sailors, yet the Japanese were also reputed to be "an exceedingly industrious and ingenious people." After arriving in Japan, commander and crewmen alike remarked favorably on Japanese etiquette, the country's natural beauty, and the people's tidiness and sense of order. Not surprisingly, after the Kanagawa Treaty, the Japanese-American relationship lost its adversarial quality, and instead a dominant view emphasizing the friendliness and generosity of the Japanese people emerged.[6]

Of course, not all Japanese welcomed the Westerners who inundated the islands after Perry, but their actions did little to change the prevailing American mind-set. In particular, a group known as the *shishi,* or "men of high purpose," tried to drive the foreigners from Japan and protect the emperor. These patriots assassinated Westerners and those government officials who had allowed the foreigners to enter the country, yet this violence did not alter how most Americans viewed Japan. When activists in the domain of Choshu fired on Western ships in 1864, for example, the *New York Times* informed its readers that the powerful "Prince of Choshu" (no such official existed) had connived to drive foreigners from Japan and that, while he deplored their actions, the "Taicoon" (the shogun) was powerless to stop him. Violence and anti-Americanism were neither inherent nor endemic, the newspaper assured its readers, and in time it predicted that with Western help the Japanese government would soon prove strong enough to keep the country open.[7]

The *Times*'s correspondent was right about a number of things and wrong about many more. Despite foreign aid, the Tokugawa government collapsed in 1868 after a brief rebellion led by the domains of Choshu and Satsuma. The new government, headed by young samurai primarily from these two provinces, proclaimed a restoration of imperial power, yet in reality the boy emperor Meiji remained subservient to the new samurai leadership. Driven by a genuine fear of Western domination, the new government sought to modernize rapidly in order to escape the fate that had befallen most other Asian nations. Modern Western states served as the model for Japanese reformers, and, once it became clear that the overthrow of the Tokugawa meant a further opening of Japan, Americans cheered.

The overthrow of the Tokugawa and the flowering of Japanese reform and modernization soon produced a unique bond between Japan and America. When an 1877 samurai rebellion threatened the new regime, for example, Americans sided with the government over the "quarrelsome, uneasy" samurai, who were "spoiling for a fight." The effusive praise that former president Ulysses S. Grant received during his 1879 visit to Japan, meanwhile, was indicative of the unique and extraordinarily pro-American attitude among the Japanese.[8]

Japan's rapid modernization reminded Americans of their own recent history, and this contributed to a positive view of Japan and a generally friendly US foreign policy. Just as the Meiji Restoration destroyed Japan's hereditary class system, so too did the Civil War and Reconstruction destroy hereditary bound labor in America. Just as the events of 1868 tolled the death knell for Japan's centuries-old decentralized government, so too did Lee's surrender at Appomattox signal the end of extreme states' rights philosophy. With the shogun deposed, Japan's new leaders rushed westward to gain the secrets of modernization, and, with the end of the Civil War, Americans resumed their relentless march across the Pacific in search of markets. Americans appreciated and understood Japan's post-1868 experience because it was their experience as well. The yardsticks that tracked Japanese modernization—rising industrial output, railroad track mileage, literacy, and wealth—were the same measurements that marked America's phenomenal postwar progress.

Perhaps because of these shared experiences, Washington displayed a willingness to work with Japan that was more often than not absent in European capitals. The new Meiji government, for example, found itself bound by a series of unequal Tokugawa treaties that the United States, alone among the major powers, proved willing to revise. Washington even agreed to cooperate with Tokyo's campaign to control antigovernment, foreign-owned Japanese-language newspapers.[9]

In addition to the shared experience of rapid modernization, Americans and Japanese shared a Protestant Christian revival that also drew the two peoples closer together. The Protestant missionaries who arrived in Japan soon after Perry found that modernization and Westernization complemented their work so much so that by the mid-1880s Japan appeared "one of the most promising mission fields in the world." Their progress in converting the Japanese might appear glacial to the contemporary observer, but the *New York Times* declared: "The Japanese are rapidly turning to Christianity—not simply Christian civilization but organic Christianity." Linking Christianity and modernization, the *Times* noted how the traditional "religions of Japan" were "loosing their hold upon that remarkably progressive nation." During the late nineteenth century, Japan occupied the place in missionary hearts that China would assume early in the next century, and these pioneer missionaries propagated both the Protestant faith in Japan and a favorable image of that country in America. Missionaries repeatedly remarked on Japanese progress under the new government and were especially quick to defend Tokyo's treatment of its Christian converts.[10]

This favorable view of Japan as a modernizing and tolerant nation proved fortuitous as it helped to both solidify the positive American mind-set and head off serious discord as both Japan and the United States sought to expand their influence in Asia. Modernization and Westernization, which were intended to preserve Japan's independence, transformed the once isolated and imperiled nation into an imperial power, and Korea, long a protectorate of China, quickly became the first nation to experience the less sanguine results of Japanese progress. Japan's penetration of Korea began in the 1870s and later accelerated as Tokyo attempted to push the enfeebled Chinese from the Hermit Kingdom and modernize the country along Japanese lines. Korean-American relations at this time were colored by the destruction of a US merchant ship and the slaughter of its primarily Chinese and Malayan crew as well as by a series of clashes that accompanied the 1871 American attempt to "open" the country in which three hundred or more Koreans died. Newspaper accounts that described Korean commerce as worthless, the people as "uncivilized," and the government as isolationist no doubt tempered America's commercial ardor as well as any jealousy resulting from Japan's more successful entrée. Normalized Korean-American relations, which came in 1882, did little to promote American trade, and, while Japan's growing position in Korea caused some friction within American business and religious circles, it did not fundamentally disturb Japanese-American relations.[11]

That Americans stood aside quietly as Japan forced open Korea is not surprising. Social Darwinist thinking and America's own genocidal wars against the American Indians conditioned many to see Tokyo's actions as part of the natural order. Indeed, by the 1880s, Japan and the Japanese people had become the Asian embodiment of America and the American people, modern, bustling, dynamic, hardworking, organized, and patriotic. Koreans, on the other hand, represented an Asian version of the American Indian, disorganized, riven by factions, and unwilling to embrace modernity. The language that the leaders of the 1871 American expedition used to describe Koreans—"savages" and a "semi-barbarous and hostile race"—was almost verbatim that used to describe American Indians.[12]

Given this shared view of Korea, American authorities were hardly alarmed when, convinced that a hostile foreign power such as Russia would soon wrest control of the kingdom, Japan precipitated a showdown with China. Watching the long approach of war from the American legation in Seoul, John M. B. Sill, the American minister to Korea, informed Secretary of State Walter Gresham: "Japan seems to be very kindly disposed to Korea. She seems only to desire once [and] for all, to throw off the yoke of Chinese suzerainty, and then to assist her weak neighbor." On the eve of war, Sill wired Gresham that the legation staff and resident Americans were in danger from both Chinese troops and Korean civilians but that the Japanese would protect them if need be. Far from an adversary, Japan was seen by officials as a protector of Americans and Koreans alike.[13]

In the ensuing 1894–1895 Sino-Japanese War, American public opinion backed Japan, and the Cleveland administration offered behind-the-scenes advice to the Japanese on reasonable war aims. As the conflict neared its end, Gresham became an unofficial mediator, and in the resulting Treaty of Shimonoseki Japan gained the Chinese island of Formosa and a sizable war indemnity totaling some $135 million. Faced with the so-called Triple Intervention, in which France, Germany, and Russia used the threat of military force to compel Tokyo to return the Liaotung Peninsula to China, Japan relinquished its most significant spoils. While the Triple Intervention robbed Japan of valuable wartime gains, America's esteem for its plucky protégé remained undiminished. In the midst of the fighting, the Cleveland administration rewarded Tokyo with a new commercial treaty that granted Japan considerable tariff autonomy and ended American extraterritoriality rights. In the intellectual climate of the fin de siècle, Japan represented the civilized West and "the Great Britain of Asia," while China remained a stubborn and decadent example of the East. Dr. R. S. MacArthur, an American missionary with extensive experience in Asia, summed up the prevailing American view of the conflict. "The war between China and Japan," he told an audience in New York City, "is really between barbarism and civilization, between hoary conservatism and modern progress, between heathenism and Christianity."[14]

In the aftermath of Tokyo's victory, however, the first significant strains intruded on the heretofore tranquil Japanese-American relationship. While missionaries continued to present a positive image of Japan, many Japanese Christians began to chafe at the control imposed by their Western brethren and sought to manage their own religious affairs. If Japan controlled its own armed forces, they reasoned, why not their own Christian churches? If this was a logical question for a successful modernizer, it was also an unpopular one in Japan's American missionary community. A second source of Japanese-US friction grew out of Japan's economic modernization. By the mid-1890s, the Meiji economy produced consumer goods for Japan and much of the Asian mainland, much to the detriment of American exporters.[15]

The subtle change in the way that missionaries and businessmen viewed Japan, and the sudden recognition of Japanese military capabilities by civilian and military officials, did not destroy the Japanese-American friendship, but it did point to future dangers. After 1895, for example, when Americans put a face to the "Yellow Peril," that face increasingly was Japanese. Victories over China on land and sea shook even a reliably sympathetic *New York Times* to speculate that Tokyo "might yet overwhelm the East and even threaten Europe." Just a little over a year after Shimonoseki, the US minister to Japan, Edwin Dun, publicly complained about the absurd number of letters that he received expressing fear over Japan's postwar power and intentions. Ominously, many of those letters singled out what after Portsmouth would become the poison pills in the Japanese-American relationship: immigration and commerce.[16]

Despite these nagging issues, Washington and Tokyo retained their traditionally good relations and successfully navigated a host of potentially difficult situations, foremost among them the future of Hawaii. On the eve of the Spanish-American War, a crisis in Hawaii precipitated by the island kingdom's decision to curtail Japanese immigration led senior officials, including Secretary of State John Sherman, to warn the American minister in Hawaii that Japan might use force against the islands. In the end, Washington and Tokyo resolved this crisis as they would many others in the decades that followed. In this instance, Washington dispatched naval forces to Hawaii in a show of deterrence while also assuring the Japanese government that after it annexed Hawaii the United States would pay any claims resulting from the ongoing immigration dispute.[17]

In the end, while the Hawaiian immigration controversy was of little historical importance, its politicization in both Japan and America was significant. The Meiji government had always, though often reluctantly, weighed the wishes of its citizens when shaping policy, and, with the inauguration of a constitutional system in 1890, the importance of public opinion grew. Opposition parties and the popular press began to scrutinize, object to, and even obstruct government programs, and in 1891, after just one year of constitutional rule, the government dissolved the Imperial Diet in an effort to push through various funding proposals. Increasingly, then, popular pressure began to shape government policy as never before, and during the 1890s public concern focused on the fate of Japanese communities overseas. The Japanese press in particular urged its government to take a strong stand, and, just days after a particularly lucid plea, Tokyo dispatched the cruiser *Naniwa* to Hawaii. While intended to mollify the public, the *Naniwa*'s sailing fueled increasingly virulent accounts of Japanese designs on Hawaii by proannexation groups within the United States that, thwarted on several previous occasions, used Japan as a cat's paw to secure Washington's takeover of the islands. Prior to the rise of Japanese military power, England served as the annexationists' bugaboo, but after 1895, the *New York Times* concluded, those pushing for annexation simply "transferred the jealousy from Great Britain to Japan." While the *Times* recognized the potential damage that the deliberately false campaign might have on "a friend and possible ally," it did not doubt the tactic's effectiveness. While the controversy in Hawaii was just a small taste of what was to come, it indicated how popular pressure in both countries could influence national policy.[18]

In addition to Hawaii, Washington and Tokyo also managed the tensions that accompanied America's even more sudden and dramatic expansion into the Pacific during the Spanish-American War. To be sure, America had since the Republic's earliest days been involved in the Far East, and by 1898 America had maintained a near continuous naval presence in Asian waters for two generations. Nevertheless, victory over Spain propelled America ever deeper into the Pacific and led the McKinley administration to annex Hawaii and take Guam and the Philippines. While the American decision to take the Philippines was not universally popular in Japan, it coincided with the wishes of the Japanese government, which encouraged American annexation because it preferred to see the United States, rather than some other, European power, perched on its doorstep.[19]

Even before the Senate approved the Treaty of Paris, the McKinley administration projected American influence onto the Asian mainland with the circulation of the First Open Door Note. This touchstone of American diplomacy grew out of a British suggestion for Anglo-American cooperation to prevent the establishment of new spheres of influence in China. President William McKinley spurned the overture, yet the British continued to enlist American support to protect the Open Door to China. McKinley, like a generation of his predecessors, valued unfettered access to China, and his third secretary of state, John Hay, believed that ever-expanding Western trade and investment in that country served the long-term interests of both Chinese and Westerners. In the summer of 1899 Hay's adviser on Far Eastern affairs, William W. Rockhill, introduced the secretary to his friend, Alfred E. Hippisley, an English employee of the Chinese Imperial Maritime Customs Service, and for the remainder of the summer Hippisley worked alongside the two Americans to promote the Open Door in China. Soon, further Russian advances into Manchuria pushed McKinley and Hay to embrace this polestar of America diplomacy.[20]

The 1899 Open Door Note sought a simple guarantee of commercial equality within the established European and Japanese spheres of influence. As realists, Rockhill and Hay hoped to salvage whatever they could for American commerce in China by gaining pledges of noninterference from the powers within both the treaty ports and the Chinese customs as well as by promoting a general agreement not to utilize discriminatory railroad rates and harbor dues inside existing spheres of influence. They recognized, however, that spheres of influence existed in China and consequently held out little hope for American investment opportunities in these areas.[21]

Despite its limited objectives, the public beatification of the Open Door began almost at once, and predictions of increased American trade in China jumped off the pages of American newspapers that foresaw "that the United States [would] greatly expand its influence and trade in the [F]ar East." Prominent dailies noted that by rejecting spheres of influence in favor of the Open Door "[Americans] have an infinitely wider scope in the Chinese markets" and that by assuring equal commercial opportunity in China Hay's policy removed "a situation which threatened a great European war." With the Open Door, argued the *New York Commercial Advertiser*, "powers that have been eager for dismemberment of China in order to secure the trade of part of it, will be eager now to prevent dismemberment in order to keep the trade of the whole."[22]

Dismemberment, however, became a distinct possibility the following year when foreign forces marched on Peking to save the international settlement from the antiforeign and anti-Manchu Boxer rebels. Even before the defeat of the Boxers in the summer of 1900, Washington grew particularly concerned that Russian forces, which reached the Chinese capital overland from Siberia, would remain in Manchuria. Accordingly, on July 3, 1900, Hay sent a second series of notes, this time requesting that the powers respect Chinese territory and the authority of the Chinese government. Once again, the powers assented, and Washington embarked on a policy that for the next forty years made the United States the guarantor of China's "territorial and administrative integrity."[23]

The twin notes, which ultimately helped drive the United States and Japan apart, drew the two Pacific powers closer together in the near term. Eager to cooperate with America and Britain, and concerned over China's disintegration, the Japanese government endorsed Hay's first note. Japan likewise approved the second note, and powerful elder statesmen, including Hirobumi Ito, one of the original samurai founders of the Meiji state, appeared genuinely wedded to promoting the Open Door. This support in turn further enhanced the empire's reputation in America, where Japan also received kudos from future president Theodore Roosevelt for its role in suppressing the Boxer Rebellion.[24]

Japan badly needed this American support at the dawn of the new century for, despite its great victory over China in 1894–1895, the empire remained far from secure. The Triple Intervention forced Japan to retrocede the Liaotung Peninsula to China, only to see Russia establish a naval base at Port Arthur. Japanese high-handedness in Korea, which culminated in the murder of Queen Min in 1895, led the Korean court to request and receive Russian military protection. That same year China entered into an alliance with Russia that obligated the tsar to defend the crumbling Manchu dynasty against Japan in return for Peking's pledge to grant the Russian navy access to all Chinese ports in the event of a Russo-Japanese war.[25]

In addition to alarming Tokyo, Russian moves in the Far East also threatened American interests and led to growing estrangement between Washington and St. Petersburg. Even Horace Allen, the anti-Japanese American minister at Seoul who initially cooperated with Russia against Japan, quickly became convinced that St. Petersburg intended to exclude wholly American interests from Korea. Meanwhile, the American minister in St. Petersburg, Clifton Breckinridge, expressed doubt that traditional Russian-American amity would appear again in the near future. Against this backdrop, predictions of a future war between Russia and the West increased as prominent intellectuals such as Henry Adams and the influential economist Charles A. Conant expressed profound concern over the growing strength of the tsar's forces. Just as Manchuria poisoned Japanese-American relations after 1905, so too did it undermine cordial Russian-American relations at the dawn of the new century.[26]

At the same time that the common threat from Russia brought Japan and America ever closer, Anglo-Japanese relations also improved. By the late 1890s, London also began to see Japan as an effective counterweight to Russian Far Eastern expansion. When attempts by the British and the Japanese to protect their Far Eastern interests through limited and specific agreements with Russia failed, both parties sought security through the 1902 Anglo-Japanese Alliance.[27]

For London, the alliance promised to stem Russian expansion in Asia while guaranteeing Tokyo the freedom to fight Russia should diplomacy fail without fear that a new Triple Intervention would rob the empire of yet another victory. Both the negotiations preceding the agreement and the terms of the pact indicate that Japanese aims were largely defensive, designed to protect the Open Door and ensure an end to Russian interference in Korea. The alliance also marked the beginning of a policy that Japan followed until 1922 and returned to in September 1940: seeking a great-power partnership to ensure national security.[28]

The American reaction to the alliance was not surprisingly almost entirely positive. The *New York Times* concluded that legitimate security concerns compelled Tokyo to seek an alliance and that US, British, and Japanese policies in China were in accord given their common support for the Open Door. For his part, President Theodore Roosevelt supported the pact because he saw that it reinforced a pro-American balance of power in the region. While the US Navy's General Board saw a potential menace in the new alliance and not surprisingly used it to push for a rapid naval buildup, on the whole most Americans supported the new entente.[29]

Japanese officials had hoped that an alliance with Britain would improve their negotiating position with Russia, but renewed efforts after 1902 proved fruitless. The tsar's government refused to recognize Tokyo's Korean sphere in exchange for Japanese recognition of Russian predominance in Manchuria. As the desultory talks dragged on, St. Petersburg strengthened its Far Eastern Fleet and occupied the South Manchurian city of Mukden.[30]

In myriad ways, the period immediately preceding the Russo-Japanese War foreshadowed the outbreak of the Pacific War. In the final months before hostilities, the Russian government and public did not believe that Japan would dare risk war. St. Petersburg had little intention of making an agreement with Tokyo, and rather than effect a compromise it redeployed its forces east while negotiations continued. Russian deterrence failed in 1904, however, because Tokyo remained convinced that national security demanded hegemony over the entire Korean Peninsula, and, consequently, while willing to forgo advantages in Manchuria, the emperor's statesmen would not compromise on Korea. When further diplomatic negotiations seemed pointless—and decidedly dangerous, given the growing strength of Russian forces—Japan launched a preemptive strike prior to declaring war.[31]

The half century between Perry's opening of Japan and the onset of the Russo-Japanese War witnessed an extraordinary flowering in Japanese-American relations and also revealed the fault lines of future crises. Rapid modernization, the shared Russian threat, a common interest in China, and a dramatic improvement in relations with Great Britain bound America and Japan together. Immigration, trade, and foreign expansion, meanwhile, clouded the horizon and generated popular pressure for government action in both countries. Serious though they were, even these issues did not disrupt the remarkably cordial Japanese-American relationship.

Only one issue, the Open Door to China, could seriously jeopardize the bond that Japanese and Americans had built since 1853, and, at the dawn of the new century, Russia, rather than Japan, seemed poised to close that door. When Japan struck the Russian fleet at Port Arthur, its future, and that of the Open Door, hung in the balance. Battles on the barren Manchurian plains and in frigid waters of the Sea of Japan tested the success of Meiji Era modernization, and victory soon brought new tests for Japanese-American amity. Could the extraordinary Japanese-American friendship survive once the victorious Japanese hoisted the Rising Sun flag beyond Korea? Could the friendship survive once Japan replaced Russia as the greatest threat to the Open Door?

Chapter 1

The Foundations of Containment

> Behold, I have set before thee an open door and no man can shut it.
>
> —Rev. 2:8 (AV)

> Japan professed belief in the open door policy . . . but the time . . . has come when Japan can disclose her real policy, that of exclusion.
>
> —George Bronson Rea (1916)

George Bronson Rea made a living off the Open Door. First, in 1905, as the founder of the *Far Eastern Review,* he championed American access to the China market. Later, as an adviser to the government of the Japanese puppet state of Manchukuo, he championed Tokyo's dominance in Northeast Asia. While Rea clearly abandoned his allegiance to the Open Door, America never did.

During the Progressive Era, long before Rea turned apologist for the Japanese, his career and America's defense of the Open Door paralleled one another. Rea launched his *Far Eastern Review* in 1905, the same year that Theodore Roosevelt inaugurated the American containment of Japan. A decade later, he penned his essay "Closing the Open Door," which highlighted Japan's wartime expansion and challenged America to defend China and its rights there. While Rea correctly drew attention to the threat that Japan posed to both China and America, he need not have worried about America's commitment to the Open Door.[1]

By 1916, three very different presidents had worked to contain Japanese expansion and protect China. Theodore Roosevelt nurtured the balance of power and employed diplomacy and deterrence in near equal measure, while Taft relied primarily on America's financial clout. While Wilson abhorred both military deterrence and dollar diplomacy, his search for a means to contain Japan eventually led him to embrace economic coercion, Roosevelt's policy of diplomatic engagement, and Taft's investment diplomacy.

These differing approaches to limiting Japanese expansion were no doubt conditioned by these presidents' more general approach to American diplomacy and their particular conception of Japan. Whereas Roosevelt did not flinch from projecting American power and using it to bend weaker states to America's will, Taft abhorred the use of force and instead preferred the rule of law and the power of the dollar. Wilson, who sought to chart a nobler course for American diplomacy, encountered both the greatest obstacles and in the end the most profound disillusionment. Roosevelt laid the groundwork for America's containment of Japan and possessed a view of that nation shaped by reality but not warped by unreasonable fear. He recognized that, while Japan had arrived on the international stage late, it was a regional power and therefore possessed, as did the Russians, English, and French, a clearly defined, if not openly acknowledged, sphere of influence. This realism contributed to Roosevelt's successful containment. Neither extreme fear nor extreme prejudice shaped Taft's view of Japan, yet the strains of commercial competition led him to see Japan as an adversary that like the other great powers in Asia could legitimately be forced from its sphere by American capital. For these reasons, neither containment nor Japanese-American relations fared particularly well during his tenure. For Wilson, Japan was a particularly troublesome adversary in that Tokyo was both a commercial and a military rival that also opposed the president's American-led diplomatic revolution. Despite the chaos that engulfed the world during Wilson's two terms, his containment of Japan was remarkably successful.

Despite their profound differences, all three leaders accepted the inherited wisdom of the nineteenth century, which emphasized that the United States must preserve the Open Door to China. Each administration searched for the Open Door's exact meaning as well as the best means for protecting it, but neither Roosevelt nor Taft nor Wilson ever seriously questioned the long-term mission of containing Japanese expansion on the Asian mainland.

Theodore Roosevelt and the Origins of Containment

Theodore Roosevelt laid the foundation for the successful containment of Japan in the midst of the 1904–1905 Russo-Japanese War, while Tokyo's modern armed forces laid waste to Russian military power. Following the American-brokered Portsmouth Treaty, which ended the war, the traditionally amiable Japanese-American relationship suddenly turned adversarial as Americans saw Japan replacing Russia as the primary threat to the Open Door. After Portsmouth, Roosevelt the peacemaker now worked to contain Japan. During the remainder of his second term, the president successfully limited Japanese expansion by nurturing the balance of power and employing a combination of military deterrence and diplomatic engagement. Virulent racism, the machinations of imperial Germany and junior American diplomats, and the growing politicization of Japanese-American relations complicated his task, but, when Roosevelt left the White House in 1909, he bequeathed a record that his successors would have been fortunate to equal.

Part of Roosevelt's success was rooted in the common admiration and respect that the president and his closest associates had for Japan. In the early years of the twentieth century, many policymakers held Japan in uniquely high esteem, and this mind-set unconsciously, almost reflexively, helped maintain amicable Japanese-American relations even as Washington sought to limit Tokyo's territorial, political, and commercial expansion in China. When Japan attacked Russian forces at Port Arthur prior to declaring war, Tokyo's ardent admirer Secretary of War Elihu Root declared: "The way the Japs began the fight [was] bully." Just as avowed Anglophiles willingly overlooked British excesses during the Boer War, Root and others eagerly approved Japan's preemptive strike at Port Arthur. The president's personal relationships with Japanese statesmen, meanwhile, paralleled those he had with English leaders. During the war, for example, the British diplomat Cecil Spring Rice, then serving as secretary of the British embassy in St. Petersburg, conferred as regularly with Roosevelt as did Baron Kentaro Kaneko, the president's friend and Harvard University classmate and the former Japanese minister of justice.[2]

The Russo-Japanese War was a fight that, at least on paper, Japan should not have won. Victories over the Russians in Korea and then in Manchuria, the destruction of Russia's Far Eastern Fleet at Port Arthur, and the staggering annihilation of its Baltic Fleet in the May 1905 Battle of the Tsushima Straits assured Japan victory and forced Tsar Nicholas II to accept American good offices in the summer of 1905. Before the summer ended, Russia and Japan made peace, and, despite profound public disapproval of the Portsmouth Treaty, Tokyo gained a great deal. Russia recognized Japanese control over Korea, agreed to withdraw all troops from Manchuria except a limited number of railway guards, and ceded to Japan the Liaotung Peninsula and South Sakhalin Island. While Japan failed to gain an indemnity from Russia, Portsmouth nonetheless provided the solid defense perimeter that it had sought for over a decade.[3]

As it turned out, the Portsmouth Treaty was no less important in protecting America's Far Eastern interests, and in retrospect it is clear that America's long and largely successful effort to contain Japanese expansion in Asia began in the summer of 1905. Roosevelt, the avowed Anglophile, sought at Portsmouth to create in Northeast Asia the very balance of opposing powers that British strategists had long sought in Europe.

At the war's outset, Roosevelt believed that a Japanese victory would protect the Open Door, but Russia's disastrous defeats quickly led him to question whether a victorious Japan might threaten China every bit as much as St. Petersburg. By the end of 1904, the specter of a victorious Japan turning on America concerned the president, as did the possibility of some future Russo-Japanese rapprochement followed by a division of Northeast Asia. Roosevelt understood that, while US military power could not protect the Open Door, a balance of opposing power could. He also recognized that, the longer the war continued, the less chance he had of achieving this balance, especially if revolution destabilized Russia. The new American ambassador to St. Petersburg, George V. L. Meyer, who arrived at his post in the final months of the conflict, closely monitored the growing antitsarist furor that swept Russia in the summer of 1905. On July 3, he cabled the president that, while he still considered revolution unlikely, "should Japan refuse an armistice [and] inflict a defeat to the Russian Army" events might get out of hand. As if this was not enough to give the president fits, Roosevelt also worried that prolonged hostilities would shatter the Anglo-French-Russian containment of imperial Germany, which, with its recently acquired sphere in Shantung Province, also threatened the Open Door. Finally, Roosevelt feared that a prolonged war could reawaken latent Japanese xenophobia.[4]

American mediation proved critical in restoring peace and a semblance of the balance of power in Northeast Asia. In August, Meyer, along with Roosevelt and Germany's Kaiser Wilhelm II, convinced the tsar to compromise over Sakhalin Island and strike a deal while he still could. The Portsmouth Treaty served Washington's ends by securing Russian and Japanese pledges to respect China's territorial integrity and the equality of commercial opportunity. The combatants had in effect endorsed the Open Door. Most importantly, this American-imposed peace, which came prior to the complete destruction of either combatant, meant that the rivals for control of Northeast Asia now faced one another across what the historian Raymond Esthus so aptly termed a "line of friction . . . in Manchuria." After Portsmouth, Roosevelt worried that defeat and revolution had so weakened Russia that it could no longer contain Japan, yet by the end of 1906 conditions had stabilized, and the Russian military had recovered enough that the president told Edward Grey, the British foreign secretary, that Japan might one day be "overwhelmed in Manchuria."[5]

Roosevelt built containment's next pillar, diplomatic engagement, gradually and in response to a series of crises that threatened Japanese-American, and by extension Anglo-American, relations following the outbreak of war between Japan and Russia. In 1905, while in Tokyo on Roosevelt's behalf,

Secretary of War William Howard Taft successfully concluded a secret executive agreement with the Japanese government that "served as America's recognition of Japan's position in Korea and Manchuria" in return for Tokyo's recognition of American control in the Philippines. Taft informed the president that Japan had no intention of challenging the United States in the Philippines and that he had agreed to both Japanese control in Korea and an informal Anglo-Japanese-American alliance. The secretary of war had some concern that he had exceeded his authority, but the president assured him that he agreed with everything Taft had told Katsura. In truth, none of Taft's statements were terribly astonishing in that Washington had given up Korea at the outset of the war and that Roosevelt had worked for closer Anglo-American cooperation for years. In the near term, Taft-Katsura helped define the respective Japanese and American spheres in Asia. However, in the long run, the agreement probably did more harm than good. Because the accord remained secret, most Americans did not know that Washington had once more agreed to grant Japan a free hand in Korea. Its flaws notwithstanding, the agreement showed that diplomatic engagement strengthened containment and safeguarded peace.[6]

The Roosevelt administration's engagement with Japan, and Taft's personal diplomacy on the president's behalf, did not end with the Taft-Katsura agreement. Two years later, when nagging immigration problems contributed to the first of many Japanese-American war scares, Roosevelt again diverted the Philippines-bound Taft to Tokyo. This time, the president needed him to work out the details of proposed Japanese immigration restrictions, and on his arrival the secretary of war held a series of meetings with senior Japanese officials. Taft soon secured a pledge from Foreign Minister Tadasu Hayashi to voluntarily restrict emigration to the continental United States, which, given the comparatively large remittances that Japanese expatriates regularly sent home, was no small concession.[7]

While his use of personal diplomacy during the California crises deserves kudos, the realism that Roosevelt applied to the problem of Manchuria is a far greater, though largely unappreciated, accomplishment. After Portsmouth, Manchuria quickly became a source of friction between Japan and the United States because, for both nations, the region had become the vital western frontier. As early as 1895, Foreign Minister Munemitsu Mutsu sought to incorporate into the Shimonoseki Treaty the Chinese cessation of South Manchurian ports, and, while Prime Minister Katsura attempted a Manchuria-for-Korea agreement with Russia prior to 1904, neither he nor Foreign Minister Jutaro Komura stopped hoping for a Japanese foothold north of the Yalu River. In the aftermath of the First Sino-Japanese War,

Manchuria's strategic and economic importance to Japan continued to grow, and, in the midst of the Russo-Japanese War, Japanese intellectuals began refining the basic outline of a Japanese-dominated Greater East Asia Co-Prosperity Sphere in which Manchuria loomed large.[8]

Meanwhile, the critical search for markets and investment outlets and support for an *expanded* Open Door naturally led Americans to look to Manchuria. As was the case with Japan, American interest in Manchuria also dated back to the late nineteenth century. At a time when the worst economic depression in its history, accompanied by violent clashes between capital and labor, convulsed the Republic, the United States led all industrialized nations in exports to Manchuria. Those economists who recognized that both overproduction and a corresponding lack of viable export markets for capital were the root causes of the 1893 panic saw the Far East as key to ridding America of its unwanted abundance. Indeed, Washington based its support for Tokyo in 1904 on the assumption that Japanese troops were keeping the Manchurian door open for American trade and investment. Not surprisingly, when they heard the rickety hinges of the Manchurian Open Door begin to close, Americans turned their ire on Japan.[9]

As Americans widely suspected, Tokyo's postwar Manchurian policy sought to promote Japanese economic supremacy in the region. Foreign Minister Komura had decided that Japan could not religiously follow the Open Door because the policy penalized nations that were not as industrially advanced as either the United States or Great Britain. Acting on this belief, and in an effort to neutralize an American foothold in Manchuria, Komura successfully blocked an initiative by Japan and an American investment syndicate headed by E. H. Harriman—an initiative that Tokyo initially approved—for the joint ownership of the South Manchuria Railway and its accompanying coal mines. The Harriman plan, which may well have originated with then American ambassador Lloyd Griscom, promised a closer Japanese-American relationship through the joint development of Manchuria.[10]

Despite the decision to depart from the Open Door in Manchuria and block the Harriman syndicate, Japan did not systematically violate the tenets of Hay's policy. Initially, Hay recognized that spheres of influence existed and that American investment opportunities within these spheres were limited at best. Japanese officials did, however, sometimes violate the commercial clauses of the Open Door, which Hay had intended to apply within the various powers' spheres of influence, but these violations were not systematic and probably did not adversely affect American trade. US officials in Tokyo and Peking agreed that the Japanese were not using the military occupation of South Manchuria to thwart foreign commerce, and William Rockhill, then minister to Peking, argued that economic conditions in Manchuria, rather than Japanese violations of the Open Door, were responsible for the decline in American exports. In the end, Roosevelt succeeded, albeit only in the near term, in removing Manchuria as a source of friction when he reached an agreement with Tokyo that placed the region within the Japanese Empire.[11]

Well before the 1908 Root-Takahira agreement, the Western powers helped Roosevelt pursue this pragmatic approach to Manchuria by recognizing Japanese control in the region in a series of agreements that Washington apparently supported. In 1907, the US ambassador to Japan, Thomas O'Brien, unmistakably signaled American recognition of Japanese control there when he informed Foreign Minister Hayashi that he equated Manchuria with Korea, then a Japanese protectorate, and Formosa, then a Japanese colony. The following year, the Root-Takahira agreement once again unequivocally signaled Washington's recognition of Japanese dominance in Manchuria.[12]

The agreement began as a private initiative undertaken by Japan's ambassador to the United States, the Viscount Shuzo Aoki, who in October 1907 proposed that Washington and Tokyo improve bilateral relations through a mutual guarantee of Pacific Ocean commerce, respect for the status quo in Asia, and adherence to the Open Door. While President Roosevelt seriously considered Aoki's proposal, Foreign Minister Hayashi did not, and, consequently, the initiative foundered.[13]

Almost a year to the day after Aoki approached Roosevelt, the Japanese government formally introduced a remarkably similar proposition. From late October through mid-November 1908, Secretary of State Root and Ambassador Kogoro Takahira hammered out an agreement whereby both sides pledged to respect one another's Pacific trade and Asian territories, the Open Door, and the status quo and to consult in the event the status quo was threatened. The most critical aspect of the new executive agreement—meaning that only Roosevelt, not his successors, was bound by it—concerned the fate of Manchuria. Did the president once again place this vital region within the Japanese sphere? England, France, and Russia recognized that the status quo in Asia meant Japanese control over South Manchuria, but did Roosevelt?[14]

The preponderance of evidence suggests that he did. Recognizing Tokyo's control over Manchuria would, as the president hoped, focus Japanese attention toward Manchuria and away from the Philippines. Moreover, it seems unlikely that, during his several weeks of negotiations with Takahira, Root failed to see that the agreement might appear to place Manchuria somehow outside the Open Door. While his is not the last word on the subject, A. Whitney Griswold persuasively demonstrates in his magisterial *The Far Eastern Policy of the United States* "that in return for a Japanese pledge to respect the security of the Philippines, the United States had given Japan a free hand in Manchuria."[15]

While Roosevelt deserves praise for laying the foundation for two of containment's most constructive pillars, maintenance of the balance of power and diplomatic engagement, his administration also oversaw containment's early militarization. Prior to 1905, when Russia appeared the greatest threat to the Open Door, Japan consistently appeared as either an ally or a friendly neutral in American war plans for Asia. War plans envisioned, for example, a joint Japanese-American defense against Russian attacks as well as a combined Japanese and American offensive in Siberia. All this changed after the Russo-Japanese War, and not long after Portsmouth the American military drew up revised war plans that, for the first time, designated Japan as a hypothetical enemy.[16]

Containment's militarization accelerated in 1907 when the Army-Navy Joint Board recommended both sending the fleet to the Far East and deploying additional ships and troops to the Philippines. Rather than reject this suggestion as needlessly provocative, the president embraced the idea as an instrument of deterrence. By the time the fleet arrived in Japan as part of its world cruise, the latest Japanese-American war scare had passed, and the president unfortunately attributed this outcome to naval deterrence. Worse still, reports of secret Japanese support for Philippine insurgents, and even more inflammatory suggestions that Japanese troops and spies were infiltrating the United States, contributed to the Joint Board's decision in 1908 to recommend building a major base at Pearl Harbor, which Congress quickly agreed to fund. The following year, in order to ensure the success of naval deterrence and match English, German, and Japanese building programs, the Navy Department recommended a major new building program.[17]

The Japanese military showed as much concern as its American counterpart over the prospect of a Japanese-American war, and in 1907 the army designated the United States number two on its list of hypothetical enemies, behind Russia and ahead of France. Because it would face the brunt of fighting in any war with America, the navy exhibited far more concern than did its sister service, and, although its leaders doubted the inevitability of war with the United States, it also worked to upgrade its capabilities following the fleet's 1908 visit.[18]

These early war scares and the military planning that accompanied them had several unfortunate long-term consequences. The war scares were very public, and, however much responsible officials on both sides of the Pacific downplayed the likelihood of armed conflict, the prospect of a Japanese-American war remained a concern to the public thereafter. American concern was further heightened by Russian, French, and German publications, which, since 1905, had taken the lead in predicting a future Japanese-American clash. Graf von Reventlow, a former German naval officer and not infrequent contributor to the *New York Times,* did much to arouse American suspicions with his repeated and all-too-well-publicized predictions of a Japanese-American war. French dailies did their part too, with one especially prescient editorial predicting that Tokyo's long-range goal was to "organize in the Middle Kingdom a sort of moral and economic protectorate" and then expel all Westerners. Not to be outdone by the Europeans, American writers also tapped into the growing anti-Japanese market in 1909 with the publication of two books featuring the common theme of a Japanese-American war, Homer Lea's *The Valor of Ignorance* and E. H. Fitzpatrick's *The Coming Conflict of Nations; or, The Japanese-American War.*[19]

Senior officials, including the president, tapped into and exacerbated this growing suspicion of Japan. In 1908, for example, in a clear bid to increase the size of the standing army, General Frederick Dent Grant, commander of the Department of the East, publicly argued that the US Army would need 100,000 men to throw back a Japanese invasion of California. Even President Roosevelt used a policy of "calculated exaggeration to facilitate his naval program" when he inflated both the troubled state of Japanese-American relations and the threat that the Japanese navy posed to the United States.[20]

With the exception of Dent and a few other doomsayers, popular accounts of a Japanese-American war not only heightened tensions; they also made a Japanese-American war appear all too staid. After World War I, for example, most military planners, civilian policymakers, and the general public saw future wars as yet more bloodbaths, and the Kellogg-Briand Pact, Anglo-French appeasement, American isolationism, and finally the 1938 Munich Conference indicated the extraordinary lengths to which nations and their citizens would go to avoid a repeat of 1914–1918. Unfortunately, for Japan and America, as early as 1909 commentators and war planners envisioned a Japanese-American conflict in which opposing navies and a limited number of troops carried on the brunt of the fighting and blockades, rather than massed armies, carried the day. For Americans, the worst-case scenario saw the initial loss of the Philippines followed by a major engagement with the Japanese navy and the liberation of the colony. Early Japanese war plans envisioned the possibility of defeat but never the staggering death toll, ruin, and occupation that visited the home islands during the Pacific War.[21]

The first Japanese-American war scare and early American war planning also indicate that policymakers were convinced—without reason—that American military power could deter Japan. This exuberant and irrational belief continued to influence containment until the Japanese attack on Pearl Harbor. Japan was not deterred in either 1894 or 1904 from going to war against nations with numerically superior forces, yet somehow policymakers believed that American military power would succeed where Chinese and Russian power had failed. Tokyo went to war against China and Russia because both countries threatened vital Japanese national interests. Conversely, Japan chose not to go to war in 1907 because no vital national interests were at stake. American deterrence clearly had little if anything to do with keeping peace in the Pacific.[22]

In addition to an overreliance on military deterrence, the Roosevelt years were noteworthy for the rise to power of a younger generation of diplomats who had come of age after 1894. These men, who did much to undermine Japanese-American relations, had no memory of the halcyon days and consequently tended to view Tokyo in strictly adversarial terms. Among the more prominent of these young Turks was Willard Straight, the vehemently anti-Japanese former vice consul at the American legation at Seoul and later consul general at Mukden, who hoped to enlarge American investment and commercial opportunities in Manchuria while weakening Japan's hold on the region. Not yet twenty when the Open Door notes were first circulated, Straight was conditioned by an expansive interpretation of the policy to see Japanese continental expansion as an explicit threat to American interests. In late 1907, as Hayashi and Roosevelt attempted to solve the immigration controversy, Straight worked with Chinese officials and American investors to free the region from reliance on Japanese capital and build a competitor to Japan's South Manchuria Railway. In the end, his efforts to create a bank and a competing railway in Manchuria failed, but his story illustrates two problems that clouded future Japanese-American relations. First, Straight believed that the Open Door provided for American investment opportunities within existing spheres of influence, and his beliefs guided many in the diplomatic corps long after 1909. More critically, his perception of Japan as an adversary, rather than a junior partner, in Asia reflected a generational problem that increasingly plagued Japanese-American relations in the decades to come.[23]

Similar generational conflicts within the Japanese government also exacerbated divisions over policy and perceptions of the United States. On the one hand, the president benefited from the generally pro-Anglo-American policy of successive Japanese cabinets that respected American interests in Asia, within reason, and cooperated with Washington and London. At the turn of the century, Tokyo cast its lot with the Anglo-American powers, as evidenced by the Open Door notes, the Anglo-Japanese Alliance of 1902 and 1905, as well as Taft-Katsura and Root-Takahira. No Japanese administration sought to impose its will on China through force, and, despite war plans, no Japanese cabinet planned to make war against America.

On the other hand, a generational shift is, in retrospect, clearly apparent, and it did not bode well for future relations. Jutaro Komura, the Japanese foreign minister who since 1904 had charted a course away from the Open Door, was born almost two years after Perry's arrival and knew little of the time when Japan was virtually defenseless. Former prime minister Hirobumi Ito, on the other hand, was a product of a very different era. Born a full decade before Perry's arrival, Ito came of age when Japan's future was far from assured, and this very different mind-set made him more sensitive to rising American criticism of Japanese policy in Manchuria. Accordingly, he convinced the Katsura cabinet that, given Japan's financial dependence on the United States and Great Britain, every effort must be made to improve relations with Washington and London. To this end, Tokyo ended military rule in the Kwantung Territory, established a new free port at Darien, and opened interior areas for foreign residence and trade. Ito also persuaded his government to give the Roosevelt administration a free hand in regulating Japanese immigration. Unfortunately, by the time a Korean nationalist assassinated him in Harbin in 1909, a new generation had risen to power in Tokyo whose worldview had not been tempered by the sobering memories that Ito took with him to the grave.[24]

Despite these many problems, the Roosevelt administration retained a weltanschauung that made Japanese-American differences seem the exception rather than the norm. Even though Japanese-Americans relations turned adversarial during Roosevelt's tenure, a generalized fear of Japan remained far more ingrained at the popular level than at the policymaking level. Roosevelt and his closest advisers had come of age when the Japanese-American relationship was generally far more positive and when Japan's place in the American mind was, however clouded by racism, not distorted by fear.[25]

President Roosevelt unhesitatingly accepted the Open Door, and, from 1904 to the approach of spring 1909, he successfully limited Japanese expansion in Asia by rebuilding the Far Eastern balance of power and combining realism with diplomatic engagement. His policy was not perfect, yet, when placed next to those of his successors, his mistakes seem small in comparison.

Containment, Liberal Expansion, and the Taft Administration

William Howard Taft's containment of Japan was spectacularly unsuccessful. This might come as something of a surprise, given that, when Taft took the oath of office in March of 1909, he was no stranger to either Japan or the Japanese. The new president had traveled to Japan four times, and on two occasions, the 1905 Taft-Katsura agreement and again in 1907 during talks with Prime Minister Kimmochi Saionji, he received Tokyo's recognition of American hegemony in the Philippines. While his visits, and successful talks, provided him with substantial goodwill for Japan, the new president also felt a sympathy for China that Roosevelt lacked. Taft also believed that the United States had to play a greater role in Chinese affairs than it traditionally had. Accordingly, he allowed younger men like Willard Straight, who did so much to undermine Japanese-American relations during the Roosevelt presidency, far too much power and authority to make mischief. He also abandoned the realism that typified Roosevelt's successful containment policy. In time, his sympathy for China and belief in America's civilizing mission there led him to forsake containment in favor of a strategy designed to roll back Japan's sphere of influence in Manchuria as well as Tokyo's commercial and political influence in China proper. This strategy backfired, containment suffered, and Japanese-American relations sank to a new nadir. Worse still, Taft's policies undermined multinational—particularly British—support for the Open Door. Where Roosevelt drew Washington, London, and Tokyo together to support the status quo in Asia, Taft drove a wedge into the heart of the unofficial entente.[26]

No epiphany explains Taft's decision to depart from containment. Instead, the president's unbridled confidence in American economic power and his conception of both liberal-commercial economic expansion and the Open Door led to disaster. Under Secretary of State Philander Knox, the administration turned the Marxist equation of capitalism and inevitable war on its head. Knox argued that capitalism linked all nations together within a system that made war obsolete. His world order mirrored Charles Conant's, who saw the Open Door as an investment system in which capitalist nations possessed shares in developing regions. Conant maintained that the Open Door prevented war, in that excess capital could be spent on productive investments rather than on unproductive and in the end destructive military growth. For Conant and Knox, *investment* expansion was a win-win situation. By finding productive outlets for excess capital, the system ensured the continuance and vitality of the capitalist order while at the same time meeting the capital requirements of developing regions. The Open Door also promoted good governance in that political modernization inevitably went hand in hand with economic modernization. Under Knox, the administration applied Conant's view of the Open Door to China and, most importantly, Manchuria. Unlike Roosevelt's carefully calculated realism, their policy sought to roll back, rather than simply contain, Japan. For its part, while Tokyo sought to maintain amicable relations with the new administration, Japanese policymakers were determined to simultaneously strengthen their rights in Manchuria and expand the empire's influence in China.[27]

The Taft administration's most ambitious project for the Far East grew out of Willard Straight's work with private American financiers, most prominent among them E. H. Harriman, for entrance into a loan consortium to build railroads in Manchuria and China proper. Straight and his supporters hoped that American capital would increase Washington's influence in China, undermine Japan's, and open Manchuria and China to further American trade and investment. Knox supported the scheme confident that loans "will be attended by enormous internal development," while Taft believed that dollar diplomacy "will present countless commercial opportunities to American manufacturers and capitalists." Straight's plan involved the purchase of the Russian-owned Chinese Eastern Railway and the construction of the Chinchow-Aigun Railway, a line parallel to and therefore competing with the Japanese-owned South Manchuria Railway. Straight also resurrected an earlier pet project, an American-financed Manchurian development bank that would substantially lessen the region's reliance on non-American capital and allow for the "development of Manchuria and Mongolia under American and British auspices." Charles Vevier, the foremost authority on early twentieth-century American economic diplomacy in China, calls Straight's policy nothing less than a bid for "American financial supremacy in Manchuria and Mongolia."[28]

At the same time that Straight worked for American financial supremacy in Manchuria, Knox announced a no less ambitious plan to further American interests in both China and Manchuria while simultaneously undermining Japan's position throughout the region. Convinced that the Open Door in Manchuria could best be protected by placing both Japanese and Russian railroads under international control, Knox called for a multinational financial syndicate to loan China the necessary funds in order to purchase all foreign-owned railroads in Manchuria. The international group would in turn manage the Manchurian rail network during the life of the outstanding loan. The plan was aimed at Tokyo, in that, without ownership of the South Manchuria Railway, Japanese influence in the region would suffer immeasurable decline. To the alarmed and somewhat flabbergasted British, argues Lloyd C. Gardner, the leading historian of early twentieth-century Anglo-American relations, Knox's proposal represented an effort "to establish a protectorate over all China."[29]

The Japanese, not surprisingly, held an equally uncharitable view of these

American plans and refused to participate in either the Chinchow-Aigun line project or in Knox's plan to neutralize the Manchurian railroads. Foreign Minister Komura informed Knox that his plan would overturn the key parts of the Portsmouth Treaty that awarded Japan the South Manchuria Railway and that the internationalization plan would harm Japan's sizable investments in the region. The French, eager to maintain cordial relations with the British, rejected Knox in early February. Russia, meanwhile, consumed with dread over German military power and concerned as well by Austria's renewed interest in Bosnia, sought only to support France and Great Britain, its partners in the Triple Entente. London signaled its formal opposition a few weeks later.[30]

American and foreign observers quickly grasped the damage that the Taft-Knox-Straight policy had done. From Peking, the first secretary at the American legation, Louis Einstein, warned Taft that, while Japan presented the single greatest threat to China and the Open Door, the United States could not dislodge Tokyo from Manchuria. Roosevelt also cautioned the president late in 1910 "not to take any steps as regards Manchuria which will give Japanese cause to feel, with or without reason, that we are hostile to them." The following spring, J. K. Ohl, the head of the *New York Herald*'s China bureau, wrote Knox that his Manchurian policy caused many Japanese to believe that the Taft administration was "spurring China on to an anti-Japanese policy." Had these warnings come sooner, they might have spared Washington a good bit of trouble, for in the end Taft, Knox, and Straight did much more than inflame the Japanese and divide the United States from the powers that traditionally had worked with Washington to contain Japanese expansion.[31]

While neither the Straight nor the Knox railroad plan ever reached fruition, together they nonetheless reshaped Asia's geopolitical map in ways that their authors surely did not intend. Announcement of the multinational loan to build the Hukang Railway sparked a gentry-led revolt, and the following year, when revolution spread, the crumbling edifice of Qing rule collapsed in favor of an equally rickety facade of republican government. In addition to hastening the end of Manchu rule, Knox and Straight also produced what no Russian or Japanese diplomat had yet accomplished, a true Russo-Japanese rapprochement. Knox was fully cognizant that his neutralization plan could force Japan and Russia into a weary embrace, and he urged W. W. Rockhill, then the American minister to St. Petersburg, to prevent any Russo-Japanese agreement that might threaten the project. He might just have well have asked Rockhill to keep the world from turning. Given that neutralization threatened both Japan and Russia, St. Petersburg willingly cooperated with Tokyo after Japan offered an alliance that guaranteed mutual respect for each nation's Manchurian sphere. The accord, signed on July 4, 1910, was far from Tokyo's final effort to enlarge its sphere of influence in Northeast Asia.[32]

The following month Japan formally annexed Korea, and, while many observers, both at the time and subsequently, viewed this as an example of Japanese perfidy, Washington and London had already approved the move. Taft-Katsura, for example, signaled American recognition of all steps short of outright annexation, while Anglo-Japanese discussions over renewal of the alliance in 1905 also indicated a singular lack of British interest in Korea's fate. In Manchuria, meanwhile, Tokyo moved forward with its efforts to bring the region firmly within the Japanese economic orbit. The semipublic South Manchuria Railway increased its investments in both its core railway and sister enterprises in the region—shipping, hotels, mines, and power stations—by over half in less than four years, and during this period Japan's overseas direct investments became so terribly one-dimensional that by 1914 nearly 70 percent were concentrated in Manchuria.[33]

In addition to these officially sanctioned efforts to draw Manchuria closer to Japan, groups within the Japanese army initiated their own efforts to secure the empire's position in the region. Taking the outbreak of revolution in China as their cue, elements of the Kwantung Army attempted to create an independent Manchuria and Inner Mongolia during the winter of 1911–1912. While the Saionji cabinet quickly quashed the plans of the Kwantung agitators when it refused to dispatch additional forces to the region, the plot highlights the ongoing role that Manchuria played in undermining Japanese-American relations. The Saionji cabinet's decision to oppose the army, meanwhile, illustrates that successful containment still required a degree of Japanese cooperation.[34]

Despite the Saionji cabinet's cooperation, Taft failed to contain Japanese expansion. Worse still, his administration oversaw the politicization of Japanese-American relations to a level not seen during the Roosevelt years. Supporters of government subsidies for the shipbuilding industry, for example, argued that Japan's commercial dominance in the Pacific and sizable merchant fleet threatened US national security. Former Treasury secretary Leslie Shaw told audiences how Tokyo's massive commercial fleet could easily land hundreds of thousands of troops on the lightly defended Pacific coast. In that event, he argued, America's rail network could not transport forces west quickly enough. Only a large and apparently amply subsidized merchant fleet could.[35]

In 1912, when news broke that private Japanese interests were seeking land in Mexico to support commercial fishing, Senator Henry Cabot Lodge of Massachusetts used the lingering fear that Japan might use Mexico as a "stepping stone for . . . [an] invasion of the United States" to undermine Taft and Knox, enhance his bid for the presidency, and rally recalcitrant senators to support a pending naval expansion bill. While Lodge may not have wanted to do much more than embarrass the president and secretary of state and further his political ambitions, the Hearst chain's decision to become involved in the controversy influenced him to take an increasingly aggressive stand. Soon, he introduced legislation—which his colleagues overwhelmingly supported—that in effect forbade foreign corporations or foreign nationals from doing "what the Monroe doctrine was intended to prevent." In 1912, this apparently meant allowing a Japanese corporation to own Mexican land.[36]

While Shaw and Lodge were clearly guilty of using Japan as a bogeyman to promote their respective interests, they were rank amateurs in comparison to Richard Henry Hobson, hero of the Spanish-American War turned Alabama congressman, who, for over a decade, relentlessly pursued naval expansion by constantly beating the anti-Japanese drum. In 1903, Hobson left the navy and joined the lecture circuit, where he warned a skeptical public that the threat of European militarism required an enlarged navy. Americans remained unconvinced, however, in that, since the conclusion of the Venezuelan crisis nearly a decade earlier, Anglo-American relations had steadily improved. Two years later, just after the start of the Russo-Japanese War, Hobson's quest for increased naval appropriations led him to abandon his Europe-first strategy and concentrate on Asia. War between Russia and Japan, he now warned his audiences, could ignite a wider war in which American naval inferiority would prove disastrous. This strategy also failed to rally a doubtful public, especially after the wider war failed to materialize. Undaunted, Hobson found a winning formula soon after Portsmouth. Decrying Japanese restrictions on American trade in Manchuria, Hobson, now a congressman, declared that the only "remedy for this audacious invasion of our prerogatives in the Far East" was a prompt military buildup. While he occasionally returned to the threat posed by European fleets, especially Germany's, his bread and butter remained Japan. Efforts in 1908 to secure greater naval funding led to an irreparable split with President Roosevelt after Hobson leaked details of a conversation in which the president revealed his fears of an impending war with Japan.[37]

While Shaw, Lodge, and Hobson contributed to the rising anti-Japanese climate in America, events in China drew increasingly positive attention to that distant country and in the process weakened Japanese-American ties. In the aftermath of the Boxer Rebellion, the Manchu court embarked on a series of ambitious reforms that infused Protestant missionaries with hope that the

Middle Kingdom might become a more receptive, not to mention safer, place for their work. When Manchu reformers abolished the Confucian examination system, which emperors had used in one form or another to select bureaucrats for over a thousand years, the tempo of reform and missionary activity in China increased. By the end of the Taft administration, what the historian James Reed calls "Christian China's American constituency" had grown to some fifteen million souls, and Americans listened to some "30,000 missionary addresses on China every year." While Japan was not without its missionary supporters, Reed notes that *rural* Protestant Americans showed far greater interest in the needs of the struggling *rural* Chinese. Given the relative absence of authoritative expertise on the Far East, American missionaries in China rushed in to fill the gaps in the public's knowledge of the region so that, by the time Woodrow Wilson reached the White House in 1913, public understanding of China and Washington's China policy was largely the creation of American missionaries. Indeed, by 1913, Reed concludes, even the "Open Door policy, as popularly conceived, rested upon a conception of America's proper role in East Asia that was missionary in character."[38]

By 1913, Americans also looked to China as the place where not only Christianity but also democratic-republicanism would at last flourish. They believed that the collapse of Manchu rule would usher in democratic government and further modernization. John Leighton Stuart, the Presbyterian missionary who served in China from 1905 to 1949, first as a pastor, later as president of the missionary-established Yenching University, and finally, in 1946, as US ambassador to China, equated Chinese revolutionaries with the founding fathers. Even after General Yuan Shikai seized power following his defeat in the 1912 parliamentary elections, Stuart and others continued to support the autocrat because he alone provided the order and stability that missionary and business interests required. By the end of Taft's presidency, Japanese-American relations continued to founder, while Sino-American relations began to tack in a very different direction.[39]

Even though Japanese-American relations sank to an all-time low during Taft's presidency, his decision to embrace diplomatic engagement produced one major accomplishment. Despite the increasingly toxic climate in which Hobson and others forced him to work, the president, along with Knox, brought the Japanese-American relationship into the twentieth century through the 1911 Treaty of Commerce and Navigation. Influenced by the widening rift with Japan, Taft and Knox actively supported treaty revision, and, within a year, Washington abandoned explicit immigration restrictions and gave Japan the right to set its own tariffs a year earlier than expected. When West Coast senators raised objections on this point, Knox trudged up to Capitol Hill to plead for their cooperation, and the Japanese government issued a pledge to continue voluntary emigration restrictions. The successful negotiations highlight the importance of diplomatic engagement, and, indeed, the treaty so impressed Taft that he considered it among the year's great achievements.[40]

Taft's adulation notwithstanding, the 1911 accord could mask neither the failure of containment nor the deterioration in Japanese-American relations that occurred during his presidency. Confident that American financial power could roll back Japanese gains in China, the president abandoned Roosevelt's strategy and in the process undermined international support for the Open Door and the balance of power in Asia. Japanese-American ties suffered along with containment, and, at some point during Taft's presidency, relations reached the tipping point. Diplomats still could and, indeed, tried for nearly a generation to improve ties, yet all they could do was slow down the decline. Something intangible, but nonetheless terrible, had occurred in just four years, for, while Japanese-American relations were often adversarial before 1909, after Taft Americans saw Japan only as an adversary. It would take nearly a half century before Japanese-American relations stood again at the level at which Taft found them on entering the White House in 1909.

Woodrow Wilson and Wartime Containment

Taft's successor, Governor Woodrow Wilson of New Jersey, abhorred disorder, chaos, and revolution. Disorder offended his cerebral nature, and chaos assaulted his faith in a divinely created universe. As for revolution, it simply inspired dread. Unfortunately, Wilson faced all three during his presidency and perhaps nowhere more acutely than in Asia, where the 1911 Chinese Revolution, World War I, and finally the Bolshevik Revolution and the Russian Civil War destroyed the balance of power in the region and realigned the geopolitical map. Despite these upheavals, the Wilson administration struggled successfully to contain Japanese expansion and protect the Open Door.

Wilson successfully restricted Japanese expansion during his two terms in office, and his accomplishments in this regard are remarkable, especially given the conditions that he faced. The president resisted military deterrence, which Roosevelt had overemphasized, and instead relied heavily on diplomatic engagement. The Wilson years, however, did include the use of economic sanctions and the further deterioration of Japanese-American relations.

The first test for Wilson's Far Eastern diplomacy was a familiar one rooted in West Coast hysteria over Japanese immigration and Tokyo's perceived military superiority. By 1913, Californians were especially suspicious of Japanese immigrants, whom they saw as a fifth column biding its time until the start of an American-Japanese war. It mattered little to Californians that Japanese immigration to the Pacific coast had declined dramatically since the 1907 Gentlemen's Agreement or that the 1911 Treaty of Commerce and Navigation returned tariff autonomy to Tokyo in return for continued Japanese pledges to restrict emigration to the United States. Despite these measures and the scars left by earlier fracases over Japanese immigrants, California legislators debated and later approved an ordinance, the Webb-Heney Alien Land Act, barring resident alien Japanese from owning land. Wilson tried but failed to get Sacramento to see reason, and the results were predictable. J. Russell Kennedy, the Associated Press's longtime Tokyo correspondent warned that tensions were unusually high because of the California legislature's scheming, and J. Ingram Bryan, a professor of English at Tokyo University, cautioned that the Japanese press had turned virulently anti-American. Ambassador George Guthrie informed William Jennings Bryan, Wilson's first secretary of state, that the combination of Knox's dollar diplomacy in China, which convinced Tokyo that the United States favored Peking, and now Webb-Heney made his new job unusually difficult. "There does exist in official circles an opinion—almost a conviction," Guthrie warned, "that America's purposes toward China conflict with Japan's interest, and that sooner or later there will be a clash."[41]

Military planners, well aware of the heightened danger, urged the new president to augment American naval strength in both the Philippines and Hawaii. The Joint Board unanimously supported reinforcing the Philippines by transferring ships from China, and after heated debate in the cabinet Wilson forbade the transfer. Two days later, on May 17, when it called for reinforcing Hawaii, Wilson, who unlike Roosevelt, saw naval deterrence as a dangerous option, defied his military advisers and threatened to disband the Joint Board should it bring up redeploying the fleet a third time.[42]

The second major problem that Wilson faced in the Far East dealt with American participation in the international banking consortium for China that Taft had originally supported. Within days of his inauguration, Wilson showed himself a friend of China and a foe of the American bankers when he withdrew support for their activities in China. The president understood that bowing out of the consortium would cost the United States influence in China, yet he maintained that withdrawal would provide the United States with the moral high ground. Wilson, like Taft before him, also believed that unilateral American action would bring more benefits than cooperation with the English, French, and Japanese. While many American businessmen saw his announcement as a retreat from China, with the outbreak of World War I the administration demonstrated that supporting the Open Door remained a priority.[43]

From the start, Tokyo used its involvement in World War I to further its long-term objectives in China. Japan had worked, since the beginning of the 1911 Revolution, to both preserve its rights in Manchuria and increase its political and economic influence in China proper. To achieve these ends, the Saionji cabinet first proposed in 1911 to expand the existing Anglo-Japanese Alliance into an economic as well as a political-strategic instrument. Tokyo also cultivated close relations with China's short-lived provisional president, Dr. Sun Yat-sen, and on the eve of World War I officials were busy seeking British support for rights to build a major railway in central China as well as for plans to extend the Manchurian and Liaotung railway leases. Efforts by the Japanese through the summer of 1914 indicate a concerted attempt to vastly expand their influence in China proper and preserve existing rights in the north. With the onset of World War I, Tokyo pressed for even more.[44]

The decision to enter the war was not an easy one, but Komei Kato, now foreign minister, confidently predicted an Entente victory and brushed aside the opposition of some in the army who forecast a repeat of 1870, when Prussia quickly brought France to its knees. The opportunity to take Germany's valuable Shantung concession as well as its strategically vital central Pacific islands also influenced Tokyo to wage war against Prussian militarism on land and at sea.[45]

The spread of war to Asia both complicated containment and exposed fissures within the new administration. Anxious to protect China, the State Department reminded Japan on August 19 of its obligation to consult with Washington regarding events that might threaten the Open Door. While Wilson and Bryan shared an almost missionary interest in China, Robert Lansing, the number two man at the State Department, held a more limited view of America's role there. Lansing, who believed that American policy should promote equality of commercial opportunity rather than Chinese territorial integrity, reacted to the spread of war with less alarm. Far more than Bryan or Wilson, he was a realist cut from the same cloth as Theodore Roosevelt and was therefore prepared to write off those parts of China now under Tokyo's control in return for Japan's support for the Open Door within its sphere of influence.[46]

After routing German forces in Shantung and sweeping the kaiser's navy from the high seas, Japan next attempted to once and for all secure its position in Manchuria and Inner Mongolia and expand its interests and influence throughout China with the Twenty-one Demands of January 1915. Divided into five sections, the demands dealt with a host of issues. The first section focused on securing Japanese rights in Shantung as well as mechanisms for its eventual return to China. It also included a guarantee from China that no part of the coast should be leased to a third power. The second section, which clearly reflected Kato's 1913 conversation with the British regarding Manchuria, gave Japan, among other things, a ninety-nine-year lease on the South Manchuria Railway. The third and fourth sections were actually quite limited. The third focused solely on Japanese control of selected mining interests, while the fourth sought to solidify Tokyo's control over its existing sphere in Fukien Province, opposite Formosa. Like the first section, the fourth can also be interpreted as essentially security minded in that it sought a Chinese pledge not to lease or cede any portion of the Fukien coast to a third power.[47]

The fifth section of demands included both the innocuous and the obnoxious and clearly threatened the Open Door. Some of Tokyo's wishes were hardly unreasonable. Japan, for example, sought the right to own land in China so that its citizens could build schools, hospitals, and shrines. The government also sought permission for its Buddhist missionaries to proselytize. The fifth section, however, also included the "desire" that Peking establish a joint arsenal with Japan, replace the then current multinational advisory staff with only Japanese economic, military, and political experts, and approve a joint Chinese-Japanese police force in selected areas.[48]

Much has been written on the meaning of the Twenty-one Demands that need not be repeated here. Suffice it to say the demands represented *part* of an ongoing Japanese policy—one that continued for another generation—to safeguard the empire's interests in Manchuria and Inner Mongolia. Plans to enlarge Japan's economic and political influence in China proper were also a *continuation* of earlier policy. The Twenty-one Demands, then, differed from earlier policy primarily in form rather than in substance. Moreover, they must not be interpreted as part of a unified, long-term plan to subjugate China and expel all Western influence, although clearly some requests in the fifth section were intended for just that purpose. Rather, as Ian Nish indicates, while the fifth section was presented as a unified block of requests, it actually represented the myriad wishes of various sectional interests.[49]

Wilson responded slowly to the Twenty-one Demands, in large measure because the administration was not sure exactly what Tokyo was demanding. As details emerged, however, the president and his associates quickly grasped the dangers inherent in Japan's claims. From Peking, US minister Paul Reinsch, who maintained that the demands jeopardized the Open Door, warned Washington that Tokyo would modify its aims only when "it comes against a dead wall of sufficiently powerful resistance." Given the gravity of the situation and the advice of men like Reinsch, Wilson concluded that Washington must now redouble its efforts to contain Japanese expansion in China. The question remained how.[50]

Reinsch suggested that Great Britain could bring its ally to heel, and E. T. Williams, his former first secretary and now head of the State Department's Far Eastern Division (FE), concurred. Williams argued that, if Washington released the contents of the Twenty-one Demands and noted specifically how American rights were jeopardized, surely England would "be glad and aid in bringing about a modification" of Japan's terms. Williams could not have been more wrong. With Japan now an important Entente ally, London could not jeopardize relations with Tokyo. Lansing, still the realist, warned that, since the United States could not compel Tokyo to modify its demands and with relations strained over pending anti-Japanese legislation in California, Idaho, and Oregon, Wilson should tread softly. Lansing carried the day, and in mid-March Bryan handed over to Tokyo a lengthy, if lukewarm, protest that highlighted how the Twenty-one Demands violated existing Japanese-American agreements, with special attention given to those demands pertaining to Manchuria, Inner Mongolia, and Shantung.[51]

Neither missionary zeal nor morality prompted Wilson to defend China. Nor did the president act out of some deep-seated anti-Japanese proclivity. Rather, he viewed China through the particularly well-developed lens of benevolent American economic and commercial expansion. While he and Taft differed over means, he mirrored the Taft-Knox-Conant position regarding the intimate connection between economic expansion and, in this instance, the health of American civilization. Should Japan block American economic expansion in China, both countries would suffer. For Wilson, Conant, and others, the Open Door was no mere policy. It was the backbone of a world system that secured progress and prosperity for all. An attack on any part of the Open Door would reverberate down to the core of the world economic system and threaten American security. Stanley Hornbeck, a young scholar under Paul Reinsch at Wisconsin and the future FE chief, articulated the link between the Open Door and America's well-being in his 1916 *Contemporary Politics in the Far East.* Hornbeck maintained that a Japanese conquest of the China market would bring about manifold problems, chief among them a threat to the Monroe Doctrine. If Japan closed the Open Door, he noted, European exporters would seek markets in Latin America, where, in the process, they would endanger both the Monroe Doctrine and the United States.[52]

In the end, Tokyo dropped the fifth section from its list of demands entirely, and under duress Peking acceded to the bulk of the remaining demands on May 7, 1915. In response, Lansing immediately drafted a nonrecognition doctrine, and on May 11 Washington notified Tokyo that it would not recognize any agreement that China entered into in violation of the Open Door. This did nothing to deter Japan, which over the next eighteen months extended its influence in China further. In 1916, the Shigenobu Okuma ministry moved to strengthen ties with St. Petersburg by concluding an alliance in which Russia recognized Japanese control over South Manchuria and eastern Inner Mongolia as well as the newly acquired sphere in Shantung in return for badly needed Japanese military supplies.[53]

A month after concluding the alliance, Tokyo used a clash between Chinese and Japanese troops at Chengchiatun in eastern Inner Mongolia to further bind north China to the empire. Japan demanded that China employ Japanese military advisers in Manchuria and Inner Mongolia, Japanese instructors in Chinese military schools, Japanese police in regions with a heavy Japanese population, and Japanese advisers for police forces in Manchuria and Inner Mongolia and order its troops not to interfere with Japanese forces. As was the case with the Twenty-one Demands, Peking settled the matter without consenting to the most egregious conditions. Chengchiatun, however, clearly demonstrated Tokyo's continued interest in controlling north China.[54]

In April 1916, before the Russo-Japanese Alliance and the clash at Chengchiatun, Wilson admitted to Lansing that Japan's continuing advance in China was "the trouble that gives me in a way deepest concern just now, because I do not see what is to be done." Reinsch, who believed that American capital could halt Japan's march across China, thought that a multinational financial effort could block the "Manchurianization of Shantung."[55]

Rather than use capital to contain Japan, however, the Wilson administration unveiled a narrow and unsuccessful program of economic sanctions. E. T. Williams and Third Assistant Secretary of State Breckenridge Long, successfully led the effort to employ economic deterrence in the forlorn hope that sanctions would force Japan to modify its China policy. While their plan was a failure, it did briefly reinvigorate Anglo-American cooperation in defense of the Open Door, for powerful elements within the British government backed their idea.[56]

Wilson's executive order of July 1917, which placed critical war matériel on a wartime embargo list, allowed sanctions advocates to move ahead with their plans, and while Lansing, now secretary of state, opposed economic coercion, a new entity, the US War Trade Board (WTB), possessed statutory authority to override his objections. Granted sole authority to issue export licenses for goods placed on the July embargo list, the WTB embarked on a policy that sought to deny Japan critical American steel plate, the kind used in shipbuilding, in order to coerce that country both during the war and quite possibly after. The embargo, however, quickly backfired as Tokyo promptly dispatched an economic mission to China to find sufficient iron ore deposits to "free Japan from dependence on the United States or Great Britain." Japan also worked to increase production of iron ore in existing mines both in Japan and within newly conquered Shantung.[57]

The American steel embargo appeared to end in March 1918 after Tokyo agreed to build cargo ships for the United States in return for export licenses. The WTB, however, continued to use its control over export licenses to influence Japanese policy. By July, the board still had not approved any export license for steel, despite the fact that most American observers had already concluded that the embargo had failed. Japan had so increased its production of steel plate that it no longer required American imports. Moreover, British patience for the protracted embargo had evaporated, and by November even the WTB concluded that the steel embargo must end.[58]

The long-term damage occasioned by the embargo proved considerable. While admitting the failure of a specific embargo in November 1918, the WTB did not reject economic coercion in general, and that same month it "decided not to issue export licenses for cotton or . . . silk." Worse still, the embargoes highlighted Japanese economic vulnerability and, according to the State Department, led "the Japanese to work with feverish energy to develop what metals they have in their own islands and privileges in the mining areas of China." From Tokyo, the embassy concluded that economic coercion had provided Tokyo with greater incentive "for territorial expansion."[59]

Japanese actions clearly concerned Lansing, who informed Wilson early in 1917: "Japan evidently aims to . . . obtain control of China." He advised the president "that a firm stand . . . will compel a modification of Japanese demands upon China," but, rather than confront Japan with sanctions, he sought a compromise, similar to earlier successful understandings, that recognized de facto Japanese control in parts of China in return for a firm Japanese commitment to the Open Door. The secretary of state viewed Japanese hegemony in Manchuria, Inner Mongolia, and now Shantung as analogous to US dominance in the Caribbean and hoped that, in return for Washington's recognition of Japan's "special interests," Tokyo would agree to reaffirm the Open Door and end its protests over California's anti-Japanese legislation.[60]

While powerful elements within the State Department and Washington's wartime bureaucracy sought to coerce Japan, Lansing continued to support a policy of diplomatic engagement. America's entrance into World War I, with its rapid military buildup, convinced many Japanese that Washington was marshaling its forces for an eventual showdown with Tokyo. The likelihood that the war would also foster closer Anglo-American relations, which might mean postwar cooperation to oppose Japanese expansion in China, also concerned Tokyo, as did economic sanctions and Reinsch's push for a Sino-American alliance. These concerns finally prompted Prime Minister Masatake Terauchi to dispatch a joint civilian-military delegation, headed by the Viscount Kikujiro Ishii, to the United States in the summer of 1917. Terauchi wanted Ishii to secure agreements to protect Japanese citizens living in the United States and reach an understanding to end the conflict between Japanese expansion in China and the Open Door. His confidential instructions reveal the depth of Japanese interests in China and the lengths to which the empire would go to protect those interests and therefore must be quoted at some length. Foreign Minister Ichiro Motono informed his plenipotentiary:

> Japan's relation's with China, economically speaking, the amount of our capital investment and the volume of our trade are incomparably greater than those of the United States, while in the political field Japan's interests far outweigh those of the United States and the European Powers, being of a special and vital nature closely linked to the security and future welfare of our country. Consequently, should any Power attempt to establish political influence in China in disregard of, or in a manner harmful to, Japan's position, Japan would as a matter of course be compelled to resort to measures of self-defense.

Over nearly two months of on again, off again talks, Lansing and Ishii successfully negotiated agreements that both affirmed Washington's official Wilsonian opposition to spheres and recognized, although not openly, Japan's spheres of interest in Manchuria, Inner Mongolia, and Shantung, in return for Japanese adherence to the Open Door.[61]

In their first major meeting on September 6, Lansing proposed a mutual reaffirmation of the Open Door, and, while Ishii agreed in substance, he informed the secretary that his government would require some recognition of Tokyo's special interests in China, which remained a major Japanese goal for the duration of the talks. Discussions between Lansing and Ishii on this point, like Ishii's original instructions, reveal a great deal regarding Japan's so-called Monroe Doctrine for China. During the negotiations, Ishii argued that "the relationship of Japan and China was more important than that of the United States and Mexico," that "disturbances in China had an immediate effect on Japan[,] and that the collapse of China would mean the collapse of Japan." In an amazingly frank speech given on October 1, during a luncheon hosted by the journalist Oswald Garrison Villard, Ishii expanded on the theme of Chinese importance to the safety of the empire and the meaning of Japan's Monroe Doctrine. Japan, Ishii argued, would "not only not seek to assail the integrity or the sovereignty of China but eventually will be prepared to defend the integrity or the sovereignty of China against any aggressor."[62]

While Ishii's interpretation of Japan's Monroe Doctrine clearly glosses over its less seemly side, namely, that Japan would exercise dominant influence over China just as Washington did over the Western hemisphere, his explanation was remarkably close to that developed by other, more neutral contemporary observers. The American-educated Indian social scientist Sudhindra Bose, for example, maintained, like Ishii, that Japan's Monroe Doctrine sought only to prevent the further spread of imperialism to Asia. While recognizing that Japanese dominance would likely destroy the Open Door, the Harvard historian Albert Bushnell Hart likewise saw clear similarities between the Japanese and the American Monroe Doctrines. "Japan will henceforth stand against all countries as the leader of the Asiatic spirit and the defender of Asiatic empire in Eastern Asia," Hart maintained, "exactly as the United States considers herself the champion of true Americanism in the Western Hemisphere."[63]

Japan's Monroe Doctrine reveals the Janusian nature of Japan's China policy, at once defensive and aggressive, motivated by fear and ambition, insecurity and vanity. For decades, successive administrations sought to ensure Japanese access to Chinese markets, raw materials, and investment outlets. On another level, forward movements like the Twenty-one Demands reveal a Japanese effort to ensure that no hostile foreign power could ever position itself to dominate China. Unfortunately, the best way to forestall this eventuality necessitated an aggressive Japanese response, which, if successful, would have undermined Chinese sovereignty in order to secure Japan's.

Lansing-Ishii also revealed the continuing importance that Wilson placed on the Open Door and that Lansing and Ishii placed on crafting an agreement that reflected basic geopolitical reality. Despite the urging of Colonel Edward House, the president's close adviser, that he moderate his demand for an explicit Japanese pledge to respect the Open Door, Wilson rightly held out until the end, determined to secure formal Japanese recognition for the American shibboleth. On September 22, Ishii informed Lansing that his government opposed openly reaffirming the Open Door because, if it did, both the public and the Diet would demand a parallel American recognition of Japan's special interests on the continent. Lansing explained that, while Washington would never offer such a declaration if *special interests* meant "paramount interests," if Tokyo "meant a special interest based upon geographic position," then he would consider the matter. Lansing honestly believed that such a position would not violate traditional policy toward China in that two years earlier Bryan had recognized Japan's special interests on the basis of the recommendations of E. T. Williams. Lansing and Ishii required another month of talks to produce what remains a remarkable, if short-lived, agreement. In the final exchange of notes, Washington recognized Japan's special interests, especially in Manchuria and Inner Mongolia, while Tokyo reaffirmed its support for the Open Door. While neither side got exactly what it wanted, neither walked away empty-handed. The wording of the agreement was also sufficiently vague as to offer a victory or a fig leaf, depending on which was needed most. As Lansing the realist told a chagrined Chinese official apropos Japan's special interests: "I thought . . . that he would agree with me that to concede a truth, which could not be successfully denied, in exchange for a declaration of a policy which restrained the other party [was a good bargain]."[64]

In the end, Lansing-Ishii may have done more harm than good, and it certainly did little to enhance Robert Lansing's reputation. A generation after the agreement's conclusion, American officials who opposed a prewar settlement with Japan used the accord, and the controversy concerning "special interests," to argue against a deal. Japan, they claimed, would twist the language as they had twisted the wording of Lansing-Ishii to suit their needs. Nobody seemed to remember that Lansing had intended that *special interests* be sufficiently vague to provide "ample room for suitable interpretations on both sides." Worse still, on the eve of the next global war, no senior Roosevelt administration official seems to have recognized the most important lesson of the Lansing-Ishii story. American pressure and Japanese fear produced the opportunity for diplomatic engagement. While Japan came to Washington unwilling to abandon its spheres of influence, it evidenced a willingness to accommodate Washington. Perhaps, had the agreements been reached at another time, they might have contributed to a sense of trust and accomplishment and therefore could have served as a bridge to better relations, but the protocols were signed on November 2, 1917, and events half a world away were already overshadowing the work of Messrs. Lansing and Ishii.[65]

Land, Bread, Peace, and Paris

The Bolshevik seizure of power in October 1917 promoted insecurity within Japan, division within its government, and insubordination within the military. This is not surprising given that the Russian Revolution presented the most ominous challenge to Japanese national security since Perry's arrival three-quarters of a century earlier. Lenin immediately undermined Tokyo's position in Northeast Asia by repudiating the 1916 Russo-Japanese Alliance, including the key provisions regarding mutual respect for spheres of influence. Instead of an ally, Japan now faced an old enemy animated by a new and dangerous ideology. Worse still, Tokyo feared that the Bolshevik takeover might inspire far-Left elements within Japan and China's Kuomintang Party. Soon after Lenin's takeover, Japan's European allies began to pressure Tokyo to dispatch troops to secure Siberia, yet, with Russia out of the war and the prospects for a German victory increasing exponentially, the Terauchi cabinet wished desperately to avoid the increased friction with Washington that Japanese military intervention in Northeast Asia would surely bring.[66]

In Washington, meanwhile, Wilson weighed the costs of military action, Japanese and American, in Russia against the costs of inaction. America's allies and many of its Russian-based diplomats wanted the president to send troops. Wilson's military advisers and the State Department, on the other hand, opposed intervention, claiming that it would antagonize the new Russian government. In March 1918, however, Lansing dropped his opposition to military action and claimed that the spread of German influence into Siberia necessitated a Japanese landing, which the United States should support. Wilson, still reluctant to encourage Japan or send American forces, disagreed and maintained his resistance until he relented to Allied pressure in July and agreed to send US forces to Russia.[67]

Several factors led to Wilson's change of heart in the summer of 1918, foremost among them the need to dispatch troops to Siberia in order to contain Japanese expansion. Since 1905, Tokyo exercised de facto control in southern Manchuria, and in May 1916 Japan and China agreed to cooperate in restoring order in Siberia as well as to the "joint defense of the Chinese border." This agreement, which facilitated a massive, long-term increase in Japanese military personnel in Manchuria along the border with Siberia, allowed Tokyo to expand its control from southern Manchuria to the entire region. Still, Wilson refused to intervene. In July 1918, Lord Reading, Britain's ambassador to the United States, presented the president with an appeal from the Allied Supreme War Council that requested immediate American intervention in Siberia. To put Wilson's mind at ease, the Allies' request included a pledge from Tokyo to respect Russian territorial integrity. The following day, Wilson received Lansing's approval for intervention and at last relented. The president pushed for a joint landing where American and Japanese forces numbered one division each, with operations restricted to the port of Vladivostok. This, he reckoned, would serve to limit Japanese expansion.[68]

Lansing hoped that joint action would contain Japan, but he did not realize that Tokyo lacked full control over its armed forces. Army officials, including Vice Chief of Staff General Giichi Tanaka, hoped to establish an independent anti-Bolshevik buffer state in Siberia, and in September, just a month after the intervention began, Japanese officials entered into negotiations with White Russian leaders in which they promised greater troop commitments in return for economic concessions. The army, meanwhile, acting without official approval, dispatched as many as eight additional divisions and deployed troops as far east as Lake Baikal.[69]

Wilson failed to contain Japanese expansion in Siberia, so the job of rolling back Tokyo's gains in Russia fell to his defeated opponent in the 1916 presidential election, Charles Evans Hughes, who became secretary of state in the Warren G. Harding administration. Hughes's success in securing a Japanese pullback in 1922 highlights the continued importance that a cooperative Japanese government played in the success of American containment. Kei Hara, Japan's prime minister since September 1918, opposed the Siberian intervention, and his new army minister, General Giichi Tanaka, who earlier had supported an open-ended intervention, had a change of heart and began to cut Japanese troop strength in Russia by the end of 1918. Aritomo Yamagata, the last of the Meiji oligarchs and the father of the modern Japanese army, supported the withdrawal, and, while the massacre of Japanese soldiers and civilians by Russians at Nikolaevsky in May 1920 no doubt prolonged the Japanese troop presence, government opposition to continued intervention proved relentless. In May 1921, influenced by rising costs as well as foreign and domestic opposition, a combined civilian-military council called for a withdrawal, which Japan completed in October 1922. In the end, the Siberian imbroglio is critical in that it highlights the extraordinary difficulty that Japan's military posed to the architects of American containment as well as the continued importance of a cooperative Japanese government.[70]

While hardly a sideshow, events far to the west quickly eclipsed Siberia. The failure of the German spring offensive and the successful Allied counterattack led at last to an armistice. That was the easy part. Now the Allies had to make peace. Wilson hoped that the Versailles Conference would establish a new order based firmly on his Fourteen Points. For Japan, however, the Fourteen Points were a mixed blessing at best. None of those points dealt specifically with the Far East, and while the third, which concerned the removal of economic barriers and free trade, and the fourteenth, which dealt with the future League of Nations, interested Tokyo, Japanese delegates at Versailles sought first and foremost to confirm the empire's wartime gains.[71]

Its victories early in the war, especially its conquest of the Caroline, Gilbert, and Marshall Islands as well as the Micronesian island of Yap, allowed Japan to expand its presence deep into the Pacific. Incorporating these islands into its empire, however, quickly raised the ire of Australia, New Zealand, and the United States. The State Department's Breckenridge Long, who worried that Japanese retention of the islands threatened Guam, the Philippines, and ultimately Hawaii and the Pacific coast, recommended that the US push for the return of the islands to Germany and then arrange for Berlin to transfer them to Washington. Hornbeck, now an adviser to the American delegation, pushed for a direct transfer to Washington or London, and E. T. Williams, who along with Long recognized the impossibility of Hornbeck's suggestions, argued that at the very least the islands must go to a power agreeable to both Japan and the United States. Tokyo, meanwhile, had already secured critical Anglo-French backing for its claim, but, given its greater desire for Shantung, Hara's cabinet accepted a lesser degree of control over the former German islands in return for firm control on the mainland. Wilson opposed the decision to make the islands Class C League of Nations mandates under Japanese control, yet, like later practitioners of containment after the next world war, he accepted the reality that, once a nation occupied territory, the options for dislodging it were few and unattractive.[72]

Negotiations over the disposition of Shantung Province proved even more acrimonious and protracted than those over Berlin's Pacific islands. Chinese delegates quite naturally opposed Japanese plans to acquire German rights in Shantung, and Tokyo foolishly linked retention of the peninsula to membership in the league. Japanese delegates clung to the position that no rights in Shantung meant a league without Japan, and, while Wilson wanted to place Japan squarely in the League of Nations, he did not want it to control Shantung. The president had few good options on the Shantung question in that Tokyo occupied the peninsula and neither London nor Paris would help roll back Japan's wartime expansion. In the end, Tokyo effected a compromise that closely reflected the agreements contained in the Twenty-one Demands and gave Japan selected German interests in Kiaochow in return for concessions elsewhere in the province. Even this created problems for Wilson in that Republicans in Congress began to use the Shantung question as justification for their opposition to the Versailles Treaty.[73]

While Japan gained most of the territorial concessions that it had sought, it lost out in the long run as the conference reinforced the growing perception of it as an adversary. Robert Lansing, once the advocate of compromise, became disgusted at Japanese threats not to join the league. He was almost as disgusted with Wilson for giving in to Japan, a step that amounted to "abandon[ing] China and surrender[ing] our prestige in the Far East." After

Versailles, E. T. Williams proclaimed that "the spirit of Japan is that of Prussia, whom the Japanese leaders openly admire," and on the floor of the US Senate, Medill McCormick of Illinois told his colleagues: "Japan's foreign policy in Asia has been one of consistent perfidy and aggression."[74]

Versailles also did nothing to improve Japanese views of the United States. Japanese delegates had hoped to obtain a racial equality clause in the League of Nations charter that would "secure racial equality for Japanese nationals" living overseas. Wilson, however, blocked the proposal owing to his fear of domestic opposition and desire to maintain an Anglo-American common front. Even as Hara attempted to mend fences over this and other irritants, his armed services developed new plans to wage war against the United States. In a sign of just how far relations had slid since 1900, these plans designated America Japan's number two hypothetical enemy behind only the Soviets, while the navy, alarmed by the growth of the American fleet, stepped up its planning as well. Ominously, the navy soon designated the United States as its most likely opponent.[75]

In the United States, meanwhile, the politicization of Japanese-American relations accelerated as Japanophobes worked to secure support for the postwar military. Thomas Millard, a newspaper correspondent and editor with over a decade of experience in Asia and a longtime critic of Japan, informed the Senate Foreign Relations Committee in August 1919 that Japan and the United States would likely be at war within a decade and that moral force would not deter Tokyo. "The only thing that will terrify Japan is force," Millard told the committee. Four months later, Congressman Julius Kahn of California, a longtime advocate of universal military training and the chair of the House Military Committee, publicly declared that, while he hoped for peace between Japan and America, adequate military preparedness might be the best way to secure such a laudable end. With Germany defeated, Russia in revolution, and England and France bled dry, advocates of an American military buildup continued to justify their requests almost solely with reference to Japan.[76]

The Circle Is Complete

In the final years of Wilson's presidency, his search for a means to contain Japan at last led back to the moribund China consortium, abandoned five years earlier. In the years after the American withdrawal, the United States attempted, with limited success, to aid Chinese development and roll back established spheres of influence by aggressively, and unilaterally, loaning money to the Chinese republic. The former American members of the banking consortium, however, refused to compete against their onetime partners, and nonmembers showed little interest in making loans to Peking. Consequently, between 1913 and 1917, American corporations and financial houses made only five substantial loans to China, totaling just over $21 million. While it is difficult to set a price on limiting Japanese expansion and fostering Chinese development, suffice it to say the American loans fell well short of the mark. Moreover, much to Washington's alarm, Japanese loans to, and by extension influence in, China continued to grow. During the last two years of the war, Japan pumped nearly ¥200 million (over $90 million) into seven major projects. Faced with this successful commercial expansion and the likelihood that more loans were in the offing, Washington admitted defeat. In June 1918, with Lansing's backing, Wilson asked the American group to form a new consortium.[77]

Publicly, the new consortium represented a return to the Roosevelt-Taft years, and the House of Morgan's Thomas Lamont, senior representative of the consortium's American group, saw the organization as a continuation of Hay's Open Door policy. He frequently described the group's mission as an attempt to carry out a Republican policy that began under Theodore Roosevelt and continued under Taft and Knox. Lamont argued that the consortium would help preserve peace in the Far East, aid Chinese development, and, perhaps most importantly from the administration's standpoint, undermine existing spheres. Given that Roosevelt never seriously entertained rolling back Japanese spheres, the new consortium really aimed at achieving what Taft could not accomplish, rolling back Japanese expansion, and this goal was no less dangerous in 1918 than it was in 1909.[78]

While the consortium's goals were dangerous, its specific proposals to aid Chinese development were merely unimaginative. While Lamont claimed that loans would enable China to develop its public enterprises and transportation system and provide the necessary funds for a general currency reform, policymakers had considered these undertakings for decades, and tens of millions of dollars had already been spent in a futile attempt to develop Chinese infrastructure. A Lamont confidant privately informed the Morgan partner in early January 1919 that repeating the old loan pattern would produce few results. "Lending money to China," he told Lamont, "was a good deal like pouring water into a rat's hole. What she needs is administrative help in the first instance." Unfortunately, a decade passed before a stable Chinese government capable of receiving such help rose to power.[79]

Japan soon found that it had little to fear from the consortium, yet its early opposition nearly killed the new organization and earned Tokyo untold ill will.

Japanese leaders quickly objected to any loans in the southern half of Manchuria, especially in territory near the South Manchuria Railway Zone, or eastern Inner Mongolia, and, with the recent Lansing-Ishii understanding in mind, they felt sure that Washington would not object to exempting these regions. Given the Wilson administration's hope, however, that international loans would roll back spheres, Washington did not give Tokyo a sympathetic hearing. Moreover, while the normally understanding Lamont publicly worked to hold the consortium together, privately he fumed at Tokyo's reservations and expressed astonishment that Japan should even be treated as a great power.[80]

By March 1920, Lamont's patience was near an end, and in a last-ditch effort to gain Japanese membership he employed both the carrot and the stick. He informed Tokyo that continued objections might cost it future American financial assistance while at the same time joining the US ambassador to Japan, Roland Morris, and the British ambassador to Tokyo, Beilby Alston, in an effort to address what all three believed were legitimate Japanese national security concerns. Tokyo, in turn, made their task somewhat easier by paring down its list of demands. Its Washington embassy informed the Department of State on March 2 that only selected railroads north of the Great Wall, including the South Manchuria Railway, its branches, and adjacent mines, should be exempt from international loans. In Tokyo, meanwhile, Lamont privately assured Japanese bankers that, because Manchurian railroads were vital to Korea and by extension Japanese security, "it would be quite contrary to the ideas of the American banking group that in Southern Manchuria and Eastern Inner Mongolia [corresponding roughly with parts of contemporary Hebei and Liaoning Provinces and portions of the Inner Mongolia Autonomous Region] the consortium should undertake the construction of new railway lines without the unanimous [consent] of all four banking group members of the consortium." Despite Tokyo's shrinking demands and Lamont's assurances, Breckenridge Long and John Van Antwerp MacMurray chafed at granting Japan veto power over Consortium loans.[81]

Their opposition soon caused Lamont to turn his anger from Japan to a still intransigent Washington. He realized, and believed that the new Harding administration should too, that the consortium would never attempt to fund competing railways in Manchuria and Mongolia and that recognizing Japanese preeminence in these areas did not entail a surrender of principles but represented instead a recognition of reality. In the first week of May, faced with the choice of either accepting Tokyo's reservations or seeing the consortium crumble, Washington admitted defeat. Without specifically recognizing Manchuria and Mongolia as Japanese spheres, the State Department agreed to Japanese terms.[82]

The consortium's prolonged and difficult birth produced a somewhat disappointing heir to the prewar group, for it never made a single loan to China. Civil war, Peking's inability to make good on previous loans, and obstruction on the part of successive Chinese administrations, coupled with reluctance and, after 1929, the inability of the consortium to make loans, spelled the end of the group's grand plans. That the consortium never made a loan to China, however, does not mean that it was without great historical importance.

Initially, the American goals for the consortium reveal that the new diplomacy of the 1920s was in some respects not so new after all, inasmuch as, a decade after the machinations of Knox and Straight, American officials still sought to use capital to roll back Japanese spheres. Japanese insistence on excluding large sections of Manchuria and Inner Mongolia, meanwhile, reveals Tokyo's continued determination to exercise unquestioned authority in these regions.

Consortium negotiations also reveal Washington's extreme reluctance to recognize what John Hay accepted a generation before: the Open Door did not extend to foreign investment within a power's sphere of influence. Lamont's experiences also illustrate the tendency, prevalent throughout the interwar period and continuing today in accounts of the era, to divide Japan between reasonable, cooperative civilians and aggressive, unreasonable militarists. After Junnosuke Inoue, the governor of the Bank of Japan, reportedly pressed his government to drop its demands regarding Manchuria and Mongolia, Lamont expressed extreme distaste for the Japanese military, which he blamed for Tokyo's policy and tremendous confidence in the goodness of Inoue and his fellow financiers. Both Lamont and leading American statesmen, however, failed to recognize that Manchuria was a poor litmus test for reasonability, one that very few Japanese could pass. The emperor's subjects could and did disagree on the methods for preserving Japanese hegemony north of the Great Wall, but even "reasonable" Japanese such as Inoue or Foreign Minister Kijuro Shidehara would not dispute the empire's need to retain control of the region. The majority of Japanese, civilian and military alike, believed that Manchuria and Mongolia were the shields of the empire, and woe to the government that willingly gave them away or was forced by the West to cast them aside.[83]

The End of an Era

By the time a stroke-ravaged Wilson left office in March 1921, Japanese-American relations and America's perception of Japan scarcely resembled those of twenty years earlier. Contempt, fear, and mistrust had replaced earlier respect for Japanese modernization and force of arms. Once seen as the champion of the Open Door, Japan now appeared its greatest despoiler. Once the Great Britain of Asia, it had degenerated into the Prussia of the Far East. Attempts to resolve outstanding differences with Japan continued, yet diplomacy alone seemed insufficient. By 1921, all too many placed undue hope in the chimera of American economic and military might.

Japan's perception of America had also changed a great deal by early 1921. Increasingly, it appeared to many Japanese, civilian and military alike, that the United States had taken the lead in opposing Japanese expansion, first in Hawaii and along the American Pacific coast, then in Manchuria and China proper. Immigration restrictions and prohibitions on land ownership inflamed Japanese public opinion and produced repeated war scares, and, while diplomats continued to secure agreements with Washington concerning expansion in China, immigration, and the rights of Japanese in America, they increasingly came to value alliances with the great powers of Europe as the best means of safeguarding vital interests. The military, meanwhile, continued to revise plans for an eventual war with America.

For twenty years, Japan and the United States had pursued policies designed to secure fundamental national objectives. These objectives stemmed from a curious combination of insecurity and confidence and rested on a firm ideological foundation. For the United States, fear of economic stagnation and confidence that American commercial expansion would benefit both the Republic and foreign lands drove the search for trade and investment outlets. In Tokyo, an even deeper preoccupation with national security and an unshakable belief in the inseparable destinies of China and Japan pulled the empire inexorably onto the Asian mainland. Successive American administrations resolved these competing imperatives and safeguarded the Open Door with a multifaceted policy that, with active cooperation from Japanese civilian authorities, had, by and large, successfully contained Japan.

If the years between Portsmouth and the conclusion of the Versailles Conference tell a cautionary tale of gradual and steady estrangement, they also impart an instructive lesson in how to secure sweeping national objectives with limited resources. Unfortunately, in the coming years, too many, on both sides of the Pacific, remembered only the estrangement while forgetting the useful lessons.

Chapter 2

The Rise and Fall of the Washington Conference System

> If there is a genuine feeling of good-fellowship and mutual trust [such as that created by the Washington Conference], nothing very serious can go wrong.
>
> —Sir Miles Lampson (May 1922)

> I really fear the Japanese have got themselves inextricably entangled in a situation that will in the end suffocate and ruin them.
>
> —John Van Antwerp MacMurray (June 1933)

Warren G. Harding is not remembered as a particularly brave or daring man. But, at the outset of his presidency, the United States embarked on a bold plan to contain Japanese expansion and protect the Open Door. The 1921–1922 Washington Conference brought representatives of the major powers to the nation's capital for four months of talks designed to end the ongoing Anglo-American-Japanese naval building program and resolve differences over the future of the Anglo-Japanese Alliance, the Open Door, and Shantung Province. The Washington Conference inaugurated the most successful period in America's long containment of Japan, and, in its aftermath, Japanese expansion on the Asian mainland receded, most notably in Siberia, northern Sakhalin, and Shantung.

The success of American containment, however, did not bring about a fundamental change in Japanese-American relations. Instead, Americans' deep affection for and sense of mission in China, which had developed during the Progressive Era, increased. Tokyo's pro-Western policies and cooperative diplomacy could not arrest the precipitous decline in relations, soften American attitudes, or change US policy.

In Japan, meanwhile, the Washington Conference undermined the very moderates who, since 1905, had ensured containment's success and by doing so acted as a catalyst to militarists and ultranationalists. Within a decade of Hughes's invitation, extremists assassinated three prime ministers, while the military's penchant for unilateral action increased exponentially, most notably in Manchuria. At the start of the Washington Conference, civilian moderates firmly controlled the Japanese government. A decade later, the military held sway at home and in their puppet state of Manchukuo.

Disenchantment with the conference fueled extremism, but so too did events in China, where long-simmering nationalism undermined both the Open Door and the multinational cooperation on which it rested. Antiforeignism in China, which often manifested itself in strikes, boycotts, and sometimes violence, further undermined Japanese moderates and emboldened ultranationalists, who called for resolute, unilateral action.

The Washington Conference and the New Far Eastern Order

In the aftermath of World War I, the Far Eastern balance of power lay shattered. The Chinese Revolution, which had begun with such promise in 1911, had devolved, first into a dictatorship, then into warlordism and chaos. Yuan Shikai, the general turned provisional president, betrayed the revolution when, following his drubbing in nationwide elections, he outlawed the Kuomintang, muzzled the parliament, and provoked a revolt in the south that his army quickly crushed. In 1915, at the urging of his American constitutional adviser, Yuan prepared to name himself emperor but abandoned the idea the very next year following nationwide opposition. With his death in June 1916, central authority in China collapsed, and the nation sank into more than a decade of warlord rule.[1]

Neither Britain nor France, exhausted and traumatized by war, could offer China much protection, and Russia, the traditional counterweight to Japanese expansion in Asia, still suffered from the ravages of defeat, revolution, and civil war. Only the United States could fill the void created by war and revolution, and in November 1921, with the opening of the Washington Conference, Secretary of State Charles Evans Hughes acted to protect both China and the Open Door. While Hughes undeniably determined the course of the conference, the impetus for the talks came not from the State Department but rather from the US Senate and Idaho's William Borah. Borah, who supported disarmament and opposed American membership in the League of Nations, proposed an Anglo-American-Japanese naval disarmament conference in order to weaken support for the Versailles Treaty. The senator believed that, when London and Tokyo balked at holding talks, which he fully expected them to do, resistance to American membership in the league would grow. In May 1921, the Senate overwhelmingly approved Borah's resolution, and the Harding administration, which initially refused to support this legislative foray into the executive domain, bowed to overwhelming congressional and public support for disarmament and began laying the groundwork for an international conference.[2]

Hughes, who cared far more about the Open Door than about naval disarmament, intended to use the conference to limit Japanese expansion and soon added a discussion of outstanding Far Eastern political issues to the agenda. Harding and his secretary of state clearly sought to use the upcoming talks to check, and in some cases even roll back, Japanese political, economic, and territorial expansion in China. By mid-July, Hughes already envisioned giving the Open Door, Shantung, Yap Island, and the Anglo-Japanese Alliance serious attention, and, while he gave British leaders the impression that he would respect the status quo in Manchuria, even this region's fate was open to discussion. From the start of the conference, Hughes was determined to correct what he believed were a generation of America's diplomatic wrongs, including Lansing-Ishii and Root-Takahira, the very agreements in which Washington tacitly recognized and defined Japan's Manchurian sphere.[3]

As their first order of business, the conferees set about ending the dangerous naval arms race then under way between the United States, Britain, and Japan. Beginning in 1916, as US entry into World War I appeared increasingly likely, Washington embarked on a colossal building program designed to add over 150 new ships to the fleet. Four years later, when the Navy Department recommended building an additional eighty-eight warships and the British Admiralty responded with its own expansion program, a race began that "threatened to make the Anglo-German competition of the early 1900s look like a lobster quadrille." Japan's decision to embark on its own postwar program, which envisioned a core fleet of eight modern battleships and a like number of cruisers, made the postwar arms race even more perilous.[4]

Given the extraordinary cost and danger of the buildup, few were surprised when Hughes opened the meeting with an exposition on the subject. His bold proposal to declare a ten-year moratorium on capital shipbuilding, however, coupled with the call to scrap over sixty vessels, either existing or under construction, exhilarated the delegates, dumbfounded the British, who knew nothing of the plan, and generated immediate congressional and public support. Under the Hughes formula, the American, British, and Japanese capital fleets would correspond to a 10:10:6 ratio. Japanese naval authorities, the Imperial Diet, and public opinion, however, all favored a 10:7 ratio, and the Japanese plenipotentiary Admiral Tomosaburo Kato, who earnestly desired an agreement, immediately found himself in a corner. Tokyo's desire to better relations with Washington soon came to the admiral's rescue because Prime Minister Korekiyo Takahashi would not let the 10:7 issue stand in the way of improved Japanese-American ties. By the end of the month, authorities cabled Kato to "strive to settle the ratio to 10 to 6.5" but that a 10:6 ratio would prove acceptable with "a firm understanding of reducing Pacific defenses or at least leaving them as they are now." British and American representatives also brought considerable pressure on the admiral to agree to the Hughes formula. British foreign secretary Arthur Balfour informed Kato that failure to reach an accord on the naval question could doom the entire conference, while Elihu Root told him that intransigence on the ratio question meant a renewed arms race and a possible American-led economic embargo of Japan.[5]

While it is doubtful that economic deterrence contributed to the final success of the negotiations, the threat is significant in that it indicates Washington's continued faith in the possibilities of economic coercion, despite the debacle of the recent steel embargo. Tokyo had already expressed its reluctant willingness to accept a 10:6 ratio precisely because, as Balfour warned Kato, the remainder of the Washington Conference depended on the success of the naval talks. Moreover, because he rejected the premise of an inevitable Japanese-American war, Kato accepted the 10:6 ratio without fear that it compromised national security. He informed the Navy Ministry that, given Japan's financial dependence on Washington, "a contest between Japan and America is unthinkable" and, therefore, that Japan must "avoid war with America." The final agreement, signed in Washington on February 6, assured Japan naval supremacy in its home waters and spared Tokyo an arms race it could ill afford and could not possibly win. Despite these notable successes, the Washington Naval Treaty also had several unfortunate drawbacks.[6]

The agreement immediately divided the Japanese navy into treaty and fleet factions, and by the middle of the decade withering attacks by the latter mortally weakened the moderate treaty camp. Second, while enhancing Japanese naval security, the accord undermined Japanese security on the continent. Following the conference, Tokyo slashed its military budget, and, while naval authorities could accept a reduction because their most likely foes also had ceased building new capital ships, the army had no illusions that the Soviets or the Chinese would enact a similar moratorium. Moreover, even a cursory reading of Japanese diplomatic traffic reveals that Tokyo often saw the United States and Britain acting in concert against Japan, especially on such critical issues as the proper ratio for capital ships and areas to be included in the nonfortification agreement. Finally, because the naval agreement dealt with the effects, rather than the causes, of Anglo-American-Japanese tension, it did not completely halt the naval arms race. Instead, arms limitation stimulated a technological revolution in naval construction as nations attempted to build lighter warships in order to remain within treaty limits. Hughes's treaty also contributed to increased submarine and aircraft carrier construction, which, however critical, paled in comparison to the new cruiser building race. In 1922, Japan launched a cruiser building program, and, two years later, the United States and Great Britain followed suit. This new breed of warship, with a displacement just under ten thousand tons and sporting eight-inch guns, did not violate the letter of the Washington Naval Treaty, however much it mocked its spirit.[7]

Hughes's naval agreement still faced an uphill battle in the Senate as long as the Anglo-Japanese Alliance remained operative. Never popular in the United States, the alliance was seen in Washington as an outmoded relic and a shield that facilitated Japanese expansion. The navy General Board, in particular, sought its termination, and, as Thomas Lamont learned during the consortium negotiations, the Chinese so dreaded the alliance that its very existence made it next to impossible to gain their trust. Hughes and other supporters of some form of Anglo-American entente also saw the termination of the pact as a necessary precursor. London did not share any of these convictions, and, while the alliance's supporters recognized that renewal would arouse the suspicion of both Washington and the American public, which they wished to avoid, they also understood that, without it, England would lose influence over Japanese policy in Asia. The historian M. G. Fry neatly summed up London's dilemma when he noted how "Britain had to contain Japan yet maintain her friendship." To further complicate matters, London had to contend with the conflicting wishes of the British dominions. Australia and New Zealand supported renewal, while Ottawa, worried that the alliance could lead to an Anglo-American war in which Canada would reprise Belgium's unhappy role in the 1914–1918 drama, vehemently opposed continuing the partnership.[8]

And what of Japan? Tokyo favored continuing the alliance for myriad reasons, not the least of which was the fear that, in the increasingly Anglo-American dominated post-Versailles world, Japan would grow isolated without its decades-old accord with Britain. Tokyo, however, walked a tightrope at Washington, for it had to balance these needs with its desire to achieve a rapprochement with the United States.[9]

In the end, while Japan and England allowed their pact to expire, Hughes's victory proved illusory. In reality, the United States had no reason to fear an Anglo-Japanese combination because the Third Anglo-Japanese

Alliance, signed in 1911, stipulated that neither signatory had to fight a third party with which it had an existing arbitration treaty. Washington and London signed such a treaty in 1914, and it is all but impossible to conceive of any postwar British government choosing to wage war with America on Japan's behalf. Moreover, while a renewed pact would have made a naval limitation agreement more difficult, enlightened statesmanship no doubt could have prevailed. The 10:10:6 ratio would have posed a threat to American security only if Washington believed that London would willingly fight the United States in the event of war with Japan. The unnecessary termination of the alliance also contributed to the immediate growth of pro-German sentiment within the Japanese navy. The officer corps, in particular, found London's lack of support for renewal disconcerting, and, by mid-decade, Tokyo sent promising young naval engineers, traditionally assigned to the Royal Navy yard in Greenwich, to Germany. On the eve of World War II, these officers exerted considerable pro-Axis influence within naval circles.[10]

In retrospect, killing the Anglo-Japanese Alliance may well have been Washington's greatest diplomatic blunder of the decade. The Four Power Pact, consisting of the United States, France, Japan, and the United Kingdom, which Hughes created to take the place of the Anglo-Japanese Alliance, did little to stabilize the Far East or assuage Japan's sense of isolation. For twenty years, Tokyo enjoyed the benefits of and discharged the obligations inherent in a great-power alliance. Given this diplomatic tradition, how long would Japan remain alone? And which nation would it join in the future? The United States did not enter peacetime alliances, and, while some future Anglo-Japanese alliance remained possible, it appeared unlikely unless Washington and Ottawa had a change of heart. If Japan continued its custom of a great-power alliance, only two choices remained: a defeated Germany or an isolated Soviet Union. In 1922, neither appeared likely, but the possibility of a Tokyo-Berlin-Moscow alliance already haunted London.[11]

It is interesting to speculate, if only for a moment, about how a renewal of the alliance might have changed subsequent events. If the pact survived the Manchurian Incident and what no doubt would have been stormy debates over renewal in 1931, would Japan have entered into the Anti-Comintern Pact in 1936? Would England have extended, and would Japan have accepted, the good offices of its ally of thirty-five years sometime after July 1937? Would Japan have turned its back on its ally of nearly four decades and joined the Axis in 1940? While it is impossible to answer these questions, one thing is clear: if the alliance had survived the Washington Conference and led to successful negotiations after the Marco Polo Bridge Incident or helped Tokyo spurn German advances in 1940, there would have been no Pacific war in

December 1941. Admittedly, these are big ifs, but Hughes squandered them at Washington and gained nothing in return.

The third major political agreement to emerge from the talks, the Nine Power Treaty, which reaffirmed the status of the Open Door and recognized Japan's sphere of interest in South Manchuria, emerged from a host of often competing and contradictory proposals. Japan's representatives had hoped to avoid any discussion of China at the conference, and, while Hughes deferred Chinese questions in order to ensure the success of the naval limitation agreement, China's future was never far from anyone's mind. As early as July 1921, Britain proposed an Anglo-American-Japanese declaration of common principles for China, and, after the delegates arrived, Balfour, in a move that surely marks him as one of history's great optimists, submitted a draft proposal for a multinational agreement designed to ensure peace in the Far East through consultation and, if need be, the use of force. The US Senate had already voted down American membership in an Anglo-French defensive alliance aimed at Germany, so Balfour's plan did not have a ghost of a chance. Later, Chinese delegates offered a formula for ensuring the peaceful development of their country, and, although the plan focused largely on traditional American Open Door principles, it received little attention. Hughes's subordinates, meanwhile, bombarded him with proposals for a comprehensive agreement designed to ensure peaceful and orderly development in China. Admiral William L. Rodgers, the former commander of the US Asiatic Fleet, put his trust in the new China consortium. Secretary of Commerce Herbert Hoover, meanwhile, fearful of spreading Bolshevism, proposed a massive American loan for China contingent on, among other things, "the elimination of the Communists." The State Department's assistant solicitor, J. Rueben Clark, called for giving Japan greater economic opportunities in China while limiting its political freedom of action on the mainland. From these proposals came the Nine Power Treaty, approved on February 3, 1922.[12]

The signatories pledged to respect Chinese sovereignty and the Open Door, aid Chinese development, and refrain from seeking any special privileges in China at the expense of either that country or the other treaty members. In many respects, then, far from breaking new ground, the Nine Power Treaty represented the culmination of two decades of American China policy and the elevation of the Open Door from American ideal to international law. Indeed, Stanley Hornbeck, still a bitter opponent of Japanese continental expansion and a key Hughes adviser, wanted the secretary to exhume the grisly remains of Knox's railroad neutralization scheme and inter it in the new treaty.[13]

The final agreement, minus Hornbeck's railroad plan, represented in microcosm the better part of a generation's worth of hopes and contradictions. Initially, the Nine Power Treaty did not resolve the central question of just what the Open Door really meant. Was it Hay's limited version or Knox's uncompromising idea? More importantly, did the agreement threaten or uphold Japanese rights in South Manchuria?

Sadao Asada has argued that, despite Washington's contention that the new agreement superseded Lansing-Ishii and therefore any hope for American recognition of Japanese special rights, Tokyo believed that Washington had recognized Japan's Manchurian sphere. Moreover, he persuasively demonstrates that the elder statesman Elihu Root deliberately crafted draft portions of the Nine Power Treaty to assure Japan of continued American support for its special position in Manchuria. Root's work, Asada concluded, represented "yet another example of ambiguous Japanese-American compromise in the tradition of the Root-Takahira Agreement and the Lansing-Ishii Agreement." The noted American historian Warren Cohen also contends that, while officials publicly described an Open Door that encompassed Manchuria, privately they assured the Japanese that this was not the case. Betty Glad's extensive study of Hughes's diplomacy supports Cohen's contention that Manchuria lay outside the Open Door.[14]

Harry Wray, on the other hand, maintains that the Nine Power Treaty signaled "a less generous interpretation [for Japan] of the Open Door," and Thomas Buckley, the foremost authority on the Washington Conference, contends that neither American nor British archives reveal any agreement exempting Manchuria. Given that General Kunishige Tanaka made no mention of a Manchurian exemption in his official report, Buckley concludes that Tokyo's contention that US representatives agreed to recognize a Japanese sphere "existed in the minds of the Japanese and not the Americans." In the end, it seems most likely that Tokyo simply read what it wanted to read and heard what it longed to hear and that Washington allowed it.[15]

The ink had barely dried on the Nine Power Treaty when the Japanese embassy informed Hughes that, while Tokyo would cancel Lansing-Ishii in light of the accord, it did not see how the agreements conflicted. The note went on to declare that Japan would continue to enjoy a special relationship with China, whether or not other powers recognized it. Shidehara and his political masters sought to cooperate with Washington, but there were limits to how far they would go. Manchuria remained vital to Japanese national security and increasingly important to the economy, especially after the postwar economic slump. For the United States, meanwhile, Manchuria's economic importance remained slight and its future, whether as a part of the Chinese republic or a Japanese sphere of influence, uncertain.[16]

The last major issue covered at Washington, the status of Shantung Province, clearly indicates Washington's continuing distrust of Japan, Hughes's commitment to rollback, and the lengths to which Tokyo would go to defend its wartime gains. Japan occupied Shantung in 1914 and pledged at Versailles to eventually restore the region to China, retaining only Germany's former economic concessions. China, however, counted on American support to settle the Shantung dispute on favorable terms. Hughes did not approach the Shantung question from a pro-Chinese position, but he did view it as a test of Japan's willingness to embrace the new American Far Eastern order. His chief advisers, on the other hand, including J. V. A. MacMurray, the chief of the State Department's Far Eastern Division, E. T. Williams, and Stanley Hornbeck, all believed that Wilson erred at Paris and therefore consistently supported China. Throughout December and January, as Japanese and Chinese delegates met in the presence of British and American observers, Washington's Far Eastern experts weighed in on China's behalf. When Japan proposed joint ownership of the province's railroads, Hughes's advisers convinced him to press Tokyo for greater concessions. Eager to improve relations with Washington, Japan finally proposed to evacuate its troops and sell its railroad interests to China. When negotiations deadlocked over the terms of the sale, Britain and the United States brought considerable pressure to bear on both parties, and chastened negotiators signed the Shantung Treaty on February 4, 1922.[17]

Its business concluded, the Washington Conference ended two days later. But what had been accomplished? The dangerous contest to build faster, stronger, more deadly battleships ended, only to be replaced by a somewhat less dangerous contest to build faster, stronger, more deadly cruisers. The Open Door found a home in the Nine Power Treaty, yet nobody really knew, after twenty years, just what the Open Door meant or precisely where it should be applied. America broke the Anglo-Japanese Alliance and reaffirmed its affection for China, but these were pyrrhic victories. Tokyo's efforts at the conference to secure American favor, like its subsequent withdrawal from Siberia and Shantung and generally cooperative policy in China, earned it little in American goodwill. Influential public figures—men who in the next decade shaped US policy in the Far East—remained wedded to the belief that foreign expansion, militarism, and duplicity defined Japanese diplomacy. Future secretary of state Cordell Hull believed that the conference "would cripple us in the Pacific" and that agreements with Tokyo "will amount to practically nothing." Seeing Japan as basically untrustworthy and dedicated to a predetermined policy of expansion in Asia, he predicted that Tokyo "will agree on paper and then proceed with her fixed policy of economic penetration of China, Siberia, Manchuria, and other portions of the Far East."[18]

The Washington Conference could not reorient American thinking because Hughes and others saw it as a means to contain, and in the case of Shantung even roll back, Japan rather than improve Japanese-American relations. Previous examples of diplomatic engagement, including Taft-Katsura, Root-Takahira, and Lansing-Ishii, sought to limit Japanese expansion, yet all three agreements recognized Japan's formal and informal empire. This was not the case at Washington. Sadao Asada best described the fundamental shortcomings of the conference when he noted that "the basic clash between the Open Door and Japan's claim to special interests in China" received little attention and consequently remained unresolved. The talks were less an example of diplomatic engagement where the root causes of Japanese-American differences could be examined and rectified and more, in the words of the Pulitzer Prize–winning historian Herbert Bix, an opportunity "to restrain Japan in China and *roll back* the advances it had made there during World War I." Rather than herald a new era, the Washington Conference indicates the extraordinary degree to which both Tokyo and Washington remained wedded to their traditional policies and tactics.[19]

Despite its shortcomings, the Washington Conference did point to two positive harbingers of the future. Initially, while war planning, mutual suspicion over China, and racial enmity persisted throughout the 1920s, Japanese and American attitudes improved. However limited, a clear psychological shift is apparent in both Japan and the United States, and in all likelihood this attitudinal change would have continued if not for American immigration policy and competition in China. This psychological shift is also important because in the months preceding Pearl Harbor Japanese negotiators argued that any agreement, no matter how imperfect or limited, would produce profound attitudinal changes in Japan and decrease the likelihood of war. It is also important to note that, on the basis of the Washington Treaties, the United States could, in late 1941, have reasonably expected Japan to meet its treaty obligations. Even as the Kwantung Army violated the Nine Power Treaty in Manchuria, Tokyo still honored both the Washington and the London Naval Treaties. Moreover, British debates in 1921–1922 over the future of the Anglo-Japanese Alliance reveal that London considered Japan a reliable, trustworthy ally. Both the Anglo-Japanese Alliance and the Washington and London disarmament agreements indicate a long history of Japan's fidelity to its treaty partners. As J. V. A. MacMurray observed during the mid-1930s: "The Japanese government for almost 10 years was, in the belief of the diplomatic representatives of all countries in China at the time, scrupulously loyal in its adherence to the letter and spirit of the Washington Conference." While it is impossible to know whether a limited Japanese-

American agreement—say, a Japanese pledge to suspend offensive operations and open negotiations with Chungking in return for a relaxation of the trade embargo—would have prevented war in 1941, the 1920s provide tantalizing clues.[20]

In the end, the Washington Conference must be evaluated both for what it did and for what it did not do. Unfortunately, the core issues that had bred Japanese-American enmity for the past fifteen years went unresolved at Washington. Worse, these issues went virtually unaddressed. The United States remained committed to containing Japan, while the Japanese Empire remained equally committed to solidifying its hold on South Manchuria and Inner Mongolia.

During the 1920s, rising Chinese nationalism made the competing designs of Washington and Tokyo increasingly irrelevant, and, as the spirit of Anglo-American-Japanese cooperation withered in the face of Chinese nationalism, the three powers increasingly abandoned cooperation and tried, often desperately, to save what they could at their partners' expense. If the aim of the Washington Conference was to contain Japan, then it began to break down only in 1931. If, however, the conference sought to create a framework for Anglo-American-Japanese cooperation in China, then it failed much earlier.

Chinese Nationalism and the Limits of Cooperative Diplomacy

For Japanese-American relations, the nine years between the end of the Washington Conference and the Kwantung Army's seizure of Manchuria were relatively calm. To be sure, American diplomats and businessmen accused Tokyo of interfering with American trade in China, but they also knew that ongoing civil war and recurrent antiforeignism interfered with export and investment opportunities far more than Japanese violations of the Open Door. Likewise, while the National Origins Act, which all but ended Japanese immigration to the United States, outraged most Japanese, it did not generate the same level of outrage as the multiple California crises of the Progressive Era. The period following the Washington Conference represented a welcome change in the familiar pattern of US-Japanese relations; yet, beneath this tranquil surface, decades-old problems lurked. Manchuria continued, as it had for a generation, to sap the strength of Japanese-American bonds, and rising Chinese nationalism led American policymakers to shy away from their treaty partners despite the agreements made at Washington.

In the end, while the Washington Conference may have mellowed attitudes, it did not change beliefs. Consequently, while containment succeeded, Japanese-American relations suffered.

Japan approached the Washington Conference hoping that improved relations would enable it to secure badly needed American capital for overseas development, yet, despite Japan's generally cooperative attitude, Washington soon disappointed Tokyo. While American banks lent money to Japan that ultimately found a home in Manchuria, this was the exception rather than the rule, for the Coolidge and Hoover administrations were no less committed to the Open Door than were their predecessors. In order to weaken Japanese spheres and earn Chinese goodwill, Washington consistently opposed loans destined for Japan's mainland empire. In 1923, Hughes and the State Department repeatedly refused to back a loan by the Riggs National Bank for the Japanese-owned Oriental Development Company. The State Department opposed the loan even after Riggs offered guarantees that Oriental Development would buy only American raw materials for its American-financed projects. Four years later, the State Department again opposed a similar Manchurian loan, but by this time its opposition also took into account a newfound fear of offending China. Kuomintang officials informed Admiral Mark Bristol, commander of the American Asiatic Fleet, that, if consummated, the loan "would give evidence of a change from the past friendly American attitude toward China." Fear of possible Chinese retaliation haunted American businesses engaged in the Far East, even titans like Standard Oil. In December 1927, company officials informed a Lamont confidant that, owing to their fear of a Chinese boycott, they wished to see the proposed Manchurian loan dropped.[21]

Japan's long and ultimately futile bid to secure American loans for Manchurian development is important in several respects. Initially, it indicates that Washington had essentially abandoned Hay's original Open Door concept in favor of the far grander Taft-Knox idea. It also reveals a continued interest in rolling back Japan's sphere in Northeast Asia. Some diplomats, including the American ambassador to Japan, Charles MacVeagh, argued that the State Department's refusal to back loans ran counter to the spirit of the Washington Conference and would gravely disappoint Tokyo. He insisted that the United States must prove to Japan that "we have an honest desire to help them in reaching a solution of their difficulties when we can legitimately do so." MacVeagh's argument, however, went unheeded. The Manchurian loan controversy also indicates important issues regarding American relations with, and perceptions of, China. Where previously Washington opposed Manchurian loans because of its historic objection to spheres of influence, by 1927 it combined this traditional argument with a renewed faith in, and fear of, China. Despite endemic civil war, attacks on foreigners, and America's disappointing lack of progress in gaining a share of the China market, Peking's wishes still counted in Washington. Moreover, American public opinion still weighed in on China's side. If Americans would stand beside a divided, often antiforeign China in the 1920s, how would they react when a united China and a Kuomintang purged of Communists faced a far less accommodating Japan beginning in 1931?[22]

While Manchuria remained a stumbling block, the powers nonetheless made admirable and often successful attempts to maintain the Washington Conference spirit. In the spring of 1922, for example, when the Bethlehem Steel Corporation and Peking appeared ready to execute a 1911 agreement for upgrading the Chinese navy, Washington queried the French, British, Italian, and Japanese governments to ascertain whether they objected to the contract's fulfillment. When Japan raised a formal objection in late May, Washington scotched the deal. Tokyo, likewise, fulfilled its obligations and abstained from supporting any of China's many warlord factions. When Kenkichi Yoshizawa, Japan's minister to China, pressed for a large loan to the Tuan Ch'i-jui administration, Foreign Minister Kijuro Shidehara refused, citing the need to cooperate with the powers, which had also declined to loan Tuan money. In addition, Shidehara refused to send troops either to prop up the pro-Japanese warlord Chang Tso-lin or to protect Japanese-owned businesses from increasingly effective and often violent strikes and boycotts.[23]

Beginning in 1925, however, the loose skein of Japanese-American cooperation in the Far East began to unravel in the face of Chinese nationalism. On May 30, a memorial for a slain Chinese protestor sparked a violent clash between British police and Chinese residents of Shanghai. In the weeks following the May 30, or Shanghai, Incident, the powers and Chinese authorities attempted to settle the matter but made little progress, so in June Peking seized the initiative and issued identic notes demanding immediate treaty revision.[24]

Yoshizawa leapt into action immediately after receiving Peking's demands, and, in a vitally important and potentially promising meeting with his American counterpart, Ferdinand Mayer, the American chargé d'affaires, he explained Tokyo's desire for closer Japanese-American cooperation. Mayer cabled Secretary of State Frank Kellogg that, while Manchuria would not be part of any agreement, Japan seemed serious about maintaining a policy of noninterference in China and therefore urged the secretary to cooperate with Tokyo.[25]

Two weeks later, J. V. A. MacMurray, the newly appointed American minister to Peking, reversed direction and wrote Kellogg that, while there existed "substantial agreement in points of view between the Japanese and us that we can work in harmony with respect to the general situation in China," he "would consider it unfortunate . . . to become involved in any new understanding which would in any degree revive the effects of the Anglo-Japanese Alliance and the Lansing-Ishii Agreement." Specifically, he warned the secretary that an agreement might limit American freedom of action or lead to pressure to recognize Japan's special interests in Manchuria. While conceding that the United States should not distance itself from either of its beleaguered Washington partners, MacMurray saw no compelling reason to draw closer to them. After all, he informed Kellogg, in China "hatred first of the British and secondly of the Japanese is the consuming passion."[26]

MacMurray carried the day, and in retrospect this is no surprise. While the Washington Conference changed attitudes, it did not change convictions, and statesmen base policy on the latter. By 1925, MacMurray had already begun a journey that led him from fierce anti-Japanese critic at Versailles to advocate of a sympathetic policy during the 1930s. He recognized that the Japanese "have shown themselves disposed to put aside mutual distrust and rivalry and to cooperate loyally with us in our traditional Far Eastern policies," but he could not transcend two decades of history. MacMurray, and many others, remained trapped in a weltanschauung that precluded a fundamental readjustment in Japanese-American relations.[27]

The degree to which Washington based policy on a preexisting weltanschauung, rather than present conditions, is startlingly evident given that, in the mid-1920s, Chinese nationalism, combined with its attendant antiforeignism and the Kuomintang's substantial Soviet influence, threatened the Open Door every bit as much as Russian expansion had in the late nineteenth century. Hornbeck realized that revolutionary nationalism threatened American interests in China and argued that the Open Door's health ultimately rested on Peking's willingness and ability to uphold its treaty obligations. The failure to abolish the likin—an internal transit tax—impeded the free flow of American goods, and the Kuomintang's avowed policy of treaty revision threatened to undermine the very system, however archaic and unfair, that supported the Western position in China.

For Japan, China's assault on the treaty system, and by extension the Open Door, represented an even greater threat. By 1925, China accounted for over 20 percent of Japan's total export share, second only to the United States. Moreover, the success of its textile manufacturing, Japan's core industry in China, depended on the maintenance of the treaty system. On the basis of current threats to shared interests, Washington and Tokyo should have enjoyed relations similar to those of 1899–1904, when Russian expansion threatened to slam shut the Open Door in north China. But two decades of mistrust, disappointment, and rivalry stood in the way, and the United States and Japan had to wait another twenty-five years for a new weltanschauung, a new Russian threat, and a renewed civil war in China to bring them closer together.[28]

After rejecting Japan's bid for closer cooperation, Washington next rejected both the advice of its Peking-based diplomats and the wishes of its treaty partners and accepted Chinese demands for conferences on treaty revision. When MacMurray advised that treaty negotiations would prove counterproductive, a view shared by both London and Tokyo, Kellogg remained unmoved. Nelson Johnson, Kellogg's adviser on Far Eastern affairs and future ambassador to China, argued that, by accepting the inevitable and taking the lead in promoting treaty revision, the United States would gain Chinese goodwill. In all likelihood, however, Kellogg needed little prompting to agree to treaty revision even if it meant breaking the weak chain of Anglo-American-Japanese cooperation in China. For the secretary, traditional American liberal expansion dictated that Washington take the lead in aiding China. He no doubt took comfort from the fact that, despite recurrent civil war and spasms of antiforeign violence, China still retained considerable public sympathy, especially among the Protestant missionary societies, which were early and articulate supporters of the Nationalists' demands. The Reverend John Leighton Stuart, the president of Yenching University, saw treaty revision as "the supreme question in what may otherwise become an impending cataclysm." Stuart conceded that tariff reform and an end to extraterritoriality could lead to "some loss of property or even of life." He maintained, however, that revision remained "the best way to help China put her own house in order." In the Senate, William Borah noted that he "would favor the withdrawal of extraterritorial rights in China as speedily as practicable." When the Hankow branch of the American Chamber of Commerce, perhaps concerned over Stuart's use of the words *loss, life,* and *property* in the same sentence, forcefully opposed revision, Borah charged them with being "part of the imperialist combine which would oppress and exploit the Chinese people." He and other progressive senators, including Montana's Burton K. Wheeler and Nebraska's George Norris, pressured the administration to promptly recognize the Nationalist government, whose leaders they compared to the American founding fathers.[29]

With these considerations in mind, and with Johnson's full support, Kellogg moved closer to China and abandoned multinational cooperation when the Peking Tariff Conference began the following October. Before the talks convened, MacMurray urged Kellogg not to make any promises regarding tariff autonomy and pointed out that Tokyo shared his opinion. The following month, however, Washington instructed its delegates to consider eventual tariff autonomy, which, after protracted negotiations, the powers agreed to grant China, effective January 1, 1929. Multinational cooperation suffered even more, however, when discussions turned to the thornier issue of interim tariffs. Although the American delegation and Kellogg sought to cooperate with the other powers, this became impossible given the differing aims of Japan, Britain, and the United States. Washington hoped to use revision to improve China's international credit as a necessary prerequisite to enhanced trade and development, while London hoped that a revised schedule would enable Peking to make good on its substantial foreign debt. Meanwhile, because it feared the effect that higher tariffs would have on exports, Japan hoped to keep any revisions within the modest guidelines established by the Washington Conference. With the beginning of the Northern Expedition, the combined Kuomintang and Communist military campaign to defeat the warlords and unify China, the talks broke up without any decision regarding interim tariff rates. Unfortunately, by this time, the American delegation came to see Japan as the chief stumbling block to an agreement and informed Kellogg that Tokyo had attempted to dictate terms and take unilateral action. In the end, the tariff conference produced meager results for China, undermined Anglo-Japanese-American cooperation, and added to Washington's continuing suspicion of Japanese aims in China.[30] The Northern Expedition, meanwhile, further challenged what remained of effective Anglo-American-Japanese cooperation in China. As Chiang Kai-shek's forces swept north, antiforeignism and the Kuomintang's determination to end the unequal treaties increased. And, while London, Tokyo, and Washington for the most part remained neutral in the conflict, all three pursued a policy of one-upmanship in an effort to secure Chinese friendship.

London opened the bidding for Chinese goodwill when, a week before Christmas 1926, its minister at Peking, Owen O'Malley, presented the treaty powers an early, unwanted gift from home. London's "Christmas Memorandum" called for immediate and unconditional granting of the tariff surcharges denied China at the Peking Tariff Conference and declared that the powers should announce their willingness to renew negotiations on ending extraterritoriality, once a Chinese government emerged with the authority to carry out talks.[31]

The State Department, which not surprisingly saw London's gambit as a threat to its cherished position as China's true friend, quickly responded. From Peking, MacMurray cabled home that, rather than placating the Kuomintang, London's actions would likely encourage further Chinese demands. Nonetheless, he advised his superiors that, once the Christmas Memorandum became public, Britain "will have forced our hands in view of the impossibility of our maintaining consistently or with any hope of success an attitude ostensibly less liberal than theirs." He repeatedly warned Kellogg, however, not to promise China too much or to engage in a diplomatic game of one-upmanship with London. As in 1925, Kellogg's natural inclination to champion Chinese modernization, and the pull of forces far closer than the distant MacMurray, led him to disregard the counsel of his man on the scene.[32]

In retrospect, MacMurray saw the Christmas Memorandum as a defining moment in the history of both great-power cooperation in China and Sino-Japanese relations. Up to the autumn of 1926, MacMurray argued, the powers had cooperated in crafting a common response to rising Chinese nationalism as well as demands for treaty revision, as evidenced by the identic notes sent to Peking in September 1925 in response to Chinese demands for tariff reform. But, after the Christmas Memorandum, Washington distanced itself from London and Tokyo and pressured MacMurray to suspend his regular informal talks with British Ambassador Miles Lampson and Japanese Ambassador Yoshizawa. In the end, MacMurray argued, the Chinese demand to repudiate the unequal treaties not only prompted the damaging Christmas Memorandum but also "was a primary contributory cause of the discrediting of liberalism in Japan and the consequent series of calamities which began in September 1931."[33]

While surprised by the Christmas Memorandum, Kellogg was clearly shaken by Representative Stephen H. Porter's January 1927 resolution, itself a response to the new British policy, which both authorized and requested that the president begin negotiations with the Nationalists to end the unequal treaties. Porter's resolution, which explicitly recognized that the United States *could act independently* of its Washington partners, received as much, if not more, public and editorial support than China's call for treaty revision two years earlier and tends to confirm that, despite escalating violence, the vast majority of popular and editorial opinion remained remarkably sympathetic to China. Kellogg quickly responded to Porter and by the end of January informed Peking that the United States would negotiate an end to extraterritoriality in China once the government proved that it could protect American lives and property. While initially popular, Kellogg's sop to Chinese nationalism proved ineffective, and within months many Chinese who were normally supportive of American policies bemoaned Washington's lack of progress in terminating extraterritoriality rights.[34]

In fairness to Kellogg, the Chinese proved unable to protect American lives and property. The following March, Kuomintang forces attacked foreign concessions in the so-called Nanking Incident, which, while it neither derailed Kellogg's plans nor cost Chiang and his followers much support in America, did have a profound effect on Japanese policy. When American and British warships pounded Nationalist positions in Nanking in response to the attacks on the foreign enclaves, Japan refused to join its erstwhile allies. Foreign Minister Shidehara recognized that Nationalist violence invited disaster both for Chiang and for Japan's China policy, should either the United States or Britain decide on large-scale intervention. Accordingly, he worked to quickly settle the incident. Shidehara refused to blame Chiang for the violence and insisted that he and the Kuomintang, rather than Anglo-American warships, restore order. His diplomacy paid immediate dividends, and the crisis passed, but the moderate Reijiro Wakatsuki cabinet paid dearly for its role as peacemaker. In Japan, popular agitation against Shidehara's "weak-kneed" diplomacy grew dramatically, and by early April even the progovernment *Asahi* newspaper suggested that Tokyo take more vigorous action to protect Japanese lives and property. Further criticism from the Privy Council left Prime Minister Wakatsuki and Shidehara with little political capital, and, when a financial panic swept the country that spring, the hobbled moderates fell from power. As it turned out, their successors practiced neither the cooperative diplomacy nor the kind of self-restraint that had destroyed the moderates.[35]

To replace Wakatsuki, the Genro, Japan's elder statesmen, chose General Giichi Tanaka, the leader of the minority Seiyukai Party. From the outset, Tanaka made clear his determination to pursue a more aggressive strategy in China "in order to defend . . . [the] Empire and to protect its rights and interests." Events soon gave him a chance to act. When victorious Nationalist forces approached Peking in May, Tokyo responded by dispatching two thousand troops to Tsinan to protect Japanese lives and property and, critics charged, block the Nationalist advance north. London and Washington, hitherto waffling on whether to dispatch troops to north China or evacuate their nationals, took heart and followed Japan's lead. The United States, in particular, evidenced concern that the summer of 1927 not be a repeat of the summer of 1900, when, at the height of the Boxer Rebellion, the foreign legations at Peking faced annihilation. Washington need not have worried, however, about Americans' safety, for Chiang had already decided to halt the Northern Expedition in order to finish his extermination campaign against Communists and Kuomintang leftists.[36]

Tanaka's intervention, however brief, proved just onerous enough to spark renewed anti-Japanese boycotts and protests from Chiang as well as his rivals at Peking and Wuhan. While the new prime minister's "positive policy" generated considerable criticism abroad, it did not deter Tanaka from running on an aggressive foreign policy platform the following year. In the months preceding Japan's first election under new universal manhood suffrage provisions, the Seiyukai forcefully declared: "Manchuria and Mongolia, because they are the areas which have special relations with our country, under no circumstances do we plan to let the military disorders of China proper spread in these areas." The platform left no doubt that a Tanaka ministry would use force, as it had the previous summer, to protect Japanese lives and property within China. The message proved popular, and in the spring of 1928 voters returned a narrow Seiyukai majority. The events that followed the general election were not the product solely of Tanaka or the military or the ultranationalists. Intervention in China, and especially Manchuria, reflected the popular, electoral will of the Japanese people.[37]

Given his pledge to aggressively protect Japanese rights and interests in China and Manchuria and the Seiyukai's narrow electoral victory, Tanaka did not have much political room to maneuver. Powerful elements within the military and civilian bureaucracy also circumscribed his options. The previous summer, representatives from the Army General Staff, the Kwantung Army, the Foreign Ministry, and Kwantung Territory met to map out Japan's China policy, and their consensus reflected and, given the publicity that the conference generated, may even have solidified the Seiyukai's narrow electoral majority. The conferees determined that, if disorder spread to Manchuria and Mongolia and threatened Japanese interests, the government "must be prepared to take immediate and appropriate means to protect the area and maintain it as a peaceful land for development by both natives and foreigners." Regarding China proper, the delegates recognized the probability of early unification and argued that Japan and the powers should endeavor to cooperate with the Nationalists. At the same time, however, the conferees endorsed taking aggressive steps to safeguard Japanese rights and interests in China and called for resolute action to break the cycle of anti-Japanese strikes and boycotts. Most importantly, the discussions indicate Tokyo's determination to follow two policies on the continent, one for China, the other for Manchuria and Mongolia.[38]

Neither the 1927 summer conference nor the 1928 general election determined Japan's subsequent actions in China and Manchuria. Tanaka, for example, met with Chiang, and the two agreed that, in return for the latter's promise not to advance into Manchuria, Japan would not interfere with the Northern Expedition. Their agreement, however, did not survive for long, and, by the following spring, as Nationalist armies once again approached

Manchuria, both the War Ministry and the Seiyukai demanded Tanaka make good on his campaign promises. On April 18, the cabinet agreed to dispatch five thousand troops to Tsinan to protect Japanese residents, and the Army General Staff, which opposed intervention, ordered its forces not to intervene. By May 3, the danger to Japanese citizens had passed, but as Japanese forces prepared to leave the city fighting broke out with Nationalist troops. Chiang, eager to avoid a clash, worked out a cease-fire on May 5, yet three days later Japanese forces, acting without orders from Tokyo, took the offensive. While the fighting proved short-lived, the expeditionary forces' unsanctioned action caused considerable damage to Japan's image in the West and acute damage to Sino-Japanese relations. MacMurray succinctly summed up the enormous cost of the Tsinan intervention when he noted that after May 1928 "the principal onus of anti-foreign feeling was shifted from the British to the Japanese." Unfortunately, Tsinan was not the last time in 1928 that, acting without orders from Tokyo, the Japanese army did untold harm.[39]

Once Chiang put his enemies to flight in Tsinan and made peace with the Japanese command, he resumed his drive north. By this time Tokyo had devised a comprehensive plan to perpetuate Japanese control in Manchuria that focused on the northern warlord Chang Tso-lin. Tanaka convinced Chang to retreat into Manchuria, where, protected by the Kwantung Army, he would retain authority free from Kuomintang interference. On May 18, Tokyo ordered its forces to allow Chang and his military to enter Manchuria, but members of the Kwantung Army assassinated the warlord as he withdrew north. Tanaka, who had hoped to safeguard Japanese interests by protecting Chang, now cast about for an acceptable substitute.[40]

Washington, meanwhile, recognized that, taken to its logical conclusion, Tanaka's policy would divide China at the Great Wall, with Chang ruling the north and Chiang and the Kuomintang governing the south. Some, including Hornbeck, argued that, if Tokyo "is successful in bargaining with or coercing both [regimes], she will practically have China subject its political matters to Japanese dictation." While Hornbeck and others had become disenchanted with China, Chiang could still count on American support. Washington continued to block loans for Manchurian development and remained wary of reaching any concrete political understandings with Tokyo. Japan, on the other hand, could not count on the support of its Washington Conference partner. When Count Yasuya Uchida, the former foreign minister, met Kellogg in September 1928 in an effort to garner American support for Japan's treaty rights in Manchuria, the secretary showed little sympathy for Japan and instead expressed his continued confidence in the Nationalist regime. MacMurray concluded that Uchida must have left the meeting convinced that a "pro-Chinese" administration had decided to abandon its Washington Treaty partners in order "to advance . . . [its] own interests."[41]

Chiang's triumphant entry into Peking during the summer of 1928 marked the end of another chapter in the Nationalist unification of China. The Washington Conference system had survived the Northern Expedition, yet, by 1928, the fires of Chinese nationalism had consumed Anglo-American-Japanese cooperation. Soon the Nationalist flag flew over Manchuria, and, though multinational cooperation might have prevented a crisis, the unofficial Anglo-American-Japanese entente had long ago ceased to exist. As successive Japanese cabinets struggled to find a solution to the Manchurian problem, the military, as it had so often done before, acted decisively and without orders from the government.

On to Mukden

Between 1928 and 1931, Japanese civilian and military officials developed three distinct yet interrelated policies for ensuring continued dominance in Manchuria. First under Tanaka's Seiyukai, then administered by successive Minseito cabinets, Tokyo utilized diplomacy and occasional intimidation. The army, meanwhile, adopted a three-tier plan that, on the one hand, allowed for diplomacy and, on the other hand, envisioned the use of force. The Kwantung Army, along with allies in the home islands, also plotted to destroy the Kuomintang north of the Great Wall and bring all Manchuria under direct Japanese control.

The Tanaka ministry increased the likelihood of some kind of clash in Manchuria when it selected a successor to the late General Chang in the summer of 1928. In the mid-seventeenth century, English Roundheads executed Charles I and, some years after Oliver Cromwell's death, made the strange error of placing the beheaded king's son on the throne. Three centuries later, the Tanaka ministry repeated their curious mistake in Manchuria. In an effort to protect its interests following Chang's assassination, Tokyo threw its support behind Chang Hsueh-liang, the elder Chang's son. Very quickly, however, this plan's obvious faults materialized. By the end of July, Chang and Chiang had reached an agreement to unite Manchuria with China proper. Fearful that unification would mean an end to its treaty rights, Tokyo immediately warned Chang not to hoist the Nationalist flag. The young marshal heeded the warning and opted to suspend unification talks until October. Tokyo, meanwhile, used this window to secure Chiang's recognition of Japanese rights in Manchuria.[42]

Chiang's agreement notwithstanding, Kuomintang leaders soon determined that the time had come to press the powers to abandon all their economic privileges in China, including those in Manchuria. Tanaka, however, did not have to face these latest crises. After delivering a false report to the emperor exonerating the army of any part in the elder Chang's death, he was forced to step down in July 1929. The opposition Minseito formed the next cabinet and brought Shidehara back as foreign minister.[43]

Together with Prime Minister Osayuki Hamaguchi, Shidehara immediately set out, with mixed results, to repair Japan's strained ties with China and the wider world and solve the growing crisis in Manchuria. In September, Tokyo proposed a nonaggression pact with Nanking and between January and May 1930 successfully negotiated an agreement on tariff autonomy. Fulfilling its pledge to forsake military intervention on the continent, Hamaguchi and Shidehara twice reined in the military during April 1930: once when recalcitrant northern rebels rose against Chiang and again when Communist forces occupied Changsha in central China. Neither Hamaguchi nor Shidehara, however, could solve Japan's most pressing problem—maintaining the country's rights in Manchuria. By December 1930, Chang developed plans to build competing rail lines in South Manchuria and a port to rival Japan's facility at Darien. Even Nelson T. Johnson, no friend of Japan's and now American ambassador to China, warned Secretary of State Henry Stimson that, while "the Japanese are disposed to a policy of cooperation in railway matters," this could change if "pushed too hard by a Chinese policy which may seek to hamstring the South Manchurian Railway." From Tokyo, the American embassy reported that Japanese officials feared that the United States would continue to withhold loans for Manchurian development while making funds available to Nanking. Worse still, Foreign Minister C. T. Wang, widely seen as an uncompromising opponent of improved relations with Japan, bluntly informed Tokyo's acting minister to China, Mamaoru Shigemitsu, that his government included both the Kwantung leased territory and the South Manchuria Railway within the category of unequal treaties that Nanking sought to either revise or abrogate.[44]

In an extraordinarily frank meeting with Johnson, Shigemitsu explained that the new Soviet five-year plan made control of Manchuria essential and claimed that if treaty revision were limited to China proper "it would be not so very difficult to reach an understanding but if Manchuria was injected into the picture then it was going to be very difficult." Echoing a decades-old argument, Shigemitsu stressed that "Japan's position in Manchuria was a military position and Japan could not afford to see her first line of defense destroyed." When Johnson reported the conversation to Stimson, the secretary proved no more sympathetic than his predecessors.[45]

In addition to undermining Japanese national defense, China's intensified efforts to regain lost rights in Manchuria further weakened Shidehara and the moderate Minseito. In January 1930, in an effort to further integrate his country into the world economy, Junnosuke Inoue, Thomas Lamont's old friend at the Bank of Japan and Japan's current finance minister, led his country back onto the gold standard. Inoue's economic orthodoxy was sound, but his timing was terrible. With the onset of the Great Depression, Japan's American market dried up, and, having returned to gold, Tokyo could not devalue the yen to make Japanese exports more attractive. As America sank deeper into the economic abyss, Congress attempted to break the nation's fall in July 1930 with the Smoot-Hawley Tariff Act. Trade protection proved wholly inadequate to help the American economy, and the steep rise in rates (23 percent for Japan) further undermined Japanese access to its largest export market. When Britain deserted the gold standard the following summer, Japanese shipping and manufacturing suffered further losses, and the already precipitous flight of gold accelerated. Within two years, Japan's wholesale price index fell 35 percent (during the same period, the US index declined 27 percent), and, with the end of the gold embargo, the Bank of Japan hemorrhaged a full third of the nation's reserve.[46]

The government's decision to enter into further naval limitation agreements with the West in January 1930 also cost support it could ill afford to lose. Following the conclusion of the Washington Conference, Britain, Japan, and the United States began a new race to build warships, especially the ten-thousand-ton Washington Treaty cruiser. While Britain and Japan rejected American demands at the 1927 Geneva talks to scale back the number and types of cruiser that each nation could possess, the three nations renewed their talks later in London. Once again, as at Washington, Japan demanded a 10:7 ratio but settled for less. Under a compromise formula worked out by Japan's ambassador to London, Tsuneo Matsudaira, and Senator David Reed of Pennsylvania, the United States agreed to delay building cruisers up to treaty limits until 1938. This delay gave Japan the 10:7 ratio that it sought, yet by 1938 America's gradual buildup would give Washington the 10:6 ratio it demanded. The new treaty proved so controversial that President Hoover had to call the Senate into special session to ratify it. The debate in Tokyo over whether to accept the compromise made Hoover's difficulties pale in comparison.[47]

Kanji Kato, head of the Navy General Staff and an old opponent of the

Washington Treaty, violently, and with good reason, opposed the agreement. By 1930, Japan held a twelve-to-one advantage in heavy cruisers, and every American naval officer who testified at the Senate ratification hearings conceded that, over time, Reed-Matsudaira would undermine Japanese security by compromising the navy's superiority within its home waters. Hamaguchi and Shidehara, however, stressed that, for both fiscal and diplomatic reasons, Japan must accept the compromise. Once the Privy Council approved the agreement, the Seiyukai and Kato charged the cabinet with violating constitutional guarantees by ignoring the general staff's wishes. Several moderate officers who supported Hamaguchi either retired or were cashiered from the navy. The army, already concerned over Moscow's latest five-year plan, also opposed the agreement. In the end, the successful ratification fight hobbled the Minseito and cost Hamaguchi his life.[48]

At a time when the Minseito desperately needed all the political capital it could muster to deal with the mounting crisis in Manchuria, it found its coffers depleted and its leaders drained by the twin crises of the Depression and the London Treaty fight. By the summer of 1931, the Minseito policy of safeguarding rights in Manchuria through diplomacy faced intractable military opposition. That June, Army Minister Jiro Minami convened a top secret meeting to determine a strategy to meet the growing emergency on the continent. After agreeing that the Foreign Ministry should continue negotiations, the participants concluded that, should the diplomats fail, the military must step in. The "General Outline of a Solution for the Manchurian Problem" concluded that the general staff should begin preparations for a military solution while the Foreign Ministry would "acquaint the Japanese people and foreign powers with the true facts of anti-Japanese activity" in order to ensure domestic support and "prevent outside countries from exerting preventative pressure." The outline determined that preparations, including negotiations, would continue until spring 1932. There was, however, a third group working to solve Japan's Manchurian predicament, and this group would not wait.[49]

In response to World War I, continued Western dominance in Asia, and the pitfalls of modernization, a small but important group of civilians and military officials developed plans to prepare Japan to wage war against the West. Kanji Ishiwara, a brilliant young officer and future leader of the plot to seize Manchuria, became convinced of the inevitability of a Japanese-American war and argued that victory in the coming conflict required effective control over Manchurian resources. Far from being dismissed as an extremist, Ishiwara rose through the ranks of the officer corps and soon became one of the most popular lecturers at the Army Staff College.[50]

Predictions of a future war with the West, coupled with the compelling question of how best to prepare, were not solely within the purview of the military, and ultranationalism, sometimes referred to as *Japanism,* flourished within the home islands in the interwar period. Often assailing their countrymen for their supposed slavish adulation of Western ideas and mores, ultranationalists attacked party governments for their corruption and continued inability to solve scores of pressing domestic social problems. Like the officers and men who often found inspiration in their writings, these intellectuals stressed that Japan must undergo a thorough social, political, and cultural renovation in order to perfect society. While not united by a belief in the inevitability of war with the West, many, including Ikki Kita, the period's most influential ultranationalist thinker, saw such a conflict lurking just around the corner. Ominously, Ikki argued that, given the life or death nature of the coming struggle, loyal Japanese could legitimately employ terror and disobey their superiors in order to perfect society and prepare for war.[51]

The leaders who set in motion the events that led to Japan's violent seizure of Manchuria in 1931 belonged to this fertile intellectual tradition and were linked to the activists who, since 1912, had tried various schemes, the latest being the assassination of Chang Tso-lin, to bring all Manchuria firmly within Japan's orbit. And, while the men who laid the charge along the tracks of the South Manchuria Railway were members of the Kwantung Army, the "conspiracy at Mukden" ran much deeper. Indeed, the Issekikai, a study group consisting of some forty junior officers from the Kwantung Army as well as the Army General Staff and War Ministry, determined in May 1929 that diplomacy had failed and that the army must drive Chang Hsueh-liang from Manchuria. Within two years, these conclusions echoed throughout the corridors of the headquarters of the general staff, which maintained in its April 1931 "Situation Estimate" that Japan must drive Chang from Manchuria, create an independent Manchurian state, or forcibly wrest both Inner Mongolia and Manchuria from Nanking.[52]

By September 1931, all Japanese had compelling reasons to fear for their nation's future should control of Manchuria revert to Nanking. Had the Kwantung plotters not acted when they did, the army, as per its 1931 assessment, may well have forced the issue the following spring. And, had Nanking made good on its promise and unilaterally abrogated the Manchurian agreements, it is unlikely given the totality of the region's importance—human, strategic, and economic—that any government, whether Minseito or Seiyukai, would have sat idly by. In September 1931, after thirty years of ambiguity, Chinese nationalists and the Japanese military at last settled the Manchurian question.[53]

The Far Eastern Crisis, 1931–1933

On September 18, 1931, elements of Japan's Kwantung Army staged an explosion along the tracks of the South Manchuria Railway and quickly engaged nearby Nationalist forces, whom they blamed for the attack. For the next several days, Wakatsuki, Shidehara, and even Minami tried in vain to restrain the renegade troops, while, in Manchuria, Kanji Ishiwara and his supporters browbeat into submission those superiors who opposed them. Soon Japanese forces widened the conflict and by year's end had all but driven Chinese units from the region. The following year, the military established the puppet state of Manchukuo.[54]

Throughout the crisis, Secretary of State Henry Stimson, far more than President Hoover, shaped America's response, and he crafted policy to support China and preserve the postwar peace structure. Seeing China as "an important friend of the United States," he declared that America's substantial commercial, educational, and missionary stake could not be ignored. The secretary also maintained that, in order to prevent either a Sino-Soviet or a Sino-Japanese rapprochement, either of which would prove inimical to American interests, Washington must support Chiang. From the earliest hours of the crisis, the State Department also saw the emergency as far more than a local matter between Japan and China or even as an assault on the Open Door. Manchuria, it argued, represented a deliberate Japanese assault on the entire peace structure that the West had painstakingly constructed over the last thirteen years. Even those who showed compassion for Japan's position in Manchuria believed that neither the United States nor the League of Nations could allow Tokyo to adjust the status quo through force of arms. Joseph Grew, who sympathized "with Japan's legitimate aspirations in Manchuria" but not "at all with the illegitimate way in which Japan has been carrying them out," summed up the dominant position of his government in May 1932. While on his way to Tokyo to begin his long tenure as US ambassador, he confided in his diary: "We hold no brief for either side in the Sino-Japanese dispute; we hold a brief for the inviolability of the international peace treaties and the Open Door."[55]

During the first months of the crisis, Stimson pursued a conciliatory policy in the hope that Japanese moderates could control the military. On the basis of their recent success in winning battles for universal manhood suffrage and naval disarmament, the secretary believed that the moderates had more power than they actually possessed. He wanted to help Shidehara and Wakatsuki "and not play into the hands of any nationalist agitators," and, while he wished to support the League of Nations, he feared that cooperation with Geneva would stir up "the excitement of national feeling behind the military elements in Japan." Rather than confrontation, he and Hornbeck preferred direct Sino-Japanese negotiation. Neither party, however, showed much inclination to talk, and American diplomats remained divided over exactly what negotiations should produce.[56]

As the crisis wore on, domestic forces in China and Japan made a negotiated settlement increasingly difficult to achieve. In a fiery speech delivered to the nation in late September, Chiang declared that he would "lead the army to fight for the preservation of our race," and, when Stimson suggested two months later that Chinese forces try to avoid a clash with the advancing Japanese, former foreign minister Wellington Koo told Nelson Johnson that domestic opposition made it impossible to carry out his request. A month later, Koo informed Willys Peck, the US consul general of Nanking, that it was still too early to begin negotiations. In Japan, meanwhile, military opposition forced the government to oppose both talks and the creation of a Sino-Japanese neutral zone monitored by foreign observers.[57]

This same military opposition also made a mockery of Stimson's strategy of supporting Japanese moderates, both civilian and military, who took extraordinary, if fruitless, steps to limit hostilities in Manchuria. The Army Ministry, in particular, repeatedly warned the Kwantung Army to limit operations and went so far as to order the evacuation of Japanese nationals from danger zones in an effort to remove any casus belli. In November, in order to gain control over the Kwantung Army, Chief of Staff Hanza Kanaya received the emperor's approval to exercise temporarily the right of supreme command normally entrusted to Hirohito. Even with this almost unheard-of power, however, Kwantung leaders continued to defy Tokyo. The sense of powerlessness and foreboding that gripped Japanese statesmen during the autumn is clearly evident in the diary of the Marquis Koichi Kido, the future lord keeper of the privy seal. In November, Kido bemoaned the present "weak-kneed" cabinet and argued that "staff officers such as Itagaki and Ishiwara are acting with full powers" in Manchuria. While recognizing the need for a change in government, he speculated that even a coalition cabinet or a Seiyukai administration "would cringe before the army." If this happened and the army were to "push its own plan, the country would stand on the brink of ruin."[58]

In December, a Seiyukai cabinet led by former admiral Tsuyoshi Inukai replaced Wakatsuki and, in an all too often overlooked yet significant episode, two months later in nationwide elections received an overwhelming electoral mandate that indicated vast public support for the army's hard-line policy in China. Despite the election results and his reputation as an ardent nationalist and vehement opponent of the 1930 London Naval Treaty, Inukai made considerable efforts to limit the scope of Japanese operations once fighting broke out in Shanghai and refused to recognize Manchukuo. For this and other supposed crimes, naval officers murdered him on May 15, 1932.[59]

Well before Inukai's murder, however, Stimson abandoned hope that either direct Sino-Japanese negotiations or Japanese moderates would end the crisis and contain Japanese expansion. Consequently, while unsure of what steps to take, the secretary was determined to take stronger action. Many factors, including Stimson's own suspicion of the League of Nations, Anglo-French opposition to sanctions, lack of public support for bolder action, smoldering isolationism, and a divided leadership, precluded a more forceful response. Walter Lippmann, the dean of American journalists, labeled both Japan and China aggressors in Manchuria, and major dailies, even those sympathetic to China, warned Washington not to be pushed into war by the league. Stimson's closest associates, meanwhile, if not openly sympathetic to Japan, at least gave every indication of sympathizing with its position. Former vice president Charles Dawes, then the American ambassador to London, told British foreign secretary Sir John Simon and Tsuneo Matsudaira, Japan's representative to the league, that Tokyo's interests in Manchuria were analogous to American interests in Nicaragua. The elder statesman Elihu Root, a friend of Stimson's, explained that Manchuria was Japan's Cuba, and General William Lassiter, who had recently commanded US forces in the Panama Canal Zone, warned the secretary that Washington "ought to measure . . . [its] words (to Japan) very carefully because tomorrow we may be up against the same sort of conditions ourselves." From the Oval Office, President Hoover, who by this time saw Stimson as prone to reckless action, reminded him that Japan was the West's anti-Bolshevik buffer. Undersecretary of State William Castle, a former US ambassador to Japan who shared many of the president's concerns regarding Stimson, described Tokyo as Washington's "one useful friend in the Orient."[60]

Stimson gave indications that he too appreciated Japan's position as a bulwark against revolutionary nationalism, and, while he pursued a conciliatory policy in 1931, both the secretary and his inner circle began to consider economic and military action in order to contain Japan. In October, Stimson first suggested sanctions to the president, and by the following month, with Tokyo controlled by "mad dogs," support grew within the State Department for some measure of economic punishment. Hornbeck predicted that an embargo would bring Japan to heel within six months with little risk to the United States. Stimson thought in terms of days or at most weeks. The League of Nations, however, refused to take the lead, and Hoover, who thought that

Japan could never control China and feared that an embargo would lead to war, refused to back sanctions. While economic action became more acceptable during 1932, the fighting in Asia simply ended before an effective public and political mandate materialized. It is significant, however, that the limited and brief fighting of 1931 and 1932 spawned vociferous calls for economic reprisals. If short-lived fighting in Manchuria and Shanghai led to increasing public support for an embargo, what might a much more protracted and widespread conflict produce?[61]

Stimson's second containment option, a naval demonstration, received serious attention in January 1932 as hostilities spread in Manchuria and fighting erupted in Shanghai. The secretary, who now believed that the time had come to give Japan reason to "fear this country," proposed leaving the US fleet in Hawaii after it completed its scheduled maneuvers. Much to his dismay, however, a comparative review of Japanese and American naval strength revealed that the American fleet would be hard-pressed to successfully engage its Japanese counterpart. Certain that competition in China would inevitably lead to a Japanese-American war, the secretary urged the administration to build up the fleet's strength, and Hornbeck, only slightly more alarmed than his superior, argued that, if the United States did not immediately enlarge the navy, it would be compelled by Japan and the other leading naval powers to "modify or abandon" the Open Door.[62]

In addition to naval and economic deterrence, Stimson and Hoover had a third option—the power of moral force and diplomatic protest—to contain Japan. In early November, Hoover proposed that the administration publicly declare that it would not recognize the validity of any treaty brought about through force, and, while the idea received lukewarm support within the State Department, Stimson quickly recognized the wisdom of the president's suggestion. He informed Dawes: "We do not see how we can do anything more ourselves as a government than to announce our disapproval and to announce that we will not recognize any treaties which may be forced by Japan under the pressure of military occupation." By early December, the secretary began drafting an official nonrecognition statement, and on January 7, 1932, following the Japanese occupation of Chinchow, a city some two hundred miles south of Mukden, the epicenter of the Far Eastern Crisis, Washington made public the final draft, which invoked the Kellogg Briand Pact and declared Washington's support both for China and for the postwar peace structure. Two leading State Department officials, the historical adviser Hunter Miller and the legal adviser Green H. Hackworth, also argued that Stimson's policy would contain Japan by isolating Tokyo from the world community and preventing it from acquiring American capital.[63]

Unfortunately, as Stimson later conceded, nonrecognition did little to support China or contain Japan. Instead of words, Chiang wanted a concrete example of American goodwill, but his request for surplus American military equipment, loans, or a conference of the Nine Power Treaty signatories all fell on deaf ears. The Stimson Doctrine also did little to isolate Japan from American or foreign capital, and the world community failed to embrace nonrecognition.[64]

Stimson and Hoover predicated their doctrine on the assumption that the postwar peace machinery deserved backing, a proposition that at least one key diplomat did not support. In the privacy of his diary, as the crisis in China came to a close, Joseph Grew asked the question that neither of his superiors could ask: "The more one mulls over the whole problem, the more one is inclined to question whether the peace machinery which the world has been trying so earnestly and painstakingly to erect these last fourteen years is basically sound, or rather whether it is basically practical." The one-time defender of the entire postwar order now questioned "whether the peace machinery is sufficient to deter *any* country, even our own, from hostilities if the urge is sufficiently strong." By the time Grew finished penning his missive, he began to sound dangerously like his counterparts at the Japanese Foreign Office, who often argued that existing treaties no longer corresponded to present conditions. "The peace machinery of the world," he argued, "must be far more radical, far more prescient, far more concerned with facts, conditions, and circumstances than with theories than it is today, if it is ever to succeed in abolishing war." Far from wanting a radical peace structure, Grew really advocated a radical shift in American diplomacy that rejected idealism in favor of realism. The Stimson Doctrine, however, precluded such a shift, precisely because, as Thomas Millard reassuringly informed Nanking, "Mr. Stimson's utterances have put the American Government in a position from which it cannot back down without humiliation."[65]

Unfortunately, the Stimson Doctrine was not the last time that the secretary resorted to moral force in order to contain Japan. A month after Washington swore an oath on the altar of nonrecognition, Stimson escalated his war of words in response to the spread of fighting to Shanghai. The Japanese attack on China's largest city stemmed from many issues, including escalating Sino-Japanese tensions, the massing of Chinese troops near the foreign concessions, high-handed Japanese demands, and the conviction within Japanese naval circles that, in order to match the army's accomplishments in Manchuria, the navy had to show equal initiative in Shanghai.[66]

Stimson quickly turned to London for help, confident that an Anglo-American common front would contain Japan. He found, however, that

Prime Minister Ramsay MacDonald, who shared Hoover's view that Japan was the key to East Asian stability, had no interest in confronting Tokyo. Unable to secure British support, Stimson decided that he had to issue "a formal statement of the case against Japan" in order to rally public opinion at home and abroad.[67]

On February 24, 1932, Stimson made his case in a letter to Senator William Borah that, by prior arrangement, the Idahoan immediately made public. The letter reviewed traditional American Far Eastern diplomacy as well as Japan's repeated depredations in China and warned Tokyo that continued violations of the Nine Power Treaty would release the United States from its obligations under the Washington Naval Treaty. Stimson, who maintained that Washington needed to exert some greater effort to galvanize world opinion against Japanese aggression, believed that the Borah letter was a natural sequel to his nonrecognition policy. He also hoped that it would help rebuild the old Roosevelt-era multinational coalition, which had protected the Open Door a generation earlier. The Borah letter did not accomplish any of these meaningful ends. Instead, it influenced the Inukai cabinet to withdraw its request for American good offices to end the fighting in Shanghai and sparked a "minor war scare" with Japan.[68]

Despite Inukai's decision to abandon American good offices, Sino-Japanese negotiations, conducted in the British consulate in Shanghai under the watchful eyes of Western observers, produced an end to the fighting and a Japanese withdrawal from the city during the spring and early summer of 1932. While Hoover credited nonrecognition with the pullout, Warren Cohen concluded that Japan's decision stemmed less from Western pressure and more from the fact that "Japanese military leaders never intended more than to bloody the Chinese." Japan's retreat at Shanghai, however, did not mean the end of the Far Eastern crisis.[69]

In December 1931, in its last scene and final act, the Wakatsuki cabinet agreed to a league-appointed commission, headed by a British diplomat, the Second Earl of Lytton, to investigate the Manchurian crisis. A year later, the Lytton Commission delivered a report recognizing that Chinese "propaganda has been pushed to such lengths that it has contributed to creating the atmosphere in which the present dispute broke out" but rejecting Japanese claims that the Manchurian campaign was justified by the right of self-defense. The report, which reaffirmed that league members would not recognize Manchukuo, also established an altogether fair set of recommendations designed to restore Manchuria to Chinese administration while guaranteeing legitimate Japanese treaty rights. In February, when the league approved the Lytton recommendations, future foreign minister Yosuke Matsuoka led the Japanese delegation out in protest. The following month, Japan formally withdrew from the league.[70]

Aftermath

The Far Eastern crisis conditioned Chinese, Japanese, and US foreign policy long after the fighting in Manchuria and Shanghai ended. In China, the scathing denunciations that accompanied the Shanghai truce convinced the leadership that in the future it must avoid the appearance of weakness or face the public's wrath. T. V. Soong, Chiang's brother-in-law and then the current finance minister, and Wellington Koo, the architects of Chinese diplomacy, determined that China's image abroad had suffered owing to the poor showing of its army as well as Nanking's acquiescence in the Tangku Truce, in which Chiang agreed to withdraw Chinese forces south of the Great Wall. They agreed "that an active policy of steady resistance against Japan and speedy preparation for the coming international crisis was essential" and that in order to obtain effective Western aid China must forcefully resist Japan in the future.[71]

The Far Eastern crisis proved no less important in shaping Japanese foreign policy. At the height of the crisis, Japan attempted to end its diplomatic isolation by concluding some kind of formal rapprochement, political agreement, or even alliance with one of the great powers. During the typically festive Moscow winter of 1932, for example, the Japanese and German ambassadors discussed improving ties, and, while no formal agreements were reached, Berlin did not dismiss Tokyo's overture out of hand. Japan next turned its eyes to France, where, beginning in July 1932, Japanese military and civilian officials launched a multipronged effort to secure a Franco-Japanese reconciliation. Although favored by the French ambassador in Tokyo, the Quai d'Orsay quickly found that the price of closer relations meant formal recognition of Manchukuo, a step Paris found unthinkable. The Foreign Ministry favored an accord with Moscow after Soviet diplomats suggested a nonaggression pact in 1932, but lingering distrust of Soviet designs in the Far East, particularly within the army, led Tokyo to spurn the overture. The very nature of the debates, however, clearly indicates that, in response to international isolation and Western pressure, forces that in the coming years typified Japan's international position, Tokyo seriously considered a move that only a few years earlier would have been unthinkable.[72]

The crisis of 1931–1933 also had a profound effect on Japanese perceptions of, and policies toward, the United States. Fleet faction officers increasingly saw America as both a near- and a long-term threat and accordingly opposed further naval limitation agreements. At the height of the crisis, Japan's naval attaché in Washington reported that a Japanese-American clash over Manchuria appeared increasingly likely, and, when a sizable portion of the US fleet remained in Hawaii following its spring 1932 maneuvers, Tokyo received ominous reports of its "warlike preparations." Japan's increasing isolation and the navy's growing conviction that the Washington Treaty no longer afforded it adequate security also increased the fleet faction's determination to impose its will on moderate treaty faction officers. Fleet faction officers believed that the navy's deterrent power kept the league and the United States from intervening after Mukden, and, therefore, they pushed for "a rapid expansion of naval power," which "would compel the United States to accept Japanese leadership in Asia." The army's policy on relations with America, meanwhile, displayed a degree of farsightedness that made the navy's myopic reasoning look downright prescient. Predicated on the idea of certain conflict with the Soviet Union, and fresh from victories in Manchuria, army policy sought to develop Manchukuo, support pro-Japanese movements in China proper, and also improve relations with Washington.[73]

The Far Eastern crisis affected the Gaimusho as well. By 1933, even those who actively supported the army's continental adventure showed genuine concern over the state of Japanese-American relations and realized that steps must be taken to arrest the decline. Well before the publication of the Lytton Report, the Foreign Ministry concluded that, in order to improve relations with America, Japan must indicate its willingness to support the Open Door in Manchuria. This attitude indicates, of course, that Tokyo understood the Open Door to mean equality of commercial opportunity, while by 1932 Washington interpreted Hay's notes à la Straight and Knox. More important, by this time, Japanese assurances regarding the Open Door meant nothing in Washington, and, rather than reassure American officials, Tokyo's avowals served only to reinforce the belief that Japanese diplomacy was inherently duplicitous.[74]

Finally, and most importantly, the Manchurian and Shanghai crises shaped both America's immediate and its long-term containment strategy. Hoover's decision to retain additional American warships in Hawaii and deploy the Asiatic Fleet to Shanghai reinforced Washington's faith in military deterrence by convincing policymakers that naval deterrence drove Japan from the city. Stimson, for one, firmly believed that "the presence of the entire American fleet assembled at a port which placed it on the flank of any such outbreak southward towards Hong Kong, French Indo-China or the Philippines, undoubtedly exercised a steadying effect" on Tokyo.[75]

In addition to reinforcing Washington's belief in deterrence, the fleet deployment also paved the way for the sword of Damocles style of diplomacy. In convincing Hoover to leave elements of the fleet in Hawaii, Stimson argued that "Japan was afraid" of American military power, and he "was willing to let her be afraid of that [military power] without telling her that we were not going to use it against her." The inherent danger in Stimson's policy, of course, comes when the object of deterrence—not realizing that it is all a bluff—becomes convinced that war is sufficiently likely to warrant a preemptive strike. In 1932, the bluff policy convinced many Japanese that the United States was planning a war that it had no intention of fighting. The Damocles theory produced frightening results in 1932. Within a decade it helped produce tragedy.[76]

Even as the fleet's redeployment reinforced belief in the value of military deterrence, it simultaneously highlighted the comparative weakness of the American navy vis-à-vis Japan. The following year, the Roosevelt administration began to redress the imbalance when it appropriated some $240 million in relief funds to construct thirty-two warships, including two aircraft carriers. A year later, Congress began a ritual of sorts when it appropriated additional funds for naval expansion under the first Vinson-Trammell Act.[77]

The Far Eastern crisis also led to renewed interest in exploiting Japan's economic vulnerability in order to contain Tokyo. Prominent Americans, including Harvard president A. Lawrence Lowell, stimulated the sanctions' debates with a public call for economic restrictions, and, while Hoover opposed them, the debates over economic deterrence help explain the evolution of American policy four years later. By 1932, while business and labor generally opposed sanctions, senior State Department officials, including Stimson and Hornbeck, were united in believing that economic deterrence would bring Japan to heel in a relatively short period of time. There were of course naysayers, principal among them Ambassador Grew, who believed that Western economic sanctions would force Japan to expand in order to acquire alternative supply sources, but they were a distinct minority within the State Department. They became an even more distinct minority in the new administration, especially after key embargo proponents, including Hornbeck, stayed on to serve Roosevelt and Hull. Policymakers, not surprisingly, accepted the prevailing wisdom that an embargo would quickly contain Japan and began immediately to consider trade sanctions after the Marco Polo Bridge Incident in July 1937.[78]

In addition to naval deterrence and economic coercion, the Roosevelt administration also inherited a growing interest in reconstituting a multinational coalition to support the Open Door and contain Japan. Stimson's disappointment notwithstanding, Hornbeck began agitating for closer Anglo-American cooperation in the spring of 1932, and within months he had come around to supporting a general alliance of Western powers against Japan. By the end of the crisis, he also endorsed calls from within the State Department for normalizing US-Soviet relations as a means of restoring the balance of power in Asia. On Capitol Hill, interest in using Russia as a counterweight also grew in concert with crises in Manchuria and Shanghai, and, in August 1932, William Borah personally appealed to Stimson for a reexamination of Washington's policy of withholding recognition from Moscow. While little came of these campaigns for multinational cooperation during the Far Eastern crisis, within a year of taking office President Roosevelt normalized relations with Moscow and began his push for closer Anglo-American cooperation in support of the Open Door.[79]

In addition to new strategies for containing Japan, the Roosevelt administration also inherited overly gloomy assumptions concerning the inevitability of a Japanese-American conflict. Forecasts of a Japanese-American war were hardly unique to the 1930s, yet by March 1933 senior statesmen increasingly believed that general, structural forces, rather than isolated, heated controversies, such as American immigration restrictions, would lead to conflict. The navy General Board, for example, concluded that the "dissimilar foundations" of the Japanese Empire and the American Republic made "permanent adjustment of controversial problems . . . difficult." Structural differences were so great, the board concluded, that only force would permanently solve "controversial problems." Throughout the 1920s, the board continued to see Japan's goal as "political, commercial, and military domination of the Western Pacific" and American support for the Open Door as the most controversial of the "controversial problems."[80]

By 1933, however, all too many civilian policymakers had come around to share the assessment that war was inevitable unless Japan or America abandoned their decades-old national policies in the Far East. In March 1932, Stimson went so far as to confide in his diary that America would have to fight Japan if Tokyo did not alter its China policy. That Stimson's views grew so dark by 1932 is especially significant. His mind-set, more than that of any other senior official, should have been formed by his experiences during the halcyon days of Japanese-American relations. Then, America was Japan's mentor, and Tokyo was Washington's junior partner. If time and experience had worn away Stimson's positive view of Japan, what could reasonably be expected of other, younger leaders?[81]

Franklin Roosevelt, for one, shared many of Stimson's concerns. The president-elect, claims the noted historian Justus Doenecke, "often gave the impression that the United States must do everything possible to stop Japanese expansion in Asia." In an early January 1933 meeting with Stimson, Roosevelt assured the outgoing secretary of state that he would continue to support the nonrecognition doctrine, and, when trusted aides Raymond Moley and Rexford Tugwell tried to convince him to abandon it, the president explained that his sympathy for China made that impossible. Roosevelt's mind-set did not soften after entering office, and in the summer of 1934 he confided to Arthur Krock: "Militarist[s] control Japan." Three months later he told Krock: "The present rulers of Japan cannot be trusted." For the new president, supporting China and the Open Door and containing Japan defined America's role in Asia. The Far Eastern crisis destroyed what little confidence American officials had in the value of Japanese-American political agreements, and, once Makino Saito's cabinet led Japan out of the league in 1933, even Ambassador Grew wrote that the "Japanese are fundamentally incapable of comprehending the sanctity of contractual obligations when such obligations conflict with what they conceive to be their own interests." Not surprisingly, the Roosevelt administration exhibited little interest in concluding new political agreements with Japan.[82]

The postwar Far Eastern order began with great promise and ended in even greater disappointment. The Washington Conference created a number of lasting agreements, but, because it sought only to contain Japan rather than to harmonize competing policies, as earlier agreements had done, it proved wanting. Despite this major limitation, the conference survived the withering heat of Chinese nationalism and the turmoil generated by China's reunification and civil war only to meet its sad end sometime after September 18, 1931. In retrospect, however imperfect the Washington order had been, its death was indeed a mournful event. In less than a decade, continued rivalry in China, a new European war, deeply ingrained mutual suspicion, and a misguided American belief in Japanese vulnerability led the US government to abandon containment in favor of a strategy that sought to roll back Japanese gains on the Asian mainland. In a short time, this change in strategy brought on a war far more brutal, terrifying, and costly than anyone imagined.

Chapter 3

Into the Abyss

> [Hull's] attitude with respect to Japan seems to be entirely different from that with respect to other countries with which we have diplomatic relations.
>
> —Harold Ickes (1937)

> Hornbeck had two supreme passions. One was a feeling of affection and sympathy for China. And the second was a pathological hatred of Japan and things Japanese.
>
> —Eugene Dooman (1962)

For the better part of a decade, the Washington Conference order governed Japanese-American relations, but by 1933 the system lay in ruins. The death of the order signaled far more than the triumph of Japanese militarism over Shidehara diplomacy or the intensification of the now institutionalized Japanese-American estrangement. It meant the end of a spirit that, whatever its limitations, was predicated on the belief that diplomatic engagement and cooperative diplomacy could contain Japan more effectively than economic sanctions and military deterrence. After 1933, Washington had no such illusions, and for eight years the Roosevelt administration consistently shunned Tokyo's efforts at a Japanese-American rapprochement and actively opposed efforts by the British and the Chinese to improve their relations with Japan. Throughout the 1930s, as diplomatic engagement gave way to a complex and ultimately futile reliance on economic coercion and military deterrence, tensions between Japan and the United States increased, and both nations prepared for the war that neither sought.

Franklin Roosevelt accepted his predecessors' faith in the material and moral rectitude of the Open Door as well as their belief that Japan's pursuit of commercial and political hegemony in the Far East represented the greatest threat to US interests in Asia. He also soon concluded that, while neither Japanese moderates nor the postwar peace structure could restrain Tokyo from its headlong march, American military and economic power could contain Japan. Before employing these traditional tools of containment, the new administration had to first arrest the decline in American naval power and then convince an increasingly isolationist public and Congress to look beyond the unrelenting Depression and once again take up the burdens of international leadership.

Between the president's first inauguration and the start of the "China Incident," four and a half years later, the administration secured sufficient funding to build a blue-water fleet capable of deterring Japanese expansion in the Far East and shored up the Far Eastern balance of power both by normalizing relations with the Soviet Union and by supporting Chiang Kai-shek. Unfortunately, Washington's active resistance to a Sino-Japanese détente also helped set the stage for a full-scale Sino-Japanese war that devastated China, threatened the Open Door, and inexorably drew Japan and America into a far greater and even more destructive maelstrom. Japanese expansion ground slowly to a halt from 1933 to 1937, but containment's victory was wholly pyrrhic.

No Time for Détente: The United States, Japan, and China, 1933–1935

The new administration quickly demonstrated its opposition to improved Sino-Japanese relations when, in a dramatic departure from 1932, American diplomats refused to work toward ameliorating Sino-Japanese differences. Shortly after Roosevelt's inauguration, Alfred Sze, Nanking's minister in Washington, approached Stanley Hornbeck in order to determine the administration's attitude regarding a new Sino-Japanese dialogue. During the meeting, Hornbeck, who showed Sze the kind of detached attention and respect with which undertakers usually treat their subjects, promptly set about preparing the Chinese proposal for the diplomatic afterworld. Hornbeck informed Cordell Hull, the new secretary of state, that any American initiative "would . . . re-invigorate Japanese animus against this country" and that successful negotiations were bound to create a lasting bitterness "on the part both of the Japanese and of the Chinese (in general) towards us." He predicted that negotiations would likely fail yet argued, quite significantly, that the United States had far more to fear from successful talks.[1]

Japan, Hornbeck noted, had long demanded negotiations with China, and their success could mean only "a capitulation on the part of China in terms of recognition of the new *status quo* in Manchuria and a pledge to refrain from any further efforts to upset that *status quo*." The Far Eastern chief maintained that China's capitulation would mean a defeat for the policies that the League of Nations and Washington had developed in response to the Far Eastern crisis and would allow "the Japanese to consolidate their position on the Continent and prepare for their next move (either further coercion of China or conflict with Russia or conflict with the United States)." In effect, Hornbeck began to enunciate a theme that, eight years later, still governed the ill-fated Hull-Nomura discussions of August–November 1941. To wit, a Sino-Japanese peace would serve neither Chinese nor American interests and would instead act as a springboard for further Japanese aggression and conquest.[2]

If Hornbeck opposed direct Sino-Japanese negotiations, what were the alternatives? "Better," he reasoned, "that the situation between Japan and China remain fluid, even though it mean further suffering for the time being for the Chinese and a continuation of uncertainty and apprehension by and on behalf of foreign nationals in China and foreign powers in general." Hornbeck believed that continued Chinese resistance would eventually force Tokyo to abandon its continental expansion. Therefore, he reasoned that successful negotiations were counterproductive in that an agreement would end Chinese resistance and thereby strengthen Japan for its next round of conquests.[3]

Hornbeck further advised that Japanese duplicity and Tokyo's appetite for expansion made any negotiation worthless and that it was better for everyone—in the long run even China—to keep Japan bogged down. The longer Japan stayed in China, the more world opinion would turn against Tokyo, and, after the bitter disappointments of the last two years, Hornbeck desperately wanted more nations to line up foursquare against Japan. In time, Hornbeck argued, "the flood tide of her invasion will reach its height and the ebb will follow," and, in the meantime, "our interests would be best served by a complete exposure of Japan's program, her strength and/or weakness, and as complete as possible involvement of herself in the situation which she has created and is developing there." He recognized that his was "not a humanitarian view," yet, given Japan's ultimate aims, he saw no other viable option.[4]

The logical extension of Hornbeck's position—use China to contain Japan and force Tokyo to abandon foreign expansion—immediately led the administration to embark on an ambitious program to provide Nanking with the tools to resist Japan. In the spring of 1933, Washington gave Chiang a $50 million credit to purchase American cotton, wheat, and flour. Officially designed as a recovery measure to sell off America's burgeoning surplus, the credit also represented an early and extraordinarily unpopular attempt to strengthen China. Britain and Japan immediately fired off angry protests alleging that the credit violated the 1920 Consortium agreement, and Japanese-owned mills in China quickly ceased using the so-called loan cotton. Tokyo's real worry, however, concerned how Nanking would spend the proceeds once it sold its American bounty on the world market, and, while Chiang's government promised to plow any profit back into developing Chinese infrastructure, Tokyo suspected that Nanking would use the money to upgrade its armed forces. In fact, Japan had reason to fear an American-sponsored buildup of the Nationalist army. During Roosevelt's first twenty months in office, Washington approved export licenses for some $6 million in military hardware, compared to less than $500,000 in 1932, the peak year of the Far Eastern crisis.[5]

While the commodity credits further undermined Anglo-American cooperation, the League of Nations decision in July 1933 to establish a special committee to coordinate the international development of Chinese infrastructure breathed new life into multinational efforts to contain Japanese expansion in China. Geneva named Ludwig Rajchman, a Polish physician with close ties to Chiang Kai-shek and T. V. Soong, to lead the mission. Rajchman's appointment, however, was not well received in Tokyo, where officials remembered his part in obstructing Sino-Japanese peace talks. In the early hours of the Far Eastern crisis, when Soong wanted direct Sino-Japanese negotiations, Rajchman convinced him instead to work through the league, confident that the world body could compel Japan to abandon its assault on Manchuria.[6]

Not surprisingly, Rajchman remained unpopular in Japan, and within days of his appointment the counselor of the Japanese embassy in Washington, Toshihiko Taketomi, informed Hornbeck "that the powers were apparently embarked on an enterprise for the assistance of China from which Japan was excluded." Taketomi warned "that the Japanese people would not tolerate Japan's being excluded from any efforts made with regard to assistance to China." He further asserted that American and league assistance strengthened the hand of anti-Japanese officials, such as T. V. Soong, who consistently opposed plans to ease Sino-Japanese tensions. Taketomi bluntly told Hornbeck that the league should stop extending technical assistance to China and that at the very least Washington should cease unilateral aid to Nanking. To a limited degree, both the Far Eastern Division (FE) and the secretary agreed with Taketomi in that both Hornbeck and Hull recognized that Tokyo would not tolerate massive Western aid to China for very long. Both men also understood that the United States was in no position to stop Japan if it attempted to block foreign assistance from reaching Chiang. In the end, Hornbeck refused to make Taketomi any promises or hold out much hope, and under the circumstances neither he nor Hull could do anything else. If Taketomi was right and foreign aid did prevent Chiang from making terms, then Washington *had to continue aiding* China.[7]

Tokyo continued to make veiled warnings regarding Western aid, and in the spring of 1934 the Foreign Ministry spokesman Eiji Amau inadvertently declared publicly that his government opposed such programs. Foreign Minister Koki Hirota rushed to make amends, assuring Grew that Amau's statement had no official sanction. Three days after his mistaken démarche, Amau found himself back in front of the cameras, this time to assure the foreign press corps that Japan had "no intention of interfering with the legitimate interests of other powers in China" and would "object only when the action of a third power threatens Japan's position." He explained that Japan wished neither to close the Open Door, nor to interfere with existing treaties, nor to circumscribe Chinese sovereignty in any way.[8]

Grew informed Hull three days after the initial press conference that, while he believed Amau had accurately explained Japan's position regarding foreign aid to China, he was convinced that the statement did not mark a significant departure from Japan's prior position. In a similar vein, Hornbeck told Hull: "Mr. Amau's statement to the press was not a declaration of policy; it was a *disclosure* of policy." As such, he continued, it merely "shows what Japan's 'China policy' is." Grew explained—and in a separate memo Hornbeck concurred—that Japan's policy stemmed from resentment over the 1933 commodity credit and the alarm produced by Curtiss-Wright's construction of an airplane factory near Hangkow. Hull's men stopped short of telling their chief that foreign aid to China justified Japan's response, but Sir Victory Wellesley, Britain's deputy undersecretary for foreign affairs, flatly informed Robert Bingham, Washington's ambassador in London, that "in the present instance he felt Japan had a fairly strong case." Grew, meanwhile, assured Hull that, given Hirota's determination to improve relations with China and the West, he found it unlikely that Tokyo would make good on Amau's declaration. He went on to note, however, that "the implications contained in the Foreign Office statement [were] very serious" and that, if they were carried out, China would be put "in a state of tutelage under Japan."[9]

Given that the Amau declaration presented Hull with a vague, uncertain, and ill-defined threat, formulating a response was no easy task. Certainly, the other Nine Power Treaty signatories, however dismayed by Amau's démarche, had not offered vigorous protests, and even Great Britain, which had far more at stake in China than did the United States, preferred appeasement over an Anglo-American common front. London appeared content with a Japanese reaffirmation of respect for the Open Door in China, and Sir John Simon made repeated references both in his official note to Tokyo and during parliamentary interpellation to Japan's special rights in China. While Washington had shed the language of Lansing-Ishii, London had not, and by mid-1934 Anglo-American cooperation to contain Japanese expansion appeared dead.[10]

While Hull "utterly detested" the British strategy, London based its Far Eastern policy on considerations entirely different from Washington's. The English—far more vulnerable in the Pacific than the United States and from 1933 on consumed with dread over the prospect of German resurgence—sought to keep peace in Asia and forestall a German-Japanese combination. As early as 1925, British diplomats forecast that Japan would be a danger only if it aligned itself with one of the dominant European powers because such an alliance, strategists reasoned, would increase the likelihood of both an Anglo-Japanese war and a Japanese victory. Once Germany and Japan withdrew from the league in 1933, the vague buzzing sound that Australian prime minister William Hughes first heard following the end of the Anglo-Japanese Alliance became a deafening klaxon of alarm. While the Australians—who would be among the first members of the Commonwealth to master the etiquette required to welcome properly the conquering Japanese—saw their own ruin in case of a German-Japanese alliance, many British were equally alarmed. Although Simon predicted victory over Germany, he contended that if England "had to enter upon such a struggle with a hostile instead of a friendly Japan . . . then not only would India, Hong Kong and Australasia be in dire peril, but we ourselves would stand in far greater danger of destruction by a fully armed and organized Germany."[11]

Sir John argued that an Anglo-Japanese agreement "which definitely called a halt to Japanese penetration into China" would benefit China, Great Britain, and the cause of peace in the Far East. He believed that an Anglo-Japanese nonaggression pact might lead Japan back into the league and, especially if Washington signed on, cause Tokyo to scale back its naval expansion. Britain's comparative weakness in the Pacific increasingly led London to pursue a frankly accommodationist policy with Tokyo in the hope that a limited sacrifice of British principles in Asia—recognition of Manchukuo, for example—would stabilize the Far East, keep Germany and Japan apart, and allow Britain to fight a one-front war.[12]

If Britain was in no mood to denounce the Amau declaration, it was not alone, for neither was the American public. Even William Randolph Hearst's reliably anti-Japanese *San Francisco Examiner* defended Tokyo's policy of continental expansion. Lacking both the support of its overseas partners and the public, the State Department's only options were to bide its time and redouble its effort to bring to the public's attention the danger that Japan presented to American interests worldwide.[13]

Despite the decision to trim support for China, the United States was not in so critical a position that, like Britain, it actively sought to appease Japan. Instead, Washington consistently spurned Japanese efforts to improve relations. During the first half of 1934, as Tokyo sought to strengthen Japanese-American ties before the next round of naval limitation talks, Washington became a kind of diplomatic Lourdes to which repeated Japanese "goodwill" missions flocked seeking a cure for Japanese-American estrangement. Distinguished visitors, including Prince Iyesato Tokugawa and Prince Fumimaro Konoe (of whom Grew noted, "there is every probability that he will eventually become Prime Minister of Japan"), came to test the waters, and, while their visits were generally positive, the State Department quickly came to question their motives. From Tokyo, Grew cabled Hull that these unofficial visits represented a Japanese effort to go around the secretary's back and gain direct access to the president. He informed Hull that the Foreign Ministry had concluded that Roosevelt would give Tokyo a far more sympathetic hearing than would the State Department and that many of the Japanese visitors were "either persons who, because of student-days association with the President, are in a position to request a friendly visit with him, or persons who, because of their high rank in Japan, cannot well be refused permission to call upon the President." He continued, however, that, since Tokyo was "endeavoring to open new channels directly to the President," he would discourage any more unofficial visits.[14]

At the same time that he worked to discourage unofficial visits, Grew did his best to encourage Hull to see that Tokyo's efforts to improve relations with Washington were sincere. He explained that all signs indicated declining military influence on both the cabinet and especially the Foreign Ministry. "If the Diet session, recently concluded, accomplished nothing else of particular importance," he informed Hull, "it did demonstrate unmistakably the existence of a strong feeling in Japan against the abuse of power by the military." In particular, the ambassador saw Hirota's willingness to transfer powerful, anti-Anglo-American diplomats, including Toshio Shiratori, to out-of-the-way posts (Shiratori got Stockholm) as a sign of the cabinet's desire to mend fences with America. Yet in his diary Grew gave no indication that he expected a dramatic breakthrough or that he had any illusions that the State Department would strike while the opportunity existed. He seems to have recognized that advocates of conciliation—both Japanese and American—would receive no encouragement from the FE chief and that, as he noted in his diary, the mere rumors of a

Japanese-American deal meant that "Stanley Hornbeck's hair must be getting whiter and whiter."[15]

Grew's initial efforts, much like his subsequent work in 1940 and 1941, to create a profitable Japanese-American dialogue failed owing to the prevailing a priori opposition to any political agreements with Tokyo as well as to the unspoken conviction that the United States had no pressing reason to make terms. The Far Eastern crisis convinced many in the new administration of Japan's inherent duplicity and thirst for expansion, and neither Tokyo's conciliatory gestures nor Grew's timely dispatches altered this mind-set. Moreover, in 1934, the architects of American containment saw no compelling reason to engage Japan. While America had to avoid an immediate confrontation, there was no need to so fear Tokyo as to make a useless, counterproductive agreement. Hull and Hornbeck saw very little that Washington needed from Tokyo yet much that an increasingly isolated Japan needed from America. This mind-set governed their attitude when, during February and March 1934, the State Department learned that Tokyo hoped to conclude a nonaggression pact with Washington and divide the Pacific into Japanese and American spheres.[16]

"Nothing could have been more discouraging to China, or more disastrous later to us and other countries interested in the Pacific area," Hull wrote in his memoirs, "than for us to sign a pact with Japan." The secretary interpreted Japanese efforts in 1934 as part of a pattern established over the past generation in which, after every round of foreign expansion, Tokyo sought some political agreement with Washington that would serve as American recognition of Japanese gains. Hull resolved not to repeat this error, as his predecessors had in 1908, 1917, and 1922. To some extent, he painted an accurate picture, linking the 1907–1908 war scare with Root-Takahira, the Twenty-one Demands with Lansing-Ishii, and the post-Versailles war scare with the Washington Treaties. Perhaps another secretary would have seen a different pattern, one that would have been more helpful to the advancement of peace, but this secretary saw no tangible benefit to successful Japanese-American negotiations.[17]

Hull did not recognize that, in 1934, an aggressive, expansionist Japan, preparing for war with the Soviets and slowly, deliberately eroding Nanking's control over north China, could still want improved relations with Washington. A genuine concern over the course of Japanese-American relations motivated Tokyo in each of its many approaches, and, while there is no need to romanticize Japan's desire for improved relations—for hardheaded diplomacy and self-interest figured prominently in every instance—it was equally important that Hull not demonize the Japanese. In 1934, moderates, including Hirota and Prime Minister Makoto Saito, sought improved ties for countless reasons, including their interest in successful naval talks and the desire to preempt the formation of an anti-Japanese Western bloc. Japanese-American talks would never have led to an abandonment of Manchuria, and, while an agreement would have signaled an American willingness to deal with the creators of Manchukuo, it would not, as Hull later claimed, have made the United States "a kind of silent partner in Japan's aggressions."[18]

When Ambassador Hiroshi Saito approached Hull with a proposal for a joint Japanese-American declaration on trade and mutual respect for Pacific territory, the secretary took all of seventy-two hours to formally reject the proposal. To be sure, Washington could not have signed off on a partition of the Pacific into Japanese and American spheres, but other parts of the ambassador's proposal, and the reasons underlying his diplomatic gambit, had considerable merit. FE, which recognized that Saito's proposed joint declaration really aimed at securing a Japanese-American rapprochement and a recognition of Japan's "special position" in Asia, offered no counterproposals. Instead, it noted that the Root-Takahira agreement covered the same ground as Saito's new proposal and that over the last twenty-five years Japan had failed to live up to this accord. FE leaders argued that new proposals were another Lansing-Ishii, an agreement that, they noted, had not only hurt American prestige but, in the end, also actually damaged American relations with both China and Japan.[19]

When Hull sat down with Saito on May 19, he informed the ambassador that his proposals were unacceptable. He may have detected some faint sign of hope in Saito, or perhaps he was unwilling to leave anything to chance, for three weeks after he sent the ambassador packing he warned Roosevelt to stay clear of him. "We have indications that the Ambassador is not inclined to accept as final," Hull told the President, "[our] view that we cannot act upon his suggestion." Then, in an extraordinarily bizarre moment, he rewrote history and warned Roosevelt not to repeat the mistake that Wilson made seventeen years earlier when Ambassador Ishii convinced him, over Lansing's objection, to conclude a bilateral agreement that "resulted in no end of confusion and embarrassment." If Hull's history was fuzzy, at least his message was clear. Do not repeat Wilson's mistake. Heed State's advice. Do not enter into any political agreements with Japan.[20]

Soon after Hull blocked Saito's bid to improve Japanese-American relations, the American diplomat with perhaps the greatest experience and insight in the Far East, John Van Antwerp MacMurray, a former ambassador to China and FE chief, sat down to write the most penetrating memorandum of his career. MacMurray first proposed writing a thorough review of

American Far Eastern policy in 1934, and a year later, with Hornbeck's backing, he prepared a comprehensive study of American diplomacy in Asia. He concluded that Japanese expansion, Chinese nationalism, and the growth of Soviet power had fundamentally reshaped the East Asian geopolitical map. While recognizing that Japan created no small share of problems in the Far East, the veteran diplomat asserted that the United States had failed to support Japan during the 1920s and that "Chinese abrogation of the Japanese treaties of 1896 and 1903" had fatally undermined the Washington Treaty system. He predicted that Japan would continue its policy of expansion, both territorial and political, in China and maintained that, while Washington should not abandon the Open Door or the Washington Treaties, it must avoid executing containment in such a way that it inadvertently brought about a Japanese-American war. MacMurray, the consummate realist, advocated building up American power without threatening Japan and cautioned against becoming China's cat's paw. Unfortunately, few policymakers other than Hornbeck, who apparently disregarded MacMurray's counsel, read the memorandum.[21]

The Race Begins

MacMurray was entirely correct when he called for an American military buildup in the Pacific. On entering office, President Roosevelt learned that Japan possessed "the most complete, well balanced, coordinated and therefore powerful fighting machine in the world today," while the United States possessed an army of barely 140,000 men and a navy that in many respects was vastly inferior to Japan's. A naval buildup soon became an administration priority, but congressional isolationists—the same isolationists who had the power of life and death over New Deal recovery measures—opposed increased defense spending. How to build up American naval power and secure congressional support in the midst of the worst depression in nearly half a century proved no easy task, but Roosevelt soon found a way.[22]

Three months after taking office, the president reversed Hoover's policy of beating swords into plowshares and earmarked nearly $250 million in relief money for naval expansion. One suspects that, despite his early fiscal conservatism and public pronouncements in favor of further disarmament, the president wanted an expanded fleet to protect the nation's vital interests. Early in his career, as Woodrow Wilson's assistant secretary of the navy, Roosevelt became, and remained ever after, a "big navy" man. The young Roosevelt believed that the navy was key to national security and that national security meant defending the American Empire. "Our national defense," Roosevelt argued, "must extend all over the Western Hemisphere, must go a thousand miles to sea, must embrace the Philippines and over the seas wherever our commerce may be." While the future president became an enthusiastic supporter of naval limitation during the 1920s, his enthusiasm died along with the Washington Conference spirit.[23]

Roosevelt did not share all of Stimson's or the General Board's assumptions regarding the inevitability of war with Japan, but he and his principal aides shared a sufficient number to convince them that America needed to build the fleet to treaty strength. A year after deciding to use relief money for naval construction, Roosevelt secured congressional authorization to fund fleet construction up to treaty limits by 1942. The Vinson Bill, premised on sustained naval building for the next eight years, created a storm of domestic protest, especially from isolationists and pacifist groups. The president publicly explained that the measure was an authorization rather than an appropriation, which meant that, if the upcoming London talks produced an accord, the Vinson funds might not have to be used. In other words, Washington would spend and build only if other nations required it to do so. In reality, Roosevelt and his chief diplomatic and naval advisers intended to use the recently approved funds, and in the coming months they actively worked to deadlock the London Conference. In his first year in office, Roosevelt had secured sufficient funding to nearly double the fleet's size, and neither money nor the fate of the next round of naval disarmament talks, scheduled for 1935, would deter the United States from achieving naval supremacy over Japan.[24]

After the Japanese takeover of Manchuria, the General Board, which even during the heyday of Japanese internationalism warned of Tokyo's Far Eastern ambitions, appeared prescient. On the eve of preliminary London Conference discussions, it echoed the familiar argument that Tokyo sought unbridled political, commercial, and territorial control in the Far East and therefore recommended that Washington stand firm in demanding retention of the existing 10:6 ratios. If the existing ratios were revised in Japan's favor, members noted, the navy could no longer fulfill its strategic doctrine and fight its way across the Pacific, defeat the Japanese main fleet, and relieve the Philippines. While the board realized that Japan might very well reject preserving the current ratio system, it confidently predicted that, if talks broke down, the United States could win the ensuing race. While this position appeared extreme, senior State Department officials were prepared for a naval arms race and much more.[25]

By early 1934, concern over Japanese expansion had grown so great that senior State Department officials increasingly looked to Moscow as a partner in containing Japan. With Anglo-American cooperation at its nadir, Soviet-American relations recently normalized, and Soviet-Japanese tensions at the point of war, Hornbeck became an outspoken yet by no means lone advocate of aid to Moscow. He advised that, in the event of war, Washington should remain neutral at the outset and at the right "*psychological moment throw our armed forces in on the side of the Soviet Union.*" William Bullitt, Washington's first ambassador to the Soviet Union, sent the president a toned-down version of Hornbeck's memo in which he informed Roosevelt that overwhelming naval superiority provided Washington the best insurance against having to fight on the Soviet side. Bullitt's message indicates that he shared the bulk of Hornbeck's opinions, especially concerning the value of naval deterrence, and differed only in not advocating fighting on the Soviet side. For Bullitt, naval superiority still provided "the best insurance against the United States being drawn into a war between Japan and the Soviet Union." Naval superiority was so important that he urged his friend, the president, to watch and wait. If "Japan begins to build above her present ratio," the United States "should speak softly and build three ships to her one."[26]

The Bullitt-Hornbeck analysis of American options in the event of a Soviet-Japanese war offers a fascinating glimpse into the sea change that had quietly overturned many of Washington's Far Eastern calculations. During the Manchurian crisis, Hoover's conviction that Japan blocked the spread of Bolshevism moderated Washington's response, but within three years FE concluded that America had far more to fear from Japan than from Russia. The Japanese threat appeared so much greater than the Russian threat, in fact, that Roosevelt's senior advisers maintained that America should "see to it that Japan does not emerge the victor" in the event of a Soviet-Japanese clash.[27]

Hornbeck's concerns over Japan and Bullitt's faith in naval deterrence were widely shared convictions, and, in the fall of 1934, a joint State–Navy Department committee agreed that the United States must reject Japan's bid for parity at the upcoming London Conference or abandon US rights and interests in the Far East. Hull, who showed an uncanny ability to shed his commitment to disarmament when Japan entered the picture, joined Hornbeck in agreeing to the hard line. The meeting revealed that, by 1934, State's upper echelon accepted both the General Board's reliance on naval supremacy and its long-held assumptions regarding Japanese expansion. By the time the conference adjourned, the committee reached a "consensus that Japan's policy was definitely to continue its aims at dominating Eastern Asia." From Tokyo, Ambassador Grew also voiced support for an expanded fleet and his confidence in the power of naval deterrence. He contended that Japan could not afford a naval arms race and that the United States had no choice but to "build up [its] Navy and [its] airforce to the limit or withdraw from the Far East." An expanded military capacity, he noted, remained "the best possible restraining influence on further Japanese imperialist aggression."[28]

Japan also approached the London talks in an inflexible mood, in part owing to smoldering discontent over the Washington and London ratios, and in part owing to the supposed success of naval deterrence during the Far Eastern crisis. Yet these issues explain only part of the story. By the mid-1930s, Tomosaburo Kato's followers in the treaty faction were waging and losing a rearguard action to Kanji Kato and the fleet faction. Structural revisions, which went into effect in 1933, elevated the general staff over the more moderate Navy Ministry, home to the bulk of the elder Kato's moderate disciples. The general staff, long jealous of the Navy Ministry's power and influence, purged scores of influential moderates who "might conceivably have exercised a measure of rational restraint" over both the high command and the even more dangerous junior officer corps. In the aftermath of the purge, convinced that tensions with America would invariably become greater and that deterrence, which had succeeded earlier, would, with adequate resources, succeed in the future, fleet faction officers pushed for an upward revision of the battleship and heavy cruiser ratios and complete parity in light cruisers, destroyers, and submarines.[29]

The growing power of the fleet faction, however, does not fully explain Tokyo's decision to depart from the treaty structure. Technological advancements and Washington's commitment to build a great blue-water fleet were new factors that swung the decision in favor of ending the Washington and London agreements. By June 1934, navy leaders concluded that the existing treaty system failed to adequately provide for national security and that Japan need not fear a naval arms race with the West. Japan's commitment to build its fleet to treaty limits, combined with Washington's earlier halfhearted replenishment program, gave the fleet an 8:10, rather than a 6:10, ratio. This ratio, of course, provided in fact what the 10:6 ratio provided in theory—Japan's naval superiority within its home waters. Washington's 1933 relief appropriation and the far more ambitious Vinson authorization threatened the 8:10 ratio, but only if the ratio system continued. If Japan abrogated the Washington agreement and allowed the London accord to lapse, it could continue to maintain an 8:10 ratio, provided Japanese industry matched American output.[30]

Japanese strategists confidently predicted that, by fighting close to home with an 8:10 ratio and superior Japanese technology, including a recently developed torpedo with a cruising range in excess of twenty miles, the long-range Mitsubishi 96 bomber, the Yamato class battleship, and new short- and long-range submarines, the fleet would emerge victorious. Moreover, naval authorities determined that with rising productivity Japan could match American quantitative output for at least a decade. Consequently, on June 8, 1934, the Navy Ministry concluded that Japan must seek an end to the entire naval treaty structure.[31]

In the aftermath of its June démarche, the Navy Ministry spent the next three months convincing the army and the civilian ministers to support its position. In July, the cabinet rejected navy demands that Japan abrogate the Washington naval agreement in advance of the preliminary London talks. Following the vote, Kato warned the cabinet that its failure to meet his demands made it impossible to maintain order within the ranks. In 1934, just two years after naval officers had joined in the assassination of Prime Minister Inukai, this was no empty threat, and six weeks later the cabinet agreed that before the year ended Japan would, as the 1922 Washington Treaty required, give formal notice that it was abrogating the agreement. If negotiators failed to achieve some sort of binding Anglo-Japanese-American agreement at London, a Pacific arms race would come hard on the heels of New Year's Day 1937.[32]

Preliminary disarmament talks quickly foundered over the Japanese demand for parity with the Anglo-American fleets. The American delegation opposed parity, and Britain, fearing a complete breakdown of the conference, floated an idea between the extreme Japanese and American positions. London's plan, which allowed for certain qualitative restrictions on capital ships and aircraft carriers, nonfortification of Pacific bases, and public notification before constructing any new ships, quickly ran afoul of Hull, who not only kept to his extreme position but also convinced Roosevelt to oppose the British. At this point the conference was doomed. It is of course impossible to know whether Japanese negotiators would have accepted any compromise, but the bulk of evidence suggests that they would not have. Foreign Minister Koki Hirota, for example, maintained that Japan would abrogate the Washington Treaty no matter what concessions Washington and London offered.[33]

The question of who was to blame for the complete breakdown of the talks seems less important than understanding the significance of the impasse. Japan's insistence on parity certainly signaled a desire for full equality and an end to the stigma of naval inferiority, but, while fleet faction officers had howled stigma before, farsighted Japanese leaders prevailed in 1922 and again in 1930. By late 1934, however, Japan's power brokers and the general public understood internationalism and cooperative diplomacy as bankrupt policies that brought Japan little in the way of tangible results. Bold unilateral action in Manchuria, on the other hand, secured in one stroke what cooperation had failed to achieve. While unilateral action had also added to Japanese security concerns and international isolation, the fleet faction argued that the navy could deter the West from intervening against Japan. In short, the decade following the Washington Conference presented Japan with two choices for achieving national security: international cooperation or unilateral action backed by naval deterrence. On the basis of its experiences between 1922 and 1932, Japan chose the latter.

Deterrence and the ideas supporting the theory also explain the American position as well as Hull's hard-line approach to the talks. Convinced that Japan had no intention of supporting the Washington order, the secretary saw no reason to reward it with a naval treaty. Rather than reward Tokyo, Hull acted on the basis of Grew's analysis of Japanese financial and productive capabilities. Tokyo could neither afford nor win a naval race, and, once this became known, Hull thought that the Japanese people would become so incensed that they would force the military to beat a hasty retreat. He also realized that for American naval deterrence to succeed it had to have popular support, and, as the secretary's memoirs make clear, he did not believe such a mandate existed. If such a mandate did not exist, then it would have to be created, and Hull believed that the London talks were a good place to begin this arduous task. If the conference broke down, and if the public saw Japanese intransigence as the reason, then Hull hoped it would support the administration's naval expansion program. Hornbeck, in his typically blunt language, suggested that, with the London talks, "the American people are being enabled to take clearer cognizance of the facts . . . with regard to the situation in the Far East" and that a breakdown of the talks would provide much-needed support "to the policy which this Administration has adopted . . . of enlarging and improving our naval equipment." By the same token, neither the public nor Congress would likely support naval expansion in the event of either a Sino-Japanese or a Japanese-American rapprochement. The United States simply could not afford a successful naval limitation agreement and the consequent easing of US-Japanese tensions.[34]

However important, naval expansion remained only a part of the new administration's strategy for containing Japan. Consequently, as Hull and the admirals strengthened American power in the Pacific, others worked to shore up the balance of power in Asia.

The Battle for China, a Search for Allies, and Preparation for War

"And over the week-end," Secretary of the Treasury Henry Morgenthau informed his adviser, the Harvard professor John Williams, "I'm going to take a hand at writing a financial program for China." As if this were too great a weekend endeavor for even Morgenthau to contemplate, he added, almost as an afterthought: "That is from a currency standpoint." Judged by any number of criteria—intelligence, force of personality, strength of will, accomplishments in office, and character—Henry Morgenthau stood shoulder to shoulder with his fellow cabinet officers, many of whom were among the finest citizens ever to serve the Republic. Schooled in social reform at New York's Henry Street settlement, the gentleman farmer from the bucolic Hudson Valley first made his mark in the early New Deal when, as director of the Farm Credit Administration, he oversaw the refinancing of nearly a quarter of the nation's farm mortgages and rescued thousands of farms from the auctioneer's gavel. In November 1934, following then secretary of the Treasury William Woodin's resignation, Roosevelt named his friend and Duchess County neighbor of nearly twenty years to head Treasury.[35]

Morgenthau's ambitious plans for China stemmed both from a short-term Chinese emergency—largely of American making—and from the secretary's long-term goal of building a grand dollar bloc. If successful, Morgenthau's currency reform plan would also enable China to stand side by side with the United States as a partner in containing Japanese expansion.

The roots of Morgenthau's reform plan lay deep within the barren landscape of Depression-era America. In December 1933, as the country faced what in all likelihood would be its bleakest winter ever, the president signed an inflationary silver purchase bill that directed the Treasury Department to buy all newly mined American silver for the next four years. Intended in part as a thinly disguised recovery measure for western mining states and a palliative to co-opt more radical action, the silver purchase legislation, in conjunction with the devalued gold dollar, also sought to break the dangerous deflationary spiral that gripped the nation. The measure proved sufficiently successful and popular, especially in the western mining states and in Congress, that Roosevelt approved even more ambitious silver legislation in June 1934.[36]

The Silver Purchase Act of 1934 required the government to buy silver until the metal formed a quarter of the nation's specie reserve or until its price doubled to $1.29 per ounce. While earlier legislation approved only domestic purchases, the 1934 measure authorized purchases of foreign silver as well. Backers of the law argued that both the United States and foreign suppliers would benefit from overseas purchases in that silver standard nations, such as China, would see the value of its money supply expand in conjunction with silver's rising value. China could then afford greater American imports, while the sale of silver would simultaneously leave it a sizable dollar cache, which in turn would further facilitate the purchase of American exports. The theory, much like the plans of Robert Burns's mouse, did not work, for, as the historian Allan Everest noted, China "was the world's most important buyer not *with,* but *of* silver," and, while low silver prices allowed China to purchase specie and other vital commodities, high silver prices made such purchases increasingly difficult. In fact, heavy American buying produced a highly unstable silver market and also gave China unwanted firsthand experience with severe deflation. American legislation authorized the purchase of foreign silver so far above its nominal monetary value that Chinese citizens gladly sold their silver money for its higher commodity value. China's money supply quite literally began to melt down during 1934, and, as the ensuing deflation gutted the Chinese economy and weakened the Nationalist government, a chagrined Morgenthau confided to William Bullitt that he felt like a Japanese agent.[37]

In December 1934, Morgenthau submitted a confidential memo to the White House that noted: "Our present silver policy is tending to produce an early and major economic crisis in China." Failure to help, he maintained, would mean further hardship for the Chinese people and would likely lead to rising anti-American sentiment. The secretary predicted that American silver purchases might force China to abandon its silver-based currency in favor of either gold or the sterling standard, which, in turn, would mean "the withdrawal of the United States as an active influence in Far Eastern affairs, leaving that field to Japan, Great Britain, and other countries." Morgenthau then explained that, if China could be induced to adopt a bimetallic currency and peg it to the American dollar, it "might be the first step in the establishment of [a] bi-metallic monetary group, under dollar leadership." He noted that China could remain exclusively on silver and still form the core of a dollar bloc if Nanking devalued its currency and linked it to the dollar. In either instance, he informed Roosevelt, the United States would need to make funds available through loans and the purchase of additional Chinese silver.[38]

Alarming reports from the Far East during early 1935 confirmed Morgenthau's warnings of a looming financial crisis. From Nanking, Ambassador Nelson Johnson's top lieutenant, Willys Peck, predicted an economic meltdown and warned that Chiang might already have signed on for Japanese financial help. H. H. Kung, Nanking's finance minister, meanwhile, informed Hull that, while he wanted to abandon the silver standard in favor of a bimetallic currency linked to the American dollar, China needed a $100 million currency stabilization loan and a $100 million credit guaranteed by future silver deliveries. Hull, clearly alarmed over the possibility that China might strike a deal with Japan and frustrated over the Treasury Department's purchases of Chinese silver, informed the president that American policy was weakening China and that Japan was gleefully exploiting the situation. FE argued that, while the United States could not turn Kung away hat in hand as this would likely force China into Japanese arms, Washington could not, on its own, honor his request. Better, it informed Hull, Morgenthau, and Kung, that China bring its request to the consortium. A frustrated Morgenthau, who opposed multinational solutions in China, reluctantly told Hornbeck that, until the State Department informed him otherwise, he would maintain a hands-off policy.[39]

The Morgenthau-Hull clash over aid to China is illustrative of subsequent Hull feuds with Morgenthau, Stimson, Ickes, and other so-called hawks. Historians often portray Hull as a moderate who fought a valiant yet ultimately futile rear-guard action against the administration's fire-eating, interventionist faction. Nothing could be further from the truth. Hull possessed a keen understanding of both the limits of American military power and the importance of securing public backing before openly challenging Japan. In 1935, Washington possessed neither the martial power nor the requisite public support for a showdown, and, accordingly, Hull continued, as he had since the Amau declaration, to support efforts to avoid a conflict with Tokyo. Japan's ability to ruin any Chinese aid package also made a far greater impression on Hull than on Morgenthau, and, while Hull was more cautious than Morgenthau, more aware of the requirements of a successful policy, in his enmity toward Japan, his distrust of the Japanese government, and his desire to see Japan contained, he was certainly Morgenthau's equal.[40]

As the Chinese economy continued its meltdown, the State-Treasury feud paralyzed action on Nanking's behalf. China, meanwhile, requested a currency reform loan from Great Britain and in due time received another disappointing reply. London, however, did express interest in enlisting the consortium, and, while the State Department initially favored the British proposal, it soon tempered its enthusiasm after learning the wider implications of Britain's policy. In part, London's decision to explore aid options on China's behalf reflected its determination to protect Britain's considerable material interests in the Far East, but protecting trade and investments was only one motivation.[41]

Whitehall, which envisioned consortium aid as a continuation of Simon's earlier conciliatory policy, believed that a multinational solution would lead to political discussions and, it was hoped, an eventual Sino-Japanese and Anglo-Japanese rapprochement. The State Department, however, showed no inclination to back a policy that flew in the face of American strategy. Undersecretary of State William Phillips informed Roosevelt that Britain's goal of forging a Sino-Japanese agreement "would be highly gratifying to the Japanese, but probably not so to the Chinese," once they learned the price. Phillips told the president that the British hoped to use a Sino-Japanese modus vivendi on Manchuria as a catalyst for reducing Far Eastern tensions and drawing "Japan into some naval agreement that could be accepted by Great Britain and the United States." Since Washington wanted neither a rapprochement nor a naval agreement, it declined to send an American financial expert to China, as London requested, and made it abundantly clear that Britain's financial expert for China, Sir Frederick Leith-Ross, should steer clear of Washington. Sir Frederick, as amusing as he was brilliant, wrote years later that as "Washington in August is not altogether a paradise . . . [he] was relieved" that Hull "did not intend to extend an invitation to [him]."[42]

Despite Washington's lack of interest, Leith-Ross proceeded to Tokyo, where he found tepid support at best for any cooperative effort to aid China. While a few of the doyens of Japanese finance favored currency reform, government officials told Leith-Ross that China "must rely on her own resources and learn to help herself." The Foreign Ministry "did not disguise their opposition," while the army regarded his efforts "in China with jealousy if not with open hostility."[43]

When the Leith-Ross mission broke down, Chiang turned to the United States, and, when Chinese officials showed up on Morgenthau's doorstep late in the evening of October 28, 1935, the delighted secretary informed Roosevelt that the time had come to hook Nanking. He told the president that he could link China to the dollar and demand such stringent supervision as to ensure that American funds would go only to currency stabilization and not, as many feared, to the purchase of war matériel. A week after the midnight rendezvous, Morgenthau, Undersecretary of State Phillips, and Ambassador Alfred Sze met to finalize terms. The secretary laid out five strict demands, including a pledge to use American funds solely for currency stabilization and an understanding that credits would stay in American banks. Nanking also had to agree to keep Washington fully informed of how it spent its American funds and establish a multinational consultative committee with American members. And, finally, it had to tie the yuan to the dollar. When Sze balked at the prospect of a formal currency tie-up, Morgenthau bluntly told him that the United States would not "invest $65,000,000 and have you tie your money to the sterling." Nanking's decision to move forward with a new paper currency and the administration's desire to strengthen China trumped Morgenthau's interest in creating a dollar bloc, and on November 13 he agreed to buy fifty million ounces of Chinese silver without any guarantee from Nanking that it would tie the yuan to the dollar.[44]

The secretary's close association with Chinese currency reform and his growing influence over the direction of the administration's China policy continued the following year. In April, a new round of talks commenced in Washington, and the following month Morgenthau agreed to buy seventy-five million ounces of Chinese silver and extend a $20 million loan backed by Chinese silver in order to help Nanking stabilize its new currency and fend off Japanese efforts to undermine China's monetary system. By this time, Treasury officials had become deeply involved in containing Japanese expansion, and Morgenthau's aide, Harry Dexter White, armed his boss with a detailed, forty-four-page study of the situation in China. White's report warned of increasing Japanese control over large parts of China and predicted that Sino-Japanese economic "cooperation" would lead to the end of the Open Door and ever-greater Japanese assaults on Chinese sovereignty. White went on to note that, while a formal yuan-dollar tie-up did have certain inherent risks, such a move "would indicate to Japan that the United States is not wholly unconcerned in her expansion program in Asia" and "would encourage China and possibly cause Japan to proceed more warily in her attempt to swallow China." He argued that the United States should purchase Chinese silver "at as favorable a rate as possible" and predicted that such a move would afford the Nationalists "enhanced prestige at home" and give China "somewhat increased political strength in her relations with Japan and England."[45]

As alarming reports continued to arrive on Morgenthau's desk, the Treasury Department extended further aid to China. The secretary's personal representative in China, Professor J. Lossing Buck, whom Morgenthau dispatched with Roosevelt's approval in early 1935, quickly concluded that "the Japanese are slowly but surely gaining control of Hopei and Chahar," provinces in north China. In September, he ventured a guess that whether Japan and China go to war "depends entirely on aggressiveness of Japanese" and that "China's increased strength is having its effect on Japanese policy in China." In what can be interpreted only as a bid for stronger American support, Buck argued that "a stiff attitude on part of other nations . . . should help curtail Japan." Over the next year, Morgenthau and the president took Buck's words to heart.[46]

Tokyo's attempt to drive the Kuomintang from north China and create a buffer for its Manchurian prodigy marked the continuation of the basic policy first approved in autumn 1933. At the close of the Far Eastern crisis, Japan found itself trapped in a reverse domino theory, driven inexorably to topple more dominoes in order to ensure the security of those that had already fallen. Progress in north China remained slow, but by the spring of 1935 Japanese military commanders had all but eliminated the Kuomintang from the region. In the aftermath of this victory, Tokyo tried to induce Nanking to join Japan in an anti-Soviet alliance, recognize Manchukuo, and end anti-Japanese movements throughout China. It also directed its troops in north China to avoid the overt use of force and follow a gradual, peaceful approach in order to lessen the likelihood of conflict with Nanking, the West, and the Soviet Union. This cautious strategy survived even after many of its architects fell in February 1936, when the worst internecine bloodletting since the Restoration rocked Japan.[47]

On the morning of February 26, 1936, Ambassador Grew cabled ominous news to Washington. "The military took partial possession of the government and city early this morning," he informed Hull, "and it is reported have assassinated several prominent men." The previous evening, as a light snow fell on the capital, some fourteen hundred soldiers and several flying assassination squads belonging to the army's imperial way faction fanned out over the city and took up positions. Hoping to bring about a new imperial restoration and a complete restructuring of the nation's political and economic system, the mutineers murdered key officials, including former prime minister Saito, Finance Minister Korekiyo Takahashi, and General Kazan Watanabe, the inspector general of military education. Rebel units, which by dawn occupied central Tokyo, issued a call for a domestic revolution or "Showa Restoration," which like the earlier Meiji model would save the nation from internal breakdown and foreign conquest. There would be no second restoration in 1936, however, for the government, military, and court soon rallied. Emperor Hirohito moved with speed and assurance and pressed the military to end the rebellion, and loyal units from the combined services quickly surrounded the rebels. The mutiny collapsed, and, after a series of quick, secret military trials, the army executed nineteen of its own as well as the fervent nationalist intellectual Kita Ikki.[48]

Postwar historiography, taking its cue from the Tokyo war crimes trials, contends that the February 26 Incident marked a turning point in interwar Japanese history, one at which the proponents of domestic fascism and military adventurism in China gained the upper hand. True, the imperial way faction collapsed, and its rival, the control faction, which stressed national mobilization under the guidance of supportive bureaucrats and zaibatsu, gained undisputed power within the army, but the failure of the February 26 Incident did not signal the beginning of a radical shift in either Japanese foreign policy in general or China policy specifically. The veteran diplomat Koki Hirota, who returned as prime minister, continued to stress a cautious policy in China, as did the War, Navy, and Foreign Ministries. Following the collapse of the Hirota cabinet in February 1937, Prime Minister Senjuro

Hayashi and Foreign Minister Naotoke Sato further moderated China policy and all but abandoned long-range plans for detaching north China from Nanking.[49]

Increased Chinese resistance and internal political developments in China pushed moderates to continue their velvet-gloved approach. In November 1936, Mongolian separatist forces backed by Japanese airpower were all but annihilated by Nationalist troops, and, in an even more ominous development the following month, Chang Hsueh-liang kidnapped Chiang Kai-shek and held him until the generalissimo agreed to end his war against the Communists and concentrate his, and the nation's, resources on the far more serious Japanese menace. After Sian, the Hayashi cabinet knew that it had to tread carefully or risk a military conflict with Nanking, and both the prime minister and control faction leaders sought to avoid war on the continent. Hayashi recognized that war with China, and further estrangement from the West, would doom planned military and economic reform, leaving Japan vulnerable to the Soviet Union.[50]

By any measure, American containment succeeded beyond all expectations during the first Roosevelt administration as Japanese expansion in north China slowly ground to a halt. Despite a rising tide of isolationism and the Depression's continued hold on the country, by the summer of 1937 the rise of Soviet and Nationalist power had forced Japanese civilian leaders and cautious control faction military officers to abandon adventurism in China and accept, at least for the time being, the central tenets of the Open Door.

The Marco Polo Bridge and Brussels

While Tokyo sought to avoid an armed conflict on the continent, Nanking did not share the same goal. For nearly two generations an often helpless and divided China fell prey to Japanese depredations, and in the aftermath of the Far Eastern Crisis Chinese leaders resolved to strengthen the nation, confident that the future would afford a rubber match with the Japanese Empire. While China did not seek war with Japan in 1937, Nanking believed that at long last it had, quite literally, a fighting chance. Chinese nationalism stood near flood tide, and Nationalist finances stood on solid ground owing in large part to extensive American support for currency reorganization. Acting on the beliefs first enunciated by Soong and Kung in the dark days of 1933, Nanking believed that by resisting Japan it would secure Western and Soviet support. Perhaps most important of all, of course, Chiang had to resist Japan. After Sian he had no choice.[51]

Japanese officers stationed in China, who were notoriously second-rate and had a penchant for seeing anti-Japanese plots where none existed, suspected that Chiang was planning a campaign to retake Manchuria, but no such plans existed. Just a month before the outbreak of fighting in north China, Kanji Ishiwara sent a trusted aide to Peking to ascertain whether the Nationalists were massing forces to retake Manchuria, and, while he discovered unusually high Sino-Japanese tension, the aide saw no signs of an imminent Chinese offensive.[52]

Tension and miscalculation, however, soon produced tragedy, and on July 7 a skirmish—a rather common occurrence—erupted around midnight between Japanese Boxer Protocol forces and local Chinese troops on the outskirts of Peking. The following day Japanese troops twice attacked the nearby Chinese garrison. Japanese officials, acting on orders from both the government and the general staff, rushed to settle the incident and on July 11 concluded an agreement with local Chinese officials. The incident, such as it was, appeared over.[53]

Nanking, however, balked at a local settlement that increased Japanese influence in north China, and, fearing that Japan sought to detach north China, Chiang took the unfortunate step of violating the Ho-Umezu agreement by dispatching four divisions to Hopei Province. Tokyo responded by mobilizing three divisions in Japan and warning Nanking not to interfere with the Peking settlement. Control faction officers worked to avoid a clash with Chinese forces, and Ishiwara Kanji, the architect of the Mukden Incident, canceled the mobilization order once he learned that local commanders had settled the episode. From the mainland, however, Japanese military attachés reported that Chiang had augmented his limited mobilization with a general mobilization of all troops north of the Yangtze.[54]

While Chiang was committed to resistance, he remained willing to use Western diplomatic pressure to contain Japanese expansion. On July 13, he requested British and American mediation, and, two weeks later, Chinese diplomats asked Western governments to inform Japan that, while Nanking no longer opposed a local settlement of the Marco Polo Bridge Incident, it would not agree to Tokyo's expected terms, which included recognition of Manchukuo and joint defense against communism. Unfortunately, these were the Konoe cabinet's exact terms. Not surprisingly, when the British forwarded them to Chiang in September, he rejected them. Hull, meanwhile, refused to join in with the British when London proposed joint mediation to end the fighting.[55]

The growing crisis in China, meanwhile, could not have come at a worse time for the Roosevelt administration, beset as it was by the sudden onset of the so-called Roosevelt Recession. Vice President John Nance Garner took the extreme position of calling for the abandonment of American interests in north China, while Hull's approach to the crisis, according to Interior Secretary Harold Ickes, appeared clouded by his enmity for Japan. Ickes was struck by how Hull "said a great deal about 'insults'": "As I listened to him, it occurred to me that on other occasions he has seemed to be obsessed with the idea that if we did or refrained from doing certain things in the Far East, the Japanese would 'insult' us." To Ickes, Hull's "attitude with respect to Japan seems to be entirely different from that with respect to other countries with which we have diplomatic relations." Obsessed as he apparently was, Hull still understood that any move to confront Japan with crippling sanctions would likely fail or, if it was successful, would invite a war that the United States could not possibly win. Morgenthau, on the other hand, contended that Japan would never militarily challenge the United States and maintained that a firm display of American power would force Tokyo to back down.[56]

In the face of a divided cabinet, the President chose the wise course, which in the summer of 1937 meant splitting the difference between competing ideas. Much to the relief of the Nationalists, Roosevelt refused to invoke the Neutrality Acts, thus allowing China to purchase critical war matériel from the United States. In a major blow to the Chinese, however, he subsequently forbade government-owned vessels from transporting war matériel to either belligerent. In October, at Hull's urging the president traveled to Chicago to explain to the public, and to the world at large, the vast problems that international lawlessness presented to peace-minded people everywhere. Written largely by Hull and Norman Davis, Roosevelt's speech was no statement of policy, for he had none to make. Instead, it was part of the ongoing effort to build a procontainment consensus in the United States and abroad. Coincident with the League of Nations decision to convene a conference of the Nine Power Treaty members in Brussels, the president's speech, and the rationale behind it, took on added significance.[57]

The Australian and British governments successfully pushed for a meeting of the Nine Power Treaty signatories, and, in hurried meetings in advance of the talks, the president, Hull, and Norman Davis, the chief American delegate, agreed that, while the United States should attempt to bring about an end to the fighting, neither the public nor the Western democracies would support sanctions. The president and his senior advisers were indeed correct about public and Western reluctance. At preconference meetings, the Soviets alone called for giving "China substantial assistance," while the British government reluctantly agreed that it would pursue sanctions only if Washington committed the United States to defend British interests in Asia. Prime

Minister Neville Chamberlin, meanwhile, clung to the hope "that Japan, if treated diplomatically might consent to some possible terms."[58]

The Brussels Conference adjourned in just three weeks and accomplished little. The Soviets continued to insist that "no steps short of adoption of pressure methods would be of any value," while the Italians supported Japan with what Davis called a "defeatist and obstructive" policy. Britain and France hinted that they might pursue sanctions, while "the smaller powers were apprehensive lest the larger powers decide upon measures of pressure" and wished "that the Conference do little and be brought to an end quickly." Before leaving, the delegates agreed to two resolutions; one outlined the deliberations, and the other, as the historian James Crowley notes, meekly "offered a vacuous profession of sympathy" to China.[59]

For well over a decade, Anglo-American cooperation in Asia suffered, and Brussels succeeded in pushing Washington and London further apart. After the meeting adjourned, Chamberlin reckoned that the "main lesson to be drawn [from the conference] was the difficulty of securing effective cooperation from the United States of America." Davis and Hornbeck made cooperation difficult by ignoring Washington's clear instructions, especially on the sanctions question. Both men wanted to go further than Roosevelt and Hull and, thus, disregarded their instructions and spent endless time lobbying for action that neither the president nor the secretary of state had any intention of pursuing.[60]

The gulf separating Washington and London widened further shortly after Brussels when, on December 12, Japanese artillery struck the HMS *Ladybird* and warplanes, perhaps mistakenly, sank the USS *Panay*. Morgenthau immediately called for a freeze of Japanese assets, but the president preferred to use the crisis to rebuild an Anglo-American common front. In pursuit of that end, the navy soon dispatched a mission to London, and, while it quickly produced plans for a joint Anglo-American blockade of Japan, none materialized. The British, initially heartened by the president's firm stand, grew increasingly disillusioned by what senior officials saw as Washington's naïveté and lack of consistency.[61]

While neither the Nine Power Treaty signatories nor Washington and London could end the fighting in China, Japan enlisted Germany, an ally of both Nanking and Tokyo, in an effort to end hostilities. On November 2, Tokyo asked Berlin to relay Japanese peace terms to China, but, as the Brussels Conference was just under way, Chiang refused to bargain. In early December, with nothing to show from Brussels, Chiang informed the German ambassador in China, Oscar Trautmann, that he was willing to begin negotiations, but by then it was too late. With the fall of Nanking, during which Japanese troops went on a weeks-long rampage murdering from 200,000 to 300,000 civilians, Tokyo hardened its peace terms and in doing so helped sentence its people, and those of China, to seven more years of war.[62]

While the Army General Staff remained committed to an early end to hostilities and hoped that through generous terms Nanking could be induced to make peace, the Konoe cabinet approved uncompromising terms and then demanded that Chiang immediately accept them. By early January, with the war still raging, Konoe appeared before the press to announce that Japan no longer recognized Chiang and the Nationalists as the legal government of China. The Army General Staff, which remained anxious to end the war, warned Konoe that, rather than weakening Chiang, nonrecognition would increase his international support and lead to a longer and more costly war for Japan.[63]

In an effort to contain Japan in the aftermath of the Far Eastern crisis, the Roosevelt administration steadfastly refused repeated Japanese attempts to improve bilateral relations and build a new foundation on the shattered ruins of the Washington Conference system. Instead, convinced of Japanese duplicity and Tokyo's unquenchable appetite for aggressive foreign expansion, the administration opposed both a Sino-Japanese and an American-Japanese rapprochement, which it saw as chimerical, if not downright dangerous. Rather than repeat the mistakes of Taft, Root, and Lansing, the administration embarked on a vast naval replenishment program designed to deter Japan. Simultaneously, it moved closer to Moscow in an effort to rebuild the balance of power in Asia. Finally, and to that end, Washington strengthened Nanking, confident that Chinese nationalism would one day triumph over Japanese militarism. After January 1938, Japanese armies put this new containment strategy to the ultimate test.

Secretary of State John Hay, ca. 1902. For forty years, successive administrations would defend his Open Door policy, first from Russian advances and then, after 1905, from Japanese expansion. (Library of Congress LC-USZ62-63963)

As this 1898 *Puck* cartoon illustrates, Japan was widely seen as standing shoulder to shoulder with the United States and Great Britain in upholding the Open Door policy. Here, the Emperor Meiji joins Uncle Sam and John Bull in protecting the Open Door from France, Germany, and Russia. (Library of Congress LC-DIG-ppmsca-28630)

In Portsmouth, New Hampshire, in the summer of 1905, President Theodore Roosevelt defended the Open Door when he brought the warring parties together and mediated an end to the Russo-Japanese War. Roosevelt's action won him the Nobel Peace Prize and brought an uneasy calm to Northeast Asia, where the two war-weary combatants faced each other in Manchuria. (Library of Congress LC-DIG-ppmsca-08199)

President Roosevelt's decision to dispatch the "Great White Fleet" on an around-the-world cruise from 1907–1908 appeared to deter Japan. Rather than fight, the Japanese prepared to welcome the fleet on its arrival in 1908. (U.S. Naval Historical Center Photograph, Collection of Chief Quartermaster John Harold)

In 1917 the Viscount Kikujiro Ishii (*center, left*) arrived in the United States on a mission to improve Japanese-American relations. Along with Secretary of State Robert Lansing (*center, right*), the two diplomats crafted a compromise agreement in which the United States recognized Japan's special relationship to China in return for Tokyo's pledge to respect the Open Door. (Library of Congress LC-DIG-hec-09434)

At the 1921–1922 Washington Conference, America once again used diplomatic engagement to contain Japan and bind Tokyo to the Open Door. President Warren G. Harding (*center, standing*) is seen addressing the conference. (Library of Congress LC-USZ62-48849)

Among Roosevelt's longest-serving cabinet officers and a Nobel Peace Prize Laureate, Cordell Hull felt that he could not risk concluding a last-minute compromise with either the Konoe or the Tojo governments. (Library of Congress LC-USZ62-94179)

A career State Department official and expert on East Asia, Stanley Hornbeck served two secretaries of state, Henry Stimson and Cordell Hull, and urged both men not to compromise with Japan. (Library of Congress LC-USW3-053766-C)

Another career official, and a former minister to China, John Van Antwerp MacMurray did what neither Hull nor Hornbeck could. The one-time implacable opponent of Tokyo urged the Roosevelt administration to heal the widening breach with Japan. (1924, Library of Congress LC-DIG-npcc-12628)

The Tojo cabinet, pictured just after its first meeting. American containment was so successful that it forced these leaders to fundamentally readjust Japanese foreign policy. (*Asahi Shimbun,* courtesy Wikimedia Commons)

Although smiling in this picture, Admiral Kichisaburo Nomura (*left*) and Saburo Kurusu (*right*) understood that time was running out to reach an agreement in Washington. (*Mainichi Shimbun,* courtesy Wikimedia Commons)

Chapter 4

Containment at High Tide

> Deterrence is the art of producing, in the mind of the enemy, the fear to attack.
>
> —*Dr. Strangelove* (1964)

> Conversation will not convince the Japanese militarists that we mean business. But the presence in Asiatic waters of a fleet more powerful than their own, would be most eloquent.
>
> —Frank Knox (1938)

From the conclusion of the Brussels Conference in the autumn of 1937 to the German invasion of the Soviet Union in June 1941, Japan challenged American containment as never before. Fighting in China and the spread of war to Europe, however, also provided the architects of American containment with the necessary tools to halt Japanese expansion. Continued Chinese resistance permitted that country's many champions in the administration, foremost among them Morgenthau and White, to successfully push for increased aid, while the joining of the Pacific and European Wars helped clear the way for the massive American rearmament that the president, Bullitt, Grew, and others believed would deter Japan. The growing global conflict also made possible economic sanctions that senior officials, including Hornbeck and Stimson, had long maintained would weaken Japan and compel it to abandon the war on the mainland. With the collapse of France in June 1940 and Tokyo's decision to join the Axis the following September, containment assumed an expanded mandate. In addition to the long-term interests of protecting the Open Door and halting Japanese expansion in China, Washington now also sought to secure immediate imperatives, namely, the protection of the West's valuable and vulnerable colonies and a weakening of the Axis Alliance.

Given Hull and Hornbeck's conviction that Japan could not be trusted, Japanese-American diplomatic engagement continued to languish. As had their counterparts at the Treasury and War Departments, these senior diplomats long ago concluded that only American power—military and economic—would contain Japan and that only by exploiting Japanese weakness—both military and economic—could America keep peace in the Pacific.

This faith in American power proved their undoing, for it was based on a fundamental misunderstanding of past policy. Prior to the outbreak of the war in China, the United States employed its military and economic power against Japan on several occasions, and, in each instance, the policy appeared successful. Theodore Roosevelt believed that the Great White Fleet's visit in 1908 deterred Japan from war, and, a decade later, the mere hint of sanctions seemed to bend Japanese policy in Siberia, in Shantung, and at the Washington Conference into less threatening shapes. In reality, these examples of American deterrence had little effect on Japanese foreign policy, yet decades later they had a most unfortunate effect on American diplomacy. By all accounts deterrence had succeeded in the past, and this unfounded belief gave policymakers a wholly unfounded and terribly unfortunate confidence. Deterrence comforted policymakers and allowed them to believe that they could achieve American ends without war. The belief that Japan both feared and needed America confirmed what so many already thought, both about American greatness and about Japanese weakness. Deterrence reinforced this illusion of strength, of the ability to achieve national policy without compromising principles, and, in a world gone mad, people needed comfort no matter how illusory.[1]

If past policy provided comfort, Japanese history did not. For those who looked at—not examined or analyzed but merely looked at—its broad outlines, Japanese history told the story of a half-century effort to expand on the Asian continent. In the wake of the 1894–1895 Sino-Japanese War, the annexation of Korea, the seizure of Shantung, the Twenty-one Demands, the Siberian intervention, Manchuria, and now the China Incident, Americans saw strewn about bits and pieces of understandings, agreements, and, finally, the wreckage of the entire postwar peace structure. Japan, they concluded, was a dangerous nation and could not be trusted.

Given the supposed success of military and economic deterrence and Japan's commitment to foreign expansion, a renewed commitment to containment, without diplomatic engagement, seemed the only rational response. The Roosevelt administration's understanding of both deterrence and the Japanese Empire, however, made American containment fundamentally unsound. If Japanese expansion and disregard for treaties demanded resolute American action, what would happen once the United States achieved its objectives? Hornbeck maintained that, when the Japanese military became discredited, moderate Japanese civilian statesmen would return to power.

Moderates had engineered Japanese expansion for decades, however, and had approved going to war in 1894, 1904, and 1914. They extinguished Korean independence in 1910 and issued the Twenty-one Demands in 1915. True, moderate statesmen guided Japan during its experiment with internationalism, but, given the American reading of Japanese history, the 1920s must have been an aberration rather than the norm. If successive Japanese governments, whether fire-eating militarists or moderate civilians, demonstrated so little regard for treaties, what value would Washington attribute to a Sino-Japanese peace agreement or a solemn pledge to abrogate the Tripartite Pact? If the militarists fell from power, would it make any difference in Washington? If Japan wanted to negotiate an end to the China Incident, would Washington prove receptive?

A particular interpretation of history, both Japanese and American, determined policymakers' answers to these questions. This is not to say that race did not play a part, for it surely did, and Americans who concerned themselves with Far Eastern affairs were constantly aware of race. Race, however, explains neither the evolution of American strategy nor the objectives of American policy nor even the dogged way in which Washington stayed the course until December 1941. A preoccupation with race may in fact obscure far more than it highlights. If race, identity, or national consciousness played a role in American calculations, then it explains far more about how Americans understood themselves and how they in turn selectively superimposed American concepts on others. Policymakers, the press, and the public predicted that in the end, and at the bitter end in the autumn of 1941, Japan would fold, not because the Japanese were Asian and therefore different, but because, like Americans, they would never start a war that could end only in their utter ruin. This conviction reassured those who consistently argued that Japan would never fight the United States and that continued American pressure would drive Japan from China and break the Axis Alliance.

Yet, if universalism—the concept that certain values and beliefs are shared by all—helped make containment appear a safer, sounder policy, so too did a belief in exceptionalism—the idea that certain values, beliefs, and institutions were, in this case, uniquely American. Repeatedly during the 1930s, Washington refused to compromise the tenets of its Far Eastern policy—the Open Door and the Nine Power Treaty. Hull, especially, saw these ideas as distinct from and distinctly superior to either the Japanese Monroe Doctrine for Asia or the Co-Prosperity Sphere, and this no doubt helps explain why the administration expected Japan to abandon its bedrock foreign policy principles for Asia.

Aid to China

If Chiang entered the war against Japan confident of Western aid, then his disappointment must have been overwhelming, for, if Brussels proved nothing else, it demonstrated in the strongest possible way that neither Paris, London, Moscow, nor Washington would give the Nationalists the tools to drive Japan from China. The West, and especially the United States, was not indifferent to Chiang's fate, for his ability to tie Japan down in the limitless Chinese interior was important in both preserving the Open Door and protecting other Western interests in Asia. For this reason, American support began to flow in late 1937 on an unprecedented scale. Rather than any fundamental policy shift, American aid marked the continuation, in vastly increased scope, of traditional American initiatives designed to contain Japanese expansion in China.[2]

Early American aid for Chiang resulted largely from Treasury rather than State Department initiatives. Given Secretary Morgenthau's interest in preventing Japan from achieving hegemony in China and his experience during the earlier currency crisis, his efforts should come as no surprise. Hull, Hornbeck, and the Far Eastern Division (FE) also hoped to keep Chinese armies in the field, and, while they recognized the importance of extending assistance to Chiang, their concern over isolationist sentiment, both in the halls of Congress and on Main Street, precluded them from taking vigorous action.

On July 8, 1937, soon after he agreed to buy sixty-two million ounces of Chinese silver, Morgenthau confided to an aide: "I honestly believe that when all this thing blows over—that ten years from now, maybe the most important thing that I did when I was here was to save China." On that warm July day, he genuinely believed "that fifty years from now the fact that China was not gobbled up by Japan and again becomes a strong nation may be the most important thing we did here." Unknown to the secretary, however, China's darkest days were just beginning, and Henry Morgenthau was just starting his tenure as China's greatest American fund-raiser.[3]

Given Morgenthau's experience in dealing with the Chinese and the prominent place that China occupied in his conception of his own worth and importance, it is no wonder that the Treasury Department took the lead, as it had done in 1935, in extending American assistance. Although Morgenthau shared with his more cautious State Department colleagues the conviction that American security was inexorably tied to an independent, pro-Western China, he never measured that country's value solely in terms of security or trade. The secretary's strong social conscience, his empathy for the underdog, perhaps nurtured by his early days at the Henry Street Settlement House or the Department of Agriculture, informed his China policy. China also remained something of a legacy, a monument to his efforts, and, from where Morgenthau sat, the Japanese were busy defacing his monument, threatening American trade and security, and trampling the spirited underdog.

In November 1937, even before the Brussels Conference ground to a halt, the Treasury Department agreed to an immediate purchase of an additional twenty million ounces of Chinese silver, and, in December, with Roosevelt and Hull's consent, Morgenthau purchased another fifty million ounces. Massive American purchases of Chinese silver continued in 1938 with the added stipulation that Chiang could now spend the considerable proceeds from Washington's thinly disguised aid program for military hardware. And the proceeds were indeed considerable. In March, May, and again in June, Treasury made additional fifty-million-ounce purchases. During 1937 and 1938 alone, American purchases of Chinese silver boosted the Nationalist war chest by nearly $175 million.[4]

All good things must come to an end, and, by the autumn of 1938, China's silver reserves were exhausted. On September 25, Morgenthau informed the president that China had no more silver to sell and that consequently the time had come to decide whether to make available to the Nationalists a $100 million credit "knowing the minute you give it to them it's gone." $100 million is a great deal of money, and the president surely knew that his own State Department, as well as Congress, would prove very reluctant to write a check with so many zeros. Before committing himself, he told Morgenthau that he first wanted to "see what happens in Europe." If war broke out, he would "definitely give them [the Chinese] credit." What if the Europeans managed to avert a crisis? "Maybe I will do it anyway," he added. Three days later, with Europe's fragile peace hanging in the balance, Morgenthau pressed the cabinet to support the Chinese loan. He told Roosevelt's inner circle that "the Chinese were busted" and that he had purchased "the last silver they had which was free." The administration, he continued, had a clear choice, and, if "they want to have peace in the Pacific," then "they ought to just come right out and lend them [China] a hundred million dollars and let them decide where they want to spend the money." After some debate, and, one suspects, on cue, the president suggested an American credit that allowed China to buy American wheat, sell it on the world market, and use the profits however it wished.[5]

Morgenthau won round one, but his victory in the cabinet lasted all of two days. The State Department's international economic adviser, Herbert Feis, broke the bad news and explained that, because of opposition from other wheat exporters, who were bound to blame the United States when the cash-starved Nationalists dumped their American wheat on the world market and prices tumbled, the deal was off. The best that he could suggest was a strict barter arrangement in which "a country, for example, Great Britain, . . . would take the wheat in exchange for munitions or something that China wished to purchase."[6]

Faced with stiff opposition from both the State Department and the Agriculture Department, Morgenthau had no choice but to consider a barter deal or find a more suitable commodity for which Washington could extend a loan. Although Chinese officials had already told him that they had no available tin or tungsten, he told his lieutenants that tung oil, a wood extract used extensively in the paint and varnish industry, might be the perfect choice for a commodity loan. While "none of the thing has jelled yet," Morgenthau explained, representatives of the paint and varnish industry were "all very much interested in a stable market for tung oil." The secretary also proposed helping Nanking establish a corporation in the United States that would function along the same lines as the Soviet's Amtorg, coordinating China's purchases in America.[7]

While the State Department predictably raised objections to Morgenthau's plan, this must not be interpreted as any great sign of moderation. Hornbeck's successor, Maxwell Hamilton, argued that the loan would only worsen American-Japanese relations and not materially affect the war's outcome. He also feared that Congress would object to the loan and vent its wrath on the Export-Import Bank, which was to oversee the project. While Hamilton opposed limited aid to China, he left no doubt that the administration must follow a long-term strategy of economic and military deterrence. In the same memo in which he spelled out the reasons for rejecting the tung oil project, he argued that the United States must bring "pressure to bear on Japan" through "retaliatory measures . . . applied patiently and judiciously over a considerable period of time." Economic sanctions alone, he noted, would prove insufficient, unless "the United States . . . keep[s] itself amply strong in arms to ensure that Japan realize[s] our strength."[8]

Hornbeck, now the State Department's Far East adviser on political relations, also preferred a "program of action" that combined "diplomatic, economic and potential military pressures" over what he termed "haphazard and unrelated steps." Specifically, he called for abrogating the 1911 Commercial Treaty and the Neutrality Acts, followed by trade embargoes and a forward deployment of the fleet, all of which, he noted, would "indicate to the Japanese Government and nation that we 'mean business.'" Even Hull, in his final plea to the president to reject the tung oil project, focused on the possible outbreak of war in Europe and isolationist sentiment at home rather than any opposition to aiding the Chinese. He maintained that, in order to temper Japan's response to an extension of credit to China, the president must first deploy the fleet beyond Hawaii. The secretary doubted, however, whether the public or Congress would approve such a move. Had China desperately needed American funds to continue the war, he would have approved Morgenthau's plan, but, as he informed the president, "China is understood to have adequate military supplies for the next six to ten or twelve months."[9]

In addition to its being premature, both Hull and Hamilton saw the loan as at best of limited value and at worst terribly counterproductive. Hornbeck, Hamilton, and Hull also resisted what they saw as Morgenthau's meddling because it jeopardized the success of their preferred policy. These men were not any more moderate than Morgenthau; they simply thought they had a better plan.

Morgenthau soon recognized that Japan's uninterrupted victories would not move Hull or the president to support the tung oil loan. Yet, if the specter of a Japanese-dominated China would not force the administration to act, what could? What could possibly frighten Hull and his colleagues more than the spread of Japanese imperialism? Perhaps only one thing. The time had come to play the Russian card.

The origins of Morgenthau's decision to use the threat of Soviet influence in China is not clear, though he certainly knew that Hull had so opposed recognition of the Soviets in 1933 that the president turned over the early courting of the Russians to him and Bullitt. It is also quite likely that Chinese officials hinted to the secretary that Chiang was getting a bit too chummy with Moscow. Wellington Koo, for example, suggested to Quo Tai-chi, the Chinese ambassador in London, that the United States "might even feel that the time is coming near . . . to pursue a more active policy now that Soviet Russia is manifesting a great deal of activity." By *activity,* Koo no doubt meant the August 1937 Sino-Soviet Nonaggression Treaty, which, John W. Garver noted, provided for "large-scale Soviet military sales and assistance" and "ensured that neither side would strike a deal with Japan."[10]

Whatever the inspiration, Morgenthau readily played his trump card in the final weeks before winning approval for the tung oil deal. On November 28, in an attempt to overcome Undersecretary of State Sumner Welles's objections, he pleaded: "No country in the world is giving them any help except Russia, and in return for that, Russia is just sending their people in and taking control of everything." The next day, he informed his top lieutenants, some of whom opposed credits for China: "There is no country in the world today, with the exception of Russia, that is doing anything, and we all sit here, and we are just driving them in the hands of Russia." Once again, the following day in a meeting with Welles, Hamilton, and Hornbeck, he stressed: "We are driving China right into the arms of Russia because they are the only people who are helping China." That Morgenthau was deliberately inflating Soviet influence is quite clear. J. Lossing Buck had only recently reported that Russian influence remained insignificant, and Buck's source, the commissioner of foreign affairs, assured him that "Russian help has not been very much."[11]

The commissioner was right. Recent Sino-Soviet aid discussions had grown so heated that Moscow demanded Chiang pay for Soviet military assistance with hard currency and the generalissimo responded with veiled threats of a separate Sino-Japanese peace. To be sure, while Morgenthau may not have known all the details, he knew a disingenuous statement when he made one. On the whole, while Buck showed little concern regarding Soviet influence in China, Morgenthau subsequently went out of his way to impress on both Treasury and State Department officials that the United States was virtually handing China over to the Soviets. Morgenthau knew better than anyone the extent of American support, yet in order to aid Chiang he gladly preyed on his colleagues' fears of Soviet influence.[12]

At the end of November, and with the president's approval for the tung oil credit in hand, Morgenthau convened a State-Treasury Department conference. Welles explained that the State Department still opposed the credit because it lacked public support and could invite a severe clash with Tokyo. He also maintained that, with the Japanese government about to make a major statement regarding the future of the Open Door in China, Morgenthau should wait before consummating his deal with the Nationalists. The secretary agreed, and two weeks later, after Tokyo moved forward with plans to create its New Order in East Asia and with Hull out of the country, the president announced the tung oil credit. The agreement, Henry Stimson wrote Morgenthau, deserved "the strong support of those citizens who believe that the action was wise and necessary." Stimson saw the "loan coming at a most critical and opportune time" and predicted that it would bolster Chinese morale and serve as "a discouragement to the military faction which now controls Japan."[13]

Success with tung oil and China's continued need for foreign assistance soon led Morgenthau to work out a second commodity loan, this time for Chinese tin. As he told Arthur Purvis, the head of the British purchasing mission in Washington, the Chinese had all but expended their $25 million tung oil credit and were hoping for more aid. He explained that they hoped to sell up to ten tons of tin through the Universal Trading Corporation, the company that Treasury helped the Nationalist government establish in the United States. While Chiang wanted a $75 million tin credit, the funds were unavailable. In the end, with Morgenthau's help, Chungking secured a far more modest $20 million.[14]

In his determination to ensure that nothing hinder China's war effort, Morgenthau quickly became not only the country's main American fundraiser but its transportation manager as well. By 1938, the Japanese navy had all but bottled up the Chinese coast, leaving only overland routes along the border with Hong Kong, French Indochina, Burma, and portions of the Soviet Union open to imports. Anxious to maximize these openings, Morgenthau arranged during the October 1938 tung oil debates for the California-Texas Oil Company, among others, to help China purchase tanker trucks "as near cost as possible" in order to facilitate transit of imported oil from Rangoon. But trucks were not enough. China also needed a dependable road network, and, in July 1939, the secretary happily informed Chiang that, "after a very thorough search throughout the United States," he had selected three transportation experts to help the Nationalists finish the 681-mile-long Burma Road, which connected Kunming, in southern China, to Lashio, Burma, and served as a key supply route for Chiang Kai-shek. Along with the transportation experts, Morgenthau also arranged, through the Surgeon General's Office, to dispatch an antimalarial team to the construction zone in order to combat a deadly epidemic.[15]

Morgenthau's substantial efforts on behalf of China must not obscure the State Department's extensive, if belated, efforts to prop up Chiang's battered regime. At the end of 1939, FE notified Hull that the time had arrived to consider new aid programs for China. The following spring, as the State Department was gripped with fear over the possible financial collapse of Chungking—Chiang had relocated his capital to this southern city after Nanking's fall—Hornbeck worked behind the scenes to secure relief for the Nationalists. On March 6, and again on April 11, he pressed Morgenthau to use money from the Chinese currency stabilization fund to prop up the yuan. Hornbeck insisted that a sound Chinese currency would prove "a decisive factor in the outcome of the conflict," especially "when increasing difficulties are causing the Japanese program to fail." Morgenthau, however, fired back that he would not consider using existing currency stabilization funds without congressional approval.[16]

Despite Morgenthau's lack of support, the war in Europe and Japan's decision to join the Axis, as well as alarming reports from both Chiang and Ambassador Nelson Johnson, finally prompted Hull to act. Hamilton informed the secretary on June 3 that any number of possible options, including increased purchases of Chinese strategic raw materials, increased credits from the Export-Import Bank, and even an outright humanitarian loan, existed. In particular, Hamilton's mention of a direct loan seems critical. For many years, State Department officials reasoned that without strong public support they could not pursue vigorous steps to aid China and contain Japan. But, by June 1940, Hamilton believed that public opinion, at last, had changed. "As the American people have during recent months and especially during recent weeks become increasingly aware of the potentialities of the international situation," he told Hull, "it might be possible now, with vigorous administration support, to have legislation passed authorizing the extension of a rehabilitation and reconstruction loan to China." By mid-September, with Japan taking full advantage of German victories in Europe to bring pressure on France and England to close their overland links to southern China, the administration acted. With Hull's full concurrence, the Export-Import Bank agreed to a $20 million loan for Chungking, and the Metals Reserve Company agreed to purchase $30 million worth of Chinese tungsten. Just over two months later, with Japan a full-fledged member of the Axis, aid to China rode the coattails of other interventionist successes, most notably selective service, and Washington granted Chiang a mammoth $100 million loan.[17]

Continuing American aid clearly helped prevent the Chinese war effort from collapsing. By 1940, Washington thought a collapse of Nationalist morale or Chiang's ouster by the Kuomintang's peace faction far more likely than a cataclysmic defeat on the battlefield, and, judging from the utterances of Nationalist officials, American aid prevented both. Chiang's minister to the United States, Dr. Hu Shi, claimed that the tung oil credit helped Chiang weather the storm following both Wang Ching-wei's 1939 defection to the Japanese and Tokyo's decision to recognize his renegade regime in March 1940.[18]

While American aid to China successfully limited Japanese expansion in that country, it inadvertently fueled it elsewhere and led Japan closer to the totalitarian states. Shortly after the start of the war in China, Japan had pressured France to close its overland link between Yunan and French Indochina, and for two years the French refused. Immediately after the fall of France, however, Vichy authorities complied with Japanese demands to close the supply route to China and allowed Tokyo to dispatch monitors to ensure compliance. Two months later, Tokyo followed up its triumph by obtaining French consent to station troops and establish air bases in northern Indochina.[19]

Expansion into Indochina clearly shows Tokyo at its most opportunistic. The Konoe cabinet had no compunction about using the German victory in Europe to further the establishment of the Co-Prosperity Sphere, yet the government limited its demands in terms of both the absolute number of troops it dispatched and the area where it based its forces. The scope of the Japanese occupation was on the whole far more consistent with an effort to end the war in China than with an effort to absorb northern French Indochina. Tokyo deployed its air force to strike supplies flowing over the Burma Road, while Japanese troops in the north would, if necessary, form the vanguard of an overland attack against Kunming.[20]

The same drive to end the war in China that contributed to the occupation of northern Indochina also influenced Japan to join the Axis Alliance. To be sure, as with northern Indochina, a good deal of opportunism as well as basic insecurity motivated the Konoe government both to join the Axis in September 1940 and to negotiate the Soviet-Japanese Neutrality Pact in April 1941. However, the specter of an endless war in China loomed large over the deliberations surrounding both agreements. During a critical cabinet debate held on September 16, 1940, Finance Minister Isao Kawada and Chief of the Cabinet Planning Board Naokoi Hoshino supported joining the Axis because, as they told their fellow ministers, "[with] this pact, we may be able to settle the China Incident." Three days later, at the September 19 imperial conference, Foreign Minister Yosuke Matsuoka assured Army Chief of Staff Prince Kan'in that an alliance with Germany would help end the war in China. Matsuoka explained that, if, as he hoped, Germany cooperated in the current peace negotiations, the government could "anticipate considerable results." No less an influential conservative than Privy Council President Yoshimichi Hara, a senior adviser to Hirohito, backed the pact owing to his conviction that the alliance with Germany was "essential to carry on the China Incident."[21]

But membership in the Axis Alliance did not facilitate an end to the war in China. Nearly a year later, with no end to the fighting in sight, Japan occupied the remainder of French Indochina. Once again, concern over ending the China Incident figured prominently. In explaining his decision to support the move south, Army Chief of Staff Gen Sugiyama argued: "In order to hasten the settlement of the Incident it will be absolutely necessary for our Empire to increase its direct pressure on the Chunking regime." Sugiyama reasoned that the occupation would put additional pressure on Chiang and that "at the same time [the] move southward . . . [would] sever the links between the Chunking regime and the British and American powers, which support it from behind and strengthen its will to resist."[22]

While Washington's policy of keeping Nationalist armies in the field succeeded, the cost of defending the Open Door and containing Japanese expansion in China proved high. Although Tokyo might have moved against the French and sided with Germany had the war in China ended by 1940, the fact remains that on three occasions Japanese statesmen chose disastrous policies that they justified as necessary to end the fighting in China.

Economic Deterrence, 1938–1941

Japan's war on China required action well beyond aid for the Nationalists, and, therefore, beginning in the spring of 1938, the United States initiated a wide-ranging and systematically planned program of economic sanctions designed to undermine Japan's ability to successfully conclude the China Incident and consolidate its control over occupied areas. For several years sanctions remained far from comprehensive, and Hull's detractors and admirers, both then and later, constantly took notice of that fact.

Initially, a fully effective embargo required the cooperation of the European democracies, and their cooperation in turn depended on collective security guarantees that Washington was in no position to offer. Moreover, after September 1939, Anglo-French policy sought as never before to avoid conflict in the Pacific, and in the critical months following the fall of France even Washington hesitated to provoke Japan. Many American experts also saw Tokyo as both able to meet the short-term strain of Western economic sanctions and willing to use force to break an embargo should it become overly threatening. For Washington, a clash in the Pacific presented a serious problem, for, despite recent naval construction, the navy was in no position to fight Japan. Hull also understood that a general embargo was more like a trip down the aisle than a first date in that one had to be very sure that the idea was sound before taking the plunge. As Ambassador Grew warned his colleagues in Washington: "To threaten sanctions and to fail to carry them through would be an act of the utmost shortsightedness, ruinous to our prestige and influence in the Far East." Practicality aside, Washington was forced by treaty to observe certain legal niceties that effectively precluded a general trade embargo. In fact, the State Department could not begin either *open* or *official* trade sanctions before first terminating the 1911 Treaty of Commerce and Navigation.[23]

In addition to these problems, Hull also faced a recalcitrant Congress and a diffident public, both of which remained a major deterrent to effective State Department action prior to the summer of 1940. Hull feared that, if Congress voted down a sanctions bill, containment would be crippled. Likewise, because the secretary had spent a lifetime in politics, he understood, better than subordinates like Hornbeck, an academic and career bureaucrat, that public support remained a prerequisite to a successful embargo. Hull realized that, if the public called for repeal of sanctions in the face of Japanese threats or a downturn in the economy, containment would collapse. Timing was everything, and, as long as the Chinese showed no sign of collapsing, Hull could afford to be patient and wait until public support for tough sanctions materialized.

Despite these many limitations on effective action, Washington crafted a remarkably strong and consistent series of restrictions that, by the end of 1940, gnawed away at the marrow of the Japanese war machine. Beginning with the moral embargo of summer 1938, Washington next moved to isolate Japan from American capital and credit and before the end of 1939 served Tokyo with the six-month notification required to abrogate the 1911 Treaty of Commerce and Navigation. When Congress approved the July 1940 Export Control Act, the administration had the legal authority to require export licenses for strategic raw materials and finished goods. These licenses were routinely denied to Tokyo, and by the end of the year, as goods under license increased, Japan found itself cut off from vital American products.

Washington fired the opening shot in America's economic war against Japan when, on July 1, 1938, the State Department issued a public letter to all aircraft and aeronautical manufacturers intended to clarify Secretary Hull's repeated, public condemnation of attacks on civilian centers. The note stated: "It should be clear to all concerned that the Government of the United States is strongly opposed to the sale of airplanes or aeronautical equipment which would materially aid or encourage that practice [aerial attacks on civilians] . . . in any part of the world." While the circular refrained from issuing a formal embargo, it added: "The Department would with great regret issue any licenses authorizing exportation, direct or indirect, of any aircraft, aircraft armament, aircraft engines, aircraft parts, aircraft accessories, aerial bombs or torpedoes to countries the armed forces of which are making use of airplanes for attack upon civilian populations." Although often maligned as ineffective, the first of the moral embargoes was remarkably successful. In mid-December, Hull informed Roosevelt that virtually without exception manufacturers were complying with the embargo. He reported not only that there were no new requests for export licenses for the current month but also that exports under license had declined from over $1.7 million in June to only $100,000 for December.[24]

With little public fanfare, the State Department quietly expanded the moral embargo the following year. Coincident with Hull's July circular, the Department of Commerce instructed American exporters to secure a "confirmed irrevocable letter of credit in their hands before accepting orders for shipment to Japan." By early January, and perhaps even before, ranking FE officers began to see to it that American business heeded the Commerce Department's "advice." In January, Hamilton put the brakes on a plan by J. and W. Seligman and Company to extend a $20 million credit to the Manchurian Industrial Development Corporation for improvements to the South Manchuria Railway. Nine months later, Hamilton was still involved in expanding the moral embargo when he brought direct pressure to bear on the Wells Fargo Bank to stop granting financial credits to Japan. Not to be outdone, Hornbeck persuaded a Pittsburgh steel company not to ship an idle plant to Japan. That Hamilton and Hornbeck involved themselves over a nine-month period in quietly expanding the moral embargo indicates that the policy was neither a knee-jerk response to a specific incident nor the product of a single overzealous officer. Rather, the expanded moral embargo became an integral part of Washington's evolving program of economic warfare. As it turned out, FE was not alone in seeing to the moral embargo's success.[25]

In December 1939, the Department's Division of Controls added processing equipment for aviation gasoline to the moral embargo list and informed major oil exporters: "The national interest suggests that for the time being there should be no further delivery to interests of certain countries of plans, plants, manufacturing rights, or technical information required for the production of high quality aviation gasoline." The Division of Controls further requested manufacturers to inform it of orders for blending agents used in the production of high-grade aviation gasoline in order to determine whether to halt such exports. Some six months later, after Frank Howard, the president of the Standard Oil Development Company, notified the State Department of enormous Japanese orders for tetraethyl lead, officials told him to suspend the sale.[26]

At the same time that the State Department began to quietly expand the moral embargo, others, in and out of the State Department, broke ground on a far more lethal form of economic coercion known as *preclusive* or *preemptive purchasing*. The primary goal of the preclusive-purchasing program was to corner the world supply of the most critical strategic raw materials, thus denying them to Japan, Germany, and Italy. Within three years, preclusive purchasing, which evolved from a small and uncoordinated array of State and Treasury initiatives, became an instrument of economic warfare, second in importance only to the July 1941 freezing of Japanese assets.

It is difficult to say exactly where to begin the story of preclusive purchasing, but late 1938 seems a promising point to start. In that year, Henry Morgenthau's brilliant aide, Herman Oliphant, began to study ways to stockpile critical raw materials. He informed his chief that army appropriations set aside over $13 million for stockpiling and that more could be had simply by having the Reconstruction Finance Corporation advance funds to the Export-Import Bank. Oliphant's plan, however, seemed genuinely focused on preparedness rather than economic coercion, and, for dyed-in-the-wool preclusive purchasers, stockpiling always played second fiddle. By the following year, Morgenthau began to toy with the idea of using preclusive purchasing, export control, or both to prevent Germany, Italy, and Japan from acquiring strategic raw materials. After mulling over the idea for a time, he handed the problem off to Harry White, who quickly produced a report that called for a combined policy of export control and preclusive purchasing.[27]

Such a combination, White argued, provided for an "effective, practicable, and relatively inexpensive" method of depriving the aggressor states of strategic war matériel. To be fully effective, preclusive purchasing needed Anglo-French cooperation, and, White warned, if Paris and London stood aside, the chief value of American purchasing would lie "far more in its political implications." White noted that even unilateral preclusive purchasing would improve American stocks of critical matériel, which, in the event of war in Asia, "may either be stopped or made subject to the will of Japan." He also saw export restriction as particularly feasible in that major supplies of eight critical raw materials lay almost completely within territory controlled by the United States, Britain, France, the Soviet Union, the Netherlands, and Belgium. Export control, however, did offer several potential drawbacks, including heavy reliance on international cooperation. The most serious drawback, White warned Morgenthau, was the possibility that international export control might lead to war.[28]

Preclusive purchasing was no doubt less provocative than export control, and it had the added advantage of being perfectly legal. The program also proved much easier to sell to congressional isolationists in that the interventionists presented it as a preparedness measure rather than a weapon of economic warfare. In the summer of 1939, the president requested $100 million from Congress to acquire strategic and critical raw materials, and legislators dutifully approved his request. It is doubtful, however, that more than a few understood just what they were approving. The minority report from the House Military Affairs Committee, for example, objected only to the size of and not the rationale for the request. Neither the War Department nor the Bureau of the Budget had officially requested such a large appropriation, the minority contended, and the president had publicly stated that $10 million would prove adequate. The report also favored an amendment that required purchases to meet the terms of the 1933 Buy American Act. The minority report never considered the possibility that strategic stockpiling would serve as the covert arm of economic coercion. Nor, for that matter, did the full House. When the bill reached the floor, the debate predictably centered on the amount of the appropriation and whether foreign purchases represented a sound method of stockpiling. Congress's primary concern may have been building up stockpiles of strategic raw materials, but, for the architects of preclusive purchasing, stockpiles were never a top priority.[29]

Despite congressional funding and Hull's backing, Herbert Feis, the State Department's economic adviser for international affairs and preclusive purchasing's leading booster, complained that support for the program was wholly inadequate. Feis envisioned preclusive purchasing as a grand program that, if successful, would starve the Axis of vital raw materials while aiding American preparedness. He also believed that massive American purchases of South American commodities would supply valuable dollar exchange to the Latin American republics and help friendly governments resist Axis pressure.

Feis believed that, if preclusive purchasing were to live up to its promise, the State Department would have to take the lead in ensuring adequate coordination and funding, and that meant bringing Jesse Jones, director of the Federal Loan Agency, on board. Feis hoped to convince Jones to support his plan to create an interdepartmental committee to coordinate the preclusive purchasing of strategic raw materials. On December 2, 1940, Feis and Jones met, and for a time all seemed well, but soon cocktail hour came, and, unfortunately for Feis, it seemed that alcohol increased Jones's caution. After the clerk whipped up "two heavy high balls" (presumably one apiece), Jones got a bit red in the cheeks and "asked for time to further think the matter through." Feis left the meeting fuming, convinced that every "day lost makes it possible for Japan and Germany to secure vital supplies for the prosecution of the war." Despite the disappointing meeting, however, all was not lost. Within weeks Feis convened the very interdepartmental board that Jones had nearly agreed to before the untimely intervention of cocktail hour.[30]

On December 23, 1940, Feis convened the initial meeting of his interdepartmental committee with full representation from the Army and Navy Munitions Board, the Procurement Division, the National Defense Commission, the Federal Loan Administration, and the Department of State. The conferees, who included such luminaries as Will Clayton, then vice president of the Export-Import Bank, and W. Averell Harriman, then serving on the National Defense Commission, quickly determined that inadequate shipping and competition between competing government agencies impeded orderly preclusive purchasing, especially of chrome and rubber. Feis then steered the discussion toward his own pet project, preclusive purchasing in Latin America. He noted that American stockpiling of Latin American commodities would aid military preparedness and extend valuable economic support to the Southern economies. Most importantly, he noted, "it was clear that purchase was suggested almost purely as a means of preventing . . . commodities from going to Japan."[31]

Within four months of the interdepartmental committee's inaugural meeting, American preclusive purchasing in Latin America was proceeding at breakneck speed. Feis was still concerned, he told Welles, that preclusive purchasing was "not making headway at anything near the rate of speed I should like," but his fears were exaggerated. During the first eight months of 1941, the United States secured "substantially the entire copper production of Chile, Mexico and Peru" and the lion's share of Bolivian tin. In La Paz, Washington and Tokyo squared off in a bidding war for Bolivian tungsten, which more than any other episode indicates the extent to which Feis and company spared no effort or expense to preempt Japanese purchases. American buyers, it seemed, were understandably reluctant to match Japanese offers, lest other producers also demand that the United States pay inflated prices. At a critical juncture in the negotiations, however, Tokyo balked at Bolivia's insistence that Japan guarantee payment in the event that the tungsten could not be shipped, and this hesitation gave Feis the window he needed. On April 30, he invited the unsuspecting Bolivian minister, Louis Fernando Guachalla, for a chat at the office. Once seated, the minister was given a display of Yankee hospitality. According to Hull's account of the conversation, Guachalla learned that, in order to win over his countrymen, Washington would increase its bid for tungsten. At the same time, officials informed him of their "natural sense of disappointment" as well as their understandable conviction "that the Bolivian Government could fairly be asked to make a special effort to conclude the sale of tungsten to us in light of our many-sided present effort to contribute to Bolivian welfare, *including recent discussions having to do with aid under the lease-lend bill.*" Even for one accustomed to La Paz's thin air, the implication that Washington might revoke Lend-Lease aid must have taken Guachalla's breath away. But State's heavy-handed tactics worked, and just three weeks later Washington secured the entire output of Bolivian tungsten for the next three years.[32]

In Brazil, meanwhile, the Rubber Reserve Company, which had already entered into an agreement with the International Rubber Regulation Company (the organization that controlled nearly all the world's crude rubber output) to purchase "*all the rubber produced which could be exported to the United States,*" stretched its mandate even further. Using the new US-Brazil Strategic Materials Agreement, which precluded Brazil from selling strategic commodities to any nation other than the United States, Rubber Reserve arranged to buy that country's entire rubber output. The importance of the Strategic Materials Agreement, however, extended well beyond American acquisition of rubber. The understanding became the first in a series of new agreements in which, rather than purchasing only select raw materials, Washington guaranteed that it would purchase a nation's entire commodity output. The Brazilian agreement, for example, committed Washington to purchase twelve commodities, and a similar agreement with Mexico, concluded in July 1941, covered twenty commodities.[33]

Washington, of course, did not limit preclusive purchasing to Latin America. By the summer of 1941, negotiations were under way around the globe to block Axis acquisition of strategic raw materials. In Turkey, American buyers concluded agreements covering chrome, while, in the Iberian Peninsula, the United States snapped up Spanish zinc and Portuguese tungsten. In Japan's backyard, Washington purchased rubber from French Indochina and Thailand as well as Siamese tin. The United States purchased nearly half of Indochina's rubber output following the fall of France and in 1941 threatened to withhold oil exports to the colony "unless Indo-China sold [the United States] a substantial share of its rubber and metals." In areas under direct American control, Japan fared even worse. By mid-1941, the Metals Reserve Company had made arrangements with the Philippines "to preclusively purchase approximately one-million tons of Philippine ore—the amount normally shipped to Japan in a year." The Philippine agreement was especially important, White told Morgenthau, because London "had agreed to stop the export to Japan of Burmese ore if we stopped the flow of Philippine ore."[34]

However effective preclusive purchasing became, it remained only part of Washington's program of economic coercion. Beginning in 1939, the United States gradually instituted Morgenthau and White's second method to deny strategic raw materials to the aggressor states when the State Department expanded the moral embargo to cover aluminum and molybdenum. By the end of 1939, the leading American producers, Climax Molybdenum and Kennecut, had turned Japan's largest purchasing agent away empty-handed, and, the following March, Canada also cut off nickel exports. Despite these achievements, early export control remained a stepchild to the moral embargo, lacking its own identity and purpose.[35]

As late as the spring of 1940, Washington had yet to construct the machinery necessary to conduct the sweeping export restrictions that, White had argued, would serve as the natural and necessary complement to preclusive purchasing. To be sure, the State Department had already taken steps toward export control when on July 26, 1939, it served Tokyo with the six months' notice required before denouncing the 1911 Japanese-American Treaty of Commerce and Navigation. January 26 came and went, however, and still export control limped along on an ad hoc basis. Hull and the State Department readily embraced economic sanctions, as the moral embargo and preclusive purchasing clearly indicate, yet for many reasons they still hesitated to push for formal export control. Hull understood that, once the administration instituted official sanctions, it could ill afford to turn back. More importantly, he remained wary of strong isolationist sentiment both in the heartland and on the Hill. The secretary worried, for example, that, if Congress debated legislation to empower the administration to proceed with sanctions and failed to come up with the necessary votes, the State Department's ability to deter Tokyo would decline immeasurably.[36]

Henry Morgenthau, of course, was not nearly as cautious and for years had fought, often alone in the cabinet, for a tougher Japan policy, but by the summer of 1940 he had valuable allies within the very heart of Roosevelt's inner circle. In June of that year, the president dismissed Henry Woodring, his long-suffering secretary of war, and replaced him with another Henry. The similarities ended there. Woodring, a cautious Kansas isolationist, repeatedly obstructed or failed to pursue aid for Britain as vigorously as Roosevelt expected, whereas his replacement, Henry Stimson, favored conscription and all measures to aid Britain short of war.[37]

Having served as Taft's secretary of war and Hoover's secretary of state, Stimson had developed a particularly beguiling mind-set on the Japanese national character and an equally enticing scheme for how to deal with the Japanese Empire. The secretary of war believed—and here he was not alone within the administration—that Japan respected force and firmness and misinterpreted anything that could possibly be construed as weakness or pacifism. He also had undue faith—and it was a deeply held faith rather than a mere belief—in the power of American deterrence. This faith extended far beyond the ability to merely check a specific move on Tokyo's part, for he believed that, just as the course of a mighty river could be changed by the construction of a dam, American power could alter the entire course of Japanese imperial development. "When the United States indicates by clear language and bold actions that she intends to carry out a clear and affirmative policy in the Far East," he argued, "Japan will yield to that policy even though it conflicts with her own Asiatic policy and conceived interests." Given his conviction that Japan would misinterpret American moderation for weakness, there seemed to be no room in his policy for diplomacy, negotiation, or compromise. If he was correct, negotiations were unnecessary, and the United

States had little to fear by pursuing a clear, measured, deterrence policy. In time, adequate American pressure would force Japan to end the China Incident and desert its Axis partners. But, if the secretary was wrong, then bold American action in the absence of compromise would produce only disaster.[38]

Stimson's views on proper American policy were well-known both to the administration and to the public well before he joined the president's cabinet. In a *New York Times* editorial published several months before his appointment, Stimson argued that repeal of the arms embargo represented the first step in an affirmative foreign policy, but only a first step and a small one at that. Stimson contended that "the merchants who are selling to Japan the ore, steel and scrap iron indispensable for her bombs, and the large oil producers who are selling to her the even more indispensable aviation gasoline for her planes," hindered the formation of an effective policy. These men who "soil their hands with this dirty traffic," he added, were aided by "those political leaders who have tried to frighten our government from doing anything to prevent the wrong by warning them that to do so would surely lead them into war with Japan." The onetime and future secretary of war discounted the likelihood of hostilities and noted: "The very last thing which the Japanese Government desires is a war with the United States." Stimson also argued that Washington could use Tokyo's commercial dependence to moderate Japanese foreign policy. The secretary explained that, when the Roosevelt administration announced its intention to terminate the 1911 commercial treaty, Tokyo responded by agreeing to reopen the Yangtze River to American commercial traffic, and, thus, for Stimson, the lesson was simple: American firmness produced Japanese concessions.[39]

This seemingly simple, yet successful, formula came to snare the secretary of war and others in a kind of deterrence mentality that precluded other containment options. Stimson rejected American mediation to end the Sino-Japanese war and instead insisted that America's national interests demanded that "the Japanese military organization should become discredited in the eyes of the Japanese people." If he sounds a bit too much like Stanley Hornbeck, that is understandable. The two had, after all, worked very closely at the State Department during the Hoover administration. Rather than compromise, Stimson called for the sweeping embargoes that Hoover had refused to approve a decade earlier, to include not only aviation fuel and scrap iron but all "arms, munitions and the raw materials out of which arms are made."[40]

Led by Morgenthau, Ickes, and, beginning in June 1940, Stimson, export restrictions continued to target Japan's warmaking potential. Typically, Morgenthau led the charge, and nowhere were his actions more significant than with regard to restrictions on oil exports. Along with Ickes and Stimson, the secretary had for some time favored an embargo on oil shipments to Japan, and one night, over dinner at the British embassy, Stimson and Lothian clashed over their respective governments' appeasement of Japan. The secretary of war focused on London's decision to close the Burma Road, while Lothian hammered away at Washington's failure to support a strong British stand in the Far East.[41]

While Morgenthau reacted mildly to the Stimson-Lothian exchange, what occurred next took his breath away. "If you will stop shipping aviation gasoline to Japan," Lothian told the Americans, "we will blow up the wells in [the] Dutch East Indies so that the Japanese can't come down [and get the oil]." Like many of his guests, Lothian confided: "We have all felt that if we put too much pressure on Japan they would go down there and take those oil wells." For the remainder of the evening, Morgenthau could not stop thinking about Lothian's comment, and, by the time he left the embassy, he had formulated a plan. He told Arthur Purvis, the head of the British Purchasing Mission, that Ickes should "say from the survey he has recently made that . . . for conservation reasons we should stop the export of American oil." This, he assured Purvis, "would keep the State Department from opposing the idea and say[ing] if we just did it against Japan it would be an excuse for war."[42]

The next day, when Morgenthau and White reviewed the previous evening's discussions, the secretary maintained that an embargo, coupled with the destruction of the Dutch wells, "would simply electrify the world and really put some belief in England." White, who doubted whether London would follow through, believed that, if Morgenthau somehow pulled it off, he would be "doing more for China than any other thing . . . [he] could do." The stakes, however, were now higher than just China, for, with the fall of Admiral Mitsumasa Yonai's cabinet, Morgenthau explained, "Japan is going to just gobble up one thing after another."[43]

When the cabinet debated an oil embargo in late July, Morgenthau and Welles quickly squared off. "The President," Stimson recalled, "raised his hands in the air and refused to participate," telling Morgenthau and Welles to "go off in a corner and settle their issue." But the two had few differences to settle because the State Department had come around to favor action on both aviation fuel and scrap metal. Morgenthau and Welles differed only on what items should be subject to export control licenses, and, while these differences were significant, they must not obscure the fact that by midsummer 1940 Hull embraced export control as a means to contain Japan. Morgenthau favored placing all petroleum and scrap metals under license, while Welles, the true moderate at State and the winner in this battle with Treasury, insisted that restrictions cover only aviation fuel, lubricants, and select grades of scrap. Two days later, the White House announced that petroleum above eighty-seven octane, steel, and scrap iron exports required appropriate licenses. Export control had begun.[44]

"No secret intelligence about Japanese affairs," Herbert Feis argued, prompted the president to place aviation fuel, steel, and scrap under license. Rather, he contended, "it was a swipe in a general direction, and not an exactly clocked and aimed blow." While he does not explicitly say so, Feis leaves no doubt that Morgenthau and Stimson delivered the "blow." While it is true that the two played a major role in bringing the petroleum question before the president, they were hardly responsible for the decision to license key exports. For several years, the State Department had envisioned building economic obstacles in Japan's path to empire, but something—lack of congressional or public support, military preparedness, and legal barriers—had always stopped it. Once Congress passed the National Defense Act on July 2, giving the administration the authority to restrict the export of goods required for national defense, the State Department had all the legal authority it needed to impose select embargoes on Japan. The president, meanwhile, had ordered the Pacific Fleet to remain on station in Hawaii, a fact not lost on Hornbeck, who explained to Welles on July 24 that the "present setup—with authority for embargoes and with the fleet in the Pacific"—made sanctions much less risky.[45]

The decision then to move forward on licensing was hardly, as Feis claims, "a swipe in a general direction." The State Department was already deeply involved in efforts to shut down the flow of aviation fuel to Japan, and export control merely made its efforts more coordinated and effective, while the fleet's forward deployment appeared to lessen the risk. On a more general level, licensing marked the logical second step in the plan first suggested by Harry White to combine preclusive purchasing, which in the summer of 1940 Feis was already pursuing, with export control. By the same token, export control also represented an orderly progression of State's program of gradual economic sanctions, first instituted with the 1938 moral embargo on aeronautical equipment, and subsequently expanded to include financial credits, raw materials, and aviation fuel. Had export control begun and ended in July 1940, perhaps Feis's argument would have merit. But the July sanctions were only the beginning.

For the next twelve months, the export control list grew at an astonishingly steady rate. In September, the White House announced that, after October 16, the United States would issue no licenses except to Great Britain and to nations within the Western Hemisphere for any type of iron and steel scrap. In December, Washington added iron ore, pig iron, ferro alloys, semifinished goods such as ingots and sheet bars, and a host of finished steel products to the export control list. During the first three months of 1941 strategic raw materials such as bronze, copper, radium, uranium, carbon black, and a range of finished goods, including petroleum refinery equipment, came under the new embargo regulations. In April, in an effort to keep peace in the Pacific, the State Department went so far as to ban the export of American caffeine to Japan. By the summer of 1941, there remained very little that Tokyo could buy from America, and US exports to Japan had fallen by half, compared to the first six months of 1940. There was really only one vital item that Japan purchased in quantity from the United States, and Washington was not yet prepared to shut off the flow of American crude oil.[46]

Like American aid to China, Washington's pursuit of economic sanctions boosted Chinese morale, lessened the likelihood that Chiang would seek a compromise peace, and made it all the more difficult for Japan to gain a strictly military solution to the war. As Hornbeck predicted, Japan's invasion had reached flood tide, and, with the bulk of the Japanese army mired in China, Tokyo, apparently, could not strike south.

But as was the case during the 1918 steel embargo, when Tokyo sought to lessen its reliance on American exports by developing supply sources in Asia, successive cabinets once again looked to the mainland in order to offset American sanctions. Although Japan had long coveted Europe's Asian colonies, it made no move to take them until 1940, when failed talks and Western sanctions made the need for vital raw materials, especially oil, tin, bauxite, manganese, and molybdenum, acute. Faced with increasing Western sanctions, Japanese negotiators worked to secure badly needed raw materials from the Dutch East Indies between December 1940 and June 1941. By spring, with their demands still unmet, successive liaison conferences (meetings of the cabinet and members of the supreme command) increasingly focused on the need to use force in order to secure strategic resources. This option required bases in southern French Indochina.[47]

On July 2, 1941, Prime Minister Fumimaro Konoe convened an imperial conference that approved the occupation of southern French Indochina. The navy's decision to move south, even at the risk of war, can of course be explained in part by personnel changes that had denuded navy policymaking bodies of their most moderate and temperate officers. Overconfidence among key junior officers as well as the conviction that neither Washington nor London would go to war for Indochina also tell part, but only a small part, of the story. As late as March 1941, the army and navy agreed that, even in the event of a British defeat in Europe, Japan should not move south. Both services recognized that an advance could lead to war, and General Okada Kikiusaburo conceded: "We are no match for the United States and Britain." Within four months, however, the leaders of both services executed a dramatic turnabout and approved the occupation of southern French Indochina.[48]

What caused this dramatic change in policy? Certainly not overconfidence, though there were men in both services who greatly overestimated Japan's chances in a war with America. Nor can personnel changes explain the shift. The strategic situation certainly did not favor such a move, especially after the German invasion of the Soviet Union gave Britain a new lease on life. If anything, Anglo-American-Dutch forces in the Far East were far more formidable than at any time since 1939. Had Japan wanted to seize Western colonies by force, the summer of 1940, rather than 1941, was the ideal time to act. Clearly, Western sanctions and the breakdown of the Batavia talks produced the July 2 decision, a decision that vastly increased the likelihood of war.[49]

Military Deterrence, 1938–1941

Since Theodore Roosevelt sent the Great White Fleet on its cruise around the world in 1907, American strategists had held an undue faith in the power of military deterrence. In spite of the president's deeply flawed conclusions, Henry Stimson absorbed the lesson of 1907–1908 and applied it to the crisis of 1931–1933. The decision to leave the fleet in Hawaii after its winter 1932 cruise, the secretary of state argued, "undoubtedly exercised a steadying effect" on Tokyo's judgment. Stimson was not alone in believing that the mere existence of a powerful American fleet could keep Japan in check. From Tokyo, even a moderate such as Grew argued that American preparedness represented the best possible deterrent to Japanese expansion.[50]

Given this mind-set, it should come as no surprise that the beginning of the China Incident immediately brought renewed calls to build on the successes of 1933 and 1934 and further enlarge the navy. Stanley Hornbeck led the charge at the State Department, but others in the administration were already well ahead of him. On July 30, 1937, Norman Davis penned a memorandum arguing: "For the sake of peace and ultimate disarmament, we should begin the construction of two or three additional battleships in replacement of existing obsolete ones." Unlike many in the administration, he envisioned a naval buildup as essential to his ultimate aim—a new naval limitation treaty. Yet, to his mind, increased naval strength also represented the best way to aid China and increase national defense. Welles read Davis's draft before sending it on to the president, and, while he agreed completely with its conclusions, he informed Davis that Roosevelt would avoid any public statement regarding increased naval spending until after Congress adjourned.[51]

Although Welles's squeamishness about a public and forceful administration endorsement for a naval buildup was understandable given the strength of isolationist sentiment, it was also a bit alarmist. For several years, a substantial public majority had backed naval expansion, and a December 27, 1937, American Institute of Public Opinion Poll registered support at a staggering 74 percent. On December 29, 1937, when the president announced his plan for a naval buildup, the *New York Times* predicted an easy triumph, and, by 1938, when Congress voted on the legislation, powerful figures outside Roosevelt's inner circle were also pushing for an expanded blue-water fleet. Frank Knox, a newspaper magnate, the GOP vice presidential nominee in 1936, and Roosevelt's future secretary of the navy, endorsed both fleet expansion and forward deployment. "Conversation," he contended, "will not convince the Japanese militarists that we mean business. But the presence in Asiatic waters of a fleet more powerful than their own, would be most eloquent." As Hornbeck had predicted in 1933, continued Sino-Japanese hostility also helped kindle support in Congress. Senator George Norris, Nebraska's progressive stalwart, gave voice to his growing concern over Japanese military expansion when, in a hauntingly prophetic statement, he claimed: "There is no doubt in my mind but what, some bright morning, we would awake to find ourselves at war with Japan [if American fleet strength fell below Japan's]." Even California's Hiram Johnson, no friend to either the president or internationalism, privately conceded that the Japanese threat required a powerful American navy.[52]

The Navy and State Departments also supported continued naval expansion as nothing had transpired to alter their earlier consensus that American naval superiority was the key to checking Japanese expansion in Asia. In many respects, then, the push for new building marked the continuation of the program that began shortly after Roosevelt's inauguration. In addition to deterring Tokyo, officials recognized, an arms race would put further strain on Japan's struggling economy.[53]

With the administration's firm backing, in May 1938 both houses of Congress passed a second Vinson Act authorizing the construction of an additional sixty-nine warships. In justifying the appropriations request, Admiral William D. Leahy, the chief of naval operations, explained that the failure of recent naval disarmament talks, the subsequent overturning of the 10:10:6 ratios, and the ongoing hostilities in China demanded an American buildup. The following year, Congress approved appropriations to increase the size of the US Army Air Corps to between fifty-five hundred and six thousand aircraft, and, two years later, in June and July 1940, Congress approved proposals for a fleet expansion that, when completed, provided the United States with a true "two ocean Navy." The third Vinson package, in particular, marked a significant departure from its predecessors in its attention to aircraft carrier construction. In addition to increased funding for the fleet, the administration also redeployed military assets and redoubled efforts to increase the nation's airpower. In May 1940, President Roosevelt both called for boosting aircraft production to fifty thousand planes a year and transferred the Pacific Fleet from California to Hawaii. By the end of the year, the administration also set about reinforcing the Philippines, both to protect the distant colony and to deter Japan from seizing the oil-rich Dutch East Indies.[54]

As early as February 1940, the US navy began to quietly press for an expanded military presence in the Philippines. At the February 20 meeting of the Joint Board, navy members, noting that American control of the islands could deter further Japanese moves south, especially in the direction of the East Indies, raised the possibility of increasing army air strength. General George C. Marshall, the army chief of staff, noted that an augmented force, whether air or ground, "would be subject to annihilation or complete loss in the event of Japanese attack." Navy members, however, refused to retreat from the thesis that "even a minor increase in the available forces would be worthwhile and might suffice to deter Japan from attack on the islands," so Marshall agreed to further study the matter. Within two weeks, Brigadier General George Strong, of the Army War Plans Division, informed Marshall that, in order to successfully repel a Japanese attack and constitute a credible deterrent, the army needed to reinforce the islands with an additional 441 planes and twelve thousand troops. By the end of the year, Stimson, Knox, Marshall, and Admiral Ernest King, then serving on the General Board, agreed to rush pursuit planes and antiaircraft guns to the Philippines. The War Department, which once derided the archipelago as a military liability, now came to see it as a forward outpost of American power along the Japanese-American frontier. By early 1941, the Philippines began to receive reinforcements, which, while in some critical areas falling well short of Strong's recommendations, were anything but "a minor increase."[55]

Throughout 1941, the administration continued to transform the Philippines from a liability into a powerful instrument of American containment. The growing availability of men and matériel, coupled with constant pressure from Major General George Grunert, the commander of the Philippine Department, General Douglas MacArthur, then a military adviser to the Philippines, and Manuel Quezon, the president of the Philippines, led Roosevelt to approve doubling the size of the Philippine Scouts from six thousand to twelve thousand men. Following this decision, Washington also rushed additional American infantry and coastal artillery to the islands, and, in the spring, Marshall and Stimson set in motion plans for naming MacArthur commander of American forces in the Far East.[56]

The most controversial decision in the entire program of military deterrence concerned that of May 1940 to leave the Pacific Fleet at Pearl Harbor over the objections of its commander, Admiral James O. Richardson. While Admiral Harold Stark, the chief of naval operations, maintained that the fleet's presence in Hawaii would deter Japan, Richardson thought that he could discourage Japanese expansion just as easily, and far more safely, from bases on the West Coast. Having received his orders, Richardson worked to improve facilities in Hawaii while he simultaneously urged the president to rescind the order. Roosevelt, however, left the fleet at Pearl Harbor and relieved Richardson early in 1941.[57]

The decision to reinforce the Philippines and leave the fleet at Pearl Harbor was part of a wider, coordinated coalition effort to strengthen Western forces in Southeast Asia in order to contain Japan. In December 1940, Stimson, Knox, and their respective service chiefs concluded that the British should take immediate steps to reinforce Singapore. At the same time, the Americans agreed that Washington should press London to release fighter aircraft to China in order to strengthen Chiang. Such a move, they argued, "would have a very important effect towards checking the withdrawal of the Japanese army for possible use in Malaya." By April 1941, British, Dominion, and Indian infantry forces in Malaya and Singapore had nearly tripled from the number in place ten months before, though even this rapid increase fell short of the number that the British believed necessary to defend the colony. British air forces in the Burma-Malaya Theater were also well short of the minimum number required to repel a Japanese attack, but, with 170 fighters on order in America, London planned to complete its initial air reinforcement by the year's end. To the south, Dutch preparations in the East Indies throughout the winter and spring buoyed American hopes. By the early summer of 1941, the Army War Plans Division concluded that Java, the principal island in the East Indies chain, would hold out against a Japanese invasion until American aid arrived.[58]

Despite its impressive appearance, military deterrence produced several unanticipated problems; foremost among these was that the Anglo-American-Dutch buildup prodded Japanese ruling circles to pursue policies that made a clash in the Pacific more, rather than less, likely. Military deterrence, for example, had a particularly corrosive effect on the navy, where the usually moderate Navy Ministry approved both the Axis Alliance and the program for southern expansion in an effort to counter the American buildup. The records of the Privy Council's Investigation Committee, for example, reveal that the Navy Ministry's single-minded concern with the cumulative effect of the Vinson programs led senior members to accept the alliance with Germany. In 1939, the navy proved decisive in beating back pro-Axis forces, but under Navy Minister Koshiro Oikawa it reversed its position and supported an alliance with Germany, in return for the army's promise to support increased naval funding.[59]

Interest in securing greater funding also led the navy to push a general program of southern expansion. As far back as 1936, the Navy Ministry supported expansion south in order to secure increased appropriations. The gambit worked, and the Diet provided funds to build over sixty new warships as well as a generous appropriation to expand the fleet's air arm. Four years later, the Navy Ministry again supported a move south for similar reasons. In the summer of 1940, the Army Ministry and the Army General Staff approved the "Outline of the Main Principles for Coping with the Changing World Situation," which called for southern expansion in order to break the deadlock on the China Front and free Japan from economic dependence on the West. The Navy Ministry approved the "Outline" because, as in 1936, it paved the way for greater appropriations. The "Outline" recognized that relations with the United States were bound to suffer when Japan moved south and that as a result the navy would require greater resources. Senior naval officials feared that appropriations would suffer if they either opposed the southern policy or admitted their concern over Anglo-American naval strength. Rather than reflect a brazen proexpansion mentality, naval support for southern expansion, Sadao Asada notes, was far "more budget-minded than war-minded."[60]

By the summer of 1940, the Navy General Staff had also become so alarmed by the Vinson programs as to call for an early start to hostilities before the full weight of American power could be brought to bear in the Pacific. For nearly two decades, Sadao Asada argues, an "almost fatalistic belief in the inevitability of war with the United States" permeated parts of the Japanese navy. Nowhere was the thesis of inevitable war held more deeply than within the Navy General Staff and the junior officer corps and among members of the First Committee, a collection of middle-echelon officers from both the Navy Ministry and the Navy General Staff. In April 1941, Admiral Osami Nagano, a die-hard believer in the inevitable war thesis, was appointed chief of the Navy General Staff. Worse still, by his own admission, Nagano heeded the advice of junior officers whose views were, if anything, even more fatalistic than his own.[61]

While the Navy General Staff needed a strong leader who steadfastly opposed fighting a war that Japan could not win, Nagano proceeded from the assumption that war was unavoidable and therefore believed that, the sooner Japan went to war with America, the better. With preparations for war complete by the spring of 1941, the First Committee, driven by the same thesis that determined Nagano's thinking, pressed for an immediate advance into southern Indochina, confident that an advance south would trigger an American embargo, the seizure of the Dutch East Indies, and war with America. The First Committee's Shingo Ishikawa argued that the navy must clarify its resolve to fight the United States and Britain and carry out the advance into southern Indochina and Thailand. He feared that, if Japan did not advance south in the very near future, "national strength will gradually decline": "When at long last we resolve to find a way out of our fatal situation, we will have already lost our power to make a comeback." Alarmed by the apparent lack of resolve shown by the Navy Ministry and the Navy General Staff as well as the army, Ishikawa contended that the committee must convince its own service that war was inevitable in order to strengthen the resolve of both the army and the government to fight the West.[62]

It is unclear whether Ishikawa's position paper convinced Nagano to support plans designed to trigger war with the West or whether the First Committee merely mirrored his preexisting views. In any event, even before Washington froze Japanese assets, Nagano argued that diplomatic efforts would fail and that American military preparations made it imperative that Japan quickly commence hostilities. "There's a chance now for victory against the United States," he informed the liaison conference on July 21, "[but] by the second half of next year we won't be a match for them anymore." Conference transcripts reveal Nagano's acute concern over how America's buildup made conquest of the Philippines ever more difficult. A successful strike against the archipelago, he explained, would make it "easier, from the Navy's point of view, to carry on the war [against the United States]." Four days later, on the eve of the assets freeze, Nagano told Admiral Seizo Kobayashi, his brother officer, that Japan must "stand resolute and break the [American] iron chain."[63]

Clearly, rather than deterring the admirals, America's naval buildup led them, and their civilian counterparts, to approve policies that exacerbated American-Japanese tensions. Navy policy may have flirted with disaster before 1939, but, faced with the colossal Vinson Acts and the deployment of additional Western forces to the Far East, naval leaders embraced a ruinous policy in the vain hope of saving the Japanese Empire.

Coalition Building

By the spring of 1941, the United States had successfully limited Japanese expansion through a wide-ranging program that included economic aid for China, attacks on the Japanese economy, and massive military expansion. At the same time, the Roosevelt administration also succeeded in building a coalition, both at home and abroad, that supported American containment.

Since 1933, officials worked to bring about public support for a firm containment policy, and, after July 1937, their task became far easier. Within a year of the Marco Polo Bridge Incident, Harry and Frank Price, the sons of former missionaries in China, formed the powerful American Committee for Non-Participation in Japanese Aggression, also known as the Price Committee. The committee worked closely with State Department officials, especially Stanley Hornbeck, who "encouraged the idea of an educational campaign," and, in August 1938, the committee began its crusade with the printing of twenty-two thousand copies of a booklet entitled *America's Share in Japan's War Guilt*. Within a year of its publication, "the overwhelming majority of Americans came to support legislative or executive action to stop the sale of war supplies to Japan." The committee followed up its efforts with an equally impressive propaganda campaign in 1940 marked by the publication of *Shall America Stop Arming Japan?* This booklet's thesis that Japan could not carry out the war in China without American support furthered the call for embargoes.[64]

Like Hornbeck and Hull, the committee also supported "action to check the flow of American war credits and American war materials to Japan." Legislation introduced in 1939 by Senators Key Pittman and Lewis Schwellenbach that sought to limit trade with Japan was written in part by the committee, as was the 1940 National Defense Bill, which eventually led to major export restrictions.[65]

Abroad, meanwhile, the threat of further Japanese expansion and the onset of the European War helped reestablish interest in an informal Anglo-American coalition to contain Japan. Even as the Brussels Conference ended in failure, the informal Anglo-American entente that had served Theodore Roosevelt so well a generation before began to reemerge. In 1938 and 1939, secret Anglo-American naval talks produced plans for a joint defense against Japan, and, following the fall of France, Washington and London formed a working group to coordinate their export control programs. As the German threat increased, so too did American support for Britain. In September 1940, the president ordered the transfer of fifty World War I–era destroyers to Britain to combat German U-boats, and, in March 1941, the United States agreed to underwrite the anti-Axis war effort through the Lend-Lease program. Well before Pearl Harbor, Anglo-American cooperation led to what one historian of the "special relationship" calls a "common-law alliance."[66]

In addition to Great Britain, the Roosevelt administration could also count the Soviet Union as an ally in the American pursuit of containment. The April 1941 Soviet-Japanese Neutrality Agreement certainly complicated Soviet-American relations, especially after President Roosevelt placed commodities heretofore bound for the Soviet Union on the export control list. Despite these differences, however, Soviet ambassador Konstantin Oumansky declared in mid-April 1941: "The Soviet Union and the United States would eventually be on the same side." As for Soviet-Japanese relations, the April 1941 agreement did little to ease tension as Japan still faced in Siberia "an autonomous [Soviet] army, steadily strengthened and enlarged since 1931," for which "the Japanese . . . acquired a wholesome respect" after their stunning defeats at Chankufeng in 1938 and Nomonhan the following year.[67]

Despite its many limitations and unintended consequences, American containment proved extraordinarily successful after the onset of the undeclared Sino-Japanese War. Almost four years after the Marco Polo Bridge Incident, Japan remained trapped in China, unable to either extricate itself or bring Chiang and the Kuomintang to their knees. To be sure, US policy contributed to Japan's decision to join the Axis and occupy northern Indochina, but, given the power vacuum that the Dutch and French defeats had created in the Far East, Washington's policies must be judged a resounding success. By the spring of 1941, the American people overwhelmingly supported a firm stand, which meant that Japan could look forward to continued, unrelenting economic pressure. On the military front, Chiang showed no sign of abandoning the war, and, in the north, Tokyo faced a Soviet military that had recently decimated its forces and continued to tie down countless divisions. To the south and east, meanwhile, the Anglo-American-Dutch buildup made seizing vital raw materials and transporting them back to the home islands an ever more hazardous undertaking.

The architects of American containment—Hull, Hornbeck, Morgenthau, Stimson, Ickes, Marshall, and even President Roosevelt—believed that aid to China and economic and military pressure would prevent a Chinese defeat and cause Japan to avoid war with the United States and its coalition partners. They were half right. In the end, to succeed, containment needed to possess, like the Roman god Janus, two faces, one coercive, the other diplomatic. Having stopped Japan, Washington now needed to wean Tokyo from the Axis Alliance and draw the Japanese war machine out of China. This required the type of realism once championed by the likes of Theodore Roosevelt and Robert Lansing. Unfortunately, this was the type of constructive engagement that Stanley Hornbeck and Cordell Hull could never embrace.

Chapter 5

Sinners in the Hands of an Angry Department

> The God that holds you over the pit of hell, much as one holds a spider, or some loathsome insect over the fire, abhors you.
>
> —Jonathan Edwards (1741)

> No promises of the Japs based on words would be worth anything.
>
> —Cordell Hull (1941)

For three decades, diplomatic engagement remained an integral part of America's containment of Japan. With the exception of Calvin Coolidge, every president from Theodore Roosevelt to Herbert Hoover achieved at least one major agreement with Tokyo designed to protect the Open Door and limit Japanese expansion. These agreements did not safeguard the Open Door, but they did help shelter it, and, in the process, diplomatic engagement kept in check the suspicion, fear, and rivalry that competition in China, American immigration restrictions, and a sustained Japanese-American naval arms race had created. Neither Taft-Katsura nor Lansing-Ishii nor even the Washington and London naval agreements solved the fundamental problems that divided America and Japan. These agreements did, however, signal that compromise, negotiation, and diplomacy took precedence over deterrence and coercion.

Although Theodore Roosevelt sent the Great White Fleet on its cruise, in part, to deter Japan, he did not hesitate to conclude Root-Takahira. The Wilson administration pursued economic deterrence, yet the president backed Lansing-Ishii, and, in the last major Japanese-American political agreement before the war, US negotiators rebuffed Japan's bid for parity at the 1930 London naval talks even as they worked behind the scenes to achieve a compromise. Just three years later, however, the days of compromise were over.

In the four years between the Marco Polo Bridge Incident and the freezing of Japanese assets, both Secretary of State Hull and Stanley Hornbeck went through the motions of engaging Japan without ever seeking a diplomatic compromise to either limit Japanese expansion or ease Japanese-American tensions. Neither man saw any need to conclude a bargain with what both believed was an inherently untrustworthy Japan, and they were not alone. Both men also understood that, in order to build a broad anti-Japanese coalition, tensions had to remain elevated if the American public and foreign powers were to continue to see Japan as a threat to Western interests. The two diplomats also believed that the United States must oppose an early Sino-Japanese peace because Tokyo's terms required Chiang's recognition of Manchukuo. Consequently, the United States continued, as it had since 1933, to eschew Japan's entreaties and repeatedly failed to use diplomacy to either support containment or improve Japanese-American relations.

The Roads Not Taken: Peace in China and the Axis Alliance

By mid-1939, continued Chinese resistance had shaken the confidence of the Japanese government and army. From the beginning of the conflict, many in the army's control faction in particular opposed the war, and, as Europe inched forward to catastrophe, moderates within the Army General Staff and the War Ministry called for a negotiated end to the fighting in China.[1]

In Washington, meanwhile, hope had long ago replaced despair as Chinese armies remained intact, retreated into the interior, and continued to take the field. Hornbeck's prediction that Japan's invasion would reach flood stage and then recede seemed at last possible. The influential American Council of the Institute of Pacific Relations concluded the previous December that China would continue "resistance over a long period" and "keep large bodies of Japanese troops in the field, thereby increasing Japan's war costs." From Chungking, Ambassador Nelson Johnson informed the president that China could continue to resist indefinitely with adequate financial help and a parallel American effort to reduce the flow of foreign financial assistance to Japan.[2]

Others close to the president, however, believed that the time had come to use American power to end, rather than prolong, the war. William Bullitt, Roosevelt's close confidant and the former ambassador to the Soviet Union, informed Hull that Washington should approach Chiang and sound him out regarding his government's peace terms. In the final hours of Europe's fragile peace, Bullitt boldly suggested bringing Japan into the Anglo-French orbit. On August 26, he notified the secretary that the Polish ambassador to France had assured him that Japan sought American help in ending the war and that, given the warm relations between Warsaw and Tokyo, Japan was in all likelihood using the Poles as a conduit. An archfoe of the Soviets, Bullitt no doubt saw Japan as a bulwark against Russian expansion in the Far East, and, therefore, his plea for an Anglo-French-Japanese condominium must be viewed with some suspicion. On the other hand, many sources indicated that the announcement of the Nazi-Soviet Pact, combined with the disaster at Nomonhan, created a groundbreaking opportunity to approach Tokyo and Chungking. From Teheran, the American chargé reported the Japanese minister's opinion that the Nazi-Soviet Pact had gutted the military party, and, from Peking, the embassy counselor wired that Tokyo now probably sought an end to the war. Finally, on September 1, as German troops streamed across the Polish frontier, Eugene Dooman, the counselor at the American embassy in Tokyo, cabled Hull the startling news that Prime Minister Nobuyuki Abe disclosed to the press that his government would cooperate with foreign powers to end the China Incident.[3]

After two years of war, it also seemed that China was willing to explore a negotiated settlement. Just hours before Dooman sent his encouraging telegram, Bullitt informed the president that Chiang also favored a conference to end the fighting and a settlement that would roll Japan back to the position it occupied prior to its 1937 occupation of Tientsin. He did not, however, require Tokyo to withdraw completely from north China. Chiang's peace plan does not appear to have been a flight of fancy, for, several weeks earlier, the Chinese Foreign Ministry, the Waichiapoa, informed its London and Washington embassies that the time had come for Anglo-American mediation. In Berlin, meanwhile, the counselor of the Chinese embassy approached the Foreign Ministry on his own initiative with a plan for German mediation. He assured his German hosts that the ambassador shared his opinion, as did Chungking. As war clouds broke over Europe, Tokyo and Chungking signaled that they desired an end to the war. Washington, however, did not.[4]

The State Department, which would have had to support any initiative to end the conflict in China, still clung to the 1933 thesis of the Far Eastern Division (FE). Hornbeck, then division chief, argued that the flood tide of Japanese expansion in China would one day reach its height and then the ebb would naturally follow. In the meantime, he insisted that Japan stay bogged down in China until its national energies wasted away, its military leaders grew discredited, and world, and especially American, opinion turned against it. Now, at the end of August 1939, it seemed that much of Hornbeck's prophecy had come to pass. Tokyo's die-hard, pro-Axis elements and the military's more reckless adventurers were thoroughly discredited. The economy lay in shambles, and Japan, long absent from the League of Nations and increasingly loathed for its brutality in China, was a pariah state. However brilliant, Hornbeck had his share of faults, and among the more serious was his profound, almost pathological distrust of Japan. This suspicion clouded his reasoning and sapped his judgment, with the result that, when pro-German, expansionist influence began to recede, he could not grasp the meaning of events.[5]

On August 26, Hornbeck wrote that he agreed with Bullitt's analysis regarding the Polish ambassador's information. Tokyo was using Warsaw as a conduit. On all other counts, he noted, Bullitt was dead wrong. "The moment has not yet arrived," he wrote, "for any effort by the American Government, whether in association with the British and the French and/or other governments or by itself, to become involved in efforts 'for the termination of the war between China and Japan.'" Any compromise peace, he contended, would be forced on China and would constitute another Munich. Whether Chiang was willing to make peace in exchange for a return to the status quo ante of 1937 and the recognition of Manchukuo was irrelevant, for Hornbeck was not. Unlike Britain and France, he noted: "We are not immediately menaced as regards territory, either overseas or at home." Here was the nub, and for Hornbeck it remained so until the first news flashes from Pearl Harbor. Japan did not directly threaten the United States and would never go to war against America, so why make a compromise peace that entailed "a sacrificing of principles" and a "betrayal of China"? Paraphrasing a fiery note from the commander of the Asiatic Fleet, Admiral Harry Yarnell, Hornbeck told Hull that, rather than compromise, "every support should be given the Chinese government to enable it to continue the war." The United States and other interested Western governments, he insisted, "should reaffirm in positive terms that no settlement will be recognized that is not in consonance" with the Nine Power Treaty.[6]

Hornbeck's analysis reveals only a part of the reasoning behind the administration's decision to oppose a negotiated end to the war in China. Chiang had survived the loss of most of China's coastal cities, the fall of Nanking, and the defection of Wang Ching-wei, and still his forces continued to resist. China, in short, showed no sign of imminent collapse. The State Department, meanwhile, had already expanded the moral embargo and served Tokyo with the required notice before denouncing the 1911 Treaty of Commerce and Navigation. Congress had passed a second Vinson Act and dutifully approved initial appropriations for preclusive purchasing. The upcoming year promised unparalleled opportunities to flatten the Japanese economy between the hammer of American economic deterrence and the twin anvils of a naval arms race and continued war in China. Had Chungking hovered on the brink of collapse, or had Congress and the public showed no willingness to support administration initiatives, then the State Department may well have moved to salvage something from the wreckage. But the autumn of 1939 was not the time to allow Japan to escape its predicament.

London, and even Berlin, shared Washington's opposition to a Sino-Japanese peace. The British chiefs of staff, in particular, reasoned that, in the event of a negotiated settlement, Tokyo could simply redeploy its forces elsewhere. In Berlin, meanwhile, the Foreign Ministry declined to mediate an end to the war, in part because of the fear "that in the course of a long German-British-French war Japan might" support its old allies. Therefore, Berlin concluded, "it would be to our interests for Japan to continue to tie up her forces in China."[7]

If Washington missed an opportunity to extend good offices to end the fighting in China, it still had repeated opportunities to keep Japan out of the Axis and improve relations with Tokyo. The State Department's first opportunity to make a constructive approach came just after the August 23, 1939, announcement of the Nazi-Soviet Non-Aggression Pact. The pro-German cabinet of Kiichiro Hiranuma quickly collapsed, humiliated, especially as Berlin concluded the pact in the midst of Japan's harrowing defeat at the hands of the Red Army at Nomonhan. With support for Germany at its nadir, General Nobuyuki Abe, who succeeded Hiranuma, lost no time harrying Axis supporters from their posts. He quickly signaled to friend and foe alike his determination to improve relations with Washington when he named Admiral Kichisaburo Nomura, a former naval attaché in Washington, his new foreign minister. Widely praised by the Japanese press, Abe's selection of the pro-American Nomura was also interpreted by the American embassy as a positive sign. Abe's obvious moves to improve relations with London and Washington so discouraged German ambassador Eugene Ott that he informed his superiors that the Anglo-American faction had routed the pro-Axis forces in their battle for control of the government. Ott, however, was not without hope. He told Berlin that Germany should bide its time and approach Tokyo for a new German-Japanese alliance once Nomura's attempt to improve relations with America failed. As it turned out, Ott did not have long to wait.[8]

Anxious to conclude a new commercial treaty with the United States, Nomura soon began a series of informal talks with Joseph Grew, who had returned to Japan in October after a five-month absence. While in Washington, the ambassador sensed "an unmistakable hardening of the Administration's attitude toward Japan" as well as an almost casual disregard for the magnitude of a Japanese-American war. When Grew warned Roosevelt that an oil embargo would trigger a Japanese assault on the Dutch East Indies, his friend assured him: "We could easily intercept her fleet." Given the prevailing mind-set at home, the ambassador determined that on his return to Japan "some sort of major operation must be performed . . . if . . . relations were to be prevented from getting steadily worse."[9]

From the outset of his talks with Nomura, Grew stressed that improved relations required a clear indication that Japan was working to end attacks on American persons and property in China. He felt certain that Abe desperately wanted to improve relations with America, but he was also convinced that the prime minister had no idea where to begin. In order to facilitate negotiations, Grew advised Hull to clarify the steps that Japan must take in advance of formal talks and suggested that, if Abe's government fulfilled Washington's conditions, he "would recommend that some trade arrangement be completed as a manifestation of American desire to bring about an adjustment of relations." Even if negotiations did not immediately lead to a new agreement, the ambassador explained, "the psychological effect of such a gesture . . . would exert a powerful and salutary influence in Japan."[10]

Days later, in an effort to move the talks forward, Grew none too gently suggested that the time had come for Hull to balance idealism—in this case support for the Nine Power Treaty—with realism. "Japan is not going to respect the territorial and administrative integrity of China, now or in the future," he informed Hull, "[and] could be brought to do so only by complete defeat." America would pay a high price for upholding its principles, and, Grew observed, measures short of war would prove ineffective. Economic coercion could not save China, for no "American embargo, even if it covered all American exportation and importation to and from Japan, would . . . bring about such a debacle as would cause the Japanese to relinquish their program in China." Grew then delivered more unhappy news. "To await the hoped-for discrediting in Japan of the Japanese army and the Japanese military system," he told Hull, "is to await the millennium." Washington's "hypothesis," he continued, was "unfortunately but unquestionably a case of the wish being father to the thought." Social upheaval would not discredit the army and lead Japan back to the 1920s, he warned, but instead would "immediately lead to a ruthless military dictatorship."[11]

Grew assured Hull that he was not calling for a sacrifice of American principles, nor did he believe that the administration or the public should consider abandoning the Nine Power Treaty. He concluded, however, that Washington had to choose between two distinct policies. On the one hand, the administration could pursue a policy of "complete intransigence," refuse to negotiate a new commercial treaty, and impose an embargo "unless and until Japan reorientates [*sic*] her policy and actions, both as regards her commitments under the Nine Power Treaty . . . and her respect of American rights and interests in China." This policy, Grew assured Hull, "would set Japanese-American relations moving on a downward slope to a point from which it would be difficult to bring them back to normal for a long time to come." Grew's second, and preferred, option was to inform Tokyo that the United States refused to sacrifice its core principles but that, with "the presentation progressively of concrete evidence that American commercial, cultural and other rights and interests are not to be crowded out of China," it would "enter into negotiations for a new treaty of commerce and navigation."[12]

In a further bid for realism, Grew argued: "[Attacks on American rights, property, and citizens] can be stemmed, but unless we are prepared to fight for it, the Open Door, as we conceive it, is not going to be kept open. We have the choice of losing everything or of saving something from the wreckage, while opening the way to a potential building up of our relations with Japan." He closed his cable with a final summation—almost a plea—for a modus vivendi and the opening of negotiations for a new commercial treaty. "Shidehara diplomacy has existed," he told Hull, "[and] it can exist again."[13]

Shortly after Grew wrote his missive, Nomura presented him with a review of Tokyo's efforts to settle Washington's protests over Japanese treatment of American property and persons in China. He then dropped hints, but did not make any formal request, that he and Grew should begin talks aimed at concluding a new trade treaty. Given that Hull had not yet approved Grew's latest suggestions or reversed his earlier decision that Japan must initiate any negotiations for a new commercial agreement, the ambassador's hands were tied. At their next meeting, two weeks later, Nomura announced that, in an effort to maintain the Open Door, his government would open the Yangtze to traffic as far as Nanking within two months. The foreign minister then formally proposed that negotiations for a new commercial treaty begin as soon as possible, and, just two weeks later, he presented his government's official draft modus vivendi. Impressed by Tokyo's efforts, Grew wasted no time cabling Hull that the Abe cabinet "is endeavoring courageously, even with only gradual success, to fight against a recalcitrant Japanese Army." He warned that, if Washington failed to support the prime minister, it would be playing into the military's hands. Although Grew understood that Abe's promise to open the Yangtze was problematic at best, he noted accurately that, if the administration failed to even consider a modus vivendi, it would be "administering a rebuff which may well bring about the fall of the present Cabinet." Two days later, he wired that, according to one of his best Japanese contacts, Abe had ventured out well past the point of no return in announcing his intention to reopen the Yangtze. Failure to receive tangible American support, the contact warned, would bring Abe's government "under such a storm of protest in Japan that it could not survive." Hull, however, remained unmoved.[14]

When Ambassador Kensuke Horinouchi delivered Japan's formal request for a new trade treaty, the secretary neither read the document nor encouraged the ambassador to come by again on a similar errand. Instead, he told Horinouchi that negotiations for a new commercial treaty were in the hands of Grew and the Tokyo embassy. He did not tell the ambassador that he had already informed Grew that he opposed both a modus vivendi and a new commercial treaty, so Horinouchi left with no idea that the game was over. Soon after Hull's decision, a gleeful Ott reported: "America's attitude brought disappointment to the initially high hopes that were nourished by the calculated optimism of the government." Even "the pro-Anglo-Saxon press," he told Berlin, "is beginning to abandon the Cabinet." Two weeks later, Abe's tottering administration collapsed.[15]

Abe, Nomura, and Grew were all victims of the State Department's inescapable and terribly shortsighted logic. Just as there had been no reason to mediate an end to the fighting in China in September 1939, there was no reason to come to Abe's rescue four months later. Chinese resistance, Hornbeck and Hull reckoned, continued to sap Japan's strength, thereby protecting the West's vulnerable Asian colonies. American moral embargoes had also begun to weaken Japan's warmaking potential, and, with the 1911 Treaty of Commerce and Navigation about to lapse, Washington could at last apply even greater trade restrictions. For Hull and his associates, there was quite simply no urgent need to strike a deal with Japan—especially a deal that might weaken Chinese resolve, derail domestic and congressional support for further sanctions, and upend the next Vinson apple cart. Hull and the State Department had handed Japan's pro-Axis elements, as well as Berlin, a great victory, and they were about to hand them another.

Abe's successor, Admiral Mitsumasa Yonai, assumed office determined to continue his predecessor's policy of resisting the lure of the Axis and improving relations with Washington and London. Long opposed to closer ties with Germany, Yonai immediately showed his determination to resist Berlin by stacking his cabinet with pro-Anglo-American statesmen. Even before he named prominent Axis opponents to his government, Washington should have recognized that Providence, or at least Hirohito's senior advisers, had given the United States a second chance. When Hiranuma fell from power the previous summer, Eugene Dooman informed Hull that Yonai "had been fighting off the Army's demands for closer relations with the Rome-Berlin axis, and that fight had been largely successful." Shortly after Yonai's elevation to the prime ministership, Grew offered a no less flattering portrait of the admiral, describing him as a "dominating personality" who possessed the navy's complete confidence. While he predicted no "drastic revision of Japan's objectives and actions in China," Grew nonetheless confidently forecast a more moderate China policy.[16]

In Washington, meanwhile, Joseph Ballantine, the acting director of FE, confirmed Grew's analysis of Yonai. In particular, Ballantine found the admiral's consistent rebuffs of the Axis and his lack of association with Japanese ultranationalism to be positive indicators. Where Grew struck an upbeat, but still very realistic, tone, however, Ballantine remained pessimistic. He too expected no significant revision of Tokyo's China policy, and, while convinced that Yonai sought closer relations with Washington and London, he did not foresee "any dramatic changes for the better in Japanese-American relations." Hornbeck, meanwhile, informed Hull that Yonai was "not likely to achieve great success" or remain in power very long. He predicted that the admiral would fail to restrain the army's more radical elements and that any hope for substantive change in Japan's China policy was completely unwarranted.[17]

From the start, Yonai's efforts to improve relations with the West faltered. A week after he assumed office, the *Asama Maru* incident, in which a Royal Navy cruiser stopped, boarded, and searched a Japanese commercial ship and removed twenty-one Germans of military age, poisoned Anglo-Japanese relations. Five days later, with neither a new treaty nor a modus vivendi in sight, the 1911 Japanese-American Treaty of Commerce and Navigation expired. While Hull gave Grew ultimate authority for negotiating a new treaty, he still refused to set the specific terms that Japan must meet in order to secure a new accord, and the reason for this tactic is clear. By continuing to raise the bar throughout the life of the Yonai cabinet, he ensured that Grew's negotiations would never bear fruit. When Japan met one condition, Hull simply added another. By February, Japanese efforts to protect American rights and interests so impressed Grew that he felt fully justified in "the recommendations . . . made to Washington, namely that Japanese efforts toward conciliation are on an upward curve and should be encouraged, not rebuffed." Hull still remained unmoved. Japan still had not done enough to merit a new treaty, and for the secretary and Hornbeck it never could.[18]

Grew was no dreamer, nor was he focused solely on Japan and the Far East. He understood that eventually American liberal expansion and Japanese continentalism were destined for a showdown. For the ambassador, the crucial question, however, always revolved around timing and conditions. He recognized that Germany welcomed an early Japanese-American war, and he feared the effect that a Pacific war would have on American support for Great Britain. Grew favored a firm policy, but he understood that sanctions would likely backfire and push Japan into the waiting arms of the Axis or into the West's rich and exposed colonies. "Time," he argued, "will play into our hands if we allow nature to take its course unhindered by us." The ambassador was right, yet too few in Washington were willing to listen, and they became even less willing after the awful spring of 1940.[19]

Grew observed that France's defeat and England's humiliating retreat from the continent made the Japanese more bellicose and demanding and that "the German military machine and system and their brilliant successes have gone to the Japanese head like strong wine." To his mind, this made it all the more imperative that Washington immediately take positive steps to improve relations. In London, meanwhile, the fall of France, the prospect of a formal Japanese-German alliance, and the increasing likelihood of a Nazi invasion of the home islands prompted His Majesty's government to approach Washington and call for determined action to settle events in the Far East.[20]

On June 27, 1940, the British ambassador, Lord Lothian, handed Hull an aide-mémoire that spelled out London's position. On the one hand, Whitehall proposed a vigorous Anglo-American common front, including a complete trade embargo against Japan and/or a dispatch of elements of the American fleet to Singapore. If Washington proved unwilling to take these steps, London proposed an equally vigorous policy of Anglo-American appeasement. According to Lothian, the British ambassador to Japan, Sir Robert Craigie, believed "that if the United States and Great Britain were to agree upon it promptly an understanding might yet be reached with Japan." Specifically, Craigie and Whitehall envisioned Anglo-American assistance in ending the China Incident "on the basis of restoration of China's independence and integrity" and a Japanese guarantee that it would remain a neutral in the European War, not reexport goods to Germany and Italy, and respect the territorial integrity of French, Dutch, British, and American overseas possessions. In return, the United States and the Commonwealth would provide "Japan all financial and economic assistance and facilities in their power both now and during the postwar reconstruction period."[21]

Hull immediately told Lothian that neither increased sanctions nor dispatching the fleet to Singapore was a viable option. A day later, he rejected Whitehall's second proposal when he told Lothian, and the Australian ambassador, Richard Casey, that the State Department saw no signs that Japan was willing to pursue a diplomatic solution. Instead, he insisted that all evidence suggested that German victories in Europe had emboldened Tokyo to expand further and that Washington would never "offer to Japan concessions or assistance at the expense of or to the injury of a third or other powers." Finally, perhaps forgetting for the moment that he was addressing Lothian and Casey rather than Saito or Horinouchi, Hull reiterated his familiar principles for any Far Eastern settlement: respect for international law and treaty commitments, peaceful settlement of international differences, noninterference in other nations' internal affairs, and equality of commercial opportunity. Even with the German army encamped on the Channel, Hull clung to his principles.[22]

Seen from the secretary's perspective, London's peace plan freed Japan from the China quagmire every bit as much as it liberated China from Japanese oppression. Since 1933, the State Department saw clear advantages in Japan dashing its head against the rock of Chinese resistance, and nothing in the intervening years had changed this attitude. Moreover, any agreement with Japan would entail some surrender on Washington's part, and, while perfectly willing to countenance a strategic retreat, Hull was unwilling to permanently sacrifice American rights, interests, and principles for what he considered an illusory peace. He took great pains to point out to Lothian and Casey that thus far the democracies had acquiesced to Japanese depredations but that they had not given their assent. In the process of negotiating, however, especially now that the democracies were on the defensive, the West would have to agree to a certain impairment of their rights that, Hull stressed, "will become irrevocable."[23]

Rather than take rash, irrevocable action, Hull preferred to wait and allow American policy to evolve. For the secretary, containment had the singular virtue of avoiding a forced solution in the Pacific at a time when Britain, the US military, and the American public were unprepared for war. Likewise, his strategy averted conducting negotiations while on the defensive. As he well knew, Congress had recently authorized a third and then a fourth Vinson program and was on the eve of approving the Selective Service Act and authorizing the president to call up the reserves. The summer of 1940 was, therefore, no time to panic.[24]

The French defeat, not surprisingly, led others besides the British to press for a diplomatic solution to the crisis in the Far East. Since December, Ambassador Grew had urged Washington to work toward concluding a new trade agreement, and, after the fall of France, he was not without important supporters. In the spring of 1940, Francis Sayre, Roosevelt's high commissioner to the Philippines, arrived in Japan on the president's orders and held a series of confidential talks with Foreign Minister Arita. His conversations with Arita convinced Sayre that Japan sought an end to the war in China, and on May 16 he advised the president to tender American good offices. While his proposal went unheeded, Assistant Secretary of State Adolph Berle had concluded that Hull should follow Grew's advice, certain that "there is everything to be gained by the attempt and little to be lost." Walter Lippmann urged the administration to negotiate not out of fear but rather from the conviction that "there is no conflict between Japan and the United States which is not reconcilable by diplomacy." Lippmann implored the State Department to recognize this fact and "enter immediately into friendly conciliatory and candid negotiations with the Japanese for the avowed purpose of preserving the peace in the Pacific."[25]

Neither Grew, Berle, Lippmann, nor even London could move American policy in a more hopeful direction. As the summer wore on and the State Department continued to prevaricate, Grew's impatience increased not so much from any drift in policy as from the rigid insistence that Japanese-American talks orbit solely around bedrock American principles. The ambassador realized that insistence on these abstract principles effectively precluded improved relations with Tokyo, and, while Grew was not a man given to desperation, he had his fingers firmly on the Japanese national pulse, which, in July, was running a mile a minute. "Japan is at present teetering on the verge of a policy of rapprochement with the axis powers," he informed Hull on July 11, and the time available "to [take] some specific step or steps which would break the impasse in our mutual relations" was running out.[26]

Like Lothian, Grew understood that the tenor of the times required bold action, yet his desultory conversations were anything but daring. The talks, he told Hull, revolving as they did around American insistence on what Japan must do, had "become a vicious circle," and, in order to break the deadlock and stem the tide of pro-Axis sentiment, Washington must offer positive inducements. Specifically, Grew renewed his call for negotiating a new commercial treaty with Japan. While he admitted that, given German victories in Europe, the Japanese press and public would interpret Washington's willingness to negotiate as a sign of weakness, he informed the secretary that "such an announcement would unquestionably afford important support" to the anti-Axis camp and "might well turn the tide which according to present trends will in all probability (in the absence of counter inducements) flow toward the totalitarian camp with increasing momentum." Hull's confidence and determination remained unshaken, however, and, while there is no way of knowing whether a concerted effort on Washington's part could have kept Tokyo out of the Axis, Grew believed that it could have. "I still believe and always shall believe," the ambassador confided in his diary, "that such a step [negotiating a new commercial treaty] might have swung the issue." The State

Department's policy, he argued, provided Japan "no hope of helpful relations with the United States and no incentive to arrest the pro-Axis tide."[27]

If Grew's efforts to keep Japan out of the Axis stemmed from his genuine concern over what a formal Japanese-German combination might lead to, then how does one explain the corresponding inaction of others? For Hull, Hornbeck, Stimson, and no doubt many in the administration, the Tripartite Pact produced little dread. While not a member of the Axis in name, Japan had long been lumped together with Germany and Italy to form the "aggressor nations." Roosevelt's 1935 disarmament plan, for example, focused on Germany and Japan, and Harry Dexter White's 1939 study of strategic stockpiling placed Japan with Germany and Italy, as did the Joint Board's Rainbow war plans. Hull did not believe he was exaggerating when he told Lothian, just three days after Tokyo joined the Rome-Berlin Axis, that Germany, Italy, and Japan "have been during recent years on a basis of complete understanding and of mutual cooperation." The recent announcement of the Tripartite Alliance, he continued, "was part and parcel of the chain of related events." For Stimson, meanwhile, the alliance meant that Japan was "making a bad face at us."[28]

While Washington reacted to the formation of the Tripartite Pact with equanimity, the decision to join the Axis caused great concern in Tokyo. While cheered by the Japanese public, the alliance was far from universally popular. The navy, for example, reluctantly agreed to support the pact, and, when news broke of the accord, the venerable *Asahi shimbun* concluded that a Japanese-American clash was now inevitable. Under the terms of the pact, the signatories recognized one another's respective spheres and agreed to cooperate if "one of the three contracting powers is attacked by a Power at present not involved in the European War or in the Chinese-Japanese conflict." While the United States was the primary target, Tokyo hoped that the alliance would also deter Britain and the Soviet Union.[29]

For the administration then, Tokyo's decision to join the Axis represented an opportunity rather than a threat. By allying itself with Germany and Italy, Japan brought its faraway war against China closer to America. Before September 27, Japan was a bellicose nation that in China had bitten off more than it could chew. After September 27, it was a bellicose empire allied with a seemingly invincible Germany. In the weeks following the announcement of the Tripartite Pact, the American public responded to Japan's new status by supporting an increasingly firm containment policy. In early September, for example, Hull backed away from an iron and steel embargo in part out of concern over public opinion. The secretary wanted "to give the American people more time to change their minds," and, by the end of the month, 88 percent of Americans supported the scrap iron ban. As late as July, just over 10 percent of the country agreed that the United States should risk war to prevent a Japanese conquest of China, but almost 40 percent approved of such measures on September 30. Looking back in May 1941 at Washington's increasingly firm stand, the Dartmouth political scientist John W. Masland noted that, as the Tripartite Pact made Americans "identify Japan as a partner of Germany," they were willing to "accept a more decisive role in the Far East." The decision to join the Axis Alliance is critical, then, because, by rallying the public to support containment, it allowed the administration to expand and solidify various elements of its policy.[30]

This is not to say that the State Department maneuvered Japan into joining the Axis in order to shape public opinion. The Konoe cabinet did that all by itself. There were, however, no compelling reasons for the State Department to pursue the policies that either Grew or Lothian called for prior to September 27. Had either of these policies borne fruit, and had Japan remained out of the Axis or begun formal negotiations with Chiang, support for a firm containment policy would no doubt have suffered. Rearmament and selective service would have proceeded, but would the administration have reinforced Hawaii and the Philippines? Would the bulk of the Pacific Fleet have remained at Pearl Harbor? More importantly, having safely buried the lifeless body of the 1911 Treaty of Commerce and Navigation, and armed with the July 2 National Defense Act, could the State Department have imposed additional sanctions on Japan? Could it have secured greater aid for Chiang had Japan not joined Germany? In the three months after Japan joined the Axis, Washington doled out $150 million in loans and credits to China. Would this have been possible without the Tripartite Pact?[31]

Moreover, would the English peace plan or any of Grew's suggestions have fundamentally altered the strategic situation in the Far East? Hornbeck thought not. He mocked the idea "that a country which is bent upon and is engaged in a major program of predatory activity and a country which is opposed to and is menaced by that kind of activity can merely by the conclusion by their governments of an agreement become 'Friends.'" He doubted whether Japan would honor American principles or respect American property in Asia and scoffed at the notion "that two strokes of a pen on one piece of paper by two diplomats will transform a predatory nation overnight into a contented, peace-loving and peace-supporting power." Hull, Hornbeck, Stimson, and Morgenthau approached September convinced that Japan was a dangerous, predatory power that had to be stopped. Whether Tokyo formally tied itself to the European Axis was irrelevant in terms of diplomatic engagement as Washington had turned a deaf ear to repeated Japanese cabinets, Grew, and the British for years. Yet, as Stimson's diary made clear, a formal Japanese link to the European Axis galvanized congressional and public support for an increasingly firm administration policy.[32]

During the remainder of the autumn, the United States continued to rearm and extend aid to Chungking while leveling ever greater economic sanctions on Japan, and, as the autumn sun raced toward its winter nadir, it seemed that Japanese-American relations were following a similar path.

The Hull-Nomura Talks

In the early winter of 1941, a curious assortment of men gave Washington yet another chance to draw Japan back into the Anglo-American orbit. Father James M. Drought and Bishop James E. Walsh, of the Roman Catholic Maryknoll order, had traveled to Japan in the autumn of 1940. While in Japan on church business, the two clerics arranged audiences with leading Japanese officials, including Foreign Minister Matsuoka, at which time they revealed details of a plan to fundamentally restructure Japanese-American relations. The clerics envisioned Japan denouncing the Axis Pact in return for the division of the Pacific into Japanese and American spheres of influence, and, in a secret January 1941 meeting with Roosevelt and Hull, they reported that containment had succeeded and that the Konoe cabinet would abandon both the Axis Alliance and the war in China. Although the president clearly understood that the information relayed was incorrect, he encouraged them to remain in touch with their Japanese contacts and report their progress through Postmaster General Frank Walker.[33]

The same day that the president met with the two clergymen, Japan's new ambassador, Admiral Kichisaburo Nomura, left for the United States. A well-respected moderate and former foreign minister, Nomura had close ties to senior American naval officers. Despite his tenure as foreign minister, however, he was very much a novice in the world of diplomacy. And, perhaps because of his experience as foreign minister, he had resisted this latest assignment. In time, his reluctance proved well founded.[34]

Over the next four months, the two Catholic clerics, their administration contact, Frank Walker, their Japanese confederates, named the John Doe Associates by an unadmiring Hornbeck, and the reluctant ambassador worked to reorient Japanese-American relations. While Hull and the State Department encouraged dialogue with Nomura and the John Doe Associates, they did so not in an effort to reach an agreement with Tokyo. Rather, they first began talks in the winter of 1941 in the hope that even the faint possibility of a diplomatic breakthrough might convince the Konoe cabinet to forgo an attack on British and Dutch colonies. State Department officers also believed that Japanese-American dialogue might alarm the Germans, weaken the Axis, and provide valuable intelligence regarding Japanese plans and intentions. On three occasions, when it seemed as if the negotiations were dangerously close to *concluding successfully,* the State Department abruptly raised new points, and, when at long last the tide turned decisively in America's favor, Hull immediately ended the talks.[35]

The president's initial meeting with Nomura took place against a fearful backdrop for the United States. It appeared that England might not survive the German U-boat blockade unless Washington convoyed ships across the Atlantic. In Asia, meanwhile, the Navy Department, the British embassy, and Ambassador Grew all reported that Japan appeared ready to seize Malaya and Singapore should the opportunity arise. Against this setting, Hull advised the president not to appear too conciliatory or too ready to close the door to further exchanges. The secretary also explained that diplomacy offered little promise in that, since 1931, the Japanese government had fallen prey to military extremists who had carried out a virtually uninterrupted assault on China. He asserted that this latest Japanese proposal was part and parcel of a Japanese program designed to bring about American acquiescence to Japan's conquests. Now that Japan found itself mired in China, Hull cautioned, Tokyo wanted to free its forces "in order that [it] may be in better position than it is at this time to embark on conquest" to the south.[36]

During his meeting with Nomura, Roosevelt worked to encourage the ambassador's hopes for a diplomatic solution. While not appearing overly conciliatory, the president did suggest follow-up talks with Hull and other State Department officials in order to "review and reexamine the important phases of the relations between the two countries, at least during the past four or five years."[37]

From the outset of the talks, neither Hull nor principal members of FE had any desire to conclude a major new agreement with Japan. Hull had little faith in the original Drought-Walsh proposal, believing that it would only free Japan from China and prove counterproductive to Anglo-American fortunes. Neither his opinion nor those of his senior advisers changed when Walker delivered a general outline of purported Japanese terms for "a settlement of all outstanding Far Eastern questions" to Roosevelt on February 28. The draft stipulated Tokyo's willingness:

> (a) To invite the President of the United States personally to initiate mediation of the China-Japan conflict; (b) To nullify the Japanese partic-

> ipation in the Axis alliance, by a refusal to send any supplies to Germany and by the assumption of an obligation to keep the Germans out of the Far East, by military force if necessary; (c) To freeze the Pacific Nations in statu [*sic*] quo, by the recognition of autonomous governments comparable to the political units in the Americas; (d) To pledge, formally, their government against any further political or military aggression in the Far East; (e) By an economic-financial agreement to coordinate action that will assure continuance of amicable relations.[38]

State Department officers did not know that the latest Japanese terms did not come directly from the Konoe cabinet, so their opposition is very telling. Hornbeck, for example, maintained that Japan must first renounce the Axis Pact and cease its program of political and military aggression before the president could mediate an end to the Sino-Japanese War. He doubted whether an agreement was necessary given "that the Japanese leaders are not at this time prepared to embark immediately upon a new and extensive move southward" or whether any agreement with Tokyo "would be acceptable to the American people and be ratified by the United States Senate." Despite these reservations, Hornbeck and Hamilton urged Hull to continue talks in order to learn "all that we possibly can regarding their thoughts and their actual or possible intentions."[39]

On March 7, Walker informed Hull that major elements of the Japanese government, including the prime minister, the Privy Council, army and navy leaders, and the emperor, had agreed "to a conditional reversal of policy." He also warned that moderates faced assassination if word of the decision leaked out before substantive progress occurred. The postmaster's memorandum further noted that Nomura knew nothing of the specifics of the Japanese initiative and must continue to remain in the dark. "It would be imperiling," Walker warned, "as well as useless, to project, at this time, progressive diplomatic conversations with members of the Japanese Embassy." Imperiling or not, given his opposition to an agreement, Hull quickly sought out Nomura, despite the danger to Japanese moderates.[40]

Although the secretary did not reveal the specifics of the John Doe Associates' work, during a meeting in early March he told Nomura just enough to alert the ambassador that some informal discussions were afoot. Next, in a clear effort to weaken support for the Axis within Japanese ruling circles, he had Roosevelt emphasize to the ambassador that Japan's membership in the Axis Alliance "had upset the American people" and that steps had to be taken to remove American "suspicion and fear regarding Japan's intentions." Hull, meanwhile, stressed that Tokyo "must make it clear by words and acts of [its] serious intentions" to remove American suspicion and doubt. Neither the president nor Hull sought a major new diplomatic accord with Tokyo. Both men, however, were content to use the John Doe Associates and their talks with Nomura to weaken the Axis and contain Japanese expansion.[41]

Throughout March and early April, Walker and the Japanese embassy forwarded to Hull proposals in which Tokyo appeared ready to satisfy American concerns over the Axis and the war in China. In particular, the Japanese proposed to abandon Berlin and seek an American-brokered Sino-Japanese peace on terms that included no indemnities, respect for the Open Door, joint Sino-Japanese defense against communism, and a coalescing of the Wang and Chiang governments. Walker, who termed the draft "a proclamation of a revolution in Japanese 'ideology' and policy" and "proof of the complete success of American statesmanship," warned the State Department to quickly conclude the preliminary negotiations and publicly announce an "Agreement in Principle." Nomura's new military adviser, Colonel Hideo Iwakura, noted that, in order to make these concessions, Japan required some economic considerations, including greater ownership of Dutch East Indies rubber, tin, and oil resources. The Japanese also cautioned that an agreement must come quickly or the moderates "will lose control and a war in the Southwestern Pacific will be started." A quick agreement, however, remained the last thing that Hull and his associates wanted. Hull wanted only to buy more time for the Western military buildup, weaken the Axis Alliance, and learn more about Japanese intentions.[42]

Hornbeck's response to Japan's April 4 draft displayed both his reasonable objections to specific Japanese terms and his more general resistance to successful diplomatic engagement. On the one hand, he conceded that the administration had no reason to fear that "Matsuoka and/or the real authorities in Japan will make of Japan a German tool," but, when it appeared that Konoe might sacrifice the alliance, Hornbeck asked whether Washington should "accept and rely upon the promise made to us simultaneously with the breaking of a promise made to another country?" His argument made it impossible for Japan to persuade Washington that it would render the alliance inoperative, for even a public denunciation of the Tripartite Pact served only as further evidence of Japanese perfidy. Hornbeck also argued that Japan would "repudiate any and all promises both political and economic if, when and as she felt strong enough politically to do so." He further maintained that Japan's sole motive in the current talks was to produce "a super-colossal political bombshell" that "would not be to the advantage of this country and would not be to the advantage of Great Britain." As to the ongoing war in China, Hornbeck continued to stress that "it would not be in the interest of the United States or in the interest of Great Britain that the Japanese-Chinese hostilities be brought to an end by any process which leaves Japan's military undefeated (undiscredited) and intact." Peace in China, he maintained, would only allow Tokyo "to have her army, her navy, her merchant marine and her resources available for possible activities in some other direction (which might be against British interests or Dutch interests or even American interests—or Soviet interests)." After half a lifetime studying the Far East, Hornbeck saw the Japanese Empire as base, devious, and, ultimately, militarily impotent. And the majority of FE apparently agreed.[43]

FE maintained that the latest Japanese proposals regarding the Axis Pact did "not go beyond what Japanese leaders have affirmed publicly on many occasions" and that Tokyo's demand for Sino-Japanese defense against communism opened the door for a continued Japanese military presence in China. In the end, despite pleas for a quick announcement of an agreement in principle, preferably before Foreign Minister Yosuke Matsuoka's return from Europe, the division urged Hull not to conclude an agreement with the Japanese.[44]

Rather than strike a bargain with Tokyo, Hornbeck informed the secretary that no agreement could lead the moderates back into power. Rather than conciliate Tokyo, Hornbeck urged Hull to adopt a firm attitude and to leave the Japanese with the "impression that we are both prepared and expecting to oppose by force any further moves southward by them."[45]

FE bolstered Hornbeck's call for a get-tough policy when it advised against "a relaxation of effort on the part of the United States" and called instead for continued aid for China and "a firm policy with regard to Japan." Of great significance was the memo's contention that, given American defense needs, "additional restrictions may reasonably be imposed upon exports to Japan." The division warned against a full embargo unless the administration was prepared for war and forecast that, barring a German victory in Europe, Japan "may of its own accord turn away from association with Germany." Until that time, FE warned, only military "force coupled with a determination to employ that force if necessary" or "the offer of alternatives of sufficiently attractive economic or political value" could contain Japan. While FE recognized the second option, it refused to endorse it and instead advised Hull to continue "to confront Japan now with determination" while simultaneously showing an "honest and sympathetic consideration . . . to Japan's legitimate desires for changes in the economic *status quo*."[46]

Had Hull been willing to offer "honest and sympathetic consideration," perhaps negotiations would have produced a settlement, but neither Hull nor his closest advisers desired an accord with Tokyo. On April 14, Hornbeck prepared a lengthy, revised response to the Japanese April 9 draft that is notable for its inclusion of terms to settle the China Incident. At the same time that Hornbeck and FE *privately* encouraged Hull to recognize that Anglo-American security depended on continued Sino-Japanese hostilities, Hornbeck, Hamilton, and Ballantine urged the secretary to entice the Japanese with terms to settle the war on the mainland that Washington would never countenance. On April 15, most likely with the active cooperation of Hamilton and Ballantine, Hornbeck urged Hull to tell Nomura that the US government believed "that the proposals as a whole offer a starting point for discussion, and that we feel optimistic that on the basis of mutual good will our differences can be adjusted and reconciled."[47]

Two days later, Hornbeck reiterated to Hull his conviction that Japan would never abandon its policy of expansion by conquest no matter what agreements it made with the United States. He contended that Japan would renounce the use of force only after its leaders possessed "a real conviction of the futility of the effort which it is making" to subdue China. In other words, only after the last defeated and humiliated Japanese soldier evacuated China could the United States even think about diffusing American-Japanese tensions. Until that day came, Hornbeck argued, Japan would use an agreement as it traditionally had in order to further the "program of imperialistic expansion."[48]

Guided by the advice of Hornbeck and FE, Hull proceeded to string the negotiations along, and on April 16 he handed Nomura a statement of his Four Principles, which, he stressed, must form the basis of any Japanese-American accord. The Four Principles sought:

1. Respect for the territorial integrity and the sovereignty of each and all nations.
2. Support of the principle of non-interference in the internal affairs of other countries.
3. Support of the principle of equality, including equality of commercial opportunity.
4. Non-disturbance of the status quo in the Pacific except as the status quo may be altered by peaceful means.

The Four Principles quickly became, and remained until Pearl Harbor, a major issue in American-Japanese negotiations. Part of the reason for them taking on a life of their own stemmed from Nomura's decision, motivated by a genuine belief that these new American conditions would only complicate his mission, to withhold their existence from Tokyo. The April 16 Hull-

Nomura meeting is also important in that, when Nomura attempted to draw Hull out on the American reaction to the latest Japanese proposal, the secretary held back. Hull did not raise any clear objections to Japan's relation to the Axis or its proposals for concluding the China Incident. Rather, as he had done during the earlier Grew-Nomura talks, he saved these and other issues for later.[49]

In May, a second round of informal exploratory talks began, but in a very different environment. Whereas Anglo-American fortunes looked grim just four months earlier, by the spring of 1941 Britain's long-range prospects had significantly improved, thereby lessening the likelihood of a Japanese assault against Singapore. In March, Congress appropriated $7 billion for Lend-Lease, and the president declared the Red Sea no longer a combat zone, thus clearing the way for American merchant vessels to begin supplying British forces in the Middle East. The following month, Roosevelt reinforced the Atlantic Fleet and extended anti-Axis patrols deep into the Atlantic. During these crucial months, the State Department also became increasingly certain that, rather than strike across the Channel, Hitler would instead throw his forces against the Soviet Union. It recognized that, since a German invasion of the Soviet Union would guarantee England's safety for the foreseeable future, there was consequently little need to make a deal with Japan. With its desperate winter behind it, Whitehall now backed Washington's hard-line policy, certain that a continued display of Anglo-American-Dutch strength would break the Axis and bring peace to the Pacific. Any chance that desperation, or, more accurately, British desperation, would force Washington to reach an accord with Tokyo had vanished. Against this backdrop, Nomura once again tried to breathe life into the stone-cold talks.[50]

On May 12, after nearly a month of delay while officials waited for Matsuoka's return from Europe, the ambassador presented Tokyo's latest response to Washington's April 16 reply. Written largely by the foreign minister, the response reiterated Tokyo's commitment to military assistance for its Axis partners and insisted that Washington persuade Chiang to open peace talks and suspend aid if he failed to conclude a treaty based on Konoe's Three Principles. Nomura explained that the Konoe principles included a joint defense against communism, Chinese recognition of Manchukuo, and a Japanese pledge not to annex additional Chinese territory, respect the Open Door, and forgo indemnities. As expected, the American reaction ranged from jubilance to outright hostility.[51]

While Drought called Tokyo's new draft "a revolution in Japanese politics and a triumph of the liberal over the militaristic forces in Japan," Grew offered a far more temperate and balanced view. Although clearly concerned by Matsuoka's demands, he nonetheless emphasized that, in the event of a German-American war, senior statesmen "would make every effort to find an interpretation of article 3 which would release Japan from the [Tripartite Pact's] mutual assistance obligation" clause. He also informed Washington that the foreign minister's increasing bellicosity might be a reaction against growing internal dissent in response to his policies.[52]

Washington, however, was far less sanguine. Hull confided to Ambassador Lothian that, while there were reports indicating that Japan seemed to be divided between forces that favored the Axis and a group that "really wants to return the policy of Japan back to one of law and order and away from military conquest," he "had not taken any of these things seriously." Despite these assurances, on May 24 Foreign Secretary Halifax felt compelled to share with Hull concerns that Tokyo had dispatched Nomura simply to divide London and Washington. By all accounts, Hull was furious at the implication that Nomura had duped him. Hornbeck may have shared British fears, for, in one particularly accusatory memorandum, the State Department's top Asia expert argued: "[Japan] 'fooled' us and other countries with treaty pledges many times in the past. So much the worse for Japan. Thus far the 'foolings' have not been fatal to us. But let us not 'fool' *ourselves*. If we let ourselves be 'fooled' both by Japan and by ourselves: if we rely for our *security* (or any part of it) on Japanese pledges—there may come fatality."[53]

While Hull and Hornbeck continued to oppose an agreement, the possibility of a German-American naval clash demanded that talks continue. On May 14, Matsuoka bluntly told Grew that such an encounter would trigger a Japanese-American war. But did Matsuoka mean what he said, or was it all bluff and bluster? Did these statements accurately reflect the opinion of Konoe and the military? Hull's discussions with Nomura could help answer all these vital questions.[54]

Despite his opposition, then, Hull continued his talks with Nomura and pressed Grew for information on the extent of Axis influence within the Konoe cabinet. Grew told Hull that Matsuoka's public statements regarding the solidarity of the Axis were all bluff and that the foreign minister was only "painting the darkest picture of what will happen if the United States gets into a war with Germany."[55]

On May 27, in what Grew considered one of the most important dispatches he ever sent, he bluntly advised Hull that he had "no doubt that any Japanese Government which assumed a bilateral commitment of the nature under reference . . . would carry out the provisions of the settlement in good faith to the best of its ability." He conceded that army or navy opposition could derail the successful implementation of the accords, yet he maintained that the embassy had "good reason to believe that both the War and Navy Ministers in general terms favor a settlement along the general lines under discussion." If Hirohito sanctioned the agreement with an imperial rescript, Grew continued, "the provisions of the settlement would thereupon become the fixed policy of the country" and would be accepted by the Japanese people "with a profound sense of relief."[56]

In an effort to preempt the naysayers around Hull, Grew advised that, should Japan fail to live up to the agreement, the United States would be released from any commitment. He assured the secretary that, during this "process of implementation," Washington's position in the Far East would not suffer. "From the point of view of constructive statesmanship," Grew concluded, "I believe that our government should proceed with the negotiations with a view to entering the proposed commitments." Should Washington fail to grasp this opportunity, he warned, "the alternative might well be progressive deterioration of Japanese-American relations leading eventually to war." He recognized that containment had succeeded and that Washington had to reach an agreement, however imperfect and morally distasteful, with Konoe. Hull, however, had no intention of concluding an accord.[57]

On May 31, Ballantine handed Nomura the American reply to Japan's May 12 proposal. The note stressed that the right of self-defense alone would govern US policy regarding the European War and that Japan would not invoke the military assistance clause of the Axis Alliance should a German-American war erupt owing to an American act of self-defense. Having clearly stated the American position regarding the undeclared naval war in the Atlantic, FE deliberately left conditions for the settlement of the China Incident vague. The American draft stated that "the question of cooperative defense against communistic activities, including the stationing of Japanese troops in Chinese territory," remained open to further discussion. Since Hull repeatedly singled out the "cooperative defense" clause as one of the major stumbling blocks precluding an agreement, the May 31 draft did little to facilitate negotiations in that, if the draft proved acceptable, Nomura and Hull still faced protracted discussions regarding the stationing of Japanese troops in China. The American reply, however, would shed light on Japanese intentions. If Tokyo agreed to Washington's latest conditions regarding the Axis Alliance, it would indicate that Konoe favored neutrality despite Matsuoka's statements. This was the type of intelligence that Hamilton and Hornbeck told the secretary he might gain by holding talks. By the same token, the last thing that Hull, Hornbeck, and FE wanted was a draft agreement or an end to the war in China. By clearly delineating the American position on Japan's obligations to Berlin while remaining vague concerning

China, Hull could achieve all that he wanted without agreeing to any version of the draft proposal.[58]

On June 4, Iwakura and members of the embassy staff sat down with Ballantine and Hamilton to air their differences over the May 31 proposal. Kaname Wakasugi, the embassy counselor, took pains to clarify that the draft understanding was not intended "to enable Japan to drift away from the Tripartite Pact," while Iwakura maintained that, by ending the war in China, it would remove one of two sources of friction between Tokyo and Washington. As to the war in Europe, the two could only hope "that the proposed agreement will improve the atmosphere between" Japan and America so that "the two countries might be expected to collaborate toward . . . the restoration of world peace." Iwakura had essentially repeated the Grew-Nomura thesis: a Japanese-American accord would not resolve all outstanding issues, but it would reduce tensions and protect the Open Door.[59]

Despite continuing differences over China and the Axis Alliance, Iwakura left the meeting convinced that the two sides "had crossed the mountain and the valley which separated us and that only a ditch remained to be bridged." Just two days later, however, the colonel "was now forced to ask himself whether the valley and the mountain had been crossed as he had hoped." On June 6, Hull backpedaled yet again when he protested to Nomura about recent Japanese pledges of fidelity to the Axis. This complaint was more than just another example of the secretary's legendary carping. Instead, it was the latest maneuver in an ongoing campaign to bring about Foreign Minister Matsuoka's ouster. Hull knew that powerful Japanese civilian and military figures favored an agreement with Washington, so, if the secretary could convince Tokyo that Matsuoka stood between them and successful negotiations, perhaps the foreign minister might soon find himself out of work. If the cabinet dropped Matsuoka, Hull could still drag out the talks, and, with the fire-eating Matsuoka gone, the likelihood that a German-American clash would lead to war with Japan would diminish. While Grew and Nomura provided ample assurances that Matsuoka's influence was waning, in fairness to Hull, the foreign minister remained something of a wild card, and it was not outside the realm of possibility that Matsuoka could persuade a reluctant Konoe cabinet to declare war on the United States in the event that Germany and the United States went to war.[60]

Although it is impossible to know when Matsuoka's ouster became a goal of the negotiations, it is clear that a change took place sometime around May 14, just after the foreign minister's return from Europe. On that day, Hull sounded Nomura out regarding Matsuoka's intentions and authority, and, two days later, he told him that, if the two could settle their differences over

Japan's relation to the Axis and the stationing of troops in China, he saw "no reason . . . why we could not then proceed rapidly with consideration of the proposal as a whole." Two weeks later, however, he notified Nomura that Matsuoka's consistent statements "in regard to Japan's obligations under the Tripartite Alliance" were preventing the successful conclusion of their talks. Hull suggested "that it would be helpful if the Japanese Government could offer something by way of clarification" on its relation to the Axis, and, on June 2, he complained to Nomura that "in the light of the loud statements which Matsuoka and others were daily making . . . one was forced back to the inquiry of whether Japan really" wished to conclude an agreement.[61]

While Hull continued to undermine Matsuoka, the process of refining the competing Japanese and American proposals continued. On June 10, Hornbeck informed Hull that, to the best of his knowledge, "every officer of the Department who has been associated with or who has close knowledge of the progress of the conversations" opposed entering into an agreement with Japan. While it remains impossible to test this assertion, it was not far off the mark. Ballantine argued that the secret negotiations and the whole idea of presenting the Japanese military with a fait accompli was nonsense, and Eugene Dooman, Grew's chargé, confirmed that both Hornbeck and Ballantine opposed the embassy's efforts and that only one junior FE officer, Max Bishop, supported them.[62]

Still unaware that the American side had no intention of concluding an agreement, Nomura told Hull on June 15 that "he would like to come to an understanding with the Secretary as to what were the points in the Japanese proposal on which we were agreed and what were the points on which we differed." However reasonable the proposal, Hull refused to say just where the two sides differed and contended that Nomura's request would undoubtedly "give rise to misunderstanding on the part of the Japanese Government." He advised the ambassador instead to simply use his best judgment. It is impossible to know whether Nomura wanted to know whether Matsuoka had to go in order for Washington to conclude an agreement. Likewise, it is unclear what Hull meant when he told Nomura to use his best judgment. However, after Hull repeatedly informed the ambassador that Matsuoka loomed large in their failure to come to an accord, his meaning seems clear. In any event, after two and a half months of negotiating, Hull refused even to specify where the two sides differed. The talks were essentially dead. Five days later, Hull took his final shot at Matsuoka and then ended his negotiations with Nomura.[63]

"At a time when Nazi Germany had invaded some fifteen or twenty countries," Hull told Nomura on June 21, "the Japanese Minister for Foreign Affairs was declaring in effect that measures of resistance by countries not already actually invaded would call for action by Japan under the Tripartite Pact." The time had come, Hull continued, for "the Japanese Government [to] . . . decide either to assume control of those elements in the Japanese body politic which supported Nazi Germany . . . or to allow those elements to take over entire charge of Japan's policies." Hull then handed Nomura an oral statement noting that "accumulating evidence reaches this Government from sources all over the world . . . that some Japanese leaders in influential official positions are definitely committed to a course which calls for support of Nazi Germany." The statement contended that "recent public statements gratuitously made by spokesmen of the Japanese Government emphasizing Japan's commitments and intentions under the Tripartite Alliance exemplify an attitude which cannot be ignored." Given these circumstances, the statement read, "is it not illusory to expect that adoption of a proposal such as the one under consideration offers a basis for achieving substantial results along the desired lines?" Then, Hull passed judgment. "The Secretary of State has therefore reluctantly come to the conclusion," the oral statement declared, "that this Government must await some clearer indication than has yet been given that the Japanese Government as a whole desires to pursue courses of peace such as constitute the objectives of the proposed understanding."[64]

The reasons behind the decision to abruptly terminate negotiations are perfectly clear. Hull never intended for the talks to produce an agreement, especially one that the Chinese, English, and Hull's own experts opposed. Like American Far Eastern policy in general, the Hull-Nomura talks were inherently tied to events elsewhere, including the Japanese-Dutch economic negotiations and the European War. In the days immediately preceding the American decision to end the talks, events in the East Indies and Europe made it unnecessary to continue the charade. The State Department had carefully avoided taking any action on oil exports while the Dutch-Japanese economic discussions were under way in Batavia, confident that Japan, in turn, would take no provocative action against the Dutch during the Hull-Nomura talks. Had Hull abruptly ended his dialogue with Nomura while Japanese negotiators were in the East Indies, the United States would have forfeited a fair degree of subtle leverage, but Hull waited until after June 17, when the talks ended.

Events in Europe, however, proved even more significant in Hull's decision to suspend his dialogue with Nomura. The persistent rumors of a German invasion of the Soviet Union, which reached Washington throughout the winter and spring, had convinced Hull that the Nazi war machine would soon fall on Russia. On June 9, the secretary dispatched word to the American ambassador in Moscow that "reports received this weekend, principally from missions in Bucharest and Stockholm," indicate that Berlin "is making immediate preparations for an invasion of the Soviet Union to take place within a fortnight." Six days later, Churchill informed the president that all signs pointed to an imminent German attack on the Soviet Union. The implications of a Nazi-Soviet war were not lost on the State Department, and, just one day after the German invasion, FE concluded that Berlin's gamble made it less likely that Tokyo would strike south in the near future. Accordingly, Hamilton confidently told Hull that preventing "any Japanese attack upon British and Dutch possessions" may now "be realized without the conclusion of any agreement with Japan." Had the Nazis given the Soviets a midnight reprieve, perhaps Hull might have softened his tone, but Providence had nothing to offer either Moscow or Tokyo. His work done, and his health in decline from the ravages of tuberculosis and diabetes, Hull left Washington for West Virginia. Nomura and the John Doe Associates were left to the tender mercies of Hornbeck, Hamilton, and Ballantine, who, more than ever, believed that there was absolutely no need to placate Tokyo.[65]

Chapter 6

The Revolutionary Summer

> The German attack on Russia is likely to result in a postponement for at least a few months of any Japanese attack upon British and Dutch possessions.
>
> —Maxwell Hamilton (1941)

> The Russians have a mighty good army and they are making a terrific fight.
>
> —Harry Hopkins (1941)

In late July 1941, Japanese forces began their occupation of southern French Indochina. The previous September, when Tokyo sent troops into the northern half of the colony and joined the Axis, Washington responded with increased aid to China and embargoes on scrap iron and steel shipments. In September 1940, with the nation ill prepared for war and England's survival in doubt, America could not afford armed conflict in the Pacific. By July 1941, however, the world had changed a great deal, and, consequently, the Roosevelt administration's response was altogether different. Before the first Japanese soldier set foot in the south, Washington froze Tokyo's assets, and the British and Dutch Empires soon followed suit. The assets freeze, combined with preclusive purchasing and export control, meant that Japan faced a complete, almost worldwide trade embargo.[1] War in the Pacific was five months away.

Japan's latest round of expansion allowed the administration to pursue a policy that it had long considered but always held in abeyance. The question of whether to impose draconian economic sanctions had long divided both the government and the armed services, and, until the summer of 1941, concerns over congressional and public opinion, military preparedness, the immediate survival of Great Britain, and German threats to the Western Hemisphere kept Washington from ending all trade with Japan. Within a month of the German invasion of the Soviet Union, however, these concerns all but vanished.

On June 22, 1941, when Axis forces crossed the Soviet frontier along a two-thousand-mile front, the entire course of the war underwent a revolutionary change. Anglo-American strategic concerns immediately lessened in that, as long as Germany remained at war in the East, it could not invade England, take the Suez Canal, or occupy Spain, Portugal, and their Atlantic possessions. Just as the German invasion of the Soviet Union ensured England's survival, America's military buildup began to change Washington's strategic calculations in the Far East. The deployment of men and matériel to the Philippines, combined with similar British moves along the Malay-Singapore barrier, at last narrowed the gap between Japanese and Western strength in Asia. With the bulk of the Japanese military bogged down in a vast Chinese morass and the outcome of the war in Europe in doubt, American war planners argued that Japan would not take precipitous action in Asia.[2]

The Revolution Begins

Washington had anticipated a German assault on the Soviet Union for months, and some of the clearest signs of the coming war were decoded messages between Tokyo and its embassies abroad. Beginning in the winter of 1941, decrypted cables from Foreign Minister Matsuoka revealed signs of an impending German attack on the Soviet Union, and, by April, deciphered communications from Japan's ambassador to Berlin, General Hiroshi Oshima, revealed the impending strike in extraordinary detail.[3]

When war at last came to Russia, few American officials held out much hope for a Soviet victory. Both William Bullitt, Roosevelt's former ambassador to the Soviet Union, and Laurence Steinhardt, the current American envoy, expected a quick German victory, a grim assessment that the War Department shared. On July 9, a still glum Steinhardt confirmed forecasts of an early Russian defeat but noted that his British colleague, Ambassador Sir Stafford Cripps, rated the Red Army's chances as high.[4]

A month later, as the shock of the Nazi blitzkrieg receded, Steinhardt's prognosis took on faint notes of optimism. On August 5, he cabled Hull that the German drive in the north and center had ground to a halt, and, by the middle of the month, his earlier defeatism gave way to optimism and calls for Anglo-American aid. "I am persuaded that American and British support will have a very important bearing in strengthening [the Soviets'] morale," he told Hull on August 17, "and in shaping Stalin's policy, such as tending to discourage him from accepting overtures which Japan might make." By the end of the month, the once down-in-the-mouth ambassador began to sound downright upbeat, noting that, with winter just two months away, the German blitzkrieg had apparently failed. By this time, Washington-based officials also began to revise their earlier forecast of the Red Army's destruction. On September 10, Stimson informed Roosevelt that Stalin's forces would survive the autumn campaigning season and that German setbacks were affecting public opinion throughout Europe as well as morale at home. A few days later, Harry Hopkins, recently back from Moscow, conceded the severity of Russia's plight but reassured Stimson and Vice President Henry Wallace that "the Russians have a mighty good army and they are making a terrific fight."[5]

By late summer, even the War Department began to express guarded optimism regarding Russia's fate. Its "Brief Periodic Estimate of the World Situation," delivered to the president, Stimson, and Hull during the first week of September, forecast that the destruction of the Red Army before December 1 remained possible but not probable. Rather than a Nazi victory, analysts predicted that Germany would stay "immersed in the conflict with the USSR, either in terms of combat or of large-scale military reorganization."[6]

Despite their initial underestimation of Soviet chances, American officials immediately recognized the significance of June 22 for the security of Britain, the Middle East, the Atlantic, and the Western Hemisphere. For months, the prospect of a Nazi invasion of England and a successful German drive on the Suez Canal filled the administration with dread. The possibility of a Nazi occupation of Dakar in French West Africa, the Azores, and the Canary Islands, a move that would vastly increase U-boat attacks in the South Atlantic and could serve as a springboard for German landings in Brazil's Natal region, also haunted American officials. After June 22, however, these nightmare scenarios vanished. On July 7, even as it appeared that the Soviets could not long survive the Nazi assault, the head of the Army War Plans Division, General Leonard T. Gerow, informed Marshall that the German attack afforded Britain relief from both a cross-Channel invasion and any intensification of the Nazi drive in the Middle East. The general admitted that neither England nor the United States could take the offensive, but the almost complete absorption of Nazi forces in Russia more than offset the lack of any Anglo-American offensive punch. That Gerow could assure Marshall that "no German offensive operations are to be expected in any other theaters of war in the immediate future" and that "no German invasion of England or Iceland is probable during the remainder of 1941" was welcome news indeed.[7]

The Nazi invasion of the Soviet Union also promised to radically alter the strategic situation in the Far East. While smoke from German barrage guns still drifted across frontier battlefields, Maxwell Hamilton predicted that the invasion would "result in a postponement for at least a few months of any Japanese attack upon British and Dutch possessions." On June 23, Harold Ickes wrote the president: "There will never be so good a time to stop the shipment of oil to Japan as we now have." "[Japan] is so preoccupied with what is happening in Russia," Ickes argued, "that she won't venture a hostile move." On July 1, the Army War Plans Division concluded that Japan would most likely "avoid precipitate action and will continue her policy of avoiding war with Russia on the one hand and with the United States and Great Britain on the other." Three weeks later, General Gerow wrote his friend Colonel Dwight David Eisenhower, then serving as chief of staff of the Third Army, that he did not expect Japan to strike Russian forces in Siberia. Instead, he predicted that Tokyo would "sit tight in the north until Germany trims Russia."[8]

At the same time that the German attack on Russia freed England from the direct threat of invasion and promised to temporarily slow Japan's progress south, German reverses in the Atlantic guaranteed that the submarine blockade would not bring England to its knees. During the winter of 1940–1941, Admiral Erich Raeder, the chief of the German submarine fleet, convinced Hitler to extend the North Atlantic war zone as far west as Greenland, with staggering results. Between January and April 1941, monthly shipping losses doubled from 320,000 to over 650,000 tons, and Stimson, Secretary of the Navy Frank Knox, and Chief of Naval Operations Admiral Harold Stark, grew certain that America would soon have to undertake convoy duties. In early spring, a delegation of high-ranking British military officers confirmed this conclusion when they admitted that the Royal Navy could no longer protect the Atlantic convoy routes without American support.[9]

Washington responded to the growing crisis in the Atlantic with a host of measures designed to ensure the continued flow of American supplies to England. On April 10, the president and his most senior advisers agreed to extend the American-defined neutral zone, in which US Navy warships patrolled and shepherded eastbound British convoys, to the twenty-fifth meridian. The following month, Roosevelt authorized the transfer of one-quarter of the Pacific Fleet to the Atlantic, received congressional authority to requisition seized Axis and Danish vessels, and announced that the protection of Greenland had passed from Denmark to Washington. The cumulative effect of American action and British improvements in convoying proved decisive, and, by the end of May 1941, Raeder saw the writing on the wall.[10]

"The enemy has adopted a very flexible convoy system," Raeder informed Hitler, "combined with a far-reaching and excellent direction finding network." The following month, the Kriegsmarine suffered further setbacks when the Royal Navy captured U-110 and, with it, the German Enigma cipher. Raeder's woes now increased exponentially in that London could learn the whereabouts of German wolf packs and plot convoy routes accordingly. The effects of this intelligence coup changed the course of war in the Atlantic, and, during the remainder of 1941 alone, some three hundred Allied ships escaped destruction. Allied merchant losses fell from 350,000 tons in May to 60,000 tons in July, and, while German success temporarily rebounded and U-boats sent 210,000 tons to the bottom in September, for the remainder of 1941 the Kriegsmarine could not surpass the May figure, let alone the far higher April numbers.[11]

In North Africa, meanwhile, Britain's rout of the Italians during the winter of 1940–1941 brought little security to the region. Had the British merely blunted Marshal Rodolfo Graziani's advance, then perhaps Hitler would have left North Africa to the Italians, but, after Rome's crushing defeat, Berlin dispatched German reinforcements. On February 12, 1941, General Erwin Rommel, who led his panzers to victory in France the previous spring, landed in Tunisia, and within six weeks his Afrika Korps began a devastating assault that erased earlier British gains and pushed the exhausted Tommies back toward the Suez Canal. A British counterattack later that summer failed, and, with both sides spent and German reinforcements unavailable, a five-month stalemate descended on the vast North African desert.[12]

If news from North Africa was mixed, Allied governments could still take heart from events elsewhere in the region. The strategically vital Mediterranean island of Malta continued to fly the Union Jack and showed no signs of surrender, and in Iraq British forces crushed a pro-German coup and restored a modicum of order to Baghdad. The failed Iraqi coup also led Free French and British forces to attack Vichy outposts in Lebanon and Syria, where, after three weeks of bitter internecine fighting, the Allies emerged victorious. Finally, in September, Anglo-Soviet forces completed their division of Iran, thus ensuring an uninterrupted flow of Lend-Lease aid to southern Russia and the Middle East.[13]

In yet another critical theater, London and Washington succeeded in keeping Turkey out of the Axis. On the one hand, Ankara gladly accepted American Lend-Lease aid, while, on the other hand, it signed a ten-year friendship treaty with Germany. J. V. A. MacMurray, the veteran American diplomat and ambassador to Turkey, deserves the bulk of the credit for keeping Turkish-American relations on a sound basis by convincing Washington not to suspend assistance in the aftermath of the Ankara-Berlin entente. He informed Sumner Welles, who supported his farsighted policy: "[The] greatest service we can render . . . would be in helping to build up . . . Turkish confidence . . . and our Lend-Lease supplying of military materials should be made to serve primarily that purpose." Convinced that the Turks would "resist even at the cost of self-immolation any overt assault upon their national rights or dignity," MacMurray worked throughout the summer to quiet those in Washington who sought to punish Ankara "for certain imaginary 'discreditable' acts." He wrote directly to the president, describing the Turks as a "staunch and dependable" people who believed that only with a British victory could they continue "the task of national regeneration." By early autumn, the same foresight that MacMurray displayed in China fifteen years earlier paid off, and, as American-Japanese relations reached the flash point, the chance that Turkey might defect to the Axis, with all the disastrous implications that such a move held for the British defense of the Middle East, all but vanished.[14]

At the same time that American concern over the safety of the British Isles, the Middle East, and Turkey waned, so too did Washington's preoccupation with the Iberian Peninsula and control by Spain and Portugal over their Atlantic possessions. Germany's assault on the Soviet Union effectively precluded an attack on Spain and Portugal as well as an occupation of the Canary and Azores Islands. Fighting in the East, however, did not preclude a peaceful German occupation of Franco's Spain. William Langer and S. Everett Gleason's extraordinarily detailed account of the run-up to Pearl Harbor, *The Undeclared War, 1940–1941,* notes that the State Department's handling of the Franco regime in the months preceding Pearl Harbor was "one of the least impressive chapters in the history of American foreign relations." Not surprisingly, and with good reason, Hull found Franco's government repugnant, yet his quite understandable loathing of Spanish fascism did nothing to lessen the likelihood of Madrid joining the war on the Axis side. Like his colleague in Ankara, however, Ambassador Alexander Weddell pleaded, though with less success than MacMurray, for greater autonomy and freedom of action. In the end, because Germany's preoccupation with Russia precluded driving the British from North Africa, Madrid remained determined to wait on the sidelines.[15]

Franco's reluctance to commit his nation to the Axis cause as long as Britain remained a power in the Mediterranean proved of far greater importance in keeping Spain out of the war than did any positive policy on the part of the State Department. Hull, who had little love for either the fascists or the loyalists, had helped convince the president to block aid for the Republic during the Spanish Civil War, and his policy toward Franco illustrates the secretary's difficulty in dealing with governments that did not behave as he wished. Hull's Spanish policy is especially significant, however, in that it indicates that his idealism had limits. In late November 1941, as Japanese-American relations were reaching a crisis, and after months of ignoring the advice of the Madrid embassy, Hull offered Franco a new aid package designed to keep Spain neutral.[16]

In addition to easing American fears over the fate of England, the Middle East, Turkey, and the Iberian Peninsula, the German invasion of the Soviet Union also relieved Washington's concerns over the South Atlantic and the Western Hemisphere. On July 1, the War Plans Division concluded that, with the bulk of its military engaged in Russia, Germany could not directly threaten the Western Hemisphere.[17]

As the worldwide strategic situation swung in favor of the democracies, the growth of American, British, and Dutch power in Asia also promised to deter and, if need be, forcibly halt further Japanese expansion in Asia. Although far from complete, American reinforcement of the Philippines had begun to transform the islands from a liability into a forward projection of American military power. British and Dutch reinforcements, meanwhile, further bolstered Western confidence and prompted Air Chief Marshall Sir Robert Brooke-Popham, the British commander in chief in the Far East, to assure the Australian War Cabinet in February 1941 that Singapore could hold out against a Japanese assault for up to six months. For his part, Churchill believed that, should the Japanese attack Singapore, a move he considered highly improbable, the island fortress would resist for as long as one year. Dutch East Indies forces were also expected to offer stiff resistance and destroy their oil facilities if relief did not come in time.[18]

The growing confidence that buoyed coalition forces in the summer of 1941 is clearly evident in the final report of the American-British-Dutch (ABD) war planners, who had been carefully crafting coalition strategy in the Far East. The ABD 2 draft of August 1941 reaffirmed that Germany's defeat remained the coalition's primary objective and stipulated that the "Associated Powers" should maintain their defenses against a Japanese attack and continue to exert economic pressure against Tokyo. Should Japan take the offensive, the draft noted, the Philippines would probably take the first blow as "Japan would be taking great risks" in attacking either Malaysia or the Dutch Indies before first crushing the American air and naval bases in the region.[19]

Although the ABD war planners recognized that the Philippines would feel the full weight of the Japanese onslaught in the opening hours of the conflict, they concluded that, until Tokyo laid away extensive supplies in southern Indochina, simultaneous attacks south were impossible. Because Japan lacked adequate numbers of both warships and supply vessels, it simply could not "launch two simultaneous major attacks without great risks."[20]

Overall, then, the combined effect of the German invasion of the Soviet

Union and the Western military buildup in Asia provided Britain and the United States with an unprecedented opportunity to contain Japan. This is not to say that events in other theaters were unimportant, that Germany's defeat no longer remained the ultimate Anglo-American objective, or even that the ABD coalition felt strong enough to best Japan on land and at sea. Rather, it is to emphasize that, after June 22, both Roosevelt and Churchill recognized that, for the foreseeable future, Germany could not bring England to terms and that Japan would therefore wait before embarking on any new and extensive military moves in the Far East. Backed by its increasing military power and Germany's involvement on the Eastern Front, the ABD coalition's freedom of action reached its zenith. Japan, as it turned out, could not have chosen a less propitious moment to challenge the West.

But, on June 25, that is exactly what the Konoe cabinet and the military decided on when they adopted the "Measures for Advancing the Southern Policy," which approved the occupation of ports and airfields in southern Indochina. Since December, the army had called for bases in southern Indochina and Thailand, and by spring many in the navy, expecting an imminent British collapse, also endorsed the southern option.[21]

The Dutch decision to spurn Japanese demands for greater concessions in the East Indies and growing American economic sanctions no doubt influenced the Konoe cabinet to endorse further expansion. Had Batavia agreed to Tokyo's economic demands, or had Hull agreed to at least a substantive portion of the latest Japanese draft proposal, it is inconceivable that Tokyo would have expanded further. While junior officers under Nagano pushed the southern advance in hopes of triggering an early war before Anglo-American sanctions, rearmament, and deployment of forces to the Far East made victory impossible, the liaison conference did not approve the occupation in order to provoke war. Rather, the need to prepare for an advance against the British and Dutch and the illusory hope that further advances would somehow stimulate Chiang to talk peace determined the June 25 decision. What with Germany engaged in the East and Britain safe in the West, it stretches the bounds of credulity to believe that Japan would have proceeded to Saigon had Washington agreed to lend good offices or had Batavia agreed to greater exports.[22]

To the Banks of the Rubicon

By June 1941, American containment left Japan mired in China and unable or unwilling to join Germany and Italy in making war on either Britain or the Soviet Union. Despite these extraordinary successes, the Roosevelt administration moved away from containment in favor of the expansive goals of rollback. These changes led to war with Japan within six months. The decision to freeze Japanese assets and the ensuing trade embargo had little to do with the takeover of French Indochina, though the Japanese occupation certainly determined the timing of the embargo and helped the administration justify its policy.

Thanks to the extraordinary American cryptological breakthrough known as Magic, which allowed for the reading of secret Japanese diplomatic cables almost as soon as they were intercepted, senior civilian and military officials knew soon after the July 2 imperial conference that approved the measures for advancing the southern policy that Tokyo intended to strike south. Washington, however, did nothing to prevent the takeover. Grew advised the State Department that a private Anglo-American warning "might conceivably exert a deterrent effect" but warned that, "once an occupation [was] effected, Japanese prestige would render subsequent withdrawal out of the question." The ambassador also advised that the British commander in chief in the Far East had reached the same conclusion. What Grew did not know, though he may have suspected, is that both Washington and London were committed to an assets freeze and may well have welcomed the southern advance.[23]

Hornbeck and Hamilton concluded that the United States should take no action to stop Japan, and, on July 24, the State Department issued a press release that, in a clear bid to rally public opinion behind tougher sanctions, highlighted Japan's latest aggression. By occupying the remainder of Indochina, the release noted, "the Japanese Government is giving clear indication that it is determined to pursue an objective of expansion by force or threat of force." It also noted that Japan had no legitimate reasons for this latest move and warned: "The Government and people of this country fully realize that such developments bear directly upon the vital problem of our national security." This was not exactly the private warning that Grew had hoped for. Only after ignoring the ambassador's advice and publicly chastising Japan did the president meet Nomura and propose that Tokyo recall its forces in return for US good offices in neutralizing Indochina.[24]

The obvious, if unsettling, explanation for American inaction is that embargo proponents, in both the administration and the State Department, had no interest in preventing the occupation. No private admonition could have diverted Japan, but this was not known, and, therefore, Hull had to avoid acting on Grew's advice. Tokyo's move south certainly complicated the defense of ABD possessions, but it did not signal a new and ominous threat in that Japan could have struck Singapore, the Indies, and the Philippines from bases in northern Indochina. Military analysts concluded that the latest move south was "opportunistic in conception" and "strategically defensive in character . . . designed primarily to prevent British and American influence from shutting off supplies of rubber, tin and rice from Thailand and Indo China which are badly needed in Japan." Moreover, given the long-held belief that Japan would not fight the ABD coalition until Germany won the European War, continued Russian resistance reduced the chances that Tokyo would use its new forward bases to attack further south. But, if the occupation of southern Indochina was neither a necessary precondition nor an indication of further and immediate Japanese expansion, it was necessary for the administration to secure broad public and congressional support for an assets freeze. As the historians Garry Clifford and Robert Ferrell observed: "Roosevelt seemed inclined to rely on international events . . . to move public opinion." And, with the move south, Japan appeared the brazen aggressor that willingly chose to seize by force what the United States offered through diplomacy. Those who opposed a freeze of Japanese assets and the imposition of a general embargo now faced an uphill battle as embargo proponents could claim increasing public support and point out that the president offered Tokyo a way out that the militarists refused. In any event, for the embargo advocates, Japan's occupation, coming as it did just a month after the German assault on Russia, must have seemed like Providence.[25]

At the State Department, Maxwell Hamilton quickly emerged as a leading opponent of the assets freeze. Long opposed to greater sanctions, Hamilton penned a thoughtful and thorough analysis of the problem in April 1941 in which he noted that sanctions were inherently linked to wider strategic and military concerns. He concluded that, in the absence of both military power and a will to utilize force, sanctions would prove ineffective and probably counterproductive. Conversely, while recognizing that adequate military power would allow the United States to apply greater sanctions, he clearly thought that military and strategic considerations mandated caution, inasmuch as hostilities with Japan would undermine American support for the far more important war against Germany.[26]

Hamilton's opposition to greater sanctions grew throughout the spring as he became ever more certain that, rather than deter Japan, further sanctions would push Tokyo "to embark upon an all-out military effort in conjunction with Germany." In a not-too-subtle jab at Hornbeck and a somewhat more respectful reminder to Hull, he argued that the "conclusion that Japan is likely, in the present world situation, to acquiesce in measures which would deny Japan *essential* commodities would not seem to be well founded." But then he made observations he should never have put on paper.[27]

"There are those who believe," he noted, "that the Government of the

United States is making a mistake in not precipitating an immediate showdown with Japan, even though such action [would] lead to military involvement at this time with Japan. Those who hold that attitude may be correct in their view. No opinion is expressed on that." Hamilton reasoned, however, that such a policy would certainly run counter to the government's bedrock stance that, "until the position of Great Britain in Europe becomes stronger," the United States should "endeavor to avert such a development."[28]

The nub of Hamilton's argument against precipitating an early showdown with Japan was determined by his concern for the fate of Great Britain and its lone struggle against Nazi tyranny. By July 1941, however, London was no longer alone, Germany could not invade England, and the United States possessed enough military power to support an embargo. Against this backdrop, Hornbeck's call for tougher sanctions drew renewed strength and overwhelmed Hamilton's measured caution. Just days after the German invasion of the Soviet Union, Hornbeck wrote Thomas Lamont that Washington could increase sanctions with little risk. "Japan's bark," he told the influential Morgan banker, "is much bigger than Japan's potential bite." On the eve of the assets freeze, Hornbeck implored Welles to recognize that the time had come to at last cross the Rubicon. "Under existing circumstances," he argued, "it is altogether improbable that Japan would deliberately take action" that "would mean war between that country and this country." He conceded that there was a risk but concluded that, in light of "political . . . economic, social, psychological, and military facts and factors *in the existing world situation*," there was little cause to fear that Japan would "deliberately resort to measures of *war* against us."[29]

Hornbeck's arguments represented the thinking of the embargo advocates as a whole, and for this reason his analysis deserves greater attention. While Hornbeck did not delineate what "facts and factors" were important, it is not difficult to surmise his meaning. He believed that Japan would not strike south until it was certain that Germany would emerge triumphant, and, in the summer of 1941, it remained unclear whether the Wehrmacht could crush the Red Army. He also maintained that the ongoing China Incident and the deterrent power of the American military would slow Japan's march south. His call for greater sanctions no longer seemed as impractical and dangerous as it had a year before, and in the wake of the assets freeze Washington embraced an embargo, but not because of the trickery of a few midlevel bureaucrats, the president's many personal problems, Hull's poor health, or even the internal maneuverings of Stimson, Morgenthau, and Ickes. Rather, after years of gradually employing ever greater sanctions, only one step remained, and, in July 1941, this final step seemed safe and practical.[30]

The irresistible momentum toward freezing Japanese assets and imposing a complete trade embargo accelerated after the German invasion of the Soviet Union. On June 25, Hornbeck passed along to his superiors a memorandum prepared by Alger Hiss arguing that the German attack on Russia "increases the importance of our aid to China." Hiss contended that the Nazi onslaught would soon force Moscow to scale back its aid to Chungking, leaving America "the only power in a position to supply effective aid to China."[31]

Hiss urged his superiors to "immediately and substantially . . . assist China's morale by taking action adverse to Japan's economic situation." Many of the reasons for hesitating to enact greater restrictions on oil no longer existed, he argued, and others "appear to be less compelling today than they were before Germany's attack on Russia." Like many of his counterparts in the diplomatic corps and, for that matter, in the military, Hiss believed that Tokyo would in all probability await the outcome of the campaign in Russia before striking south, thus minimizing the risks associated with a freezing order. He concluded that the time had arrived for the State Department to implement the "draft directive, which was prepared some time ago, which provides for increased restrictions on the export of petroleum products to Japan," and to simultaneously freeze Japanese assets. Further delay, he argued in closing, would only make it more difficult to pursue these options and render their effect less decisive.[32]

Although Hiss did not spell out just what conditions had changed since May, it is not difficult to guess his meaning. Initially, Washington had been bound by Welles's October 1940 promise to the Dutch that the administration would not further restrict American oil exports to Japan during the Tokyo-Batavia trade talks. The negotiations concluded a week before Hiss sent his memo to Hornbeck with the withdrawal of the Japanese negotiators and Batavia's rejection of Tokyo's demands. Second, as Hiss no doubt knew, the Hull-Nomura talks had collapsed just four days earlier, and, with Congress considering several measures to limit American petroleum exports to Japan and the Eastern Seaboard up in arms over looming fuel shortages, the public would likely support greater restrictions as never before.[33]

As if to test Hiss's conclusions, Washington relentlessly increased its economic pressure on Japan in the weeks leading up to the embargo. On June 20, the president ordered an end to petroleum exports from the Atlantic coast, and, on July 11, Panama Canal authorities notified shippers that repairs required closing the canal or at the very least curtailing its use for the immediate future. This announcement was a charade, however, as repairs delayed only Japanese vessels.[34]

The decision to bar Japanese ships from the canal indicated a further step in the administration's effort to cut Japan off from foreign oil. For over a year, American-flagged tankers had been barred from the Japan trade, and, since January 1941, Stanvac and Shell claimed that they had no tankers available to ship larger-than-normal orders to Japan. In February, at Hornbeck's insistence and with Hull's approval, the Export Control Division added the metal drums that Japan typically used in shipping oil to the export control list. The following month, the secretary requested the US Maritime Commission to pressure American shippers operating foreign-flagged vessels to stop doing business with Japan. The combined program of denying Japan both tankers and metal shipping drums produced staggering results. George Walden, Stanvac's chairman, informed Hornbeck in April that a third of the oil that Tokyo contracted to purchase in the East Indies from his company and Royal Dutch Shell had not left the docks owing to inadequate shipping. By this time the State Department had already made the extraordinary decision to temporarily refuse any new export licenses for gasoline and crude oil to Japan. Restrictions on tankers, metal drums, and export licenses and the closing of the Panama Canal to Japanese traffic meant that, by the middle of July, prior to the assets freeze, the administration had succeeded in denying Japan much of the oil that it required to wage war on the Asian mainland. Containment had worked, but now, in July 1941, the Roosevelt administration abandoned this strategy in favor of rollback.[35]

Crossing the Rubicon

There is little debate among historians on either side of the Pacific that the July freezing order and subsequent Western trade embargoes led to war in the Pacific within six months. Neither the Mukden Incident, nor the Marco Polo Bridge Incident, nor the sinking of the *Panay,* nor the signing of the Tripartite Pact, nor even the clash between the Open Door and Japan's Monroe Doctrine for Asia led to war. In a story where gray rather than black and white dominates the landscape, this much is clear. Denied access to critical raw materials, and facing a physical collapse, Japan gambled all on a desperate war in which its worst fears were confirmed—humiliation, defeat, and foreign occupation. Later, it will be necessary to examine why the United States and its coalition partners persisted in applying sanctions to the bitter end. For now, however, it is enough simply to understand how the assets freeze became an embargo.

American scholars have long recognized that, on one level, the embargo evolved from a loose set of guidelines stemming from the July 26 freezing of

Japanese assets. The administration had planned to allow Japan to purchase as much oil below eighty octane as it had during 1935–1936, that is, before it began the war against China. Under guidelines written by Assistant Secretary of State Dean Acheson, Japan could purchase limited amounts of American cotton and oil through a barter exchange or by securing access to frozen funds in an amount equal to the value of the reduced American exports. A joint Treasury–Justice–State Department Foreign Funds Control Committee, however, consistently refused to release any of Japan's frozen assets, so the administration's trade restrictions evolved into a full-scale embargo. On this point, there is general agreement. Opinion diverges, however, on who is to blame for transforming additional sanctions into a complete trade embargo.[36]

Dean Acheson has become the patsy who bears responsibility for transforming the freeze into an embargo. Clearly, Truman's future secretary of state and eventual "wise" man was an embargo hawk who in the spring of 1941 went so far as to manipulate public opinion in order to pressure Hull into approving further restrictions. Other studies, somewhat more charitable to him, argue that, within the tangle of bureaucracies that carried out the latest restrictions, the intent of the new policy somehow became lost. Such arguments, however, tend to shortchange Acheson, who, along with other embargo proponents, understood what his superiors wanted.[37]

The July sanctions turned into an embargo because a complete cessation of trade was always the preferred option of the president and his inner circle. The embargo grew directly out of the administration's decision to adopt an open-ended policy designed to take advantage of favorable political, strategic, and diplomatic trends. Had Congress, the public, the military, or the British and the Dutch retreated in horror from an embargo, the assets freeze allowed for continued trade. Likewise, if Russia collapsed, or if Magic revealed an imminent Japanese attack, Washington could take steps to avoid war. If the freezing order, which the public widely interpreted as an embargo, caused little uproar at home, and if the global-strategic situation continued to swing in the Allies' favor, the loose July 26 guidelines could easily harden into an embargo. Finally, should Magic reveal that Tokyo contemplated a diplomatic rather than a military offensive, the administration would know that, for the time being, it could pursue an embargo with no risk of immediately triggering war in the Pacific.

The president approached the July embargoes with a distinct lack of clarity or, perhaps more charitably, an admirable sense of flexibility. There is ample evidence to suggest that Roosevelt opposed an embargo as late as July 1, and, just days before Magic intercepts revealed Tokyo's intention to move south, he cautioned Ickes not to impose further petroleum export restrictions just yet. "I think it will interest you to know," he wrote, "that the Japs are having a real drag-down and knock-out fight among themselves and have been for the past week—trying to decide which way they are going to jump." Within a week of learning Tokyo's plan to move south, however, Roosevelt indicated that the time for sweeping embargoes was at hand. Welles informed Halifax that, according to the president, "the United States would immediately impose various embargoes, both economic and financial," should Japan move south. Morgenthau, Stimson, and Ickes had long called for an embargo, and now the president appeared willing to join them. On July 18, he informed the cabinet "that if Japan went overboard, we would ship no more oil." Just six days later, however, a more cautious Roosevelt approved measures to freeze Japanese and Chinese assets while allowing continued petroleum sales.[38]

This decision must not be taken as an indication that the president had given up on plans for an embargo, for those present recognized that the assets freeze allowed for one if conditions turned favorable. "The President," Harold Ickes complained, "was still unwilling to draw the noose tight. He thought that it might be better to slip the noose around Japan's neck and give it a jerk now and then." Dean Acheson was a bit less picturesque, but every bit as accurate, when he claimed that Roosevelt kept the possibility of limited trade open so that the administration could "feel our way along . . . until we got a sense of Japanese reaction to it [the freezing order]." Assistant Secretary of the Treasury Daniel Bell, who attended the cabinet meeting in Morgenthau's absence, recorded that, while the president was prepared to allow Japan to continue importing American oil, this policy "might change any day and from there on we would refuse any and all licenses." Roosevelt's handling of the freeze paralleled that of Atlantic convoying—the great question dominating American policy for the European half of the world war. On this issue, as with the embargo, "the president watched and waited."[39]

Just as the president had signaled his tentative acceptance of sanctions to his cabinet, Hull, still recuperating at White Sulphur Springs, West Virginia, told Welles, Acheson, and Hamilton on July 17 that Washington should increase sanctions. The secretary, who clearly understood that few interim steps remained, surely realized that further sanctions would likely mean a complete trade embargo. Like Roosevelt, who also vacillated, Hull, despite waffling, favored cutting off oil. There is, moreover, compelling evidence suggesting Hull believed that the administration's initial response did not go far enough. On July 28, well before the freeze became a complete embargo, Mrs. Hull wrote Norman Davis that the Hulls were returning to Washington the following Monday. She explained that she dreaded returning, "particularly as the Jap situation was handled so badly in W." She noted: "Some one 'big W.'

would not listen to advice given over phone." Since Hull and Welles spoke regularly, Mrs. Hull's "big W" could only be Sumner Welles. But what advice did Welles reject, and what part of the "Jap situation" was bungled?[40]

Welles, far more than Hull, was always the true moderate on the embargo question. In the summer of 1940, when Morgenthau, Knox, and Stimson called for an immediate oil embargo, Welles persuaded the president to license only certain grades of aviation fuel, lubricants, and select grades of scrap metals and steel. With Hull recuperating in West Virginia, the undersecretary again proved the true moderate when he oversaw drafting the directives for implementing the freeze and export restrictions. During the drafting process, he turned down Acheson's plan to implement a general embargo until the State and Treasury Departments put in place the cumbersome machinery needed to coordinate release of Japanese funds and administer a silk-for-oil barter system.[41]

The key question remains, however, just what advice Welles refused to heed that forced the Hulls' return to Washington. During a July 18 cabinet meeting, Welles suggested freezing Japanese assets should Tokyo take the remainder of French Indochina. It is unclear when Hull learned of this suggestion, but, if this were "big W's" sin, it is unlikely that Hull would wait until after the freeze was announced to return home. It is far more likely that his suggestions reflected Hull's wishes. "Big W" could have failed to listen to Hull ten days later when he met Nomura and told the ambassador that the Treasury Department would release sufficient funds to allow Japanese merchant vessels marooned in port to buy food and fuel for the journey home. It is doubtful, however, that this small issue drew Hull back to Washington. Instead, he returned to the capital because his undersecretary had not pushed the embargo strongly enough.[42]

Feis, for example, recounts how the secretary burned the wires between White Sulphur Springs and Washington in an effort to get the Latin American republics to follow the new American hard line. Circumstantial evidence also indicates that, even before his return to the capital, Hull moved Welles in a more hawkish direction. On July 26, two days before the "big W" letter, Welles was willing to release funds for newly approved export licenses. Just five days later, however, the undersecretary submitted a memorandum to FDR, which the president approved, proposing to halt the processing of Japanese export licenses and revoking existing export licenses for oil.[43]

A second, equally remote possibility is that Hull objected to the revised Acheson drafts because they went too far toward an embargo. Yet, if this were the case, why did Hull not carefully review the new orders after his return on August 4? In other words, if he worried that Acheson or even Welles might have gone too far, why did he not check immediately to see whether oil was flowing to Japan? Hull's defenders have claimed that he was simply too busy after his return to Washington and "had neither the time nor the inclination to peer over Acheson's shoulder." Rather than being too busy, it is far more likely that he objected to Welles's decision to water down Acheson's orders. This seems probable, especially given that, within days of his return, Hull assured Stimson that he was through appeasing Japan and that only a resolute policy, including possible military force, could stop the Japanese march. The reasons, both for his comments to Stimson and for his inaction, are clear. He wanted an embargo. On August 2, immediately after the White House announced new restrictions that many believed amounted to an oil embargo, he took pains to both justify the action and downplay the resulting dangers. He told Welles that "nothing will stop [the Japanese] except force" and that Japan intended to proceed south "by evasion, deceit, and all manner of avowals of friendship and peace." Sounding more and more like Hornbeck, Hull chided his undersecretary that, while "there is naturally going to continue to be an element of risk and danger in our course, if it is sufficiently firm and extensive to checkmate them," Japan's leaders "would have stood for cutting off oil entirely as a deserved penalty for going into Indo-China." Clearly, he wanted an immediate embargo, and he as much as told "Big W" this on August 2.[44]

Hull's discussions with others besides Stimson and Welles reveal his determination to pursue a complete embargo. Just a week before the cabinet approved the freezing order, Hull told Hamilton that if Japan seized "military and naval bases in French Indochina . . . we should develop a broad program designed to deter Japan." In addition to new loans to China, he maintained that the administration "should work out concrete measures" that "would . . . impose economic, financial and other restrictions upon Japan." With existing embargoes covering virtually every major export except cotton and certain grades of oil, and with no new petroleum export licenses issued since March, what restrictions could Hull have meant other than a complete embargo? Moreover, when Hamilton, who clearly recognized that Hull was calling for an embargo, questioned whether "instituting a program of drastic economic and restrictive measures against Japan" would be in America's best interests, Hull dismissed his concerns.[45]

Hull also certainly knew the most likely course of action that the men who implemented the freeze, Dean Acheson, Joseph C. Green, the director of the State Department's Division of Controls, and his assistant, Charles W. Yost, would follow. These men were in fact responding to the perceived wishes of their superiors as well as acting on nearly identical motivations. It is impossible that Hull was unaware of Acheson's hawkish views or his efforts to manipulate public opinion to support more draconian sanctions or that Green, a ten-year veteran of the department, had earned a reputation for supporting a tougher stand against Japan than had most of his colleagues. Like Hull in particular, Green also shared the sting of criticism from powerful outsiders like the columnist Drew Pearson, who publicly castigated him for his supposedly tepid support for sanctions.[46]

Hull rushed back to Washington early, not to stop Welles from going too far, but because he believed Welles had not gone far enough. The secretary always withheld support for an oil embargo not because he was a true moderate who sought to ameliorate American-Japanese differences through diplomacy. Instead, domestic and geopolitical considerations made him moderate his policies. With Congress and the public clamoring for action and Britain safe from invasion, the summer of 1941 had become the best time to turn the final screw. While the specific issue that led Hull to return home early remains open to interpretation (it might have been prompted by FDR's decision to take Welles to Argentia Bay), the reason is obvious. Already favoring an embargo, the secretary made certain that the administration acted accordingly. There was no Acheson-Welles coup in Hull's absence. Nor can bureaucratic momentum explain the embargo. Hull was neither too ill nor too preoccupied to realize that an embargo was taking shape. Nor, given Hamilton's explicit warning, was he uninformed of the potential danger.

The ABD Embargo

It is clear that the administration approached the July embargo with no precise policy. Rather, as the president made clear to the cabinet, reactions at home and abroad would determine the ultimate scope of this latest round of sanctions. At home, congressional and public hostility could have convinced Roosevelt to allow limited trade with Japan. Likewise, had the armed services come out against the evolving embargo, the administration could have moderated its policy. Halfhearted British and Dutch support or a Russian collapse would also likely have produced a different policy in Washington.

The American press immediately interpreted the assets freeze as a complete embargo, and over the next several weeks it applauded the administration's strong stand. On August 1, the *Milwaukee Journal* declared: "We want no such halfway measures as were applied to Italy when economic sanctions were declared against Mussolini for moving into Ethiopia. Halfway measures are worse than none at all." The *Washington Post* proclaimed that "there need be no qualms about public opinion" inasmuch as a majority of Americans "advocate that steps should be taken now to keep Japan from becoming more powerful even at the risk of war."[47]

The *Post*'s analysis was correct as polls indicated strong public support for a complete embargo. A significant percentage also approved direct American action to defend Australia as well as Dutch and British Far Eastern possessions. Congress likewise supported the evolving embargo. As the historian Wayne S. Cole notes: "[The freeze] aroused very little criticism from congressmen. Even Burton K. Wheeler . . . the leading Democratic isolationist in the Senate, approved the decision."[48]

Despite public and congressional acquiescence, military opposition to an embargo could have forced the president to soften the latest round of sanctions. Neither branch of the armed forces, however, acted as a moderating force despite the embargo's apparent contradiction of existing military strategy, which placed priority on Europe rather than the Pacific. Even Admiral Harold Stark, who authored the November 1940 Plan Dog, which articulated the Europe-first strategy, did not question the wisdom of sanctions. Instead, he maintained that America should wage a defensive war in Asia and deny Japan vital raw materials.[49]

Indeed, while many high-ranking officials urged the administration to forgo a complete cessation of trade, neither branch of the armed services presented a united front on the embargo question. Military opinion, in short, remained divided, and only a clear consensus could have prevented the oil embargo. On July 19, Director of the Navy War Plans Division Admiral Richmond Kelly Turner warned that an oil embargo would likely result in an early Japanese invasion of the Dutch East Indies. Less than a week later, however, Acting Chief of Army Intelligence General Sherman Miles concluded that the time for "moral embargoes and export control" had passed. Japan, he told Marshall, "has now burst through these mild restraints imposed by the United States Government and is now embarked upon new aggression." With the latest move south, Miles argued, "the last reason for withholding effective sanctions against Japan has been brushed aside." Moreover, Miles reasoned, there seemed no reason to shy away from embargoes in that "effective economic sanctions against Japan imposed by us, today, would not, in the opinion of this Division, force Japan to take any steps in the way of aggressive action which she does not plan to take anyway, when a favorable opportunity arises, nor would they precipitate a declaration of war on us by Japan." He then gave a nod to Admiral Stark and Plan Dog: "Such action on our part need not and should not distract our attention from the main theater of operations. On the contrary, by adopting such a policy we will be able to conserve for Britain and for ourselves supplies which from the viewpoint of our national defense, are being worse than wasted when we place them in Japanese hands."[50]

As the freezing order gradually hardened into an embargo, neither service provided a compelling reason to modify policy. An August 16 memorandum that Miles wrote for Marshall, the president, and others called for increased sanctions and concluded: "Forceful diplomacy vis-à-vis Japan, including the application of ever increasing military and economic pressure on our part, offers the best chance of gaining time, the best possibility of preventing the spread of hostilities in the Pacific area and of the eventual disruption of the Tripartite Pact. The exercise of increasingly strong 'power diplomacy' by the United States is clearly indicated."[51]

During the crucial few weeks that the July freeze evolved into an embargo, the Red Army's continued survival acted as yet another green light for embargo advocates. By August, estimates from both military and civilian sources indicated that Germany would not knock the Soviets out of the war before winter, and, with the culmination of the Anglo-Soviet Alliance, Konoe had some reason to fear that any move south against the British would invite a Soviet response in the north. Accordingly, beginning in mid-July, Tokyo undertook a massive reinforcement of its forces in Manchuria, which at the time were outnumbered two to one by the Soviets. American analysts, meanwhile, concluded that continued Soviet resistance in Europe only lessened the likelihood that Japan would strike south.[52]

America's coalition partners likewise provided no reason to modify policy. Even before the president announced the American freeze, the British embassy assured the administration that London would immediately abrogate existing trade treaties and urge the empire and the dominions to do likewise. While a majority in both the British government and the British military favored a much less draconian response, in keeping with the long-held belief that sanctions should be used only to deter Japan and not as part of a policy of economic warfare, their concern with supporting Washington determined policy. Churchill's closest associates, Eden and the members of the War Cabinet, agreed that they must back the Roosevelt administration, and Churchill, in particular, had in fact become so concerned with securing American favor that for some time he often judged a policy's merits largely on the basis of how it might draw Washington closer to London. The Dutch East Indies authorities also played a crucial part in the evolving embargo. Under the terms of their latest trade agreement with Tokyo, Batavia had binding contracts to supply Japan with critical raw materials, including oil and bauxite. Just two days after Washington announced the freeze, however, the Dutch amended their agreement and announced a new license export policy for all Japan-bound goods, effectively nullifying the existing understanding.[53]

In the summer of 1941, Washington abandoned a measured and careful containment strategy in favor of policy that sought to break the Tripartite Pact and drive Japan from China. This dangerous shift was without precedent in the history of Japanese-American relations. A strange confluence of events—Germany's strategic blunder, Britain's new lease on life, the growing power of the ABD coalition and its gross underestimation of Japanese capabilities, the understandable sense of indignation and frustration that the American people felt toward Japan, and the willingness of the Chinese, British, and Dutch to pursue forceful actions—came together to produce catastrophe. After a generation of suspicion, rivalry, war scares, and war planning, the stage was set for a war more awful than anyone could imagine.

On both sides of the Pacific, men of goodwill spent the dying days of summer and the painfully short autumn that followed searching for a way to avoid disaster. Yet, if Washington saw no reason to prevent the freeze of Japanese assets from hardening into an embargo, neither would it see any reason to end the petroleum ban and reach a settlement with Japan.

Chapter 7
Rollback

> History will determine whether this opportunity was missed by an attempt to achieve at once our long-range objectives . . . at the expense of the immediately vital and essential interests of our country.
>
> —Ambassador Joseph Grew (1953)

> All I can conclude is that you all are determined to make us fight China until we are exhausted.
>
> —Hidenari Terasaki (October 1941)

During the summer of 1941, American containment succeeded beyond its creators' grandest hopes. Japan, still mired in China after four grueling years of war, faced a formidable and growing Western military buildup in Southeast Asia. Stiffening Soviet resistance in Europe, meanwhile, increased the Konoe cabinet's concerns over both Germany's future and the value of the Tripartite Pact. Worse still, the American-led trade embargo and worldwide preclusive-purchasing program cut Japan off from nearly all vital raw materials. Unbreakable Chinese resistance, growing Allied strength, grave concerns over the alliance with Germany, and a looming, catastrophic petroleum shortage forced the Japanese government and military to moderate Tokyo's decades-old policy of continental expansion.

During its final months in office, the Konoe administration undertook extraordinary diplomatic efforts to avoid war with the United States. By this time, however, the Roosevelt administration had fundamentally readjusted the Republic's policies and objectives for the Far East. As the military and diplomatic situation continued to swing in the democracies' favor worldwide and the coalition buildup closed the military gap in Asia and the Pacific, the architects of American Far Eastern policy abandoned their limited aim of containing Japanese expansion in favor of new and sweeping objectives. In the summer of 1941, it appeared within America's power to drive Japan from the Asian mainland, break the Axis Alliance, and bring about a complete restructuring of the Japanese national polity.

While the dangers inherent in this strategy were clear to many, both civilian and military leaders agreed that, in order to secure its aims both in Asia and in Europe, Washington should accept the possibility of armed conflict in 1941 rather than pursue a compromise that might succeed only in delaying a clash. Should Japan lash out in desperation in an effort to gain vital raw materials, policymakers concluded, it would not likely breach the Malay-Singapore barrier, take the Philippines, or capture the East Indies. These same men reckoned that, even in the worst-case scenario, should Japan defeat coalition forces on all fronts, it would inherit an empire where fires from a thousand burning oil wells blotted out the rays of the rising sun. Against this backdrop, the Konoe cabinet attempted for ten long weeks to avoid a ruinous war.

The American Mind-Set

Having allowed the freeze of Japanese assets to evolve into an embargo, the administration now had to decide whether to leave the embargo in place or lift it in return for specific Japanese concessions. By the summer of 1941, however, senior civilian and military leaders, including Hull, Hornbeck, Stimson, Miles, and Gerow, believed that diplomacy could neither eliminate the Japanese threat to Western interests nor remove the underlying issues that had created the current crisis in Japanese-American relations. Diplomacy, they reasoned, would likely prove counterproductive. In part, this mind-set stemmed from the unfortunate American penchant to view Tokyo's actions through a particularly unpleasant prism that distorted the last forty years of Japanese diplomacy. Seen from the American side, military expansion remained a basic part of the Japanese national fiber, one that no agreement could purge. Joseph Ballantine, assistant head of the Far Eastern Division (FE), saw the China Incident as the latest chapter in an ongoing Japanese commitment to dominate China that dated back to the last century. Secretary Hull and General Gerow, meanwhile, believed that Tokyo also sought to dominate Siberia in the north and French, British, and Dutch possessions in the south.[1]

Given the prevailing view that continental expansion was as basic a part of the Japanese national character as westward expansion had been for the United States, American officials simply could not believe the sincerity of Tokyo's peace overtures. Stimson interpreted pleas for a leaders' conference as yet "another example of Japanese duplicity" and "a pure blind" inasmuch as "[the Japanese] have already made up their minds to a policy of going south through Indo-China and Thailand." Early on in the delicate negotiations to avoid war, Hornbeck informed Hull that, "in its eagerness to achieve an agreement with us," Tokyo revealed its preeminent motive, "to weaken China, to drive a wedge between the United States and China and to strengthen Japan." When Japanese leaders requested secrecy in conducting negotiations, this too was suspect even though Japan lost two prime ministers to assassination during the 1930s. To Ballantine, the plea for secrecy was a ruse designed to "stamped[e] our government into making a snap decision." Hornbeck also warned Hull to be wary of "high pressure" tactics as well as Japanese efforts to use negotiations as a means "to size up . . . the national attitude, the national preparedness and the national capacity of this country." This relentless opposition clearly reinforced Hull's suspicion, especially given the increasing credence that the secretary gave to Hornbeck and Ballantine.[2]

In addition to doubting Japanese diplomatic sincerity, both military and civilian leaders also discounted Japanese military power and, therefore, the likelihood of a Japanese attack against British, Dutch, or American possessions. The military's "Brief Periodic Estimate of the World Situation," dated September 5, 1941, noted: "Japan, beset with uncertainties, will probably 'buy' time by entering into negotiations with the United States. A cabinet upset in Japan, a not unlikely event, will change the whole picture. The present cabinet, however, will initiate no additional aggression on the part of Japan until all diplomatic means of relieving pressure have been explored and exhausted." A month later, as the Konoe cabinet tottered on the brink of collapse, the president seemed convinced that Japan would not soon challenge the American-British-Dutch (ABD) coalition. "The Jap situation is definitely getting worse," he confided to Churchill on October 15. "However in spite of this you and I have two months of respite in the Far East."[3]

Even if the commander in chief and his best military strategists were wrong, senior officials concluded that America had little to fear from Japan. Harold Ickes, then serving as petroleum coordinator for national defense, concluded earlier that summer that the ABD coalition, plus Russia and China, "could probably crush [Japan] within a few months." Hornbeck declared that, as it considered its policy options, the administration must remember that "Japan is in a weakened and perilous position" and, consequently, "is in no position to attack, with expectation of success, either the Russians, the British and Dutch or the United States." America should not fear Japan, Hornbeck concluded. On the contrary: "Had we—which we have not—any desire to go to war with Japan, now would be the opportune moment."[4]

In the autumn of 1941, with the Soviet Union and China absorbing the full fury of the German and Japanese war machines, Hornbeck's argument was anything but extreme. Despite his many virtues, Stanley Hornbeck had a penchant for writing memoranda that, in their confidence or hysteria, bordered on the absurd. His September 2 memorandum, however, reflected a cold realism that many shared. The previous July, for example, General Miles informed Marshall that by the summer of 1942 Germany would have defeated the Soviet Union, secured effective control of North Africa, and reestablished its air and submarine campaign against the British Isles. Nazi forces could also mount a seaborne invasion of England, but they would more likely strike "through the Middle East toward the Indian Ocean, possibly in conjunction with a southward advance by Japan." Three months later, however, with Barbarossa faltering, the War Department's "Strategic Estimate" concluded: "Collaborative effort between Russia, Great Britain, China and the Netherlands East Indies . . . against Japan is now possible." The future, however, looked uncertain. "The developing situation in the Middle East," the study continued, "may cause the British to withdraw from the Far East all but the minimal security forces." If Red Army units west of the Urals were unable to stop the Germans, Moscow would likely "greatly reduce her maritime military forces to bolster her army in the European theater." The implications of a British-Soviet withdrawal from the Far East could well prove catastrophic in that it would undermine Western military deterrence and ease Japan's road to empire. While not endorsing Hornbeck's prediction, the military seemed to endorse his conclusions. The autumn of 1941 was the best time to go to war with Japan.[5]

The War Department's analysis of Japanese military strength and intentions also supported Hornbeck's conclusion that Japan would not likely strike south and challenge the coalition in the near future. Since the preceding spring, both army and navy analysts determined that Dutch forces would hold Java, the main island in the East Indies archipelago, until relief arrived. Anglo-Dutch authorities had also already assured Washington that they would destroy all oil facilities rather than allow Japanese forces to take them intact. The War Department had already concluded that Japan would not invade the East Indies before "first reducing the Philippines and Singapore," and either operation would stretch Japanese capabilities beyond their limit. Analysts concluded that a Japanese landing on the west coast of Malaya "is considered out of the question," while "the season for a landing on the east coast has passed." British forces could easily check a limited Japanese assault against Malaya and Singapore, and only in the event of "an all-out Japanese attempt, using 500–1000 aircraft, the bulk of the fleet and 10–20 divisions," would Japan emerge victorious. However, an all-out assault would strip Japan of the forces needed for use against the Philippines and the East Indies.[6]

Japan's chances for victory in the Philippines also appeared equally slim given that American air reinforcements had already transformed Washington's strategic doctrine in the Far East. In early February, Marshall all but apologized to General George Grunert, the commander of the Philippine Department, for equipping his flyers with the outdated P-40 pursuit plane. Having scotched plans to send the advanced B-17 bomber to China the previous spring, he relented late that summer to the Philippines dispatch, which prompted Douglas MacArthur to write that, with the new bombers, "no further major reinforcement will be necessary for accomplishment of defense mission." This overestimation of American strength proved disastrous. Marshall based his decision to dispatch the B-17s to the Philippines, in part, on reports that inflated British success in Europe. The supposed potential of the B-17, combined with the rising Philippine morale, convinced MacArthur that he would annihilate any Japanese invasion force, and his unfounded optimism soon spread to Washington.[7]

Several excellent studies, foremost among them John Dower's classic *War without Mercy,* argue that Western racial prejudice explains the kind of overconfidence that MacArthur and others displayed. Surely there was a good deal of individual and collective racial prejudice that no doubt warped American thinking. Yet, historically, the US military did not underestimate Japanese capabilities. For the better part of a generation, American military analysts saw little hope of defending the Philippines against a concerted Japanese invasion, and, as late as 1935, naval war games demonstrated that Japan would destroy the fleet long before it caught sight of Manila Bay. By the autumn of 1941, however, earlier pessimism had given way to a conviction that the Philippines could be defended and that Japan could never mount a simultaneous assault against the entire ABD coalition. Race cannot explain this evolution in American thinking. It can be explained only in reference to America's multifaceted containment strategy. Both the fleet and Philippine defenses were vastly more powerful than at any time previously. Japan, meanwhile, was bogged down in China and forced to strengthen its forces along the perilously long Soviet-Manchurian border while its oil reserves literally drained away.[8]

If race indeed was a determining factor in American thinking, then the military should historically have dismissed Japanese capabilities. Since it did not, the change in thinking can be explained in one of two ways. On the one hand, either American race prejudice, which led to a fatal underestimation of Japanese capabilities, was a relatively new phenomenon or one that grew tremendously in the years leading up to the Pacific War. Alternatively, a more convincing argument can be made that the growing power of the ABD coalition, combined with Western economic sanctions and Japanese preoccupation with both China and the Soviet Union, convinced both civilian and military officials to fatally underestimate Japanese strength. Either way, the results were the same. The United States misjudged the severity of the Japanese threat and in the process removed one possible motivation for an accord—the desire to avoid a military disaster.

The Konoe-Roosevelt Summit: A Most Unwelcome Idea

Washington may have had little reason to fear Tokyo and even less reason to negotiate an end to the embargo, but key Japanese leaders, including Konoe, Foreign Minister Teijiro Toyoda, and Emperor Hirohito, dreaded the prospect of waging a war that few thought the empire would survive, much less win. But, after July 26, pressure for a war against the ABD coalition increased dramatically. Faced with a near complete, worldwide trade embargo, Admiral Nagano told the emperor that Japan had "no choice but to come out fighting." Even the somewhat cooler heads at the Cabinet Planning Board recognized that the time for decision had arrived. Three days after Washington announced the freeze, the board concluded: "Up to the present we have tried to enhance the nation's strength by relying on Britain, the United States, and others to acquire resources but that is now becoming very difficult. Should present conditions continue, the Empire will shortly become impoverished and unable to hold its own. In other words the Empire stands at the point of no return and must make a final decision, immediately and without hesitation." In addition to growing internal pressure for war, Konoe also had to contend with German reverses in Russia that made a settlement with Washington more difficult. The prime minister predicted that September would prove the critical month on the Eastern Front and concluded that, if the summer passed without a Russian capitulation, then "Germany's future cannot be viewed with optimism." Konoe understood that a stalemate in Russia meant that "the American attitude will stiffen and she will no longer entertain the thought of talking with Japan." It is striking that American analysts reached the same conclusion. The War Department's October 1941 "Strategic Estimate" concluded that while German victories "jeopardized the future friendly relations between the United States and Japan . . . Russian strength stimulates Japanese efforts to conciliate."[9]

The conviction that Japan stood "at the point of no return" and that the United States would likely become increasingly intransigent soon produced extraordinary results. On August 4, Konoe approached War Minister Hideki Tojo and Navy Minister Koshiro Oikawa in order to secure their support for his plan to meet President Roosevelt, and within a day he had it. In the event that the summit failed, which Tojo thought likely, the war minister demanded that Konoe lead Japan to war. The following day, Chief of the Army General Staff Gen Sugiyama also approved the prime minister's plan, and two days later, having also secured the emperor's support, Konoe quickly cabled Nomura to "sound out the American side immediately" as to the possibility of a meeting with Roosevelt.[10]

Unfortunately for Konoe and Nomura, the most important member of the "American side" had just left Washington for his secret rendezvous with Winston Churchill at Placentia Bay, off the coast of Newfoundland. While Hull could have forwarded the Japanese proposal to the president, he did not, and, consequently, during the course of his meetings with Churchill, Roosevelt knew nothing of Japan's latest diplomatic efforts. This may have influenced him to agree to Churchill's plea to issue a stern warning to Tokyo that further Japanese expansion south could mean war with the United States. Hull and his closest aides rewrote the war warning so that the actual message, which the president handed to Nomura on Sunday August 17, bore little relation to what FDR had promised Churchill. Nonetheless, Hull's decision to withhold information, and Churchill's consistent demands for firm action, conditioned Roosevelt's response, both to the evolving embargo and to Konoe's proposed summit, on his return home. This mind-set proved especially critical given that none of the president's advisers supported a leaders' conference.[11]

Hull, for example, opposed the summit for familiar reasons and also some new ones. By the summer of 1941, the secretary found himself increasingly usurped by his own undersecretary as well as by the president's legion of unofficial foreign policy advisers. Insecure about his place in the foreign policy establishment, Hull was especially irked by what he saw as Welles's "efforts . . . [at] self-aggrandizement" as well as Roosevelt's decision to take Welles, rather than Hull, to Placentia Bay. Hull had not been asked to accompany the president, and there were certainly no guarantees that he would travel with Roosevelt to meet Konoe. Welles began his diplomatic career in Tokyo, and, with innumerable foreign policy problems to deal with, the president very likely might decide to leave Hull at home to solve them. But the secretary had nurtured American containment, prolonged negotiations, and kept hotheads like Morgenthau, Stimson, and Ickes in line long enough for American policy to succeed. Now everything very well could be wrecked if Roosevelt sat down with Konoe.[12]

Although fear of losing control over Far Eastern policy certainly underlay Hull's opposition to the summit, in the end his conviction that a meeting could produce only one of three wholly undesirable outcomes governed his actions. Hull thought that the president and Konoe could reach an understanding that would prove publicly unpopular and perhaps crippling to Chinese morale. Worse still, Roosevelt might secure a substantial Japanese withdrawal from China that would free Tokyo to strike north against the Soviets or south against the British and the Dutch. Alternatively, if the president and Konoe failed to reach an understanding, Tokyo's last hope would have vanished, and Japan would have to act. While action did not necessarily mean an assault on the ABD coalition, Hull saw no reason to force an early decision. For all these reasons, it should come as no surprise that Hull and the president's other advisers greeted Konoe's summit plan with outright hostility.

Stimson, for example, learned from Magic intercepts on August 9 that Konoe sought a meeting with Roosevelt. This news cast a pall over an otherwise pleasant day spent swimming and watching home movies of his Scottish vacation, for the secretary dismissed the summit as "merely a blind to try and keep us from taking definite action" rather than as an extraordinary attempt to avert war.[13]

With the president and Welles away at Placentia Bay and the distribution of Magic intercepts limited, the summit's opponents had a full week to prepare to sandbag Konoe's proposal. Grew urged Hull to maintain the highest level of secrecy in order to avoid leaks and not to reject the summit "without most prayerful consideration," but neither Grew nor Konoe nor the summit had a prayer. Hull had already rejected the plan.[14]

The day before Grew's telegram arrived, Hull informed Stimson and Knox that he had rejected Nomura's invitation for a Konoe-Roosevelt meeting "on the ground that, with the Japanese advancing into Indochina, any peace conference was absurd." By the time Nomura approached Roosevelt, Hull had prepared a reply for the president that "recited the Japanese provocative action" and ended with the watered-down warning that Roosevelt had promised Churchill. Hull's note, however, also contained a ray of hope.[15]

Rather than reject the proposed summit outright, the secretary elected to reopen his dialogue with Nomura. As was the case seven months earlier during the ill-fated discussions over the "John Doe" proposals, talks with Nomura could reveal a good deal about Japan's reaction to the ABD embargoes. Moreover, since the president had recently ordered the navy to shoot any German warships in the American security zone on sight, renewed conversations could once again provide clues regarding Tokyo's reaction to the evolving but undeclared German-American naval war. Moreover, Hull believed that as long as talks continued Tokyo would not likely attack the beleaguered

Soviets in the north or the ABD coalition in the south. Finally, Hull used the talks to sow seeds of dissension within the Axis. In early September, after the latest round of talks and Konoe's plea for a summit became public knowledge, he informed Hornbeck that within a few months Germany would "not be speaking to the Japanese." While the final Hull-Nomura talks served as a valuable intelligence conduit and perhaps bought time for the ABD coalition and the Soviets, Hull never wanted the talks to produce a Japanese-American accord, and in the weeks that followed Nomura's plea for a summit the secretary made certain that President Roosevelt and Prime Minister Konoe never met.[16]

On August 28, Nomura delivered Konoe's response to an earlier American request that Japan clarify its policies prior to the conference. Konoe noted that, while the earlier Hull-Nomura talks "were quite appropriate both in spirit and content," they no longer "[met] the need of the present situation which is developing swiftly and may produce unforeseen contingencies." Therefore, Konoe's note continued, it was "of urgent necessity that the two heads of the government should meet first to discuss . . . all important problems between Japan and America." In an accompanying communiqué, intended to clarify Japanese policy and advance the talks, Konoe pledged to withdraw all Japanese forces from Indochina following the conclusion of the China Incident and disavowed any intention to use the region as "a preparatory step for military advance into neighboring territories." Roosevelt expressed concern over some portions of the Japanese note as well as some pique over Japanese protests regarding American oil shipments to the Soviets via Vladivostok, but the meeting ended cordially, and the president reiterated his hope that he might have "three or four days with Prince Konoe" in Juneau.[17]

It is not clear exactly what the president had in mind when he told Nomura he wanted a few days with Konoe. Robert Dallek has argued that, like Hull, Roosevelt took a cautious approach to the proposed meeting and was concerned primarily with buying time. Dallek notes that, rather than being led by Hull, the president had his own deep reservations that a meeting "would produce only vague commitments which could be bent in almost any direction" and, thus, "followed the State Department's advice that [Hull] and Nomura resolve fundamental differences before" the summit. Other evidence, however, suggests that the president welcomed the opportunity to meet Konoe. Hull, for one, believed that FDR "would have relished a meeting with Konoe, and at first he was excited at the prospect."[18]

Based on Roosevelt's reaction, Nomura left the August 28 meeting confident that the summit would take place. Later, however, Hull raised the bar and informed him that prior to the leaders' conference he and the ambassador must reach "an agreement in principle" on Tokyo's relationship to the Axis, the stationing of Japanese troops in North China and Inner Mongolia, and nondiscrimination in international trade and commerce. The secretary also told Nomura that, while settlement of the China Incident remained perhaps the single most important issue to resolve, he would not consider extending American good offices until Japan first produced peace terms.[19]

Although Hull was a careful and patient man, his demand for a preliminary agreement in advance of the summit cannot be ascribed to innate caution. Rather, it can be explained only in reference to his clear opposition to the proposed Konoe-Roosevelt meeting. Eugene Dooman examined the secretary's opposition and concluded that his conditions were "deliberately designed to end any prospect of the meeting being held and thus eliminating any possibility of liquidating the deadlock between the two countries." Although Dooman did not elaborate, it is not difficult to follow his argument. Hull in effect required a Japanese-American agreement on the Tripartite Pact, the withdrawal of troops from China, and the application of nondiscrimination in international commerce *prior to the summit.* The Japanese pushed for a summit precisely because the Hull-Nomura talks failed to produce agreement on these issues. If Hull and Nomura could resolve these outstanding issues, there would be no need for the Roosevelt-Konoe meeting. Hull, however, never allowed the two sides to reach an agreement; therefore, Roosevelt and Konoe never met. Hull made sure of that.[20]

Dooman also contends that, in addition to setting impossible prerequisites for the summit, Hull and his intimates deliberately set out to derail the talks. Dooman explained that on September 6, after an imperial conference determined that Japan would go to war if negotiations failed, Konoe took the extraordinary step of arranging a secret meeting with Grew and Dooman at Baron Tokugawa's villa. Perhaps influenced by Hirohito's clear opposition to war with America, he held little back and emphasized that what he was about to tell them was known by no one else in the cabinet, including Toyoda, because "the foreign office staff abounded with Axis sympathizers." Dooman maintains that, in "complete disregard of Mr. Grew's stipulation that the knowledge of the contents of his report be confined exclusively to the President and the Secretary of State, Mr. Hull lost no time in calling the Japanese ambassador." This was the second time that Hull contacted Nomura (the first being in early 1941 during talks with the "John Doe Associates") about parallel negotiations after explicit warnings from Grew not to do so.[21]

Until his death, Dooman remained convinced that a Konoe-Roosevelt summit could have prevented war. During their secret meeting at Baron

Tokugawa's villa, Konoe explained that he would bring two generals and two admirals with him in order to assure the president of military support for the agreement. At the end of the meeting, Konoe also took Dooman aside and asked whether he could share in total confidence certain facts that not even Grew could be told. After some hesitation, Dooman agreed, and Konoe informed him that Hirohito had approved a plan whereby, once a deal had been struck, the prime minister would "report by radio directly to the Emperor and request that his majesty order the withdrawal of our troops from China." Konoe explained that Hirohito could not become "involved before a definite agreement has been reached" but that he was "ready to take a decisive step."[22]

It is impossible to confirm Dooman's and Grew's contention that a summit could have prevented war in the Pacific, and, indeed, a substantial body of work contends that a Konoe-Roosevelt summit would have changed nothing. Robert J. C. Butow, for example, notes in his 1961 *Tojo and the Coming of the War* that military and Foreign Ministry opposition to Hull's Four Principles would in all likelihood have doomed a meeting. He fails to note that the emperor's approval of a Japanese-American accord upholding the Four Principles would have rendered both Foreign Ministry and military opposition mute. His argument that ultranationalist opposition made a successful summit impossible, however, is far more compelling. He contends that the extreme secrecy that surrounded the proposed summit, including Konoe's clandestine talks with Grew and Dooman, indicates the strength of the opposition that Konoe faced. In his 1987 *The Origins of the Second World War in Asia and the Pacific,* Akira Iriye also maintains that the summit had no prospect of success. Specifically, he blames both Washington and Tokyo for failing to modify their foreign policy objectives. Waldo Heinrichs's 1988 *Threshold of War* likewise argues that a leaders' conference would have failed. He overlooks, however, the military's commitment to the Konoe peace plan while overemphasizing Konoe's many personal and political shortcomings. While Heinrichs raises sound points, Hirohito's backing, which Konoe no doubt received during his August 4 meeting with the emperor, rendered tepid military support and the prime minister's own personal failings relatively unimportant.[23]

In 2000, Herbert P. Bix's Pulitzer Prize–winning *Hirohito and the Making of Modern Japan* crystallized a generation of arguments supporting the "failed summit" thesis. While recognizing that Konoe was burdened with halfhearted support and questionable character, Bix focused on Japan's unwillingness to modify its ambitions in Asia, or what he termed "Konoe's set of stale positions." While Bix's characterizations are correct, his conclusion is not. A man of dubious character accompanied by sullen military men might very well have concluded a successful summit had the Americans proved willing. But no matter the quality of Konoe's product—and much of it was indeed shopworn—the Americans were not in a buying mood.[24]

While the majority of historians discount the possibility of a successful summit, others, on both sides of the Pacific, compellingly argue that a meeting could have produced an agreement. Shigeharu Matsumoto, a noted Japanese scholar-journalist, observed in 1969 that the army and navy supported Konoe and that the prime minister "would not have minded watering down the Tripartite Pact and withdrawing troops from China." Takeo Iguchi, whose father was stationed at the Japanese embassy in Washington and who lived in the United States at the time of these delicate negotiations, supports Matsumoto. Iguchi maintains that Tojo supported the summit and that Konoe made Grew aware of this shortly after his resignation. Jun Tsunoda demonstrates that, despite Konoe's failings, the prime minister had committed himself to diplomacy and that, along with Foreign Minister Toyoda, he had secured the necessary support, from both the high command and the throne, to ensure the summit's success. More recently, Seishiro Sugihara's critical study of Japanese foreign policymaking during the Pacific War, *Between Incompetence and Culpability,* makes a compelling case for a successful conference and lays the blame for the failed talks squarely on American shoulders.[25]

On the American side, the historians Hilary Conroy and Norman Graebner persuasively argue in their contributions to the 1990 collection *Pearl Harbor Reexamined* that Washington should have pursued direct talks with Konoe. Conroy stresses that Konoe's decision to send Admiral Nomura to the United States, his decision to sack Matsuoka in July 1941, and his selection of the moderate Admiral Teijiro Toyoda as foreign minister clearly indicated the prime minister's sincerity. Graebner, meanwhile, convincingly argues that, while Japanese terms remained difficult to countenance in September, under the cumulative effects of the Western embargoes Konoe would have settled for less by October, thus increasing the likelihood of a successful summit. Graebner's argument is especially compelling when considered alongside Scott D. Sagan's 1988 "Origins of the Pacific War." Sagan notes that, at the September 6 imperial conference, the military demanded that troops must remain in China, but, if Graebner is correct, then by October, with the emperor's backing, the generals may well have settled for far less.[26]

A closer look at Konoe's preparations in advance of the summit confirms that the prime minister had indeed laid the groundwork for a successful meeting. US military analysts, for example, observed: "The chief obstacle is that even if a conference were convened by the two governments there could be no guarantee of the results of such a conference unless the Japanese Army and Navy were directly represented." "Unless such representation is obtained," they concluded, "a conference at this time would be without lasting results." As early as August 5, however, Konoe had the approval of both the navy and the war ministers, and Hull knew from Grew's cables that "the Premier would be accompanied by the Vice Chiefs of Staff of the Army and Navy and other high ranking officers of the armed services who are in accord with his aims."[27]

Even some high-ranking members of the Japanese armed forces who did not necessarily share his aims believed that Konoe had a better than even chance of staving off war. The Army War Guidance Office, for example, predicted that summit talks "would probably not break down and a negotiated settlement would be reached based on a temporary compromise settlement." Akiho Ishii, of the Army Ministry's Military Affairs Section, also predicted that the talks would succeed with the emperor's expected intervention.[28]

It is equally impossible to confirm Dooman's second assertion—that Hull worked to wreck the leaders' summit. It is, however, surprisingly easy to trace a pattern indicating that, if he did not try to spoil the talks, the secretary did deliberately leak information. Once Hull learned of the proposed summit, for example, he violated Grew's plea for secrecy. On August 19, 1941, Grew cabled a carefully worded appeal in support of the leaders' conference. At the outset, he noted: "If the proposal should become prematurely known . . . it would in all probability lead to further attempted assassinations." For this reason, the ambassador noted, his information was intended only for Hull and Welles. Despite this admonition and the reasons underlying it, Hull showed Hornbeck the complete contents of the message, and within days American newspapers featured coverage of the impending Japanese-American summit. On August 28, Hull went a step further and publicly announced that Nomura had just delivered a message from Konoe to the president, and, while Tokyo temporarily suppressed publication of the reports in Japan, it could not do so indefinitely. After this fiasco, Magic confirmed what Grew had already told Hull. "There is much danger," Nomura's government warned him, "that the project will fail if information is allowed to leak out before a settlement is reached." By this time, Tokyo began to suspect that less than sincere motives drove American policy and that Washington may have wanted the information leaked. "It is quite possible," Tokyo cabled, "that the United States proposed that the announcement be made to estrange Japan from Germany and Italy."[29]

Despite Grew's warnings and his own reading of Magic, Hull continued to leak information about the ongoing talks. On September 4, he provided the Chinese Ambassador, Hu Shih, with "the chief points" contained in both the recent conversations and memoranda associated with the Japanese-American conversations. While Hull may have been trying to allay Chinese fears of an American betrayal, Chungking clearly opposed any deal to lift the embargo, so, whatever the information, it probably did not remain secret for long. The Chinese government's reputation for secrecy was such that it once prompted a member of the British Foreign Office to observe: "Anything of a confidential nature, if communicated to the Chinese Government, would reach the Japanese shortly afterwards." Hull should have known this. But, then again, he probably did. In any event, Grew tried to assure the Japanese Foreign Office that no American officials had leaked information and that newspaper reports regarding the proposed summit were based only on guesswork. His explanation, while honest, was in all likelihood not entirely correct. The journalist and author Wilfrid Fleisher informed Terasaki that the president had told him of Konoe's proposed summit. Even if this is incorrect, with Hull routinely informing the conference's most avowed enemies of critical information, any number of officials, both American and Chinese, could have leaked sensitive intelligence, so the Japanese Foreign Office remained convinced that only official American involvement could explain the detailed nature of certain press reports.[30]

In addition to persuading the president not to meet Konoe, setting impossibly high standards for the "preliminary agreement," and leaking news of the summit, Hull also did nothing to bolster the position of Japanese moderates or encourage the formation of pro-American opinion in Japan. In fact, for no apparent reason, he did the opposite. For example, as part of an American operation to strengthen the Russian war effort, Washington shipped oil to the Soviets via Vladivostok. American tankers had to pass literally within sight of Japanese shores, however, and, as the United States had already shut off the flow of oil to Japan, these fully loaded tankers had something short of a steadying effect on Japanese public opinion. Nomura first raised the issue with Hull on August 23, and within a week the Foreign Ministry formally requested Grew's help in arranging for the suspension of further tanker runs. Nomura explained that the oil shipments concerned Tokyo because it did not wish to see a significant Soviet buildup in Siberia. While this may well have been true, a Foreign Ministry official told Dooman: "The trend of the internal situation in Japan is causing the most serious concern and may develop into one of the utmost gravity largely as a result of the despatch by the American Government of supplies of oil to the Far Eastern ports of the Soviet Union." Although it is possible that the Foreign Ministry used this argument to weaken American support for Siberian forces, Tokyo seemed more interested in diverting rather than stopping the shipments. Terasaki, for example, told Dooman that, if Grew would not recommend ending the shipments, he hoped that the ambassador could at least recommend that Washington reroute the tankers.[31]

Despite the difficulties that the oil shipments created for Japanese moderates, Hull would not compromise. When Nomura again raised objections, Hull replied "that his protest did not have a thing to stand upon." Not content to let the matter rest, the secretary asked Nomura whether Tokyo would "acquiesce in any objection Soviet Russia may make to Japanese purchases of any oil from the United States." By this time, of course, the United States had embargoed oil shipments to Japan. But, even as Hull dismissed Japanese protests, he complained that "the constant agitation in the Japanese press against the United States created a source of difficulty to this government in connection with the" Konoe-Roosevelt summit. In Tokyo, meanwhile, Terasaki again asked Grew whether Washington would "postpone the sending of tankers to the Soviet Union at least pending the outcome of the proposed meeting between the President and the Japanese Prime Minister."[32]

While Hull considered the Japanese protests unimportant and refused to address them, the US military did not. As late as the final week of October, senior army intelligence officials questioned shipping oil to Vladivostok, especially as long as the port of Archangel remained open. An October 25 report noted that, should war erupt in the Pacific, Washington would have no choice but to suspend convoys to Vladivostok. "Assuming this to be the case," the report continued, "the most logical step would be not to undertake a thing that would certainly have to be abandoned later." The study also concluded that, because "the shipping of supplies to Russia via Vladivostok has been one of the major issues between America and Japan recently, the abandonment of said route may serve to keep the door of diplomacy open for a longer period."[33]

While clearly peripheral to the eventual breakdown of relations, the tanker issue nonetheless serves to highlight Hull's fundamental shortsightedness in the final months of peace. While oil shipments to Vladivostok did not materially affect Soviet strength either east or west of the Urals, they did inflame Japanese public opinion. Meanwhile, Hull's insistence that Konoe dampen the fire of anti-American opinion, even as the Vladivostok-bound tankers inflamed the Japanese public, shows the secretary at his worst. Washington could have supplied Soviet forces through alternate ports or even, as the Japanese suggested, through alternate routes. The administration never faced a Hobson's choice of either denying aid to the Russians or poisoning

Japanese public opinion, and Hull could have achieved two valuable ends with one simple decision. He could support Moscow in its epic struggle against the Nazis as well as peace in the Pacific by doing what the American military and the Japanese Foreign Office suggested; find an alternate route for American oil. At the end of October, the US Maritime Commission took the matter out of Hull's hands and announced that future deliveries would go to Archangel. By then, however, the damage was done.[34]

The Preliminary Agreement

Despite his opposition to the proposed summit, Hull continued to encourage the Japanese in order to provide the military greater time, learn more about Japanese intentions, and further undermine the Axis. Continued American-Japanese negotiations highlight the growing success of American containment as well as Washington's inability to recognize the victory that it had already won.

On September 5, for example, the Konoe cabinet met the bulk of Hull's demands when it informed the secretary that the Tripartite Pact was purely defensive, that it would withdraw its forces from China within two years of a peace accord, and that it would respect the Open Door. Tokyo also pledged to halt its southern advance and adhere to the principle of equality of commercial opportunity in the Southwest Pacific. Grew, who had received the Japanese reply first via the Foreign Office, advised the secretary "that the commitments contained in the latest Japanese proposal . . . would fulfill" the American request that Japan cease its policy of aggression. He noted that, while the administration needed more than Japanese assurances, Washington could gradually relax "the military and economic measures . . . which are now inexorably pressing on Japan" once the Konoe cabinet began implementing the proposed agreement.[35]

The State Department, however, rejected Grew's advice and instead raised new concerns. On September 10, Hull and Ballantine objected to Tokyo's terms for settling the China Incident and noted that the latest Japanese proposals no longer called for American mediation. A subsequent American note also highlighted concern over Tokyo's continued ties to the Axis and its commitment to commercial nondiscrimination throughout Asia and the Pacific.[36]

While Hull's concerns regarding China were definitely warranted, others were pointless. Tokyo's latest draft pledged "to withdraw its armed forces from China as soon as possible in accordance with the agreement between

Japan and China." The draft, however, left the way open for the continued presence of Japanese forces in Inner Mongolia and North China. It also called for the United States to "abstain from any measures and actions which will be prejudicial to the endeavor by Japan concerning the settlement of the China Affair." Under no circumstances could Washington suspend aid to Chiang and allow unsupervised Sino-Japanese peace talks. Even here, however, Hull's concerns were more shadow than substance as both State and the military opposed an end to the Sino-Japanese War, and, as the informal talks continued, military opposition became more pointed. In a memorandum distributed to Marshall, the president, and Hull, Hayes Kroner, the chief of the War Department's British Empire Section, informed Marshall: "We must cease at once our attempts to bring about the withdrawal of Japanese forces from China."[37]

Objections over the Tripartite Pact were equally disingenuous. For months, responsible Japanese officials had assured the secretary that a successful summit would render the Axis Alliance a dead letter. Grew and the military, meanwhile, reassured Hull that Japanese support for the Axis Pact was waning. The September 5 "Brief Periodic Estimate of the World Situation" confirmed that, even as Foreign Minister Toyoda publicly proclaimed Japan's adherence to the Axis, privately the "value of the Tripartite Agreement [is] at present being very seriously questioned." Hull remained unmoved even after General Miles reported that recent personnel changes in both the Japanese military and the Imperial Rule Assistance Association, which the Konoe cabinet created in the autumn of 1940 after first abolishing the existing political parties, pointed to "a trend away from the Axis and toward better relations with the United States and Great Britain." Miles concluded: "It is probable that Japan will find a peaceful way out of one of the greatest crises in her history and seek a means to realign her foreign policy in an anti-Axis direction."[38]

While Hull continued to delay, the sense of urgency that initially led Konoe to propose the summit increased, and in an effort to meet Hull's terms the government took further, extraordinary steps. On September 22, the Foreign Ministry provided Grew with the "Text of Basic Japanese Terms of Peace with China," which still included impossible conditions, including the coalescing of the Wang and Chiang regimes, and, the following day, Nomura submitted a document intended to allay Hull's concerns over commercial nondiscrimination. Four days later, Tokyo submitted yet another document "prepared along the lines of the American draft understanding of June 21, both in form and contents, and in which is incorporated all that we have since communicated to the American Government." The document explained, lest Hull raise objections, that the draft was not "intended to be a rigid formula like a treaty." Rather, Tokyo hoped "only to make all matters clearer" and, thus, prepared the document "for the convenience of the American Government."[39]

For his part, Grew, who still held out hope for the summit, launched a parallel effort to influence Hull. The ambassador knew that this would not be easy given his conviction that "the thought is prominently in the mind of our own government . . . that an American-Japanese understanding . . . would merely afford Japan a breathing spell." With Konoe's days numbered, the ambassador sent the most important, well-reasoned, and penetrating cable of his diplomatic career. Hoping to move Hull before time ran out, his mammoth report noted what should have been obvious to the architects of American containment: their policy had succeeded. Grew maintained "that Japan has been deterred from taking greater liberties with American interests only out of respect for our potential power" and that it had already seen "a regeneration of thought." The ambassador concluded that, since Matsuoka's fall, a fundamental change had occurred in the Japanese government, *but he feared that Washington had failed to grasp the full significance of events* and might repeat the mistakes of 1939–1940, when, after Hirunama's fall, Hull failed to support Abe and Yonai. If the secretary once again failed to act, after containment and the Nazi-Soviet War brought Washington to within a hair's breadth of realizing its goals of splitting the Axis and halting Japan's forward march, the results would prove catastrophic.[40]

Grew next set about demolishing the American shibboleths that stood in the way of successful diplomacy. First, he dismissed the notion that Japan sought an agreement in order to facilitate further expansion, and next he attacked the premise that continued sanctions, rather than diplomatic engagement, would force Japan to reorient its foreign policy. He stressed the need for "constructive conciliation" and reasoned that, if the president failed to conclude a final agreement during the summit or if Japan failed to abide by the agreements, Washington could then reimpose sanctions.[41]

Grew also rejected the thesis that continued American economic and diplomatic pressure would loosen the military's hold over Japan. "The only way of wholly discrediting the Japanese army and military machine is by wholesale military defeat of which," he noted, "there is at present no prospect." He warned that continued sanctions and further delays in holding the summit would not produce a more pliable cabinet: "If we expect and wait for the Japanese government to agree in preliminary conversations to clear cut commitments of a nature satisfactory to our government . . . the conversations will almost certainly drag on indefinitely." In that case, he predicted, "the Cabinet and those supporting elements who desire rapprochement to the United States will reach the conclusion that the American government is merely playing for time and that the outlook for an agreement is hopeless." In such a poisoned atmosphere, he maintained, Konoe's cabinet would collapse, a military dictatorship would take its place, and "war would be difficult to avoid." Events soon proved Grew entirely correct, yet, even as he worked to bring about a Konoe-Roosevelt meeting, the summit's foes labored to ensure that the leaders remained an ocean apart.[42]

Despite Hull's opposition, the possibility of a Roosevelt-Konoe summit continued to alarm members of the State Department, foremost among them Stanley Hornbeck, who argued that, given the disastrous Munich accord, the public would oppose the conference. He maintained that meetings that have received "popular acclaim have been 'fighting' meetings like the recent Roosevelt-Churchill conferences." Moreover, he noted, a successful conference would increase Konoe's prestige and "strengthen the position of Japan's militaristic ruling group." Rather than a diplomatic compromise, he argued, "now would be an opportune moment, whether from [the] point of view of the past or from the point of view of the potential future," to go to war with Japan. He maintained that, if the Red Army collapsed, Japan's strategic position would so improve that no American measures short of war would be able to restrain Tokyo.[43]

If Hornbeck was concerned that the administration might undertake a Far Eastern Munich, he did not worry for long. Three days after Grew's long telegram arrived, Hull passed sentence on Konoe and the leaders' summit. On October 2, he handed Nomura an oral statement that explained why Tokyo's proposals were "a source of disappointment." By this time, the reasons were familiar. Hull complained that the Japanese commitment to commercial nondiscrimination covered only "the countries of the Southwest Pacific area," rather than the entire Pacific, and that the terms for settling the China Incident, which included the indefinite stationing of troops in parts of China, "would not . . . make for peace or offer prospects of stability." Finally, despite adequate assurance from both Japanese and American sources, Hull requested that "the Japanese Government . . . give further study to the question of possible additional clarification" as to its obligation under the Tripartite Pact.[44]

Hull's oral statement clearly indicates that the division between Tokyo and Washington had not narrowed appreciably since the first round of the Hull-Nomura talks the previous April. Washington would never go to war in support of the principle of commercial nondiscrimination, and no Japanese guarantee on this point would ever satisfy Hull and his subordinates. Meanwhile, Tokyo could "clarify its position" as to the Axis Alliance until the end of time, and it would have had no discernible effect on Hull.

As for China, while no senior American official sought an end to the fighting there, differences over Japanese troop withdrawals still served as a convenient blind from which Hull could snipe at whatever terms Tokyo offered. Given the often-repeated assertion that Washington went to war in 1941 to save China from Japanese imperialism, it is necessary to dissect this comforting, if inaccurate, myth. Paul Schroeder's pathbreaking 1958 *The Axis Alliance and Japanese-American Relations, 1941* argues: "American diplomats made it clear that the United States would accept war with Japan in preference to any settlement between Japan and China which did not restore intact China's territorial and administrative integrity." Schroeder subsequently concluded that, in an effort to attain China's liberation, "the United States forfeited the diplomatic victory which she had already virtually won."[45]

Schroeder's conclusions are, in two critical respects, open to question. Initially, both the State Department and the military called for continued Sino-Japanese hostilities rather than China's prompt liberation. Second, while the United States did forfeit the diplomatic victories that containment attained, the liberation of China in no way accounts for the failure of American diplomacy. Rather, Washington squandered its gains because senior officials believed that a compromise was both dangerous and unnecessary. Hull and Hornbeck maintained that Japan would break any agreement it made when it was advantageous to do so. Both men also perceived that a compromise agreement was unnecessary in that Japan appeared unable to carry out extensive armed advances in Asia. While his scholarship remains outstanding and his interpretations extremely generous to American policymakers, Schroeder's conclusion is incorrect. America did not go to war to liberate China. Instead, Washington risked war, in part, to keep Japan mired in China.[46]

The Fall of the Third Konoe Cabinet

Not surprisingly, Hull's October 2 oral statement devastated Konoe and his supporters. Tomohiko Ushiba, the prime minister's private secretary, told Dooman: "[Now that] Konoe was at a loss to know what further he could do, the opposition had now something concrete to use in their attacks on the Cabinet, and the future looked dark." The "failure on the part of the American Government to lay any of its cards on the table," Ushiba noted, coupled with "the apparently great care being taken by the American Government not to give the Japanese any specifications was extremely discouraging." This policy had convinced "an increasing number of persons in Japanese Government circles . . . that Japan had fallen into a trap." He explained that many now believed "the United States never had any intention of coming to any agreement with Japan."[47]

An equally glum Nomura reported: "It is my sense that Japanese–United States negotiations have finally reached a 'deadlock.'" Only "a great change in the world political situation" or a radical change in Japanese policies, he maintained, could salvage the talks. Konoe quickly convened a meeting of the cabinet and the supreme command to determine whether he could secure this "radical change." Navy Minister Oikawa, who abhorred the prospect of war with America, supported Konoe and informed the prime minister that to avert a crisis the cabinet "must be prepared to do nothing less than swallow whole the United States proposal." War Minister Tojo and Army Chief of Staff Sugiyama, meanwhile, maintained that the government should not be stampeded into a hasty reply to the American oral statement. Only Navy Chief of Staff Nagano demanded "quick action."[48]

Within days, the proponents of continued negotiations suffered a stinging setback when Sugiyama informed the Liaison Conference: "The Supreme Command cannot extend the deadline beyond October 15." (Nagano had prepared a similar statement covering navy policy, but Admiral Oikawa stopped him from reading it.) Both general staffs now demanded that negotiations conclude no later than October 15. Toyoda, however, could offer no guarantee that a preliminary agreement with the Americans could be reached within a week. He told the conferees that, although he repeatedly requested that Nomura gain some clarification from Hull regarding the October 2 statement, he had yet to do so. As it turned out, Toyoda had asked the impossible.[49]

On the afternoon of October 9, Nomura met with Joseph Ballantine, Maxwell Hamilton, and Max Schmidt, an FE officer who had formerly served under Grew in Tokyo, in an effort to satisfy Tokyo's repeated requests for clarification. The ambassador had asked Hamilton and company to review Tokyo's latest proposal point by point and explain exactly what Washington found "objectionable, unsatisfactory or unacceptable." For two hours, however, the Americans dodged and parried and argued instead that Nomura should "take the [American oral statement] and . . . study it in the light of other statements which this government has made." Nomura wanted answers and was in essence told to bone up on his subject. If this strategy sounds familiar, it should. Hull employed the same tactic during the final stages of his spring talks with Nomura. Now, four months later, a different cast played out the same hackneyed drama.[50]

On October 13, Kaname Wakasugi, a career diplomat and the second man at the Japanese embassy, having just returned from Japan, met Welles in a last-ditch effort to get a clear explanation of "what in reality were the desires of the United States" as well as "what the reasons for the delay [in holding the summit] might be." If the veteran diplomat expected a straight answer, Welles soon disappointed him. "I said to the Minister," Welles recorded, "that it seemed impossible to believe that the Japanese Government did not in fact have a clear and specific understanding of the position of this Government." By this time of course, Nomura's frequent requests for a clarification of the American position, as well as Magic intercepts, revealed that Tokyo was genuinely at a loss to understand the American delay and had begun to suspect the worst. In this case, the worst unfortunately doubled as the truth. Washington was simply stringing Konoe along. There would never be a summit. Nor would there be a Konoe cabinet for much longer.[51]

With no new information regarding the American position, Konoe and his senior advisers met on October 12, the prime minister's fiftieth birthday, to determine whether to continue to work for a summit. At the outset of the meeting, Navy Minister Oikawa, who still shrank from the prospect of fighting the combined Western fleets and desperately wanted negotiations with the United States to continue, argued that the time had come to decide definitely on a policy of either peace or war. The prime minister responded that, if he had to immediately choose between war and peace, he favored "bring[ing] negotiations to fruition no matter what happens." Tojo, however, who had already lost confidence in Konoe's plan, interjected that the time had come to realistically evaluate the chances for a negotiated settlement. Toyoda replied that one major stumbling block remained: the evacuation of Japanese forces from China. This problem appeared insoluble in that Tojo and Sugiyama had already decided that Japanese forces would remain in Inner Mongolia, North China, and Hainan Island indefinitely.[52]

Proceeding from the false assumption that China remained the major stumbling block, Konoe approached Tojo two days later in a final effort to modify the army's position. On the basis of statements that Tojo made to Oikawa on October 7, Jun Tsunoda has suggested that the general considered a total withdrawal if Oikawa would admit that the navy could not successfully wage war against the United States. Oikawa, however, could not bring himself to do this. In an effort to deter the United States and match the American Vinson programs, successive cabinets spent lavishly on building the fleet, and now, at the eleventh hour, he could not acknowledge that the effort had been for naught. Consequently, when Konoe explained that the best interests of the nation demanded the swift conclusion of the China Incident and that ending the war on the continent seemed the only way of avoiding war with the United States, Tojo refused to support him. Instead, he replied: "[If Japan] yields to the United States, she will take steps that are more and more high-handed, and will probably find no place to stop." And

Tojo was right. Japan had fallen into the trap fashioned by Hull, Hornbeck, and others. In a moment of supreme crisis, the Konoe cabinet tore itself apart over the issue of withdrawing troops from China in the vain hope that concessions on this point would save the nation from a ruinous war.[53]

Had Tojo and the army agreed to a complete withdrawal from China, Washington would no doubt have asked for more, if only to delay a final agreement. On October 2 General Kroner bluntly informed the president, Hull, Stimson, and Marshall:

> At this stage in the execution of our national strategic plan, a cessation of hostilities in China followed by the withdrawal of twenty-one Japanese divisions, 20 independent brigades, and 1,000 aircraft therefrom would be highly detrimental to our interests. Such a force if returned to Japan would be potentially of such an explosive nature that only a military oligarchy could control it. These militarists would submerge or destroy the moderate element in Japan replacing it with a restless Chauvinistic element possessing neither the ability nor the inclination to continue diplomatic relations with any of the Democratic Powers.[54]

Tokyo remained convinced that ending the China Incident—the very thing that Washington did not want—remained the key stumbling block. The plain, if ugly, truth was that the administration and the armed services believed that American security depended on continued Sino-Japanese hostilities. The State Department had to keep Japan bogged down in China, prevent a Roosevelt-Konoe meeting, and keep the Pacific at peace until early 1942. This was a Herculean task—and one that it quite nearly pulled off.

On the evening of October 14, General Teiichi Suzuki, the chief of the Cabinet Planning Board, brought the Konoe cabinet its death sentence and gave diplomacy a new lease on life, both actions courtesy of War Minister Tojo. By this time, Tojo had grown convinced that the government had erred at the September 6 imperial conference when it adopted the "Essentials for Carrying Out the Empire's Policies." The war minister was particularly troubled by the decision to "immediately decide to commence hostilities against the United States, Britain, and the Netherlands" should negotiations not produce concrete results by mid-October. He had hoped that Oikawa would admit that the navy was unprepared for war, thus allowing the government to reconsider its policy, but, given that Oikawa could not, Tojo maintained that a new cabinet must be allowed to reexamine existing national policy. His letter, which Suzuki delivered, explained that, while Oikawa opposed war, he refused to say so unequivocally. Instead, Tojo continued, "it looks as if the Navy Minister is making the Premier shoulder the entire responsibility." He noted that the navy's continued vacillation meant that the policy decided on at "the conference on September 6 in the presence of the Emperor will have been fundamentally overturned." Accordingly, he argued that Konoe must step down and that a new cabinet, headed by a member of the imperial family, preferably Prince Higashikuni, form a new government. Tojo favored Higashikuni because of his well-known opposition to war with America as well as his own conviction that only a member of the royal family "has the power to keep control over the army and the navy." The next day, Konoe informed the Marquis Kido, the lord keeper of the privy seal and a top Hirohito adviser, that "he could not hold his premiership any more."[55]

But who would be the next prime minister? Kido, Suzuki, the Imperial Household Ministry, and Emperor Hirohito opposed a Higashikuni cabinet. Kido feared that the prince could become a tool of the military, while the emperor believed that the monarchy would suffer if a member of the royal family led Japan to defeat. Konoe, while not certain, supported Higashikuni because he believed that the prince favored continued negotiations and, owing to his royal authority, could restrain the opponents of Japanese-American reconciliation.[56]

Since Tojo could not overcome the opposition, the search for a new prime minister quickly focused on two men: Oikawa and Tojo. Kido reasoned that Konoe's successor must be thoroughly familiar with the pertinent issues, possess the authority to unite the military, and have the power to reexamine the decision reached at the September 6 imperial conference. It is very significant that both men's perceived opposition to war with America propelled them to the top of the short list. Shortly after submitting his resignation, Konoe told Kido that he favored a Tojo cabinet because, while the war minister appeared opposed to further negotiations with America, "he would not plunge us immediately into war." Rather, Konoe believed, as long as the navy refused to commit itself, Tojo would lead a new cabinet to reexamine the decision reached at the September 6 imperial conference. The following afternoon, Kido convened a meeting of Japan's senior statesmen to recommend a new premier, and, in a complete break with the tradition "that a privy seal hardly ever states his own opinions aggressively," he brushed aside suggestions for a Higashikuni cabinet and assured the senior statesmen: "Tojo is someone who can handle negotiations with the United States." After less than four hours of discussion, the conferees adjourned, and within hours Emperor Hirohito commanded Hideki Tojo to form a new government.[57]

War in the Pacific was seven weeks away.

Chapter 8

All or Nothing

> Down deep in my heart, I doubt whether the Japs will have the guts to go through with their program of aggression when they find they are confronted with war with both the United States and Great Britain.
>
> —Frank Knox (November 1941)

> One acts on what one believes to be reality.
>
> —William Appleman Williams (1988)

The final six weeks of peace offered the United States and Japan repeated chances to spare Asia and the Pacific a cataclysmic war. That these chances came through the ascension to power of a career military officer who years later swung from the gallows might come as something of a surprise. But, in November 1941, as Japan and America frantically prepared for the war that neither wanted, statesmen on both sides of the Pacific produced plans that could, just possibly, have averted war.

In the last desperate months of peace, Japan's most unyielding leaders considered compromise. The same, however, could not be said for America's policymakers. Instead, Washington's position hardened as continued Russian resistance, declining U-boat success, apparent Japanese weakness, and the growing power of the American-British-Dutch (ABD) coalition reinforced the determination to roll back Japanese gains in Asia and force Tokyo out of the Axis. Convinced that they could simultaneously secure the long-term goal of protecting the Open Door and the short-term imperatives of weakening Japan and breaking the Axis Alliance, the architects of American containment continued to reject Japan's proposals.

The Tojo Cabinet

Within twenty-four hours of the emperor ordering him to form a cabinet, Hideki Tojo completed the process of organizing a new government. After leaving the imperial palace, the prime minister hurried to the shrine of the

Meiji Emperor, in whose name patriots had established the modern Japanese state three generations earlier, and then on to the memorial of Admiral Togo, the hero of Tsushima. Finally, he rushed to Yasukuni Shrine to honor Japan's legion of war dead. When he at last returned home, he found his brother officers waiting with a suggested roster of cabinet officials that he immediately brushed aside. He neither needed nor desired their help. Tojo already knew the type of cabinet he wanted.[1]

The new prime minister simplified the difficult choice of selecting ministers by taking three portfolios himself. In addition to prime minister, Tojo also served as war minister and home minister. He explained that the two extra portfolios were essential in that, if negotiations with Washington succeeded, control over the home and war minister portfolios would offer the added assurance of controlling internal opponents. For foreign minister, Tojo selected the veteran diplomat Shigenori Togo, a former ambassador to the Soviet Union and chief of the Foreign Ministry's old European-American Bureau. Known for his pro-Anglo-American and anti-Axis credentials, Togo first wanted assurances from Tojo that he would pursue diplomacy and that the army would make sufficient concessions to achieve an agreement with the United States. Though the two were something of an odd pairing (perhaps not so odd in that the Allies indicted both men as Class A war criminals), Tojo had the perfect bait to hook Togo: Hirohito's command to "wipe the slate clean." Shortly after commanding Tojo to form a new government, the emperor instructed Kido to order the prime minister to reexamine the decisions of the September 6 imperial conference. With assurances from Tojo and Hirohito's injunction, Togo took on the most difficult assignment of his career.[2]

However much Togo and Tojo were determined to adhere to Hirohito's orders, others were not. The Army General Staff, for example, steadfastly opposed reversing the decisions of the September 6 imperial conference, as did Admiral Nagano, who stated: "It is incomprehensible why we should conduct a reexamination . . . at this point." Worse still, within two weeks of his appointment, Navy Minister Shigetaro Shimada, who initially favored diplomacy, threw his support to the hawks.[3]

Despite this opposition, Tojo secured support at a marathon November 1 conference for a policy that continued negotiations while simultaneously preparing for war. At the outset of the meeting, the conferees dealt with the thorny problem of allocating Japan's meager steel resources between the army and the navy. Consequently, it was late afternoon before they turned to diplomacy. Tojo first asked their opinion on three proposals. Japan should: "1. [E]xert every effort to avoid war and undergo great hardship and deprivation. 2. [D]etermine to go to war immediately and focus political and military strategies to this end. 3. [B]eing determined to go to war, continue on with diplomatic measures in an effort to reach a compromise agreement while completing preparations for military operations." The combined effect of American naval and economic deterrence made option 1 impossible. Nagano argued that "the time for Japan to go to war against the United States is now," and General Teiichi Suzuki, the head of the Cabinet Planning Board, agreed that the country could not endure the embargoes for much longer.[4]

Representatives from the Army General Staff, meanwhile, pushed hard for option 2. They claimed—not without reason—that Hull's October 2 proposal offered little hope for a diplomatic breakthrough and that continued negotiations seemed to "merely be aiding the delaying tactics of the opponent." When Finance Minister Okinori Kaya, who opposed war with America, asked Nagano when Japan had to attack if it were to have any chance of winning, Nagano answered: "Now. The time for war will not come later." That was enough to push Suzuki to openly side with the hawks. Despite their success in winning over the Cabinet Planning Board, the armed forces did not rule out diplomacy. After a twenty-minute adjournment, the meeting reconvened, and, with Tojo's support, option 3 carried the day. Japan would pursue diplomacy and simultaneously prepare for war.[5]

The conferees now moved to consider Japan's diplomatic options. It was 2:00 A.M. on November 2. The Foreign Ministry prepared two proposals in advance of the meeting. Plan A, which had been approved at the October 30 liaison conference, sought a comprehensive settlement with the United States. Bowing to army pressure, however, the plan allowed troops to remain in North China, Inner Mongolia, and Hainan Island for an unspecified period. All other troops would evacuate immediately "the minute peace is concluded." Plan A also sanctioned the complete withdrawal of Japanese forces from French Indochina "upon the settlement of the China Incident or upon the establishment of a just peace in the Far East." Tokyo also pledged to observe the principle of commercial nondiscrimination throughout Asia and the Pacific, China included, as long as nondiscrimination was applied worldwide. As for the remaining points of divergence between Washington and Tokyo, plan A flatly rejected abrogating the Axis Pact and also avoided a firm commitment to Hull's Four Principles.[6]

Togo did not hold out much hope for plan A, so he introduced a second proposal that functioned as a modus vivendi designed to buy Washington and Tokyo enough time to avoid war. Plan B called for the following:

1. Both Japan and the United States will pledge not to make an armed

> advance into Southeast Asia and the South Pacific area, except French Indochina.
> 2. The Japanese and American Governments will cooperate with each other so that the procurement of necessary materials from the Netherlands East Indies will be assured.
> 3. The Japanese and American Governments will restore trade relations to what they were prior to the freezing of assets. The United States will promise to supply Japan with the petroleum it needs.
> 4. The United States will not take such actions as may hinder efforts for peace by both Japan and China.

Plan B also contained two sets of clarifying notes that were submitted at the November 5 imperial conference and not released to the United States. These clarifying points, which were in fact indicators of further concessions, included:

> As occasion demands, it is permissible to promise that with the conclusion of the present agreement Japanese troops stationed in southern Indochina are prepared to move to northern Indochina with the consent of the French Government; and that the Japanese troops will withdraw from Indochina with the settlement of the China Incident or upon the establishment of a just peace in the Pacific area. As occasion demands, we may make insertions in the provisions on nondiscriminatory trade and on the interpretation and execution of the Tripartite Pact in the above mentioned proposal (Proposal B).[7]

Kijuro Shidehara and Shigeru Yoshida, veteran diplomats, Occupation-era prime ministers, and the architects of plan B, carefully laid the groundwork for their proposal by reviewing it with both Grew and Craigie. While the British ambassador found the plan especially promising, key military representatives present at the liaison conference opposed it. Sugiyama and Army Vice Chief of Staff Ko Tsukada insisted that a withdrawal from French Indochina would complicate settling the China Incident and obtaining raw materials. Tsukada, in particular, expressed concern that repealing the freezing order alone was insufficient. Mirroring the concern of Americans like Miles who feared what 1942 might bring, he understood that, as a temporary agreement, plan B left open the possibility of war, not in the immediate future, but in six months, when Japanese prospects for victory would have faded. When Nagano joined the army representatives in opposing plan B, it seemed that Togo might resign and bring down the government. After yet another adjournment, however, the conferees engineered a compromise in which the army backed Togo in return for the requirement that, under plan B, the United States sell Japan a specified amount of petroleum.[8]

In addition to formulating these two plans, the Tojo cabinet also decided to dispatch Saburo Kurusu to Washington to assist Nomura during the final negotiations. The admiral had requested the career diplomat's assistance since August, but the Konoe cabinet demurred for several months. Tojo and Togo, however, quickly agreed to send him. Like Togo, Kurusu did not seek his appointment and agreed to take on this latest assignment only after Tojo "'declared in a firm voice that he would keep the agreement'" should the two diplomats secure one.[9]

Tojo: The American Reaction

The initial American reaction to Tojo's appointment undercut what little hope remained for a negotiated settlement as American analysts, civilian and military alike, greeted the new cabinet with a combination of dread and equanimity. On the one hand, experts saw Tojo as pro-German, anti-American, and militant. On the other hand, nearly all agreed that the new prime minister would not immediately lead Japan to war. This interpretation meant that, while Washington had every reason to despise Tojo, it had no reason to deal with him.

With the news of Konoe's fall, American analysts immediately swung into action. On October 16, General Miles predicted that, whoever headed the next cabinet, "the trend will be toward the Axis, with the Army, rather than the Navy, exercising the controlling influence." The following day, having learned of Tojo's appointment, Miles predicted that the new cabinet "may be expected to have Axis leanings, but will be otherwise anti-foreign and highly nationalistic." Having had an additional four days to digest events, Naval Department analysts concluded: "The ultra-Nationalist element of Japan has seized control of the Government and is prepared to push collaboration with the Axis powers and the opposition to the democracies to the ultimate extent." British military observers had reached an almost identical conclusion. General Miles learned that the chief of British Far Eastern Intelligence had concluded that Tojo "is wholly pro-German" and "speeches by the . . . cabinet should be viewed as obscuring [Japan's] real intent," an attack on Siberia and the Maritime Provinces. On October 25, army intelligence reported that the new government's ties to the Axis "make all protestations of peaceful intent a sham" and declared that, with the ascension of Tojo,

Americans at least "know where we stand, what to expect, and what should be done." Echoing a familiar refrain, the report declared that Japanese "overtures should be preceded by concrete evidence of sincerity before they can be seriously considered."[10]

In general, the State Department's reaction to Tojo lacked the military's shrill alarm, and it was predicted that the new prime minister would welcome a diplomatic settlement. William Langdon of the Far Eastern Division (FE), a veteran Foreign Service officer with extensive prior service in Japan and Manchuria, argued that Tojo's "designation as Premier signifies a continuation of Prince Konoe's policies including continuations of conversations with the United States." Hamilton too agreed that Tojo's cabinet would pursue diplomacy and saw Togo's selection as indicative of "continued efforts towards a negotiated settlement with the United States and the Soviet Union." Grew, like Hamilton, maintained that Tojo's selection should be viewed as a positive harbinger rather than a sign of impending war.[11]

While differing on the meaning of his ascension to power, both military and civilian analysts concluded that, for the time being, Tojo would not lead Japan to war against America. On October 25, army analysts predicted that Japan would not embark on any new major operations for another month. G-2 concluded that the recent dispatch of Japanese vessels to pick up stranded Japanese nationals, continued Russian resistance, the onset of the Siberian winter, and the announcement that the emperor would convene a special session of the Diet indicated that "no major move will be made before the latter part of November." Even those analysts who predicted "that Japan will, in the near future, take military action in new areas of the Far East" discounted the likelihood of a simultaneous attack against the ABD coalition. London too believed that Japan would not strike south "except possibly into Thailand, because of the danger of becoming embroiled with the United States and Britain, especially in view of the firm stand taken by the U.S." At State, meanwhile, the same opinions prevailed. Langdon, who asserted "that Japan will go nowhere where her keen intuition will tell her she will be challenged by force," based his conclusion on the "belief that Japan is incapable at present of conducting a war on two widely separated fronts; incapable because of insufficient manpower and military equipment."[12]

The Marshall-Stark Memorandum

Even if Japan did not appear ready to make a move before the end of November, military and civilian leaders were concerned that an attack on the Burma

Road might drag America prematurely into war. At the end of October, when Chiang Kai-shek informed Washington that Japan intended to assault Kunming in order to sever the Burma Road, Hull, Welles, Hornbeck, and representatives from the armed forces met to consider a response. The conferees decided that Washington must avoid war with Japan and preserve Anglo-American defensive strength in Asia. Accordingly, they concluded that no American or British forces would be diverted to aid Chiang.[13]

Two days later, Marshall, Stark, Gerow, and Rear Admiral Royal Ingersoll, assistant to the chief of naval operations, concurred—Chiang would receive no additional aid. While this consensus alone was important, the meeting also revealed an increasing divergence between the army and the State Department, on the one hand, and the navy, on the other hand, concerning American military capabilities in Asia and the Pacific. This divergence had significant implications for US-Japanese diplomacy. Speaking for the navy, Ingersoll argued that any major American effort in the Pacific would tax precious resources, "materially affect United States aid to England," and require such a diversion of tanker traffic as to cause a severe domestic oil shortage. The admiral went on to note that Japan could harass American lines of communication from bases in the Mandated Islands and that as yet there was no secure anchorage for the fleet. He stressed that the United States should "defer offensive action" and fight only in the event of a Japanese attack against American, British, and Dutch Far Eastern territory. Clearly alarmed by what he felt was an overly optimistic State Department assessment of American capabilities, he added that the diplomats were "under the impression that Japan could be defeated in military action in a few weeks." Indeed, Hornbeck had only recently concluded: "With Japan as comparatively weak as she is today and with this country as comparatively strong as it is today, we need not fear unduly the military outcome—or even the immediate consequences—of such a conflict." The United States, he claimed, was "physically capable now of waging a properly conducted war with Japan and at the same time carrying on in the Atlantic all operations which it would be advantageous for us to make."[14]

Once Ingersoll finished his support for a cautious containment policy, General Marshall noted that a Pacific war would largely be a naval affair and that "due consideration should be given to the fact that the navy was now fighting a battle in the Atlantic." Continuing what seemed to be his support for the navy, Marshall concluded that the president must reject Chiang's plea.[15]

Marshall then noted "that as long as the augmented Army Air Force remained in the Philippines, Japanese action in the Philippines or towards the south would be a very hazardous operation." The general concluded: "By the middle of December, the Army Forces in the Philippines would be of impressive strength, and this in itself would have a deterrent effect on Japanese operations." Later, Ingersoll began to detail navy movements to the Philippines and explain "that United States forces and shipping now being moved to the Philippines might be in danger if a decision adverse to United States interests should be made on November 5." Marshall then interjected "that Japan could hardly take the risk of military operations with a powerful air and submarine force directly on the flank of their supply lines." The general's analysis of army airpower reveals the depth of conviction on the part of the airpower advocates. Since the previous November, when Morgenthau, Hull, and the president threw their support behind a Chinese plan to base American bombers in the Middle Kingdom, the airpower fantasy warped the minds of senior policymakers. Stimson had already concluded that Philippines-based airpower "has completely changed the strategy of the Pacific and lets American power back into the Islands in a way which it has not been able to do for twenty years." The secretary of war realized that American bombers remained an "imperfect threat," but he informed the president on October 21 that it nonetheless "bids fair to stop Japan's march to the south and secure the safety of Singapore, with all the revolutionary consequences of such action."[16]

By this time, British overconfidence matched that of the State and War Departments. On November 5, the Admiralty informed its mission in Washington that the capital ship force that London expected to send to the Far East after the outbreak of hostilities with Japan was already forming and that, astoundingly, *it could be safely based in Luzon.*[17]

By early November, Hornbeck, Stimson, Marshall, and now the British Admiralty believed that the United States possessed the might to check a Japanese move south and wage a successful defensive war against Japan. Given their convictions, no support for a compromise agreement with Tokyo could be expected from their quarter. This meant that Harold Stark bore a terrible burden. He had to do what Admiral Oikawa would not: admit that the navy could not wage a two-ocean war.

Two days after the Joint Board meeting, Marshall and Stark prepared a crucial memorandum for the president detailing their recommendations for Far Eastern policy. Initially, they proposed making no moves on China's behalf that might lead to an early war with Japan. "At the present time," the report read, "the United States Fleet in the Pacific is inferior to the Japanese Fleet and cannot undertake an unlimited strategic offensive in the Western Pacific." Any effort to bolster naval strength for offensive operations would require massive withdrawals from the Atlantic and "require tremendous merchant tonnage." Such a diversion of Atlantic-based shipping, the report warned, "might well cause the United Kingdom to lose the Battle of the Atlantic in the near future."[18]

Their memorandum then took on a curious, overly optimistic tone, *significant for its discussion of fighting a defensive war in the Pacific.* Marshall and Stark noted, for example, that current "combined naval, air and ground forces will make attack on the islands [the Philippines] a hazardous undertaking" and that by mid-December "United States air and submarine strength in the Philippines will have become a positive threat to any Japanese operations south of Formosa." The two clearly hoped to convince the president to delay taking any provocative and unnecessary action that might lead to war, and, consequently, they advised FDR against sending an ultimatum to Japan. This, however, was their only reference to diplomacy, which is odd, given what had occurred two days earlier.[19]

At the November 3 Joint Board meeting, Marshall admitted that "until powerful United States forces had been built up in the Far East it would take some very clever diplomacy to save the situation." He even suggested: "The basis of U.S. policy should be to make certain minor concessions which the Japanese could use in saving face. These concessions might be a relaxation on oil restrictions or on similar trade restrictions." But, two days later, the Marshall-Stark memorandum made no mention of either "clever diplomacy" or concessions. This is doubly surprising given that the Joint Board approved Ingersoll's recommendations, with amendments made by Stark and Marshall, which included, among other suggestions, the following points:

> Oppose the issuance of an Ultimatum to Japan. Advocate State Department action to put off hostilities with Japan as long as possible. Suggest agreements with Japan to tide the situation over for the next several months. Point out the effect and cost a U.S.-Japanese War in the Far East would have on defense aid to Great Britain and other nations being aided by the U.S. Emphasize the existing limitations on shipping and the inability of the U.S. to engage in a Far Eastern offensive operation without the transfer of the major portion of shipping facilities from the Atlantic to the Pacific.[20]

On one level, the Marshall-Stark memorandum was true to the Joint Board recommendations. Both men opposed intervention on Chiang's behalf as well as an ultimatum for Japan. Marshall and Stark failed, however, to follow the Joint Board's recommendations concerning concessions to put off war and included none of the recommendations that the army chief of staff had suggested just two days earlier. Rather than concessions, Marshall and Stark maintained that "all possible aid short of actual war against Japan should be extended to the Chinese central Government." In the portion of the directive detailing specific recommendations, the service chiefs advocated only accelerated material aid to China and the American Volunteer Group. In an earlier portion of the memorandum that concerned "aid [that] can be extended to Chiang Kai-shek by measures which probably will not result in war with Japan," the service chiefs specifically mentioned "continuation of economic pressure against Japan."[21]

Although Marshall and Stark clearly favored delaying hostilities, neither man suggested any positive steps to buy time. Marshall's actions can be explained by his faith in Philippines-based airpower, which was clearly on display during a November 15 meeting with several journalists. Marshall began the meeting by telling the assembled newsmen that what they were about to learn must be held in the strictest confidence. He then explained that Japan and America "were on the brink of war." He noted how the army was preparing for an offensive war against Japan using Philippines-based airpower and explained what would happen if war broke out: "We'll fight mercilessly. Flying fortresses will be dispatched immediately to set the paper cities of Japan on fire." More importantly, he explained how airpower would offset any deficiencies in American naval strength. "The grand strategy," Marshall said, "does not include the use of much naval force." In fact, "U.S. bombers can do the trick against Japanese Naval strength and against Japanese cities." Marshall assured the newsmen that the Philippines would be secure by December 15.[22]

While Marshall's confidence in Philippines-based airpower helps explain his position, Stark's silence is more difficult to fathom. The admiral may have been reluctant to challenge Marshall because that would require him to admit that the navy was less prepared for war than the army was. Stark may also have known that Stimson, and no doubt others, interpreted navy caution as defeatism and saw him as wary and apprehensive. He was also no brawler and would not have relished a collision with Marshall and Stimson. His conclusion that a Japanese-American war remained unlikely also colored his actions. Just after Konoe's fall, for example, he informed Admiral Husband Kimmel, who replaced Admiral Richardson as commander of the Pacific Fleet in February 1941, that he doubted "the Japs are going to sail into us."[23]

Given this conviction, Stark remained certain that no war would immediately occur as long as the president adhered to the strict guidelines on when to commit American forces. He saw little need to challenge Marshall and

Stimson, and, rather than plead for more time, he and Marshall simply provided the president with clear recommendations as to the precise events that required an American military response. They also left Roosevelt with the impression that American forces would be ready within weeks to face Japan. Most importantly, neither gave the commander in chief any reason to support a cautious containment policy by striking a bargain with Japan. And neither did anyone else.

President Roosevelt's Modus Vivendi and the White Memorandum

The Marshall-Stark memorandum clearly had a significant impact on the president, who quickly determined not to commit American forces to Chiang's defense. In order to give Marshall and Stark extra time to prepare for war, Roosevelt also considered a modus vivendi. On November 6, he suggested to Stimson that a temporary agreement with Japan might provide the armed services with more time to prepare. The secretary of war opposed the idea, however, because he thought that it might harm Chinese morale. Additionally, convinced as he was that "a strategic opportunity of the utmost importance has suddenly arisen in the southwestern Pacific," Stimson opposed anything that might disrupt reinforcement of the Philippines. Rather than use a modus vivendi to buy time, he intended to use B-17 bombers "to shake the Japanese out of the Axis." General Marshall shared Stimson's confidence, and their vision of the B-17's omnipotence was no doubt mutually reinforcing. While Stimson hoped that the heavy bombers would break Tokyo's ties to Berlin, the general believed that, if Japanese moderates learned through American leaks about B-17 deployments, they would pressure their government to avoid war. Marshall maintained that, should the Tojo cabinet learn that the Americans "really mean to bomb our cities, and they have the equipment with which to do it," it might deter the government from going to war. This conviction explains his November 15 meeting with journalists and Arthur Krock's November 19 *Times* article, which not only carried details of the B-17 deployments but speculated that either the president or Hull had told Kurusu about how the army intended to use the new bomber.[24]

Stimson did nothing to encourage the president's move toward diplomatic engagement, and, after the cabinet met the next day, Roosevelt moved the modus vivendi to the back burner. Evidently in high spirits, he began the meeting by explaining how Lincoln once polled his cabinet on a particular issue and, after all present voted nay, exclaimed: "The Ayes have it." FDR then said that today he would conduct his first cabinet poll. The question was "whether the people would back us up in case we struck at Japan down there and what the tactics should be." This time the ayes did have it. The cabinet was unanimous; the public would continue to support the administration's policy of favoring sanctions and military deterrence over negotiation, even at the risk of war. For Stimson, it was "the best Cabinet Meeting I think we ever had." Any chance that a cabinet split would move the president to support containment over rollback and offer the modus vivendi vanished that afternoon.[25]

The cabinet continued to encourage hard-line diplomacy over moderation, which further undercut compromise solutions. On November 10, Navy Secretary Frank Knox wrote John Winant, the American ambassador to London, that he had long seen the coming crisis in Japanese-American relations and was "delighted with the firmness with which it is being met by the President and the Cabinet." He informed Winant that the navy was "as thoroughly well prepared . . . as it is possible for us to be." He told his friend: "Down deep in my heart, I doubt whether the Japs will have the guts to go through with their program of aggression when they find they are confronted with war with both the United States and Great Britain."[26]

While Knox doubted Japan's willingness to attack, Harold Ickes, who shared Hull's and Hornbeck's unfortunate conviction that war with Japan would be over by spring, saw the autumn as the best time to fight. In late November, he confided to the president: "By going to war with Japan now we would soon be in a position where a large part of our Navy, as well as of the British Navy and the Dutch East Indies Navy, could be released for service in the Atlantic." Secretary of the Treasury Morgenthau likewise believed that the administration should confront Japan with a policy of "iron firmness." A modus vivendi was beyond the pale, he argued, in that "no settlement with Japan . . . no matter how temporary . . . will be viewed as consistent with the position of our Government."[27]

Even after he abandoned the modus vivendi, the president instructed Hull to keep the talks going in order to delay a crisis in the Pacific, and, while these negotiations were meant only to buy time, an unlikely peace advocate provided the administration one final chance to break the deadlock and fundamentally readjust Japanese-American relations. This final opportunity came from Harry Dexter White, one of Henry Morgenthau's bright assistants at the Treasury Department. White, a noted hard-liner and an early champion of combining preclusive purchasing and export control, distinguished himself as a farsighted proponent of compromise in the final weeks of peace.[28]

White's recommendations were extraordinary on several levels, and his idealism shone through when he proposed ending extraterritoriality in China, British rule in Hong Kong, and French control of Indochina. His plan sought "a victory that requires no vanquished, a victory that immediately would bring peace, happiness and prosperity to hundreds of millions of Eastern peoples, and assure the subsequent defeat of Germany!" But White was much more than a starry-eyed idealist. He reasoned that, if Japan rejected the plan, its mere terms would rally the country behind the administration and simultaneously "create serious division in Japan." Most importantly, he had a bold idea built on the following understanding: "If ever there was a time when diplomacy could secure its most brilliant victories for the United States, now is that time! The longer we wait the less chance we will have to use diplomacy as an aid to our defense. The patterns of relationships jell; plans become irrevocable; opportunities lost are gone forever. A nation committed irrevocably to a course of action loses the power to exercise choice, to accept offers, to make conditions."[29]

Sounding more and more like the increasingly desperate Nomura and nothing like Hull, White declared: "What is most needed at this moment is not a carefully worked out program but rather a decision to employ an all-out diplomatic approach in the current discussions with the Japanese." White's diplomatic offensive committed Washington:

1. To withdraw the bulk of the American Naval forces from the Pacific.
2. To sign a 20-year non-aggression pact with Japan.
3. To promote a final settlement of the Manchurian question.
4. To actively advocate the placing of Indo-China under the Government of a joint British, French, Japanese, Chinese, and American commission. . . .
5. To give up all extra-territorial rights in China, and to obtain England's agreement to give up her extra-territorial rights in China, and give Hong Kong back to China.
6. To present to Congress and push for enactment a bill to repeal the Immigration Act of 1917 which prohibits immigration into the United States of Japanese. . . .
7. To negotiate a trade agreement with Japan, giving her (a) most-favored-nation treatment and (b) such concessions on imports as can be mutually satisfactorily arranged. . . .
8. To extend a $2 billion 20-year credit at 2 per cent interest. . . .
9. To set up a $500 million stabilization fund half supplied by Japan and half by the United States, to be used for the stabilization of the dollar-yen rate.

> 10. To remove the restrictions on Japanese funds in the United States.
> 11. To use its influence to the full to attempt to eliminate sources of potential friction between Japan and her neighbors, and to assure Japan access to the raw materials of the world on the same basis as now enjoyed by United States and Great Britain.[30]

While his plan committed the United States to sweeping concessions, White expected no less from Japan. For its part, Tokyo would:

> 1. Withdraw all military, naval, air police forces from China (boundaries as of 1931) from Indo-China and Thailand.
> 2. Withdraw all support—military, political or economic—from any government in China other than that of the national government.
> 3. Replace with yen currency at a rate agreed upon among the treasuries of China, Japan, England and the United States all military scrip, yen and puppet notes circulating in China.
> 4. Give up all extra-territorial rights in China.
> 5. Extend China a billion yen loan at 2 per cent to aid in reconstructing China. . . .
> 6. Withdraw all Japanese forces from Manchuria except for a few divisions necessary as a police force, provided U.S.S.R. withdraws all her troops from the Far Eastern front except for an equivalent remainder.
> 7. Sell to the United States up to three-fourths of her current output of war material—including naval, air, ordinance and commercial ships on a cost-plus 20 per cent basis as the United States may select.
> 8. Expel all German technical men, military officials and propagandists.
> 9. Accord the United States and China most-favored-nation treatment in the whole Japanese Empire.
> 10. Negotiate a 10-year non-aggression pact with United States, China, British Empire, Dutch Indies (and Philippines).[31]

Taken as a whole, White's plan secured Washington's fundamental aims. An agreement based on it would render the Axis Pact a dead letter and allow the Allies to focus on the destruction of Nazi Germany. As for China, while Chiang might protest, his concerns would likely dissipate. The plan forced Tokyo to abandon Wang, protected the Open Door, and restored Chinese sovereignty by removing the Japanese military as well as Western extraterritoriality rights. It presented a workable method for achieving both long-term aims, the preservation of the Open Door, and short-term imperatives, the disruption of the Axis and the destruction of Germany.

Maxwell Hamilton, who maintained that the proposal needed revision, called it "the most constructive" proposition he had seen, and his senior staff backed him to a man. At Hamilton's urging, Hull forwarded a revised version of White's plan to the War and Navy Departments, where Gerow approved using the study "as a basis for discussion" and noted that, if the proposal were adopted, it would serve a vital American end by keeping peace in the Pacific. "Even a temporary peace," he argued, "would permit us to complete defensive preparations in the Philippines and at the same time insure . . . material assistance to the British." Gerow stressed that, from the standpoint of the War Plans Division, "it is of grave importance to the success of our war effort in Europe that we reach a modus-vivendi with Japan." For Stark, Europe also remained the top priority, and, although he found far more flaws in White's proposal than did Gerow, the admiral did not dismiss it out of hand. By November 21, the State Department's top Asian experts, save Hornbeck, the Army's War Plans Division, and the director of Naval Operations gave Hull their approval to negotiate with Tokyo on the basis of a modified version of the White memorandum.[32]

To Judgment Day

Despite his opposition to a last-minute compromise, Henry Morgenthau passed White's memorandum along to the president on November 18. Just two days later, perhaps influenced by the proposal, Roosevelt resurrected his modus vivendi plan and shared it with Hull. A rough four-point outline to delay hostilities for six months, the president's plan called for:

> U.S. to resume economic relations—some oil and rice now more later.
> Japan to send no more troops to Indo-China.
> Japan to agree not to invoke Tripartite Pact even if U.S. gets into European war.
> U.S. to introduce Japs to Chinese to talk things over but U.S. to take no part in their conversations.

At the same time, FE also turned out various modus vivendi proposals, and, on November 20, Nomura and Kurusu presented Japan's plan B. Now, in the final week of negotiations, Hull and the administration had three proposals to consider: White's plan for an overall adjustment, Roosevelt's modus vivendi, and Tokyo's plan B. Any one of these plans would have confirmed the success of American containment and secured Washington's long-term objectives and short-term strategic imperatives.[33]

Hull and the president, however, soon shelved all three options. The secretary was no doubt influenced by men like Hornbeck, who wrote Hull on November 17 that Japan's real aims in the current talks were to undercut American aid to Chiang and "size up the situation as regards the national attitude, the national preparedness and the national capacity of this country." Besides the perception of Japanese duplicity, negotiations failed because policymakers did not believe that any agreement could fundamentally adjust American-Japanese relations. After reading White's proposal, Hornbeck informed Hull that, even if Tokyo accepted the plan, he did "not believe that it would cause Japan to turn from and abandon her aspiration toward her program of conquest." Joseph Ballantine also questioned the value of any agreement with Tokyo and claimed "that by 1941 it was too late to arrest the progressive deterioration toward an ultimate breakdown of peaceful relations between the United States and Japan."[34]

Hull's own suspicion of Japanese intentions, which on any given day were as grave as Hornbeck's, had grown deeper by November and made it unlikely that the secretary would conclude an agreement. Tokyo's decision to dispatch Kurusu to help Nomura with the negotiations, for example, only reinforced Hull's doubts. Chosen by Togo for his experience in the diplomatic service, excellent English, and marriage to an American, Kurusu could not alter Hull's outlook. "I felt from the start," he wrote, "that he was deceitful." When Kurusu broached the idea of a modus vivendi to Hull on November 18, the secretary's innate suspicion took over. Specifically, Kurusu proposed a return to the status quo ante of July 1941 in which Japan would withdraw from southern Indochina in return for a modification of the American freezing order. Hull, however, told him that such a move only raised the possibility that "the troops you withdraw from Indo-China will be diverted to some equally objectionable movement elsewhere."[35]

The conviction among senior civilian and military officials that Japan would not launch a direct assault against the coalition also conditioned American policy. Even an intercepted November 5 cable from Togo to Nomura, in which the former noted that "it is absolutely necessary that all arrangements for the signing of this agreement be completed by the 25th of this month," did not change the perception that Japan would move soon, only against Thailand rather than the ABD coalition.[36]

On November 21, General Raymond E. Lee cabled an intelligence estimate that, he assured the War Department, "represents the consensus of all British intelligence services." "From the Japanese viewpoint," the cablegram read, "her best move, the one with the least chance of bringing on a general war, would probably be occupation of Thailand." The seizure of Thai bases, Lee continued, "would also pave the way for later movement against Malaya or the Netherlands East Indies." Finally, he noted, "a Japanese drive into Thailand is indicated by [Japan's] recent movements." The official report by the British Joint Intelligence Committee, which the British Embassy Annex forwarded the next day, confirmed that Thailand would be next. Lee had no way of knowing that his "reported consensus" was, in fact, misleading. A week earlier, the committee had determined that Japanese forces would soon take Thailand and possibly land in Malaya, but Brooke-Popham and Churchill dismissed this conclusion.[37]

The amended British view that Lee sent supported what American analysts had maintained for some time and continued to maintain during the last week of November. These projections clearly led both Marshall and Stark to discount the possibility of a simultaneous Japanese assault on the ABD coalition. In the last week of November, when the president's military chiefs warned that "Japan may attack: the Burma Road; Thailand; Malaya; the Netherlands East Indies; the Philippines; the Russian Maritime Provinces," they were covering all bets rather than making a prediction. Marshall and Stark also noted that Russian strength would deter Tokyo and that Japanese forces would not attack Malaya or the East Indies until first reducing American power in Luzon. If this analysis was correct, then only three likely targets remained, and neither Marshall nor Stark could venture to tell the president "whether the offensive will be made against the Burma Road, Thailand or the Philippines." It is significant, however, that their memorandum provided Roosevelt with an either/or scenario. Mirroring Langdon's conclusion at State, the leaders of the armed forces determined that Japan could not attack on widely scattered fronts. It simply seemed beyond the realm of possibility. Even Germany, far stronger than Japan, had never attacked along individual and widely separated fronts. Japan simply could not mount such an operation.[38]

If Japan did challenge the coalition in the Philippines, it would require the better part of two and a half months merely to transport the requisite forces, and as late as November 27 army intelligence concluded that Japanese forces on Hainan and in Indochina numbered fewer than 150,000, or barely enough to mount a long and difficult expedition against the archipelago. By the time Tokyo had marshaled these forces, however, Marshall's December 15 deadline would have passed, and the Philippines would presumably be completely secure. An attack on Malaya and Singapore, which required an even greater number of troops, appeared to stretch Japanese capabilities beyond the limit. If Tokyo struck directly at the East Indies, a move considered unlikely, American analysts felt certain that the Dutch could hold Java until relieved, and, if the worst came, British and Dutch authorities promised to raze the oil installations. Even the most likely Japanese move, an advance into Thailand, did not automatically mean an American-Japanese war; Marshall and Stark consistently argued that the United States should respond with force only if Japan crossed "to the west of 100 East or south of 10 North."[39]

Hornbeck also expected a new round of Japanese expansion, but he too stressed that Japan would strike Thailand or China rather than the ABD coalition. Specifically, he maintained that the Japanese military would "persevere in and intensify [its] operations toward 'bringing China to her knees.'" In part, he predicted that Tokyo would intensify its effort to conclude the China Incident because "the Japanese Government does not desire or intend or expect to have forthwith armed conflict with the United States." He fully anticipated some "new offensive operations at some point or points in the Far East" but nonetheless insisted that Japan "will endeavor to avoid attacking or being attacked by the United States." He continued: "Although there may be some armed encounters similar to those to which we have been and are a party in the Atlantic, there will not be a recognized 'state of war' such as to disrupt substantially or put an end to the present program of our Army and Navy." "The reasonable probability," he contended, "is that Japan's new military operations of the near future will be directed either toward gaining position in Thailand or operations against Yunnan and the Burma Road or both."[40]

The belief that Japan would not directly challenge the ABD coalition was shared by leading nongovernment organizations as well. William W. Lockwood, with the Institute of Pacific Relations, had concluded in midsummer that Japan would not begin any new offensives and that, while change would come slowly and might require several new cabinets, Tokyo would embrace a new, presumably less threatening foreign policy. Lockwood had, in essence, concluded that American containment had succeeded. Japan would limit its expansion, drift away from the Axis, and turn back toward London and Washington.[41]

As leading military and civilian officials and nongovernment organizations minimized the Japanese threat, thereby reducing the need for Hull to strike a deal, the chance that crumbling British or Soviet resistance might prompt Washington to conclude an agreement vanished. In early October, Ambassador Halifax assured Hull that Allied forces in the Middle East "would not be taken by surprise but would be organized to a sufficient extent to meet an attack from any direction." British forces scored victories against Rommel in November, and, as Japanese-American talks approached their denouement, the American military attaché in Cairo sent word "that the British were winning a brilliant victory." In Russia, meanwhile, Stimson learned that the Red Army was "holding hard and fast at Moscow" and that German advances on the southern part of the Eastern Front were slowing down as well. Finally, in the Atlantic, while the U-boat's success temporarily rebounded by the end of summer, that success proved temporary. In September, German attacks sent 210,000 tons of American, British, and neutral shipping to the bottom—yet even this number represented a 40 percent decline over the preceding May—and increased American Atlantic patrols cut merchant losses during the remainder of the autumn.[42]

While Hull understood that the armed forces sought more time, he believed that, if Japan limited its next advance to Thailand, or even Yunnan and the Burma Road, as expected, the army would surely have a month to prepare Philippine defenses. It is also vital to recall that by the beginning of November Hull and Hornbeck believed that coalition forces would defeat Japan in a matter of weeks. Hornbeck had little sympathy for the navy, and his ire is not difficult to understand. He believed that the State Department had bought all the time that the armed forces needed, a conclusion that Secretary Knox apparently shared.

Although Hull recognized that a modus vivendi would buy the military additional time, it came at too high a price and carried great risks. China, for example, certainly would have balked at a modus vivendi, and Washington had to avoid weakening Kuomintang morale. There was also formidable opposition within the cabinet to any last-minute deal, and by November Hull was loath to challenge the interventionists. Stimson believed that the administration had to reject any temporary agreement that barred Washington from completing its reinforcements in the Pacific. Harold Ickes, meanwhile, confided to his diary that he "would have promptly resigned from the Cabinet with a ringing statement attacking the arrangement and raising hell generally with the State Department and its policy of appeasement." While the president may not have known the depth of Ickes's feelings, he must surely have suspected. He must also have known that to act against Stimson and Ickes, two leading interventionists, might well have crippled his efforts to prepare the nation for war in Europe.[43]

Hull and President Roosevelt must also have been aware that Henry Morgenthau, another longtime Roosevelt confidant, strongly opposed a modus vivendi. In a note White wrote on Morgenthau's behalf, which Morgenthau never sent, the secretary summed up his feelings and the president's worst fears of what a modus vivendi might mean:

> Mr. President, word was brought to me yesterday evening that persons in our country's government are hoping to betray the cause of the heroic Chinese people and strike a deadly blow at all your plans for a world-wide democratic victory. . . . Oil—rivers of oil—will soon be flowing to the Japanese war machine. A humiliated democracy in the Far East, China, Holland, Great Britain will soon face a Fascist coalition emboldened and strengthened by diplomatic victory. . . .
>
> Mr. President, I am aware that many honest individuals argue that a Far East Munich is necessary at the moment. But I write this letter because millions of human beings . . . share with me the profound conviction that you will lead a suffering world to victory over the menace to all our lives and all our liberties. To sell China to her enemies for the thirty blood stained coins of gold will not only weaken our national policy in Europe as well as in the Far East, but will dim the bright lustre of America's world leadership in the great democratic fight against Fascism.
>
> On this day, Mr. President, the whole country looks to you to save America's power as well as her sacred honor. I know . . . should these stories be true, should there be Americans who seek to destroy your declared policy in world affairs, . . . you will succeed in circumventing these plotters of a new Munich.[44]

Although the president never read Morgenthau's letter or Ickes's diary, he too feared that a modus vivendi could cripple the interventionists. An unpopular accord with Japan might well have undermined the public's confidence as well as its willingness to support the administration's European policy. Roosevelt must also have been aware that, with the public straining at the leash, it might turn back to bite its master's hand should it be proffered in friendship to the hated Japanese. Certainly Harold Ickes thought so. "I have no doubt," he mused, "that the country would have reacted violently." Had the president struck a deal, his loyal friend speculated, he "would have lost the country on this issue."[45]

Ickes may well have been right as public opinion polls revealed overwhelming support for a firm stand against Japan. One November poll, for example, indicated that nearly 75 percent of the country believed the navy capable of defeating its Japanese opposite, and a November 25 survey indicated that 48 percent of the country believed that war with Japan would prove "comparatively easy." This confidence in part explains why, following the president's freezing order and throughout the autumn, leading newspapers continued their call for a strong stand. The editorials are significant for their support of an increasingly firm policy, consistent fatalism, seeming disregard for Japanese military power, discussion of specific terms that Japan must meet before an agreement could be reached, and, most importantly, impact on the president. The *Wilmington News,* for example, conceded that there were risks in firmly opposing Japan but argued: "It will be far riskier to give in to Japan now while she is relatively weak and wait to take a firm stand later on." The *New York Times* maintained that a Pacific war would amount to an unpleasant detour when it noted: "We do not want to fight Japan. We do not want to waste in the Pacific weapons and ammunition that ought to go to the more important battlefields in the Atlantic. But we will fight if Japan pushes us too far." The *Philadelphia Inquirer,* meanwhile, argued that improved American-Japanese relations required Tokyo's "complete and final withdrawal from the Axis" and its commitment to "renounce absolutely its own lawless policy of aggression, whether against China, Indo-China, Thailand, the Dutch East Indies or any other territory." Given that Roosevelt was a president who, as Clifford and Ferrell noted, often gauged public opinion through "the views of conservative [newspaper] publishers," these frank expressions of American resolve served to reinforce his increasingly inflexible stance.[46]

To be sure, not all major papers supported the administration's rigid policy. The *New York Daily News* and the *Chicago Tribune,* with combined daily circulations approaching three million, were both long-standing opponents of the administration's Far Eastern policy. To their credit, these newspapers, which often noted that Japanese violations of the Open Door's commercial protections were not as injurious as widely believed, supported diplomatic engagement long after their competitors had given up hope. Even these leading anti-interventionist organs, however, tended to minimize Japanese military power.[47]

It was ironic, given the enormous difficulty that a diffident public gave the architects of American containment in the previous decade, that a now overconfident citizenry undermined eleventh-hour diplomacy. Eight years earlier, when Nanking's minister to the United States, Albert Sze, approached Stanley Hornbeck to sound him out regarding the new administration's willingness to help mend Sino-Japanese fences, Hornbeck urged Hull to reject any American role. He was motivated in part by a conviction that continued Sino-Japanese animus would help build a domestic consensus that would allow the United States to successfully contain Japan. Seven years later, when Japan joined the Axis after the fall of Abe and Yonai, Stimson argued that Japan's membership in the Axis "will be pretty useful . . . in waking up our people to the effect that at last they have got what they have been talking about—isolation." "Clamors are being made," he continued, "for an alliance with Great Britain already." While the alliance did not come until after December 7, Roger Greene of the Committee to Defend America by Aiding the Allies noted that increased support for Great Britain prepared the public to support equally "strong action against Japan." Hornbeck, Stimson, and Greene were right. Continued Sino-Japanese animus, Japan's decision to join the Axis, and the ongoing war in Europe built a wall of solid public support for an interventionist foreign policy. But, in November 1941, the strong walls of public support had become something of a cage. A modus vivendi would raise howls of protest if it allowed Japan to remain in the Axis and on Chinese territory. And, more than any other person, Cordell Hull would have been the target of the public's fury.[48]

Hull had always been sensitive to public criticism of his Far Eastern policy. For years he had been called an appeaser, and a modus vivendi would leave him open to new, more vitriolic charges. A modus vivendi also would have forced him to confront cabinet interventionists, who, to a man, enjoyed a much closer relationship to FDR. Just days before Pearl Harbor, Hull confided the depth of his miseries to Assistant Secretary of State Adolph Berle. "Everybody was trying to run foreign policy," he lamented. "Stimson, who felt bitterly about the Far East; Knox; and pretty much everyone else. They all come at me with knives and hatchets." And they even came from State. "Acheson, yesterday morning, went at me," Hull complained, "and I had to ask him directly whether he knew what the naval force could do in the Far East." Worse still, the secretary's chronic ailments—tuberculosis and diabetes—had grown so severe that he found it difficult even to get out of bed. Tired, ill, hounded, Hull believed he had done his best.[49]

And what of the president? Twice in the run-up to war he considered a temporary agreement but ultimately backed away on each occasion. Did reasoned arguments lead him to change his mind, or did he lack the courage and the will—either personal or political—to override Hull, the cabinet, his aides, and his own fears? The answer is both and neither. Had Roosevelt been wholly committed to a temporary agreement, he would have ensured a modus vivendi with Tokyo. But, as his commitment to a modus vivendi was no greater than his earlier commitment to blockade the aggressor nations or meet with Konoe, he never felt compelled to summon the will or the courage to defy those around him. Rather than a commitment, the blockade, the summit, and, finally, the modus vivendi were mere ideas that he could easily disregard. The president was also a man, an ill and bereaved man, whose attentions were divided by two oceans. While this work has focused on one ocean, during the autumn of 1941 President Roosevelt constantly monitored the ongoing and undeclared war in the Atlantic, which consumed more of his flagging energies than did events in the Pacific. He left Asia, his secondary theater of concern, in Hull's hands and, along with Hopkins and Welles, focused on America's coming war in Europe.

The Race to the Finish

In the final week of peace, Secretary of State Hull killed the last chance to reach an agreement. He believed—and believed absolutely—that his actions were in the nation's best interests and would, far better than a temporary agreement, secure both the nation's long-term interests in Asia and immediate wartime imperatives. No doubt, his long-held distrust for Japan partly explains his decision. So too did a simple, short-term, cost-benefit analysis. A modus vivendi would buy time, but time was less important in the autumn of 1941 than it had seemed nine months earlier. Moreover, time came at a cost: Chinese morale, Anglo-Dutch confidence, public unity, a deep cabinet split. Although time had value, for Hull, the unity and determination of the Allies, the public, and the government were more important. This was especially true given that Hull could not possibly have envisioned the damage that Japan would soon visit on the ABD powers.

By November 22, the secretary had decided to reject the Japanese modus vivendi in favor of an American proposal that would rally the public behind ever more forceful measures to contain Japanese expansion. This decision ended any chance of reaching an accord and does not square with his claim that he tried until the bitter end to reach an agreement. Hull knew from Magic that plan B was Tokyo's final offer and that he had only a few days to conclude an agreement. It is difficult to understand his reasons, had he honestly hoped to reach an accord, for rejecting plan B in favor of a completely new American draft, for Tokyo's final offer was a viable option that did not differ in the most critical respects from the final draft American modus vivendi.

Japan's plan, for example, precluded attacks "into Southeast Asia and the South Pacific," whereas the American draft also applied to "Northeastern Asia . . . [and] the northern Pacific area." While the American draft protected the Russians from a Japanese attack on Siberia and the Soviet Maritime Provinces, the oncoming winter offered a more ironclad guarantee. Tokyo's plan also directed Washington to end "such actions as may hinder efforts toward peace by Japan and China." For moral and military reasons, the

United States could never terminate aid and leave China to fight Japan alone, but this was not Tokyo's intention. On November 24, Togo informed Grew that his government expected American aid to end with the start of Sino-Japanese negotiations, and the ambassador, who had no objections to this point, informed Hull that the demand was designed "largely to save face." Both plans also called for a withdrawal from southern Indochina, with the only substantive difference being that, while the Japanese draft did not set a ceiling for troop deployments in northern Indochina, the American draft called for no more than twenty-five thousand Japanese troops in the region. Finally, both the Japanese modus vivendi and the American draft remained silent as to the Axis Pact.[50]

On November 22, Hull met the Chinese and British ambassadors along with the Dutch and Australian ministers, and all agreed that it would be better to offer a substitute American modus vivendi rather than a point-by-point reply to Japan's final offer. Though not mentioned at the meeting, an American modus vivendi would have had the added advantage of public palatability, for, as Herbert Bix noted, "to have agreed to anything proposed by Tokyo would have been seen, all across the United States, as an act of 'appeasement.'" The secretary's decision, however, to withhold copies of the draft modus vivendi from the assembled diplomats belies his intention to use an American plan.[51]

Hull's subsequent meeting with Nomura and Kurusu later that same day further undermines his contention that he still hoped to conclude an agreement, for, despite the looming deadline, the secretary made no effort to lay the groundwork for *either a Japanese or an American* modus vivendi. Hull opened the meeting by telling the Japanese "that there had been a discussion of the question of whether things (meaning Japanese peaceful pledges, et cetera) could be developed in such a way that there could be a relaxation to some extent of the freezing." He happily informed Nomura and Kurusu that "there was a general feeling that the matter could all be settled if the Japanese could give us some satisfactory evidences their intentions were peaceful." Hull's comment pleased Kurusu and Nomura and led Tojo to inform the cabinet that he would enforce the provisions of the modus vivendi should diplomats conclude the agreement in time.[52]

Hull knew that Japan had set a November 25 deadline that Togo had extended to November 29, so, had the secretary honestly sought an agreement, he would have sounded out Nomura and Kurusu as to the points of divergence between Tokyo's plan B and the as yet unfinished American agreement. Hull, however, who had no intention of submitting a modus vivendi, subsequently blamed the members of the coalition for the breakdown in talks.

On November 24, Hull again met with the coalition's Washington representatives, and, if the secretary often appeared as a stern preacher to the Japanese, on this occasion he appeared as a severe father, a father terribly disappointed by the lack of initiative shown by his four wayward sons. According to Hull's account, the meeting initially went well. The representatives read copies of the revised modus vivendi and agreed that a three-month reprieve would be quite valuable to the coalition forces. While the Chinese ambassador objected to allowing twenty-five thousand Japanese troops in northern Indochina, this was far from critical. But then the meeting foundered when Hull "discovered that none of [the other representatives'] governments had given them instructions" concerning the modus vivendi. "I made it clear," he noted, "that I was definitely disappointed at these unexpected developments, at the lack of interest and lack of a disposition to cooperate." The Dutch minister broke in that his government had done its homework "and that it would support the modus vivendi proposal." Casey and Halifax could add only that, faced with a choice between submitting the modus vivendi or seeing the talks break down, London and Canberra "would wish him to use his own judgement as to terms of any such counterproposal." Not to be put off by this support, and having already decided to drop the proposal, Hull informed the chastened diplomats that he might not present the modus vivendi at all "without knowing anything about the views and attitude of their Governments."[53]

The "views and attitudes" of Hull's government, meanwhile, crystallized the next day, and, in fairness to the secretary, he was not alone in opposing the modus vivendi. At a morning meeting with Knox and Stimson, the secretary of war admitted that the modus vivendi "adequately safeguarded all our interests," but he doubted that Tokyo would ever approve it. The document "was so drastic," Stimson noted, in that it required Japan "to at once evacuate and at once to stop all preparations or threats of action, and to take no aggressive action against any of her neighbors." In return, Washington promised only "to give [the Japanese] trade in sufficient quantities only for their civilian population." Stimson made no effort to amend the draft proposal because, while he wanted additional time to prepare Philippine defenses, delay had become less important. By the time the three secretaries and Marshall met the president later that day, the modus vivendi was no longer even a topic. Instead of diplomacy, the meeting focused on the immediacy of a Japanese attack. According to Stimson, the president seemed most concerned with "how we should maneuver [the Japanese] into the position of firing the first shot without allowing too much danger to ourselves." Later that day, Stimson passed along intelligence to Hull that Japanese transports carrying five divisions were moving south. Still, neither man made any move to amend the modus vivendi. Japanese troop movements only confirmed Magic intercepts. Tokyo had set a deadline, but a deadline did not mean war.[54]

Two recent, and excellent, studies, Roger B. Jeans's *Terasaki Hidenari, Pearl Harbor, and Occupied Japan* and Takeo Iguchi's *Demystifying Pearl Harbor,* maintain that President Roosevelt stopped considering the modus vivendi only after learning that Japanese forces were moving south. No doubt, as both authors note, Tokyo's latest move outraged the president—in all likelihood because it would embarrass him, given that this latest provocative action had occurred in the midst of negotiations—but the troop movements did not lead him to alter his plans. He had already decided, before he learned of Japan's latest deployment, to drop the modus vivendi. Rather than attack an American possession, Stimson and the president believed, Japan would attack Thailand, Singapore, or the Dutch East Indies, and, therefore, the latest intelligence report merely confirmed their thinking. A week later, the president was concerned enough by the possibility of a Japanese attack on British or Dutch territory to assure Ambassador Halifax that, if Tokyo struck Malaya or the East Indies, then "we should obviously all be together." On December 3, as signs of an imminent Japanese attack on Thailand accumulated, Roosevelt informed Halifax that the United States would support Britain should it go to war to defend Thai sovereignty.[55]

Signs of an impending Japanese attack and promises to defend colonial possessions did not bode well for the administration, for public support on this point remained tepid. As the historian Richard N. Current compellingly demonstrated in his 1953 study "How Stimson Meant to 'Maneuver' the Japanese," public opposition to defending the Dutch and British Empires largely explains the president's comment about maneuvering Tokyo into firing the first shot. In order to rally public opinion, Roosevelt had to wait for Japan to strike first, but, if, as expected, Tokyo attacked Thai, British, or Dutch targets, then rallying the public might prove difficult.[56]

While the president and his closest advisers mulled over ways to unite the public, Minister Casey received instructions from home regarding Hull's plan. From Canberra, Minister for External Affairs H. V. Evatt cabled his emphatic view "that delay is so important at present that every reasonable step should be taken to avoid breakdown of Hull-Kurusu talks." Evatt clearly found Hull's demand that Canberra bless the talks more than a little awkward, for as he told Casey: "It is difficult to see how you can be authorized to bind this government in relation to an arrangement as to which we are not even suggested parties." Nonetheless, his cable left little room for doubt. "Above all," he instructed Casey, "primary consideration is to prevent breakdown of present talks."[57]

Halifax, meanwhile, delivered Whitehall's response on November 25, and, while it was not as supportive of the modus vivendi as either the Dutch or Australian answer, neither was it a hysterical denunciation. In brief, the Foreign Office, which objected to large Japanese troop concentrations in northern Indochina and the effect the modus vivendi might have on Chiang, saw Tokyo's plan B "as the opening movement in a process of bargaining" and was prepared to support the secretary if he "put forward a counter proposal." Clearly concerned lest it offend the Tennessean once again, London expressed "complete confidence in Mr. Hull's handling of these negotiations" as well as its firm faith that the secretary "is in the best position to judge."[58]

Chiang Kai-shek apparently did not share London's confidence. The generalissimo "got the impression that the United States Government . . . is still inclined to appease Japan at the expense of China." Hu Shih told Hull that Chungking "firmly opposed . . . any measure which may have the effect of increasing China's difficulty in her war of resistance, or of strengthening Japan's power in her aggression against China." Owen Lattimore, the president's adviser to Chiang Kai-shek, expressed deeper concerns when he cabled Washington "that even the Generalissimo questions his ability to hold the situation together if the Chinese national trust in America is undermined by reports of Japan's escaping military defeat by diplomatic victory."[59]

Despite Dutch and Australian support for the modus vivendi and British expressions of confidence, Hull went to the White House the next morning and announced that, owing to "the opposition of the Chinese Government and either the half-hearted support or the actual opposition of the British, the Netherlands and the Australian Governments" as well as the "utter lack of an understanding of the vast importance and value otherwise of the modus vivendi," he would submit only the plan for a comprehensive settlement. This decision did not trouble Roosevelt, and, after the meeting, Hull telephoned Stimson and told him that he had decided not to propose a modus vivendi to Japan and instead planned "to kick the whole thing over" and "tell them that he had no other proposition at all." Negotiations were over.[60]

Despite Hull's account, coalition opposition does not explain his decision. With the exception of Chungking, the other coalition partners *believed that they had approved the modus vivendi.* On November 26, Casey cabled Evatt: "The interested Governments other than the Chinese have now said in effect 'buy time as cheaply as possible.'" The following day Alexander Loudon, Dutch minister to the United States, took care to reiterate "that he had supported . . . [Hull] unequivocally in connection with the proposed modus vivendi." For his part, Halifax, who described Hull's decision to scrap the modus vivendi as a "sudden change" in direction, told Welles that he could not understand the secretary's attitude "as much as he had communicated to Secretary Hull the full support of the British Government."[61]

It is possible that the secretary misinterpreted objections to specific provisions as opposition to the entire modus vivendi. It is also quite possible that Anglo-Dutch-Australian support did not counterbalance Chinese opposition. Hull had, after all, lamented to Halifax "that Chiang Kai-shek . . . has sent numerous hysterical cable messages to different Cabinet officers and high officials in the Government other than the State Department, . . . sometimes even ignoring the President." Chiang's brother-in-law, Hull complained, "disseminate[s] damaging reports at times to the press and others, apparently with no particular purpose in mind." Arguments that a modus vivendi would cause a Chinese collapse, more recent reports that Chiang might seek a separate peace, or Churchill's plea to support China even at the risk of war no doubt influenced Hull, but his claim that Chinese opposition killed the modus vivendi was disingenuous. If the secretary is to be believed, then the reader must conclude that, all other issues aside (Hull's suspicion, his record in previous negotiations, interventionist opposition), had Chiang endorsed the modus vivendi, Hull would have submitted it for Tokyo's approval.[62]

Even before he met with coalition representatives, Stimson, Knox, Marshall, and the president, Hull had taken steps to ensure that the final week of negotiations would not produce an agreement. FE prepared both an official American draft modus vivendi and a comprehensive peace proposal. Prior to this, FE also produced a comprehensive statement of American principles *that Hull would deliver only when the administration decided to end the discussions with Nomura and Kurusu.* After Hull submitted the final American plan minus the modus vivendi, T. V. Soong worried that the secretary had sold China out. According to Morgenthau, however, Stanley Hornbeck reassured Soong that this was not the case. Rather, Morgenthau recounts, Hornbeck told Soong that the memo "had been prepared some time ago in case the United States was ready to break off with Japan." This indicates that, had Hull submitted both plans, as he told the coalition delegates he intended to do, the final plan would have functioned as a poison pill.[63]

But Hull did not need a poison pill to kill the modus vivendi. Instead, he used the remains of the White memorandum. Between November 19, when Hamilton redrafted White's proposal, and November 26, when Hull delivered his ten-point plan, the November 11 restatement of principles and the Hamilton redraft merged into a uncompromising statement known as the "Hull Note." Hamilton's redraft, which the military approved as the basis for negotiations, committed the United States to the following ten points:

1. To reduce to a normal footing American naval forces now in Pacific waters, without of course limiting in any way the freedom of action and of decision of the Government of the United States with regard to the disposition of the naval forces of the United States.
2. To negotiate a multilateral non-aggression pact with Japan, China, the British Empire, the Netherlands, Thailand and Soviet Russia.
3. To suggest to the Chinese Government and to the Japanese Government that those Governments enter into peaceful negotiations with regard to the future status of Manchuria.
4. To enter into negotiations with the British, Chinese, Dutch, Thai and Japanese Governments for the conclusion of an agreement whereunder each of the Governments would pledge itself to respect the territorial integrity of French Indochina and, in the event that there should develop threat to the territorial integrity of Indochina, to enter into immediate consultation with a view to taking such measures as may be deemed necessary and advisable to meet the threat in question. Such agreement would provide also that each of the Governments party to the agreement would not seek or accept preferential treatment in its trade relations with Indochina and would use its influence to obtain for each of the signatories most-favored-nation treatment in trade and commerce with French Indochina.
5. To give up all extraterritorial rights in China, including rights and interests in and with regard to the International settlements at Shanghai and Amoy, and rights under the Boxer protocol of 1901. To endeavor to obtain the agreement of the British Government to give up British extraterritorial rights in China, including rights in international settlements and in concessions and under the Boxer Protocol of 1901. To use its influence towards causing the British Government to cede Hong Kong to China. (This provision might take the form of an undertaking to use our influence with the British Government to cause the British Government to sell Hong Kong to China, the purchase price to be loaned to China by the United States.)
6. To recommend to Congress enactment of legislation to amend the Immigration Act of 1924 so as to place all peoples of all races on a quota basis.
7. To negotiate a trade agreement with Japan, giving Japan (a) most-favored-nation treatment and (b) such concessions on Japanese imports into the United States as can be mutually satisfactorily arranged, including an agreement to bind raw silk on the free list. To enter into a joint declaration between the United States and Japan with regard to commer-

cial policy along the lines of the draft handed the Japanese Ambassador on November 15.

8. To extend to Japan a $2,000,000,000 20 year credit at 2 percent interest, to be drawn upon at the rate not to exceed 200,000,000 a year except with the approval of the President of the United States. (Note: This provision should be prepared to extend a similar credit to China.) (Note: This provision presumably would require Congressional approval.)

9. To set up a $500,000,000 stabilization fund half supplied by Japan and half by the United States, to be used for the stabilization of the dollar-yen rate. (Note: The United States should be prepared to act similarly in regard to China.) (Note: This provision may require Congressional approval.)

10. To remove the freezing restrictions on Japanese funds in the United States.

Hamilton's redraft in turn bound Tokyo to the following eight points:

1. To withdraw all military, naval, air and police forces from China (excluding Manchuria—see separate provisions) and from Indochina.

2. To withdraw all support—military, political, economic—from any government or regime in China other than the Government of the National Republic of China with capital temporarily at Chunking.

3. To replace with yen currency at a rate to be agreed upon among the Treasuries of China, Japan, Great Britain, and the United States all Japanese military scrip, yen, and local regime notes circulating in China.

4. To give up all extraterritoriality rights in China, including rights in international settlements and concessions and rights under the Boxer Protocol.

5. To withdraw all Japanese troops from Manchuria except for a few divisions necessary as a police force, provided U.S.S.R. withdraws all her troops from the Far Eastern front except for an equivalent remainder.

6. To sell to the United States . . . Japanese merchant shipping, to be delivered to the United States within three months of the signing of the present agreement; also to sell to the United States up to 50 percent of Japan's current output of shipping, including naval and commercial ships, on a cost–plus–20 percent basis as the United States may select, it being understood that the United States will sell Japan such raw materials as it may be necessary for Japan to import for these purchases.

7. To negotiate a multilateral non-aggression pact with the United States, China, the British Empire, the Netherlands, Thailand and Soviet Russia.
8. To remove the freezing restrictions on American funds in Japan.[64]

Two days later, FE's latest redraft dropped points 6 and 8 from the American side and substituted a commitment "to take steps . . . directed toward terminating the Nine Power Treaty." While Tokyo lost ground on immigration restrictions and reconstruction loans, it gained the end of an agreement that successive Japanese cabinets had long argued no longer conformed to reality. The latest American draft also deleted points 3 and 5, thereby lessening Japanese commitments. The following day, FE's newest draft deleted point 1, dealing with the disposition of American naval forces in the Pacific, and also committed Tokyo to agree that the Axis Pact "shall not be interpreted by Japan in such a way as to conflict with the fundamental purpose of this agreement, the establishment and preservation of peace throughout the Pacific area." In a sense the latest draft increased Tokyo's commitments, yet in a more fundamental way it represented an astonishing American concession. While Hull consistently maintained that Japan's membership in the Axis prevented any fundamental readjustment of Japanese-American relations, senior members of FE now reversed course and were prepared to accept Tokyo's word just four days before the talks collapsed.[65]

Within forty-eight hours, however, Hull reset America's diplomatic compass and steered the negotiations back toward an utterly uncompromising position. By November 24, before he proclaimed his intention to drop the modus vivendi in light of the attitude of the coalition partners, the modus vivendi was attached to a comprehensive draft proposal that bore little resemblance to either White's proposal or the FE redrafts of November 19, 21, or 22. The latest draft of the comprehensive plan contained the following eleven points:

1. The Government of the United States and the Government of Japan will endeavor to conclude a multilateral non-aggression pact among the British Empire, China, Japan, the Netherlands, the Soviet Union, Thailand, and the United States.
2. Both Governments will endeavor to conclude among the American, British, Chinese, Japanese, the Netherlands and Thai Governments an agreement whereunder each of the Governments would pledge to respect the territorial integrity of French Indochina and, in the event that there should develop threat to the territorial integrity of Indochina, to enter

into immediate consultation with a view to taking such measures as may be deemed necessary and advisable to meet the threat in question. Such agreement would provide also that each of the Governments party to the agreement would not seek or accept preferential treatment in its trade or economic relations with Indochina and would use its influence to obtain for each of the signatories equality of treatment in trade and commerce with French Indochina.

3. The Government of Japan will withdraw all military, naval, air and police forces from China (excluding Manchuria—see separate provision, paragraph six) and from Indochina.

4. The Government of the United States and the Government of Japan will not support—militarily, politically economically—any government or regime in China other than the National Government of the Republic of China with capital temporarily at Chunking.

5. Both Governments will give up all extraterritorial rights in China, including rights and interests in and with regard to international settlements and concessions, and rights under the Boxer protocol of 1901. Both Governments will endeavor to obtain the agreement of the British and other governments to give up extraterritorial rights in China, including rights in international settlements and in concessions and under the Boxer Protocol of 1901.

6. The Government of the United States will suggest to the Chinese Government that those Governments enter into peaceful negotiations with regard to the future status of Manchuria.

7. The Government of the United States and the Government of Japan will enter into negotiations for the conclusion between the United States and Japan of a trade agreement, based upon reciprocal most-favored-nation treatment and reduction of trade barriers by both countries, including an undertaking to bind raw silk on the free list.

8. The Government of the United States and the Government of Japan will, respectively, remove the freezing restrictions on Japanese funds in the United States and on American funds in Japan.

9. Both Governments will agree upon a plan for the stabilization of the dollar-yen rate, with the allocation of funds adequate for this purpose, half to be supplied by Japan and half by the United States.

10. Both Governments will agree that no agreement to which either is party shall be interpreted by it in such a way as to conflict with the fundamental purpose of this agreement, the establishment and preservation of peace throughout the Pacific area.

11. Both Governments will use their influence to cause other govern-

ments to adhere to and give practical application to the basic political and economic principles set forth in this agreement.[66]

By November 24, FE had shorn the draft comprehensive agreement of nearly all its financial incentives. In less than twenty-four hours, the final version offered Tokyo nothing. Hull's November 26 statement required Tokyo to withdraw forces from all China, including Manchuria, and deleted paragraph 6, in which Washington proposed Sino-Japanese negotiations over the future of Manchuria.[67]

What explains this dramatic turnabout? Certainly, no Japanese action. Japanese troop movements clearly alarmed the administration and the service chiefs, but these movements only confirmed what Hull already knew: Tokyo had a deadline. Moreover, Grew had informed the State Department weeks earlier that the Tojo cabinet was working for peace but preparing for war should diplomacy fail. Japan, he noted, "is on the one hand seeking by peaceful means to extricate herself from the situation which she is in at present" while simultaneously preparing for war "in the event that her efforts . . . end in failure." Hamilton similarly informed Hull just days after Tojo took power that Tokyo intended to seek a negotiated settlement while preparing for war should talks fail. In short, no Japanese actions between November 19 and November 25 adequately explain the decision to gut White's proposal and Hamilton's redraft. The only compelling explanation is that Hull opposed an agreement—as he had since 1933—and no persons or events forced him to change his position. The secretary's actions during the final week of negotiations can be explained only by his consistent opposition to any Japanese-American accord. Four days after Pearl Harbor, Arthur Krock, the dean of American journalists, spoke with Hull, who admitted not only that he had supported the embargo but that "he would have embargoed everything to Japan, including oil." In an even more revealing comment, the Tennessean admitted that securing an agreement with Tokyo had not been the aim of his most recent talks with Nomura. "Well," Krock ventured, "we were playing for time until we could be strong enough to smash the Japs, and they found out and smashed us first, isn't that so?" According to Krock, "Hull said it was."[68]

In his official testimony before the Pearl Harbor Congressional Committee, Hull offered a wholly self-serving account, squarely at odds with the record. "Well, the truth is," he told the committee, "[my associates and I] were most anxious, as we have said here at different times, to go forward with the conversations, and we had every motive to desire to go forward with them." The secretary explained that his ten-point note represented "an ordinary, normal plan for international relations" and that "all they had to do was to announce that they were through with conquest and aggression and that automatically they would have become the beneficiaries of these proposals."[69]

Hull's ten-point proposal, however, bore little resemblance to a "normal plan," and its public disclosure struck Nomura like a body blow. "The State Department," he informed Togo on November 28, "which had maintained silence concerning the Japanese-American negotiations, broke its silence and made disclosure of the conversations yesterday." For Nomura, and especially for Togo, this represented an ominous change in tactics. The foreign minister interpreted Hull's decision to release the details of American-Japanese negotiations as evidence that Washington had decided on war. He was not far from the mark. The administration's decision to at last make public details of the talks can be interpreted only as a final bid to garner support in the event that the president committed American forces to defend either British or Dutch possessions. Had Hull known that in less than a fortnight the American people would unite behind any measures needed to crush the Japanese Empire, he might not have released details of the negotiations. But, then, he did not anticipate a Japanese attack on Pearl Harbor.[70]

Conclusion

> And the Japanese were right to do it. From their point of view we were their mortal enemy. As long as we existed, we were a deadly threat to them. Their only mistake was that they failed to finish us at the start.
>
> —Professor Groeteschele in *Fail-Safe* (1964)

> It should be remembered that three centuries ago a great Japanese leader started out to conquer China and that ultimately the Japanese nation gave up on that idea. . . . Not long after the Japanese Army and Navy had withdrawn . . . another great Japanese leader decided to make Japan an isolated and secluded hermit nation.
>
> —Stanley Hornbeck (1940)

In the autumn of 1941, America's carefully crafted containment strategy brought on the war its creators sought to avoid. In Washington, the dream of achieving long-term objectives and short-term imperatives, safeguarding the Open Door and breaking the Axis Alliance, led senior military and civilian leaders to reject an eleventh-hour compromise. In turn, this decision left the Japanese government with no choice but war.

In explaining why negotiations failed, Foreign Minister Togo pointed to problems that had plagued Japanese-American relations for decades. "The United States Government," he declared, "has persistently adhered to its traditional doctrines and principles . . . in East Asia." If Japan were to accept Washington's latest proposal, he argued, the empire's "very survival would inevitably be threatened." His colleague, Privy Council President Yoshimichi Hara, agreed. To accept Hull's offer meant erasing "in one stroke not only our gains in the Sino-Japanese and Russo-Japanese wars but also the benefits of the Manchurian Incident." For Tojo, Washington's final proposal simply "threatened the very existence of our empire."[1]

If US policy, especially the transition from containment to rollback, convinced the Tojo cabinet that war was preferable to diplomacy, it persuaded its American counterpart that conflict was preferable to compromise. Stimson, who continued to see Thailand as Japan's next victim, grew so anxious to prevent a last-minute accord that he badgered Marshall and Stark not to suggest "to the President that he request Japan to reopen the conversations." While "glad to have more time" to prepare for war, he "didn't want it at any cost of humility on the part of the United States or of reopening the thing which would show a weakness on our part." He need not have worried. Rather than pleading for additional time, Marshall and Stark simply told Roosevelt that the latest Japanese troop movements suggested a southern advance. While they could not specify a likely target, they did inform FDR that, rather than Malaya, Singapore, or the East Indies, the Japanese would in all probability strike the Burma Road, Thailand, or the Philippines. Despite this sobering news and their conclusion that "the desirable strength has not been reached," neither insisted on additional concrete steps to buy more time. They even noted that, from the standpoint of coalition defense, "Japanese involvement in Yunnan or Thailand up to a certain extent is advantageous" as it "leads to further dispersion, longer lines of communication and an additional burden on communications."[2]

As Japanese forces continued to move, Stimson, Knox, and Hornbeck drew up for the president to send to Congress a war warning that, like Hull's ten-point plan, sought to rally the nation should the administration decide to defend either Thailand or British and Dutch colonial possessions. The president, who left for Warm Springs, Georgia, even before his aides completed the warning, was also not overly concerned about the prospect of war. Recent intelligence indicating that Japanese troop transports were heading for Saigon rather than points further south convinced Stimson that the Japanese were "evidently not going to make the attack at once and are . . . not even going to invade Thailand at once." The coalition, he believed, had gained a further delay.[3]

At the State Department, meanwhile, rollback's most stalwart supporters were, like Stimson, more concerned with the prospect of a last-minute American compromise than with the chance of a Japanese-American conflict. Hull wanted "the President to take a stiff stand," while "Hornbeck was urging determination to act by force of arms" to defend Thailand. Harry Hopkins and Associate Justice of the Supreme Court Felix Frankfurter also sought "decisive action," and Hopkins, who enjoyed as close a relationship with the president as any man, roused himself from his hospital bed in order to lunch with FDR. After their meeting, Hopkins gave Frankfurter some good news: "The President was all right. He had not . . . weakened at all." He had no reason to weaken, for, like his senior advisers, he continued to believe that the country and its allies had more to fear from compromise than from conflict.[4]

When the bombs at last fell on Pearl Harbor and war came, when rollback had at last failed and failed completely, its supporters were stunned. Hull famously castigated Nomura and Kurusu, but he seemed less surprised than angry that Japan should attack without a prior declaration of war. Stimson no doubt was caught off guard as well, and, while he supported rollback, he was a relative newcomer to the administration and was always as focused on war plans and preparations as on diplomacy. The attack on Pearl Harbor also shocked the president, yet, as was Hull, he was as much astonished by Japan's success as he was stunned by its duplicity. Besides, Roosevelt, Stimson, and Hull were privy to Magic, and, while they did not know exactly what Japan was planning, they knew something was afoot.

Stanley Hornbeck, however, was not privy to Magic, and, therefore, his surprise was the most pure and the most profound. He had wagered just days before the attack that the odds were five to one against Japan going to war with America before December 15. His shock on December 7, however, involved much more than simply being wrong. He had nurtured containment and fought for rollback, convinced that these policies would protect America and China. More significantly, he predicted that, if containment and then rollback succeeded and Japan were defeated in China, Tokyo might once again pursue an isolationist foreign policy as it had after Japan's last failure on the Asian mainland, some 350 years earlier. His hubris, as well as his confidence in America's ability to transform nations, is familiar to Americans in the twenty-first century and should serve as a sobering, cautionary reminder of the limits of American power. Rollback was about much more than the Open Door and the Axis Alliance. It was about revolutionary change in Japan and, by extension, the entire world system. To Hornbeck more than any other man, the failure of American policy must have seemed profoundly and uniquely personal.[5]

The failure of rollback, however, was not the failure of Hornbeck alone. American statesmen had committed the same mistakes made by Tsar Nicholas II's aides thirty-seven years earlier. In the winter of 1904, Russian officials believed that Japan sought at the conference table what it would not dare attempt to win on the battlefield and that the Russian Empire had more to fear from compromise than from conflict. In 1941, far too many American officials believed the same. The Roosevelt administration, no less than Nicholas II's government, left Japan to choose between a ruinous war and a catastrophic peace.

In a fundamental sense, however, Washington's errors were greater than St. Petersburg's, for America's best and brightest were not operating in unexplored territory. In 1904, Japanese diplomacy was still a tabula rasa, but not so in 1941. America's leaders simply studied the wrong history and took away the wrong lessons. Instead of learning from 1894 and 1904 that, if pushed to its limits, Japan would lash out against a far larger enemy, Hull, Hornbeck, and even Henry Stimson, the dean of American statesmen, learned only the spurious lessons of 1907, 1917, and 1932, that American power could bend Japan to Washington's will.

Equally troubling were the many lost opportunities that litter the landscape of Japanese-American diplomacy. That Hull could not break free of an institutional mistrust born out of a generation of frustration to pursue constructive diplomacy is understandable. More disturbing, however, is the failure of American policymakers to embrace the constructive diplomacy outlined by Ambassador Grew. There is always a danger that an ambassador might "go native" and lose his or her objectivity, but that danger must be balanced by the understanding, certainly true at any time between 1933 and 1941, that Grew knew more about Japan than the president, Hull, Hornbeck, Stimson, and Ballantine did. These men, however, either marginalized Grew, ignored him, or used his recommendations when they supported their notions of what constituted proper policy; the contemporary term for this, popularized in the last decade, is *cherry-picking* intelligence. This contributed to the tragedy of the Pacific War and serves as a warning that, if Washington-area policymakers continue to marginalize, ignore, or misuse the input of senior career diplomats, then tragedy awaits America once again in some misunderstood part of the world.

In fairness to President Roosevelt and his inner circle, the habit of largely discounting the analysis and recommendations of their ambassador was shared by their counterparts in Tokyo and London. Ambassadors Craigie and Nomura were no less prescient than Grew and were no more successful in either swaying their governments to adopt conciliatory diplomacy or convincing them to forgo disastrous policies.

The American decision to ignore calls from Grew, Craigie, and Nomura, as well as from the Australian, British, and Dutch governments, for a modus vivendi takes on added importance given Tojo's insistence that such an offer would have averted war. There remains an almost a priori belief in the United States, and perhaps elsewhere, that Tojo was bent on war—a belief seemingly confirmed both by the Pacific War and by Tojo's postwar trial and subsequent execution. Yet, by fashioning its own modus vivendi, the Tojo cabinet demonstrated its willingness to accept a last-minute compromise.

Long after the war had begun and repeated setbacks had brought Japan's ultimate defeat into clearer view, Tojo told Kurusu that, had the "American note of November 26th . . . been somewhat more conciliatory, it would have been impossible for Japan to go into the war." According to General Kenryo Sato, the prime minister told him that he would have accepted an American modus vivendi in order "to carry out the Emperor's wishes and avoid war."[6]

Had Hull and the president either embraced Japan's plan B or forwarded a more temperate proposal than the Hull Note, war in the Pacific may well have been averted. A six-month reprieve ending in June 1942 would have presented Japanese policymakers with a very different environment in which to decide on war or peace. By June 1942, American shipyards were churning out the products of the third and fourth Vinson programs, and the United States was coming near producing as much war matériel as were all the Axis nations combined. The British still held Suez, and the Russians had also proved at the Battle of Moscow that Germany was not invincible. No one can be sure what policy Tojo, Togo, and others would have advocated given this strategic picture, yet there is no doubt that these changes would have made a decision to go to war more difficult in June 1942 than it was in December 1941.

Had Japan and America avoided war in 1941—*had containment succeeded*—it is altogether likely that both nations' aversion to revolution and communism would have produced a postwar relationship as strong as that which bound the nations together in an informal alliance at the dawn of the twentieth century. Germany's defeat, Russia's victory, and Mao's triumph would have left Japanese statesmen no other choice but to align their country within the American orbit. Had containment been allowed to succeed, Hornbeck's vision of a new Japan, pro-American rather than isolated, might well have occurred.

But what kind of statesmen would have led this reorientation of Japanese diplomacy, and what kind of Japan would they have led? While pro-American, the new Japan would likely be heavily influenced by the military, and there is no guarantee that postwar progressives like Shidehara and Yoshida would have led the country. It is equally unlikely that the Meiji Constitution would have been scrapped, as it was in 1946, in favor of a more progressive document that provided for women's suffrage and guaranteed basic civil liberties. Nor would Japan's rural population have enjoyed the benefits of an American-led land-redistribution program. In time, prosperity and a close relationship with Washington would have led Japan to develop along the lines of South Korea and Taiwan. A healthy, progressive democracy would have evolved, but in fits and starts, and the process would have taken fifty, rather than five, years.

Clearly, war and Japan's ruinous defeat quickly produced the stable, prosperous, democratic, and humane nation that postwar Japan became. War destroyed the Japanese Empire and the Meiji state and expunged imperialism and, most significantly, militarism from the Japanese polity. The forces that produced the Siberian intervention and the Mukden Incident, the assassinations of Prime Ministers Hamaguchi and Inukai, the February 26, 1936, Incident, and the Sino-Japanese and Pacific Wars, disappeared just after the birth of the atomic age. Militarism plagued Japan from the earliest days of the Meiji Restoration, and neither modernization, nor victory against China and Russia, nor an alliance with Great Britain, nor even America's decades-long containment policy lessened the threat that the Japanese military posed to its own people and those of neighboring countries. Only a defeat far more terrible than anything that Tojo or Nagano or even Kanji Ishiwara could imagine destroyed the specter of Japanese militarism.

If war and defeat quickly produced a stable and democratic Japan, the same cannot be said for the rest of Asia, where Japan's early victories and sudden collapse created a dangerous power vacuum. In August 1945, General Albert C. Wedemeyer, the commander of the American forces in China, described the region as "an enormous pot, seething and boiling." Containment's failure not only brought on the Pacific War; it also contributed to a generation of unrest that led directly to America's long and divisive wars in Korea and Indochina. Had containment been allowed to claim its final victory in the autumn of 1941, the end of Japanese, British, French, and Dutch colonialism in Asia might have looked like the crumbling of the Soviet Empire in 1991—troubled, and at times violent, but tranquil in comparison to postwar Burma, Indonesia, Korea, Laos, Cambodia, and Vietnam.[7]

The failure of American containment in December 1941 was neither the first nor the last time this strategy has failed. And, if the postwar history of Asia or the early twenty-first-century history of Iraq is any guide, Americans must gain a better understanding of how to make this policy work and how to avoid making it fail.

Acknowledgments

I first became interested in American-Japanese diplomacy almost twenty-five years ago. After graduating from college I took a job teaching English in Gifu, a small and lovely city in central Japan. I did not give much thought to the war, although it sometimes came up in conversations with students, coworkers, and friends. One weekend, in late July 1989, near the end of my stay, I attended a fireworks festival along the banks of the Nagara River. The next day at work one of my older students asked about my weekend, and, when I told her that I had attended the festival, she smiled and said she remembered sleeping on the banks of the same river with her mother on warm summer nights when she was a little girl. I thought that they slept outdoors to escape the oppressive heat that blankets central Honshu in summer, but then she continued her story. "We slept on the banks of the river," she told me, "to escape the bombing of Gifu." She said it matter-of-factly and without malice, and perhaps for the first time I understood why so much of Gifu was no more than forty years old. Until then, I had thought that only large cities like Tokyo experienced heavy bombings, but I soon learned that much of Gifu was leveled during the war. By the time I left Gifu, I knew that I wanted to learn more about why Japan and America went to war in 1941.

After returning home, I decided to go back to school, first for a master's at the University of California, Riverside, then for a Ph.D. at Rutgers University. At Riverside, Professors Richard Godbear and Irwin Wall encouraged my interest in diplomatic history and helped me find an appropriate doctoral program. Professor Wall also worked with me extensively on World War II diplomatic history and, along with his late wife, Sarah, offered me encouragement and friendship.

At Rutgers, Donald Roden taught me Japanese history and patiently and consistently supported my interest in American-Japanese diplomatic history throughout my graduate program. Warren Kimball brought me to Rutgers and shared with me his unparalleled understanding of Roosevelt-era diplomacy. My adviser, Lloyd Gardner, was everything that a graduate student could want. His knowledge of and insight into American diplomatic history, acquired during his decades-long career, were matched only by the kindness that he showed me and his other students. I was fortunate to end up at Rutgers with its talented and caring faculty and very lucky to have trained under three such nurturing individuals.

My work also benefited from the time and efforts of several other scholars. Thomas Buckley at the University of Tulsa read my manuscript and offered his insights into Japanese-American diplomacy and his unrivaled expertise on the Washington Conference system. John W. Chambers, who fortunately took me under his wing early in my stay at Rutgers, read an early draft of this study and helped me begin the long process of revising my manuscript. G. Kurt Piehler of Florida State University and J. Garry Clifford of the University of Connecticut read drafts and offered steady encouragement and insightful suggestions for improvement. At Fayetteville State University, my friend and colleague Stanley Johnson read the entire draft, saving me from countless errors as well as from writing that only I found clear or clever.

The staffs of many libraries facilitated my research, and two in particular deserve special thanks. A generous research fellowship from the Friends of the Princeton University Library allowed me several weeks of uninterrupted work, and the staff of Princeton's Seeley G. Mudd Manuscript Library helped me locate crucial information needed to bring my work to fruition. Finally, the staff at Fayetteville State University's Charles Chesnutt Library generously secured critical secondary source material from outside libraries and, just as importantly, ensured that these same libraries restored my borrowing privileges when I failed to return items by their due dates.

My editor at the University Press of Kentucky, Steve Wrinn, encouraged my work from the moment my manuscript landed on his desk. Steve, Allison Webster, Joseph Brown, and the entire staff have been a joy to work with, and this book has benefited tremendously from my association with them.

My wife, Melinda, and sons, Graham and Sam, consistently supported this project. The boys happily sacrificed parts of their school holidays to take research trips, while Melinda read various drafts, listened to countless ideas, and convinced me to finally send off the manuscript.

In the end, this work was made possible by my mother and father, Betty and Earl Pash, who always encouraged my siblings and me to choose courses of study and careers that made us happy. When I decided what made me happy, my parents supported my decision and made it possible for me to attend graduate school and begin this project. For a lifetime of unwavering encouragement, I dedicate this work to them.

Notes

The abbreviation *FRUS* is used throughout the notes to refer to the following source: US Department of State, *Papers Relating to the Foreign Relations of the United States* (Washington, DC: US Government Printing Office, 1861–).

Groupings of records labeled RG and WPD are held by the National Archives and Records Administration.

The epigraphs at the front of the book come from the following sources: "An Approach to the Problem of Eliminating Tension with Japan and Insuring the Defeat of Germany," folder 16 A, box 6, Harry Dexter White Papers, Seeley Mudd Library, Princeton University, Princeton, NJ; James Madison, "Universal Peace," *National Gazette,* February 2, 1792.

Preface

1. Michael A. Barnhart, *Japan and the World since 1868* (London: Edward Arnold, 1995), 34–37; John Albert White, *The Diplomacy of the Russo-Japanese War* (Princeton, NJ: Princeton University Press, 1964), 84–85.

2. R. M. Connaughton, *The War of the Rising Sun and the Tumbling Bear: A Military History of the Russo-Japanese War, 1904–1905* (London: Routledge, 1988), 22; Ian Nish, *The Origins of the Russo-Japanese War* (London: Longman, 1985), 249; Andrew Malozemoff, *Russian Far Eastern Policy, 1881–1904, with Special Emphasis on the Causes of the Russo-Japanese War* (Berkeley: University of California Press, 1958), 244.

3. Nish, *Origins,* 206–7.

4. William Appleman Williams, *The Tragedy of American Diplomacy,* new ed. (New York: Norton, 1972), 52; Walter McDougal, *Promised Land, Crusader State* (Boston: Mariner, 1997), 7; Walter Russell Mead, *Special Providence: American Foreign Policy and How It Changed the World* (New York: Routledge, 2002), 107–9; Fred Greene, "The Military View of American National Policy, 1904–1940," *American Historical Review* 66, no. 2 (January 1961): 363–65, 370–74.

5. A. Whitney Griswold, *The Far Eastern Policy of the United States* (New Haven, CT: Yale University Press, 1938). Writing in the 1930s, Griswold recognized both continuity in American Far Eastern diplomacy as well as a continued interest in restraining Japanese expansion.

6. McDougal, *Promised Land,* 116; Griswold, *Far Eastern Policy,* 126–30.

7. *New York Times,* August 3, 1917, 1.

8. Ronald H. Spector, *In the Ruins of Empire: The Japanese Surrender and the Battle for Postwar Asia* (New York: Random House, 2008), passim.

9. James William Morley, ed., *Deterrent Diplomacy: Japan, Germany, and the*

USSR, 1935–1940: Japan, Germany, and the USSR, 1935–1940: Selected Translations from Taiheiyo senso e no michi: kaisen gaiko shi, trans. James William Morley, Alvin D. Coox, and Hans Baerwald (New York: Columbia University Press, 1976), *The Fateful Choice: Japan's Advance into Southeast Asia, 1939–1941: Selected Translations from Taiheiyo senso e no michi: kaisen gaiko shi,* trans. Peter A. Berton and Robert A. Scalapino (New York: Columbia University Press, 1980), *The China Quagmire: Japan's Expansion on the Asian Continent: Selected Translations from Taiheiyo senso e no michi: kaisen gaiko shi,* trans. James William Morley (New York: Columbia University Press, 1983), *Japan Erupts: The London Naval Conference and the Manchurian Incident, 1928–1932: Selected Translations from Taiheiyo senso e no michi: kaisen gaiko shi,* trans. Arthur E. Tiedemann, Marius B. Jansen, and Akira Iriye (New York: Columbia University Press, 1984), and *The Final Confrontation: Selected Translations from Taiheiyo senso e no michi: kaisen gaiko shi,* trans. David A. Titus (New York: Columbia University Press, 1994); Barnhart, *Japan and the World;* Warren F. Kimball, ed., *Alliance Emerging,* vol. 1 of *Churchill and Roosevelt: The Complete Correspondence* (Princeton, NJ: Princeton University Press, 1984); Anthony Best, *Britain, Japan, and Pearl Harbor: Avoiding War in East Asia, 1936–1941* (London: Routledge, 1995).

10. John W. Dower, *War without Mercy: Race and Power in the Pacific War* (New York: Random House, 1986); James Reed, *The Missionary Mind and American East Asian Policy, 1911–1915* (Cambridge, MA: Harvard University Press, 1983); Williams, *Tragedy of American Diplomacy.*

Introduction

1. Francis L. Hawks, comp., *Commodore Perry and the Opening of Japan: Narrative of the Expedition of an American Squadron to the China Seas and Japan, 1852–1854* (1856; reprint, Gloucestershire: Nonsuch, 2005), 227; Walter LaFeber, *The Clash: A History of U.S.-Japanese Relations throughout History* (New York: Norton, 1997), 10.

2. LaFeber, *The Clash,* 10–13.

3. Hawks, comp., *Commodore Perry,* 8, 59.

4. Ibid., 228–70 passim; William Speiden, Journal Entry, July 8, 1853, Journals, 1852–1855, William Speiden Papers, Library of Congress, Washington, DC.

5. LaFeber, *The Clash,* 14–15, 21–22, 29–30.

6. Hawks, comp., *Commodore Perry,* 59–60, 246, 261, 367, 485.

7. Marius B. Jansen, "The Meiji Restoration," in *The Emergence of Meiji Japan,* ed. Marius B. Jansen (New York: Cambridge University Press, 1995), 156–58; *New York Times,* November 24, 1864, 5.

8. *New York Times,* May 19, 1877, 4, August 17, 1879, 8, and February 13, 1890, 6; "General Grant in the Orient," n.d., folder 10, box 2, Eli T. Sheppard Papers, Library of Congress.

9. Draft of Circular to the Western Powers, December 1877 (?), folder 15, box 1, Von Brandt to Parks, July 3, 1879, folder 7, box 2, Sheppard to Mori, June 29, 1877,

folder 5, box 2, "General Grant in the Orient," n.d., folder 10, box 2, and Sheppard to Mori, May 5, 1879, folder 7, box 2, Sheppard Papers.

10. *New York Times,* January 7, 1884, 8, April 17, 1889, 4, and August 10, 1895, 5; *FRUS, 1888–1890,* 1, pt. 2:1078–79, Hubbard to Bayard, October 25, 1888.

11. Gordon H. Chang, "Whose 'Barbarism'? Whose 'Treachery'? Race and Civilization in the Unknown United States–Korea War of 1871," *Journal of American History* 89, no. 4 (March 2003): 1335–36; McDougal, *Promised Land,* 107; *New York Times,* July 27, 1878, 1; Tyler Dennett, "American Choices in the Far East in 1882," *American Historical Review* 30, no. 1 (October 1924): 92.

12. Chang, "Whose 'Barbarism'?" 1344, 1347.

13. *FRUS, 1894,* app. 1, pp. 25–26, Sill to Gresham, June 29, 1894; ibid., 40, Sill to Gresham, July 24, 1894; ibid., 41, Sill to Gresham, July 26, 1894. For a dated but fascinating look at Japan's early penetration of Korea, see Fred Harvey Harrington, *God, Mammon and the Japanese: Dr. Horace N. Allen and Korean-American Relations, 1894–1905* (Madison: University of Wisconsin Press, 1944), pt. 1 passim.

14. LaFeber, *The Clash,* 49–52; *FRUS, 1895,* 2:969, Emperor Mutsuhito to President Cleveland, November 1, 1895; *New York Times,* January 31, 1895, 2, and October 10, 1895, 5.

15. *New York Times,* November 16, 1895, 10, and December 1, 1895, 30.

16. *New York Times,* April 1, 1895, 5.

17. Thomas A. Bailey, "Japan's Protest against the Annexation of Hawaii," *Journal of Modern History* 3, no. 1 (March 1931): 47–50, 58–59.

18. *New York Times,* December 30, 1891, 10, December 19, 1897, 3, May 31, 1898, 6, April 12, 1897, 1, April 14, 1897, 1, and May 31, 1898, 6.

19. Paul R. Schratz, "The Orient and U.S. Naval Strategy," in *The American Military and the Far East,* ed. Joe C. Dixon (Washington, DC: US Government Printing Office, 1980), 127; Griswold, *Far Eastern Policy,* 17, 22–23.

20. Griswold, *Far Eastern Policy,* 41–76 passim.

21. LaFeber, *The Clash,* 68–69; Raymond A. Esthus, "The Changing Concept of the Open Door, 1899–1910," *Mississippi Valley Historical Review* 46, no. 3 (December 1959): 436.

22. *Literary Digest,* January–June 1900, 35–36.

23. LaFeber, *The Clash,* 69–70; George Kennan, *American Diplomacy, 1900–1950* (Chicago: University of Chicago Press, 1951), 33–34.

24. LaFeber, *The Clash,* 69–73; *New York Times,* February 23, 1900, 3, October 14, 1900, 21, and July 8, 1900, 1.

25. Barnhart, *Japan and the World,* 25; Mikiso Hane, *Modern Japan: A Historical Survey* (Boulder, CO: Westview, 1992), 172.

26. Walter LaFeber, *The New Empire: An Interpretation of American Expansion, 1860–1898* (Ithaca, NY: Cornell University Press, 1963), 321–23; Charles A. Conant, *The United States in the Orient: The Nature of the Economic Problem* (1900), ed. Ralph Adams Brown (Port Washington, NY: Kennikat, 1971), 58–60; Raymond A. Esthus, *Theodore Roosevelt and Japan* (Seattle: University of Washington Press, 1966), 7–11.

27. Morinosuke Kajima, *The Diplomacy of Japan, 1894–1922,* 3 vols. (Tokyo: Kajima Institute of International Peace, 1978), 2:23–28. Kajima notes that Britain attempted to secure preponderance in the Yangtze River valley in return for recognizing Russian preponderance in the Yellow River basin. He also notes that Japan attempted to secure Russian recognition of Tokyo's position in Korea in return for Japanese respect for Russian predominance in Manchuria.

28. Ibid., 45–46, 51–52. Japan's minister to London, Tadasu Hayashi, told the Marquis of Lansdowne, Britain's foreign secretary, that "the maintenance of [Japan's] interests in Corea and prevention of other powers from disturbing them" as well as the "preservation of [the] territorial integrity of the [Chinese] Empire and the maintenance of [the] Open Door" were Japan's primary goals. Ibid., 45.

29. *New York Times,* February 14, 1902, 8; Walter LaFeber, *The American Age: U.S. Foreign Policy at Home and Abroad, 1750 to the Present,* 2nd ed., 2 vols. in 1 (New York: Norton, 1994), 251; Schratz, "The Orient and U.S. Naval Strategy," 129–30.

30. Barnhart, *Japan and the World,* 36–37.

31. Ibid., 38; Kajima, *Diplomacy of Japan,* 2:114–15.

1. The Foundations of Containment

Second epigraph: Rea quoted in Stanley K. Hornbeck, *Contemporary Politics in the Far East* (New York: D. Appleton, 1916), 349.

1. George Bronson Rea, "Closing the Open Door," *North American Review* 203, no. 726 (May 1916): 690.

2. Esthus, *Roosevelt and Japan,* 24, 40; William N. Tilchin, *Theodore Roosevelt and the British Empire: A Study in Presidential Statecraft* (New York: St. Martin's, 1997), 57.

3. Lloyd C. Griscom to Elihu Root, September 15, 1905, box 2, folder General Correspondence, R, 1905–1911, Lloyd C. Griscom Papers, Library of Congress.

4. Robert Dallek, *The American Style of Foreign Policy: Cultural Politics and Foreign Affairs* (New York: Oxford University Press, 1983), 49–50; Howard K. Beale, *Theodore Roosevelt and the Rise of America to World Power* (Baltimore: Johns Hopkins University Press, 1956), 274, 277, 312–14; Tilchin, *Roosevelt,* 56; Esthus, *Roosevelt and Japan,* 54–55, 62; George V. L. Meyer to Theodore Roosevelt, July 3, 1905, folder 2, box 2, George V. L. Meyer Papers, Library of Congress.

5. George V. L. Meyer, Diary Entries, August 23, 24, Meyer Papers; Griscom to Brother, August 9, 1905, folder 10, box 1, Griscom Papers; Elting E. Morison, ed., *The Letters of Theodore Roosevelt,* 8 vols. (Cambridge, MA: Harvard University Press, 1951–1954), 5:473–75, Roosevelt to Senator Eugene Hale, October 27, 1906; ibid., 527–28, Roosevelt to Grey, December 18, 1906.

6. Barnhart, *Japan and the World,* 42; LaFeber, *The Clash,* 85–86; Ralph Eldin Minger, *William Howard Taft and United States Foreign Policy: The Apprenticeship Years, 1900–1908* (Urbana: University of Illinois Press, 1975), 144–48; Esthus, *Roosevelt and Japan,* 97; Tilchin, *Roosevelt,* 17; Morison, ed., *Roosevelt Letters,* 5:49, Roosevelt to Taft, October 17, 1905.

7. Griswold, *Far Eastern Policy,* 353–55; Minger, *Taft,* 151–60; *New York Times,* March 7, 1909, C4.

8. Akira Iriye, *Pacific Estrangement: Japanese and American Expansion, 1897–1911* (Cambridge, MA: Harvard University Press, 1975), 97–98; LaFeber, *The Clash,* 50, 75–76. Iriye notes that in 1904 the journalist Kayahara Kazan argued that Japan must expand for economic and demographic purposes and that the Korean and other mainland Asian economies should be integrated into Japan's to form an "economic empire."

9. LaFeber, *New Empire,* 301.

10. LaFeber, *The Clash,* 75; Charles Vevier, *The United States and China, 1906–1913: A Study of Finance and Diplomacy* (New Brunswick, NJ: Rutgers University Press, 1955), 23–24; Lloyd Griscom to Father, October 26, 1905, folder Family Correspondence to Father, 1903–1907, box 1, and Memorandum, n.d. (probably written before Portsmouth), folder Memoranda, 1907, 1939–1940, box 3, Griscom Papers.

11. Paul A. Varg, *Open Door Diplomat: The Life of W. W. Rockhill* (Urbana: University of Illinois Press, 1952), 32; Esthus, "Open Door," 436–39. Esthus discusses the confusion surrounding the Open Door and Japanese vs. American rights in Manchuria. Secretary of State Root protested Japan's superior mining interests in Manchuria even though Tokyo was awarded these and other former Russian rights at Portsmouth. For more on Japanese commercial policy in Manchuria and a discussion of violations of the Open Door, see Varg, *Open Door Diplomat,* 87–88; and Vevier, *United States and China,* 37–38.

12. Griswold, *Far Eastern Policy,* 129, 147–49; Iriye, *Pacific Estrangement,* 169; *FRUS, 1908,* 1:510–11, Takahira to Knox, November 30, 1908.

13. Thomas A. Bailey, "The Root-Takahira Agreement of 1908," *Pacific Historical Review* 9, no. 1 (1940): 19–20.

14. Morison, ed., *Roosevelt Letters,* 5:135, Roosevelt to Leonard Wood, January 22, 1906; Bailey, "Root-Takahira Agreement," 22–25.

15. Bailey, "Root-Takahira Agreement," 34–35; Griswold, *Far Eastern Policy,* 129; Harry Wray, "Japanese-American Relations and Perceptions, 1900–1940," in *Pearl Harbor Reexamined: Prologue to the Pacific War,* ed. Hilary Conroy and Harry Wray (Honolulu: University of Hawaii Press, 1990), 5, 10; Ute Mehnert, "German Weltpolitik and the American Two-Front Dilemma: The 'Japanese Peril' in German-American Relations, 1904–1917," *Journal of American History* 82, no. 4 (March 1996): 1458.

16. Steven T. Ross, *American War Plans, 1890–1939* (New York: Routledge, 2004), 45–46, 79–80; Louis Morton, *Strategy and Command: The First Two Years,* vol. 10 of *The War in the Pacific* (Washington, DC: Office of the Chief of Military History, Department of the Army, 1962), 22–23.

17. Beale, *Roosevelt,* 328–33; Charles E. Neu, *An Uncertain Friendship: Theodore Roosevelt and Japan, 1906–1909* (Cambridge, MA: Harvard University Press, 1967), 227; Iriye, *Pacific Estrangement,* 163; Albert C. Stillson, "Military Policy without Political Guidance: Theodore Roosevelt's Navy," *Military Affairs* 25, no. 1 (Spring 1961): 23.

18. Akira Fujiwara, "The Role of the Japanese Army," in *Pearl Harbor as History: Japanese-American Relations, 1931–1941,* ed. Dorothy Borg and Shumpei Okamoto (New York: Columbia University Press, 1973), 189; Iriye, *Pacific Estrangement,* 146–48.

19. *New York Times Sunday Magazine,* April 28, 1907, 1; *Literary Digest,* January–June 1905, 790, July–December 1905, 788, and January–June 1907, 353; Homer Lea, *The Valor of Ignorance* (New York: Harper & Bros., 1909); Earnest Hugh Fitzpatrick, *The Coming Conflict of Nations; or, The Japanese-American War: A Narrative* (Springfield, IL: H. W. Rokker, 1909). For German fear of a Japanese attack, see *Literary Digest,* January–June 1905, 633; and William L. Neumann, *America Encounters Japan: From Perry to MacArthur* (Baltimore: Johns Hopkins University Press, 1963), 128–29.

20. *New York Times,* February 23, 1908, 10, August 23, 1908, 5, and September 7, 1908, 4; Morison, ed., *Roosevelt Letters,* 6:1342 (Morison's entry).

21. *New York Times Sunday Magazine,* June 16, 1907, 8.

22. Morison, ed., *Roosevelt Letters,* 5:18–21, Roosevelt to Whitlow Reid, September 11, 1905.

23. Vevier, *United States and China,* 28–31, 40–53, 66–68.

24. Akira Iriye, "Policies toward the United States," in *Japan's Foreign Policy, 1868–1941: A Research Guide,* ed. James W. Morley (New York: Columbia University Press, 1974), 422–23; Barnhart, *Japan and the World,* 42.

25. Beale, *Roosevelt,* 29–30, 268.

26. Raymond Esthus, "The Taft-Katsura Agreement: Reality or Myth?" *Journal of Modern History* 31, no. 1 (March 1959): 48; Charles E. Neu, "1906–1913," in *American–East Asian Relations: A Survey,* ed. Earnest R. May and Charles E. Thompson (Cambridge, MA: Harvard University Press, 1972), 158–60.

27. Martin J. Sklar, *The Corporate Reconstruction of American Capitalism, 1890–1916* (New York: Cambridge University Press, 1988), 75–76, 79–83; Ian Nish, *Japanese Foreign Policy, 1869–1942: Kasumigaseki to Miyakezaka* (London: Routledge & Kegan Paul, 1977), 80, 280–81.

28. Vevier, *United States and China,* 92, 115, 129–30; container 8, pp. 1239–40, Philander Knox Papers, Library of Congress.

29. Container 9, pp. 1604–6, P. Knox Papers; Vevier, *United States and China,* 141–43; Lloyd C. Gardner, *Safe for Democracy: The Anglo-American Response to Revolution, 1913–1923* (New York: Oxford University Press, 1984), 71–72.

30. *FRUS, 1910,* 245, O'Brien to Knox, January 8, 1910; ibid., 251–52, Komura to O'Brien, January, 21, 1910; ibid., 256, Bacon to Knox, February 4, 1910; ibid., 261–62, Memorandum from the Russian Embassy, February 24, 1910.

31. Einstein to Knox, October 17, 1910, container 11, pp. 1796–1804, Roosevelt to Taft, December 22, 1910, container 12, pp. 1923–1930, and Ohl to Knox, April 10, 1911, container 14, pp. 2290–99, P. Knox Papers.

32. Vevier, *United States and China,* 147, 162–63; Convention between Russia and Japan concerning Manchuria, in *American Journal of International Law,* vol. 4, no. 4, suppl., *Official Documents* (New York: Baker, Voorhis, 1910), 279.

33. Stanley K. Hornbeck, the future director of the State Department's Far Eastern Division and a chief adviser to Secretary of State Cordell Hull, argued in 1916 that, although Japan had repeatedly guaranteed Korean independence, it nonetheless absorbed the kingdom in 1910. From annexation, Hornbeck apparently "learned the lesson" that Japanese guarantees had little meaning. Hornbeck, *Contemporary Politics,* 199–215. For a similar view, see Henry F. Merrill, "Present Conditions in China," *Political Science Quarterly* 36, no. 4 (December 1921): 651–52. Both authors represent the camp that argues that Japanese policy had always aimed at destroying Korean independence. In any event, Washington's approval of complete Japanese control over Korea may be seen in both official and semiofficial acts. Taft-Katsura indicates American approval of steps just short of formal annexation. Moreover, in discussing the terms of the Second Anglo-Japanese Alliance in June 1905, Foreign Secretary Lansdowne informed Henry Cabot Lodge that he assumed the United States had no objections to Japan's control of Korea. Lodge, who was acting as Roosevelt's emissary, raised no objections. Beale, *Roosevelt,* 156–57. See also Kajima, *Diplomacy of Japan,* 2:435. For Japanese investment and rate of return in Manchuria, see Ramon H. Myers, "South Manchurian Railway Company," in *The Japanese Informal Empire in China, 1895–1937,* ed. Peter Duus, Ramon Myers, and Mark R. Peattie (Princeton, NJ: Princeton University Press, 1989), 109–15. For Manchuria's share of Japan's total direct investment, see ibid., 8.

34. Alvin D. Coox, "The Kwantung Army Dimension," in Duus, Myers, and Peattie, eds., *Informal Empire,* 400–401; Nish, *Japanese Foreign Policy, 1869–1942,* 92.

35. Neumann, *America Encounters Japan,* 130; *New York Times,* April 12, 1910, 3.

36. American concern over Japanese activity in Mexico did not end after Magdalena Bay. From 1913 to 1917 Japan shipped arms to the Huerta regime. The 1917 Zimmerman telegram, meanwhile, did nothing to ease American concern over the possibility of a Mexican-Japanese alliance. For Mexico's place in Japanese-American relations, see Roy Watson Curry, *Woodrow Wilson and Far Eastern Policy, 1913–1921* (New York: Bookman, 1957), 131–32; LaFeber, *The Clash,* 105–6; Iriye, *Pacific Estrangement,* 218; and Thomas A. Bailey, "The Lodge Corollary to the Monroe Doctrine," *Political Science Quarterly* 48, no. 2 (June 1933): 224–25, 232–33.

37. Clipping, *Arizona Democrat,* March 26, 1903, folder 5, box 32, Clipping, *Birmingham News,* January 3, 1905, folder 1, box 31, Clipping, *Oakland California Herald,* August 17, 1906, folder 1, box 31, Speech, "The True Relation of Our Navy to the Nation," February 22, 1913, folder 9, box 31, and Roosevelt to Hobson, July 9, 1908, folder 4, box 31, Richard Pearson Hobson Papers, Library of Congress.

38. Reed, *Missionary Mind,* 18–32, 94, 104–5.

39. Neumann, *America Encounters Japan,* 138; Yu-ming Shaw, *An American Missionary in China: John Leighton Stuart and Chinese-American Relations* (Cambridge, MA: Harvard University Press, 1992), 2–3, 28–32.

40. Robert Schwantes, "America and Japan," in May and Thompson, eds., *Relations,* 105–6; LaFeber, *The Clash,* 96–97; *New York Times,* January 27, 1911, 1, and February 25, 1911, 1; *New York Times Sunday Magazine,* December 31, 1911, 1.

41. C. T. Elliot to Attorney General Charles Bonaparte, February 5, 1908, J. Russell Kennedy to Hamilton Holt, November 17, 1914, and J. Ingram Bryan to Holt, November 16, 1914, folder 2, box 31, Hobson Papers; Guthrie to Bryan, November 7, 1914, folder 1914 October–November, box 30, William Jennings Bryan Papers, Library of Congress.

42. LaFeber, *The Clash,* 105–6; E. David Cronon, ed., *The Cabinet Diaries of Josephus Daniels, 1913–1921* (Lincoln: University of Nebraska Press, 1963), 64–68.

43. Noel H. Pugach, *Paul S. Reinsch: Open Door Diplomat in Action* (Millwood, NY: KTO, 1979), 71–72; Arthur W. Link, ed., *The Papers of Woodrow Wilson,* 69 vols. (Princeton, NJ: Princeton University Press, 1966–1994), 27:237, Josephus Daniels Diary, March 28, 1913; Williams, *Tragedy of American Diplomacy,* 80; Vevier, *United States and China,* 207–10; Burton F. Beers, *Vain Endeavor: Robert Lansing's Attempts to End the American-Japanese Rivalry* (Durham, NC: Duke University Press, 1962), 17–20, 27; Gardner, *Safe for Democracy,* 71, 76.

44. Barnhart, *Japan and the World,* 48; Nish, *Japanese Foreign Policy, 1869–1942,* 90–92; Robert Joseph Gowen, "Great Britain and the Twenty-one Demands of 1915: Cooperation versus Effacement," *Journal of Modern History* 43, no. 1 (March 1971): 78–80, 84.

45. Nish, *Japanese Foreign Policy, 1869–1942,* 94–95; Barnhart, *Japan and the World,* 50–51; Robert Lansing, *War Memoirs of Robert Lansing* (Indianapolis: Bobbs-Merrill, 1935), 281.

46. Beers, *Vain Endeavor,* 23, 27.

47. Tamura Kosaka, "The Taisho Era: The Immigration Act and World War One," in *Japan-American Diplomatic Relations in the Meiji-Taisho Era,* ed. Kamikawa Hikomatsu, trans. Michiko Kimura (Tokyo: Pan-Pacific Press, 1958), 309; LaFeber, *The Clash,* 109; Gowen, "Twenty-one Demands," 86; Nish, *Japanese Foreign Policy, 1869–1942,* 96–99; Barnhart, *Japan and the World,* 52.

48. Kosaka, "Taisho Era," 312–13; LaFeber, *The Clash,* 109; Nish, *Japanese Foreign Policy, 1869–1942,* 96–99; Barnhart, *Japan and the World,* 52; Gardner, *Safe for Democracy,* 81.

49. For information on the Twenty-one Demands reflecting the interests of various groups, see Nish, *Japanese Foreign Policy, 1869–1942,* 96–99.

50. *FRUS, 1915,* 80, Reinsch to Bryan, January 24, 1915; ibid., 82, Bryan to Paige, February 2, 1915; ibid., 105–11, Bryan to Japanese Ambassador, March 13, 1915; Pugach, *Reinsch,* 148.

51. Pugach, *Reinsch,* 65; Gardner, *Safe for Democracy,* 81–83; Kosaka, "Taisho Era," 311–13; Lansing, *War Memoirs,* 283.

52. Curry, *Wilson,* 129; Iriye, *Pacific Estrangement,* 68; Hornbeck, *Contemporary Politics,* 347.

53. Lansing, *War Memoirs,* 283–84; Barnhart, *Japan and the World,* 52; Kajima, *Diplomacy of Japan,* 3:225–30; Nish, *Japanese Foreign Policy, 1869–1942,* 108–11.

54. Beers, *Vain Endeavor,* 66–67; Kosaka, "Taisho Era," 319–21.

55. Link, ed., *Wilson Papers,* 36:428, Wilson to Lansing, April 7, 1916; ibid.,

30:509–13, Reinsch to Bryan, December 22, 1914; ibid., 37:234–35, Reinsch to Lansing, May 27, 1916; ibid., 235–36, Reinsch to Lansing, June 15, 1916.

56. Jeffrey J. Safford, "Experiment in Containment: The United States Steel Embargo and Japan, 1917–1918," *Pacific Historical Review* 39, no. 4 (November 1970): 440–42.

57. Ibid., 445–47.

58. Ibid., 449–50.

59. Ibid., 450–51.

60. Link, ed., *Wilson Papers,* 40:512–13, Lansing to Wilson, January 17, 1917; Beers, *Vain Endeavor,* 37–40.

61. Lansing, *War Memoirs,* 285; Kajima, *Diplomacy of Japan,* 3:301–15; Gardner, *Safe for Democracy,* 217; *New York Times,* October 2, 1917, 9.

62. Lansing, *War Memoirs,* 291–92; Nish, *Japanese Foreign Policy, 1869–1942,* 115–16; Kajima, *Diplomacy of Japan,* 3:307–11, 314.

63. Sudhindra Bose, "A New Situation in the Orient," *Scientific Monthly* 6 (January–June 1918): 339; Albert Bushnell Hart, *The Monroe Doctrine: An Interpretation* (Boston: Little, Brown, 1916), 298.

64. Beers, *Vain Endeavor,* 111, 116–19; Lansing, *War Memoirs,* 298–302; Lansing-Ishii Agreement, p. 10, folder 4, box 2, Lansing Papers, Seeley Mudd Library; Arthur Link, *Wilson: The Struggle for Neutrality, 1914–1915* (Princeton, NJ: Princeton University Press, 1960), 282; Memorandum of Lansing-Koo Conversation, November 12, 1917, folder 4, box 2, Lansing Papers.

65. Beers, *Vain Endeavor,* 111, 116–19; Kajima, *Diplomacy of Japan,* 3:333; Gardner, *Safe for Democracy,* 222.

66. Barnhart, *Japan and the World,* 56–65; Christopher Lasch, "American Intervention in Siberia: A Reinterpretation," *Political Science Quarterly* 77, no. 2 (June 1962): 207.

67. Betty Miller Unterberger, *America's Siberian Expedition, 1918–1920: A Study of National Policy* (Durham, NC: Duke University Press, 1956), 21–26, 52; Link, ed., *Wilson Papers,* 47:131–32, Lansing to Wilson, March 24, 1918; ibid., Wilson to Lansing, March 26, 1918.

68. Unterberger, *Siberian Expedition,* 49–51, 67–69; Ian Hill Nish, *Japanese Foreign Policy in the Interwar Period* (Westport, CT: Praeger, 2002), 22–23.

69. Beers, *Vain Endeavor,* 120–22; Leonard A. Humphreys, *The Way of the Heavenly Sword: The Japanese Army in the 1920s* (Stanford, CA: Stanford University Press, 1995), 26; George C. Guins, "The Siberian Intervention, 1918–1919," *Russian Review* 28, no. 4 (October 1969): 434–35; Barnhart, *Japan and the World,* 65.

70. Humphreys, *Heavenly Sword,* 27–28; *New York Times,* June 4, 1922, Special Features, 92; *Current History* 14 (April–September 1921): 887; Curry, *Wilson,* 247; Unterberger, *Siberian Expedition,* 203.

71. Tokyo's official opinion of the Fourteen Points can be found in Kajima, *Diplomacy of Japan,* 3:348–50.

72. *FRUS, 1919, Paris Peace Conference,* 2:513–15, Long Memorandum, December 14, 1918; Russell H. Fifield, "Disposal of the Carolines, Marshalls and Marianas

at the Paris Peace Conference," *American Historical Review* 51, no. 3 (April 1946): 472–73, 475–78.

73. Gardner, *Safe for Democracy,* 293–94; Barnhart, *Japan and the World,* 67–68; Kosaka, "Taisho Era," 408–12; *FRUS, 1919, Paris Peace Conference,* 5:245, Memorandum of Conversation, Wilson, Lloyd George, Georges Clemenceau, April 25, 1919; ibid., 363–67, Memorandum of Conversation, Wilson, George, Clemenceau, Baron Makino, Viscount Chinda, April 30, 1919; *New York Times,* July 14, 1919, 8.

74. Beers, *Vain Endeavor,* 154, 160; Curry, *Wilson,* 251–53; *New York Times,* August 21, 1919, 10.

75. Naoko Shimazu, *Japan, Race and Equality: The Racial Equality Proposal of 1919* (New York: Routledge, 1998), 166–69; Fujiwara, "Japanese Army," 189; Akira Iriye, *After Imperialism: The Search for a New Order in the Far East, 1921–1931* (Cambridge, MA: Harvard University Press, 1965), 36.

76. *New York Times,* August 19, 1919, 17, December 10, 1920, 17, and December 14, 1920, 19.

77. Warren I. Cohen, "America's New Order for East Asia: The Four Power Financial Consortium and China, 1919–1946," in *Essays in the History of China and Chinese-American Relations,* ed. Kwan Wai So and Warren I. Cohen (East Lansing: Michigan State University Asian Studies Center, 1982), 41, and *The Chinese Connection: Roger S. Greene, Thomas W. Lamont, George E. Sokolsky and American East Asian Relations* (New York: Columbia University Press, 1978), 48–51; Link, ed., *Wilson Papers,* 43:7–8, Lansing to Wilson, June 25, 1917. For a brief discussion of the Nishihara loans, see Kosaka, "Taisho Era," 389.

78. Speech, "The Chinese Consortium and Our Trade Relations with the Far East, 1920," folder 17, vol. 143, Lamont to Hughes, March 1, 1920, folder 20, vol. 209, "Preliminary Report on the New Consortium for China," August 8, 1920, folder 19, vol. 143, and Speech to Chinese and American Chamber of Commerce, Shanghai, April 2, 1920, folder 18, vol. 143, Thomas Lamont Papers, Harvard University, Baker Library, Cambridge MA. Warren Cohen, a leading authority on Lamont's role in the consortium, argues that Lamont saw Japan, rather than China, as the preferred market for American capital and undertook his role in starting the new consortium "as a public service" in the hope of gaining "good-will and prestige for himself and his firm." Cohen, *Chinese Connection,* 69.

79. Lindsay Russell to Lamont, January 9, 1919, folder 3, vol. 183, Lamont Papers.

80. Cohen, *Chinese Connection,* 52; LaFeber, *The Clash,* 131.

81. Cohen, "America's New Order," 50–51.

82. Cohen, *Chinese Connection,* 59–60, 64–68.

83. Ibid., 65; vol. 142, passim, Lamont Papers.

2. The Rise and Fall of the Washington Conference System

Epigraphs: Miles Lampson to John Van Antwerp MacMurray, May 22, 1922, folder 15, box 45, John Van Antwerp MacMurray Papers, Seeley Mudd

Library; MacMurray to Langdon, June 14, 1933, folder 1, box 50, MacMurray Papers.

1. Conrad Schirokauer, *A Brief History of Chinese and Japanese Civilization* (New York: Harcourt, 1978), 474–76; J. A. G. Roberts, *A Concise History of China* (Cambridge, MA: Harvard University Press, 1999), 214–22.

2. Akira Iriye, *The Globalizing of America, 1913–1945,* vol. 3 of *The Cambridge History of American Foreign Relations* (New York: Cambridge University Press, 1993), 75; Warren I. Cohen, *Empire without Tears: America's Foreign Relations, 1921–1933* (New York: Knopf, 1987), 46; Robert James Maddox, *William E. Borah and American Foreign Policy* (Baton Rouge: Louisiana State University Press, 1969), 86–90.

3. Maddox, *William E. Borah,* 100; Takeo Iguchi, *Demystifying Pearl Harbor: A New Perspective from Japan,* trans. David Noble (Tokyo: International House of Japan, 2010), 37; Sadao Asada, *Culture Shock and Japanese-American Relations* (Columbia: University of Missouri Press, 2007), 91; Gardner, *Safe for Democracy,* 308–11; Griswold, *Far Eastern Policy,* 299.

4. Thomas Buckley, *The United States and the Washington Conference, 1921–1922* (Knoxville: University of Tennessee Press, 1970), 6–7, 22–24; John Chalmers Vinson, *The Parchment Peace: The United States Senate and the Washington Conference, 1921–1922* (Athens: University of Georgia Press, 1955), 43; Hiroyuki Agawa, *The Reluctant Admiral: Yamamoto and the Imperial Navy,* trans. John Bester (Tokyo: Kodansha International, 1969), 27–28; Roger Dingman, *Power in the Pacific: The Origins of Naval Arms Limitation, 1914–1922* (Chicago: University of Chicago Press, 1976), 122.

5. Erik Goldstein, "The Evolution of British Diplomatic Strategy for the Washington Conference," in *The Washington Conference, 1921–1922: Naval Rivalry, East Asian Stability and the Road to Pearl Harbor,* ed. Erik Goldstein and John H. Maurer (New York: Routledge, 1994), 27; Buckley, *Washington Conference,* 71–73, 85; Betty Glad, *Charles Evans Hughes and the Illusions of Innocence: A Study in American Diplomacy* (Urbana: University of Illinois Press, 1966), 270–71; Kajima, *Diplomacy of Japan,* 3:473; Agawa, *Reluctant Admiral,* 28–30. For a remarkably full analysis of Japanese policy concerning naval disarmament, see Kajima, *Diplomacy of Japan,* 3:469–95.

6. Kajima, *Diplomacy of Japan,* vol. 3.

7. James B. Crowley, "Military Foreign Policies," in Morley, ed., *Japan's Foreign Policy,* 43. Barnhart notes that, long before the February naval agreement, army leaders feared that retrenchment in one service would inevitably lead to budget cuts for the other. In 1924 these fears came true. Barnhart, *Japan and the World,* 70–71. For a discussion of the cruiser race following the Washington Conference, see Arthur E. Tiedemann's introduction to Tatsuo Kobayashi, "The London Naval Treaty, 1930," in Morley, ed., *Japan Erupts,* 6–7; Ernest Andrade Jr., "The Cruiser Controversy in Naval Limitations Negotiations, 1922–1936," *Military Affairs* 48, no. 3 (July 1984): 113; and Richard W. Fanning, *Peace and Disarmament: Naval Rivalry and Arms Control, 1922–1933* (Lexington: University Press of Kentucky, 1995), 11. For more on

technological change, see Emily O. Goldman, *Sunken Treaties: Naval Arms Control between the Wars* (University Park: Penn State University Press, 1994), 151, 153–57.

8. Buckley, *Washington Conference,* 27–28; Vinson, *Parchment Peace,* 27; Gardner, *Safe for Democracy,* 303, 306; M. G. Fry, "The North Atlantic Triangle and the Abrogation of the Anglo-Japanese Alliance," *Journal of Modern History* 39, no. 1 (March 1967): 47–48, 59–60; Goldman, *Sunken Treaties,* 132; Wm. Roger Louis, *British Strategy in the Far East, 1919–1939* (Oxford: Clarendon, 1971), 52–78 passim; *New York Times,* November 6, 1921, Book Review and Magazine section, 44.

9. Kosaka, "Taisho Era," 432–33; Kajima, *Diplomacy of Japan,* 3:441–42.

10. Sadao Asada, "The Japanese Navy and the United States," in Borg and Okamoto, eds., *Pearl Harbor,* 228–29.

11. Louis notes that during the debates over the future of the Anglo-Japanese Alliance some British statesmen discussed the possibility of a Soviet-Japanese or German-Japanese combination. See Louis, *British Strategy,* 41, 61.

12. Buckley, *Washington Conference,* 145–51; Iguchi, *Demystifying Pearl Harbor,* 42; LaFeber, *The Clash,* 141–42; Shizhang Hu, *Stanley K. Hornbeck and the Open Door Policy, 1919–1937* (Westport, CT: Greenwood, 1995), 53–54. Hu argues that the American-sponsored Root Resolutions, which combined respect for Chinese sovereignty, territorial integrity, and independence with promises of support for the Open Door and Hughes's Open Door Resolution, formed the backbone of the Nine Power Treaty.

13. Buckley, *Washington Conference,* 152; Hu, *Open Door Policy,* 53.

14. Sadao Asada, "Japan's 'Special Interests' and the Washington Conference, 1921–1922," *American Historical Review* 67, no. 1 (October 1961): 63, 67–70, and *Culture Shock,* 98–100; Gardner, *Safe for Democracy,* 311; Glad, *Illusions of Innocence,* 291.

15. Wray, "Relations and Perceptions," 10; Buckley, *Washington Conference,* 152–53.

16. *FRUS, 1922,* 2:597–98, Japanese Embassy to Department of State, December 27, 1922.

17. Glad, *Illusions of Innocence,* 292–93; Kajima, *Diplomacy of Japan,* 3:380; Noel H. Pugach, "American Friendship for China and the Shantung Question at the Washington Conference," *Journal of American History* 64, no. 1 (June 1977): 72–74; Vinson, *Parchment Peace,* 173; *FRUS, 1922,* 1:960–65, Hughes to Schuman, February 15, 1922.

18. Cordell Hull, *The Memoirs of Cordell Hull,* 2 vols. (London: Hodder & Stoughton, 1948), 1:117.

19. Asada, "Washington Conference," 62; Herbert P. Bix, *Hirohito and the Making of Modern Japan* (New York: Harper Perennial, 2000), 148 (emphasis added).

20. Memorandum, "Developments Affecting American Policy in the Far East," folder 1, box 77, MacMurray Papers.

21. Cohen, *Empire without Tears,* 32; *FRUS, 1923,* 2:507–8, Harrison to Ailes, May 23, 1923; ibid., 508–9, Ailes to Harrison, June 7, 1923; ibid., 509, Harrison to

Ailes, June 15, 1923; ibid., *1927,* 2:483, Kellogg to MacVeagh, November 19, 1927; ibid., 482, Mayer to Kellogg, November 19, 1927; Egan to Lamont, December 21, 1927, folder 32, vol. 189, Lamont Papers; Cohen, *Chinese Connection,* 158.

22. *FRUS, 1927,* 2:484–86, MacVeagh to Kellogg, November 21, 1927; Lamont to Inoue, January 9, 1928, folder 33, vol. 189, Lamont Papers; Cohen, *Chinese Connection,* 155–57.

23. *FRUS, 1922,* 1:747–48, State Department to Japanese Embassy, May 4, 1922; ibid., 751–52, Japanese Embassy to State Department, May 31, 1922; Iriye, *After Imperialism,* 45–46. Shidehara's restrained response to the civil war in China and anti-Japanese agitation is discussed in Barnhart, *Japan and the World,* 80–81; and Nobuya Bamba, *Japanese Diplomacy in a Dilemma: New Light on Japan's China Policy, 1924–1929* (Vancouver: University of British Columbia Press, 1972), 225–44.

24. Dorothy Borg, *American Policy and the Chinese Revolution, 1925–1928* (New York: Macmillan, 1947), 20–23, 29–31.

25. *FRUS, 1925,* 1:771–74, Mayer to Kellogg, July 5, 1925.

26. Ibid., 785–87, MacMurray to Kellogg, July 16, 1925.

27. Akira Iriye, *Across the Pacific: An Inner History of American–East Asian Relations* (New York: Harcourt, 1967), 152.

28. Hu, *Open Door Policy,* 68; Toshiyuki Mizoguchi, "Sino-Japanese Trade," in Duus, Myers, and Peattie, eds., *Informal Empire,* 12; Peter Duus, "Zaikabo: Japanese Cotton Mills, 1895–1937," in ibid., 89–90; Iriye, *After Imperialism,* 58–59.

29. Warren I. Cohen, *America's Response to China: A History of Sino-American Relations* (New York: Columbia University Press, 1990), 94–97; Iriye, *Across the Pacific,* 157; Borg, *American Policy,* 26–27, 75–76; Robert David Johnson, *The Peace Progressives and American Foreign Relations* (Cambridge, MA: Harvard University Press, 1995), 147–48.

30. *FRUS, 1925,* 1:807–9, MacMurray to Kellogg, August 1, 1925; ibid., 842–47, Kellogg to Delegation, September 9, 1925; ibid., *1926,* 1:743, Delegation to Kellogg, January 30, 1926; ibid., 758–59, Delegation to Kellogg, June 13, 1926; ibid., 760–63, Delegation to Kellogg, June 28, 1926; Hu, *Open Door Policy,* 74–76.

31. Borg, *American Policy,* 146–47, 228–30; Iriye, *After Imperialism,* 98–101; Louis, *British Strategy,* 129–30.

32. Borg, *American Policy,* 231–39.

33. Memorandum, "Developments Affecting American Policy in the Far East," folder 1, box 77, Ferdinand Mayer to William Henry Chamberlin, December 6, 1954, folder 10, box 52, and MacMurray to Dorothy Borg, July 17, 1946, folder 12, box 31, MacMurray Papers.

34. Borg, *American Policy,* 242–66; Gerald Leinwand, *1927: The High Tide of the Twenties* (New York: Basic, 2002), 105; David Z. T. Yui, "China and the Pacific Relations during 1925–1927," *News Bulletin of the Institute of Pacific Relations,* August 1927, 15.

35. Bamba, *Japanese Diplomacy,* 266–82; Ikuhiko Hata, "Continental Expansion, 1905–1941," trans. Alvin D. Coox, in *The Cambridge History of Japan,* vol. 6,

The Twentieth Century, ed. Peter Duus (London: Cambridge University Press, 1988), 286.

36. Bamba, *Japanese Diplomacy,* 283–91; Cohen, *America's Response,* 100.

37. For the Seiyukai platform, see Bamba, *Japanese Diplomacy,* 326.

38. Ibid., 299–300; Crowley, "Military Foreign Policies," 45–46.

39. Barnhart, *Japan and the World,* 84–85; Iriye, *After Imperialism,* 193–205; Memorandum, "Developments Affecting American Policy in the Far East," folder 1, box 77, MacMurray Papers.

40. Iriye, *After Imperialism,* 205–14; Takehiko Yoshihashi, *Conspiracy at Mukden: The Rise of the Japanese Military* (New Haven, CT: Yale University Press, 1963), 40–51. Wempu Wang, who had served as secretary to an American member of the international banking consortium, maintained that Chang had been murdered because, while he had promised Japan additional holdings in Manchuria in return for the military's help in suppressing a rebellion, he failed to make good once the rebellion was over. Memorandum of Peck-Wang Conversation, August 14, 1928, folder 12, box 44, MacMurray Papers. See also MacMurray to Hornbeck, August 17, 1928, folder 14, box 44, MacMurray Papers.

41. Hu, *Open Door Policy,* 99–102; Yoshihashi, *Conspiracy at Mukden,* 37–38; Iriye, *After Imperialism,* 242–43; *FRUS, 1928,* 2:425–27, Uchida to Kellogg, September 29, 1928; ibid., 427–30, Johnson Memorandum, September 29, 1928; Memorandum, "Developments Affecting American Policy in the Far East," folder 1, box 77, MacMurray Papers.

42. Akira Iriye, "Chang Hsueh-liang and the Japanese," *Journal of Asian Studies* 20, no. 1 (November 1960): 33–43 passim.

43. Iriye, *After Imperialism,* 255; James Weland, "Misguided Intelligence: Japanese Military Intelligence Officers in the Manchurian Incident, September 1931," *Journal of Military History* 58, no. 3 (July 1994): 453; Barnhart, *Japan and the World,* 86.

44. Bamba, *Japanese Diplomacy,* 357–58; Barnhart, *Japan and the World,* 86–87; *FRUS, 1930,* 2:308, Johnson to Stimson, December 19, 1930; ibid., 303–8, Forbes to Stimson, December 15, 1930; Marius B. Jansen, introduction to Seki Hiroharu, "The Manchurian Incident," in Morley, ed., *Japan Erupts,* 137; Yoshihashi, *Conspiracy at Mukden,* 122.

45. *FRUS, 1931,* 3:843–45, Johnson Memorandum, May 8, 1931; ibid., 882–83, Johnson to Stimson, June 23, 1931; George Sokolsky to MacMurray, October 12, 1928, folder 4, box 65, MacMurray Papers.

46. G. C. Allen, *A Short Economic History of Japan, 1867–1937* (London: George Allen & Unwin, 1946), 96–98; LaFeber, *The Clash,* 154.

47. Fanning, *Peace and Disarmament,* 50; Andrade, "Cruiser Controversy," 115–16; Ray Lyman Wilbur and Arthur Mastick Hyde, *The Hoover Policies* (New York: Scribner's, 1937), 592.

48. Kobayashi, "The London Naval Treaty, 1930," 11–27; Crowley, "Military Foreign Policies," 47–50; Seki, "The Manchurian Incident," 157.

49. Seki, "The Manchurian Incident," 175–76.

50. Sadako Ogata, *Defiance in Manchuria: The Making of Japanese Foreign Policy, 1931–1932* (Berkeley: University of California Press, 1964), 23–29; Michael Barnhart, "Japan's Drive to Autarky," in *Japan Examined: Perspectives on Modern Japanese History,* ed. Harry Wray and Hilary Conroy (Honolulu: University of Hawaii Press, 1983), 294. For the army's impression of the lessons learned from Germany's defeat in World War I, see Mark R. Peattie, *Ishiwara Kanji and Japan's Confrontation with the West* (Princeton, NJ: Princeton University Press, 1975), 12–13, chap. 2 passim.

51. Tetsuo Najita, *The Intellectual Foundations of Modern Japanese Politics* (Chicago: University of Chicago Press, 1974), 114–15, 128–33.

52. Chihiro Hosoya, "Characteristics of the Foreign Policy Decision-Making System in Japan," *World Politics* 26, no. 3 (April 1974): 360; Seki, "The Manchurian Incident," 174. See also Weland, "Misguided Intelligence." Weland's work is especially important in two respects. Initially, his essay clearly indicates that the Mukden Incident had wide active and tacit support among both field officers and their counterparts in Tokyo. Second, Weland compellingly demonstrates that the army's unsanctioned efforts to solve the Manchurian problem went back a generation.

53. Henry L. Stimson, *The Far Eastern Crisis: Recollections and Observations* (New York: Harper & Bros., 1936), 17; Weland, "Misguided Intelligence," 447–48; Christopher Thorne, *The Limits of Foreign Policy: The West, the League and the Far Eastern Crisis of 1931–1933* (London: Hamish Hamilton, 1972), 32. Thorne notes that nearly 80 percent of Japan's total foreign investment was in China and that of this some two-thirds was centered in Manchuria.

54. Yale Candee Maxon, *Control of Japanese Foreign Policy: A Study of Civil-Military Rivalry, 1930–1945* (1957; reprint, Westport, CT: Greenwood, 1973), 80–86.

55. Justice D. Doenecke, comp., *The Diplomacy of Frustration: The Manchurian Crisis of 1931–1933 as Revealed in the Papers of Stanley K. Hornbeck* (Stanford, CA: Hoover Institution Press, 1981), 12–13; Henry L. Stimson and McGeorge Bundy, *On Active Service in War and Peace* (New York: Harper & Bros., 1947), 226; Joseph C. Grew, *Ten Years in Japan* (New York: Simon & Schuster, 1944), 3–4.

56. Stimson and Bundy, *Active Service,* 227; Masaru Ikei, "Examples of Mismanagement in U.S. Policy toward Japan before World War II," in Conroy and Wray, eds., *Pearl Harbor Reexamined,* 47; *FRUS, 1931,* 3:43–47, Memorandum of Conversation, Stimson, Davis, et al., September 23, 1931; ibid., 48–49, Stimson to Wilson, September 23, 1931; Armin Rappaport, *Henry L. Stimson and Japan, 1931–1933* (Chicago: University of Chicago Press, 1963), 13–14, 26–27.

57. Koo to Johnson, November 26, 1931, Koo to Peck, December 13, 1931, and Memorandum of Conversation, Koo-Shigimetsu, November 30, 1931, folder 1, box 4, Wellington Koo Papers, Butler Library, Columbia University, New York.

58. Toshihiko Shimada, "Extension of Hostilities," in Morley, ed., *Japan Erupts,* 272–73; Koichi Kido, *The Diary of the Marquis Kido, 1931–1945* (Frederick, MD: University Publications of America, 1984), 13, 15.

59. Maxon, *Control of Japanese Foreign Policy,* 87–92; Barnhart, *Japan and the World,* 95.

60. Herbert Clark Hoover, *The Memoirs of Herbert Hoover,* vol. 2, *The Cabinet and the Presidency, 1920–1933* (New York: Macmillan, 1952), 366–68; Rappaport, *Stimson and Japan,* 81–84; Doenecke, comp., *Diplomacy of Frustration,* 23–24; Gary B. Ostrower, *Collective Insecurity: The United States and the League of Nations during the Early Thirties* (Lewisburg, PA: Bucknell University Press, 1979), 134–35, 200–201; Wilbur and Hyde, *Hoover Policies,* 599–603; Gerald Wheeler, "Isolated Japan: Anglo-American Diplomatic Co-Operation, 1927–1936," *Pacific Historical Review* 30, no. 2 (May 1961): 172; Bernard Sternsher, "The Stimson Doctrine: F.D.R. versus Moley and Tugwell," *Pacific Historical Review* 31, no. 3 (August 1962): 282; Robert H. Ferrell, *American Diplomacy in the Great Depression, 1929–1933* (New Haven, CT: Yale University Press, 1957), 148 n. 22; Thorne, *Limits of Foreign Policy,* 139–40, 157, 185, 195.

61. Doenecke, comp., *Diplomacy of Frustration,* 19; Richard N. Current, *Secretary Stimson: A Study in Statecraft* (Hamden, CT: Archon, 1970), 80; Stimson and Bundy, *Active Service,* 232, 255; Thorne, *Limits of Foreign Policy,* 196, 246, 269; *FRUS, 1931,* 3:488–98, Memorandum of Stimson-Dawes Conversation, November 19, 1931; Warren I. Cohen, "American Leaders in East Asia, 1931–1938," in *American, Chinese and Japanese Perspectives on Wartime Asia, 1931–1939,* ed. Akira Iriye and Warren Cohen (Wilmington, DE: Scholarly Resources, 1990), 7, 10, and *Empire without Tears,* 113; James R. Herzberg, *A Broken Bond: American Economic Policies toward Japan, 1931–1941* (New York: Garland, 1988), 33.

62. Thorne, *Limits of Foreign Policy,* 196, 246, 269.

63. Ferrell, *American Diplomacy,* 151–58; Stimson and Bundy, *Active Service,* 234–35; *FRUS, 1931,* 3:498–502, Memorandum of Stimson-Dawes Conversation, November 19, 1931; Rappaport, *Stimson and Japan,* 93; Hu, *Open Door Policy,* 137–41; Doenecke, comp., *Diplomacy of Frustration,* 24.

64. Ferrell, *American Diplomacy,* 153; Thorne, *Limits of Foreign Policy,* 301; Hoover, *Memoirs,* 373–74.

65. Grew, *Ten Years,* 78–80; Millard Memorandum, November 15, 1932, folder Sino-US Relations, box 26, Koo Papers.

66. Donald A. Jordan, *China's Trial by Fire: The Shanghai War of 1932* (Ann Arbor: University of Michigan Press, 2001), 10–16, 27–28.

67. Ibid., 64; Hu, *Open Door Policy,* 142.

68. Cohen, "American Leaders," 11–12; Ferrell, *American Diplomacy,* 183–85; Stimson, *Far Eastern Crisis,* 158–75; Stimson and Bundy, *Active Service,* 246–47; James B. Crowley, *Japan's Quest for Autonomy: National Security and Foreign Policy, 1930–1938* (Princeton, NJ: Princeton University Press, 1966), 165.

69. So Wai Chor, "The Making of the Guomindang's Japan Policy, 1932–1937: The Roles of Chiang Kai-shek and Wang Jingwei," *Modern China* 28, no. 2 (April 2002): 223; Ke-wen Wang, "Wang Jingwei and the Policy Origins of the 'Peace Movement,' 1932–1937," in *Chinese Collaboration with Japan, 1932–1945: The Limits of Accommodation,* ed. David P. Barrett and Larry N. Shyu (Stanford, CA: Stanford University Press, 2001), 23; Hoover, *Memoirs,* 376; Cohen, "American Leaders," 11.

70. *Appeal of the Chinese Government, Draft of the Report,* Series of League of Nations Publications, 7, Political, no. 2 (Geneva, 1933), 15–20; Barnhart, *Japan and the World,* 98; LaFeber, *The Clash,* 173; Crowley, *Quest for Autonomy,* 185–86.

71. Maxon, *Control of Japanese Foreign Policy,* 94; Dorothy Borg, *The United States and the Far Eastern Crisis of 1933–1938: From the Manchurian Incident through the Initial Stages of the Undeclared Sino-Japanese War* (Cambridge, MA: Harvard University Press, 1964), 36–38; Confidential Summary of Koo, Quo, Soong, and Yen meeting, June 30, 1933, folder Foreign Policy, 1933–1939, box 23, Koo Papers.

72. Thorne, *Limits of Foreign Policy,* 232, 296–98; Chihiro Hosoya, "Policies toward Russia," in Morley, ed., *Japan's Foreign Policy,* 397–98.

73. Asada, "Japanese Navy," 239–40; Crowley, "Military Foreign Policies," 57–58; Maxon, *Control of Japanese Foreign Policy,* 97.

74. Seeichi Imai, "Cabinet, Emperor and Senior Statesman," in Borg and Okamoto, eds., *Pearl Harbor,* 63; Yukio Cho, "Importing American Capital into Manchuria," in ibid., 387; Crowley, *Quest for Autonomy,* 191–92.

75. Stimson, *Far Eastern Crisis,* 137–38; Stimson and Bundy, *Active Service,* 245–46.

76. Stimson and Bundy, *Active Service;* Rappaport, *Stimson and Japan,* 203.

77. Waldo H. Heinrichs Jr., "The Role of the United States Navy," in Borg and Okamoto, eds., *Pearl Harbor,* 199, 208.

78. Herzberg, *Broken Bond,* 36–37, 45–46; Joseph C. Grew, *Turbulent Era: A Diplomatic Record of Forty Years, 1904–1945,* 2 vols. (London: Hammond & Hammond, 1953), 2:940, and *Ten Years,* 70, 77, 80.

79. Doenecke, comp., *Diplomacy of Frustration,* 32–33, 35; Richard Harrison, "A Neutralization Plan for the Pacific: Roosevelt and Anglo-American Cooperation, 1934–1937," *Pacific Historical Review* 47, no. 1 (February 1988): 53; Maddox, *William E. Borah,* 210–11.

80. Gerald E. Wheeler, "The United States Navy and the Japanese 'Enemy,' 1919–1931," *Military Affairs* 21, no. 2 (Summer 1957): 62–63.

81. Stimson and Bundy, *Active Service,* 255.

82. Justus D. Doenecke and Mark A. Stoler, *Debating Franklin D. Roosevelt's Foreign Policies, 1933–1945* (New York: Routledge, 2005), 29; Sternsher, "Stimson Doctrine," 281; book 1, pp. 56 (September 13, 1934), 61 (December 8, 1934), box 1, Arthur Krock Papers, Seeley Mudd Library; Grew, *Turbulent Era,* 2:939, and *Ten Years,* 76–77.

3. Into the Abyss

Epigraphs: Harold L. Ickes, *The Inside Struggle, 1936–1939,* vol. 2 of *The Secret Diary of Harold L. Ickes* (New York: Simon & Schuster, 1954), 186; Eugene Dooman Oral History, 105, Butler Library.

1. Hornbeck Memorandum, May 9, 1933, PSF 26, Franklin D. Roosevelt Papers, Franklin D. Roosevelt Library, Hyde Park, NY.

2. Ibid.

3. Ibid.

4. Ibid.

5. Ibid.; Hornbeck Précis, "Russo-Japanese Conflict," February 2, 1934, PSF 42, Roosevelt Papers; Borg, *Far Eastern Crisis,* 62–63; Far Eastern Division Memorandum, August 2, 1933, PSF 26, Roosevelt Papers; *FRUS, 1934,* 3:516–18, Far Eastern Division Memorandum, October 25, 1934; Arthur Nichols Young, *China's Nation Building, 1927–1937: The Financial and Economic Record* (Stanford, CA: Hoover Institution Press, 1971), 383.

6. Marta Alexandra Balinska, *For the Good of Humanity: Ludwik Rajchman, Medical Statesman* (Budapest: Central European University Press, 1995), vii, 81–83, 91; Borg, *Far Eastern Crisis,* 61–63, 71.

7. *FRUS, 1934,* 3:412–14, Memorandum of Hornbeck-Lamont Conversation, September 19, 1934. Lamont informed Hornbeck in September 1934 that Tokyo believed that Rajchman had torpedoed a Soong-Shidehara meeting designed to settle the Manchurian Incident. Rajchman supposedly advised Soong against the meeting, and, according to Lamont, "the project fell through." After this episode, Lamont told Hornbeck, Rajchman was "distinctly *persona non grata* to the Japanese." *FRUS, 1933,* 3:502–5, Memorandum of Hornbeck-Taketomi Conversation, July 25, 1933.

8. *FRUS, 1934,* 3:112–13, Grew to Hull, April 18, 1934; ibid., 115–16, Grew to Hull, April 20, 1934; ibid., 126, Phillips to Bingham, April 23, 1934; ibid., 140–41, Grew to Hull, April 26, 1934.

9. Ibid., 117–21, Grew to Hull, April 20, 1934; ibid., 141–42, Hornbeck to Hull, April 26, 1934; ibid., 128–29, Hornbeck Memorandum, April 24, 1934; ibid., 135–36, Bingham to Hull, April 25, 1934. See also LaFeber, *The Clash,* 177.

10. Harrison, "Neutralization Plan," 53–55; *FRUS, 1934,* 3:142–43, Phillips Memorandum, April 26, 1934; ibid., 148–49, Bingham to Hull, April 30, 1934; ibid., 164–65, Hull Memorandum, May 7, 1934; Hull, *Memoirs,* 1:280.

11. Hull, *Memoirs,* 1:280; Louis, *British Strategy,* 207–14.

12. Louis, *British Strategy,* 207–14.

13. Borg, *Far Eastern Crisis,* 80–81, 90–91.

14. *FRUS, 1934,* 3:640–43, Grew to Hull, April 5, 1934.

15. Ibid., 644–45, Grew to Hull, April 6, 1934; Grew to Nelson Johnson, April 9, 1934, and Grew to Prentice Gilbert, May 17, 1934, Letters, vol. 69, and Diary, no. 43, pp. 958–59, Joseph Grew Papers, Houghton Library, Harvard University, Cambridge, MA.

16. *FRUS, 1934,* 3:633–34, Atherton to Hull, February 1, 1934; ibid., 634–35, Hornbeck Memorandum, February 2, 1934.

17. Hull, *Memoirs,* 1:277–78.

18. Ibid.

19. Saito to Hull, May 15, 1934, and Far Eastern Division Memorandum, May 16, 1934, PSF 26, Roosevelt Papers.

20. Hull, *Memoirs,* 1:283–85; Hull to Roosevelt, June 9, 1934, PSF 26, Roosevelt Papers.

21. Arthur Waldron, ed., *How the Peace Was Lost: The 1935 Memorandum "Developments Affecting American Policy in the Far East,"* prepared for the State Department by Ambassador John Van Antwerp MacMurray (Stanford, CA: Hoover Institution Press, 1992), 31–32, 34, 38, 126–36.

22. Stephen E. Pelz, *Race to Pearl Harbor: The Failure of the Second London Naval Conference and the Onset of World War II* (Cambridge, MA: Harvard University Press, 1974), 76–79; Russell F. Weigley, "The Role of the War Department and the Army," in Borg and Okamoto, eds., *Pearl Harbor,* 165.

23. Lloyd C. Gardner, *Economic Aspects of New Deal Diplomacy* (Madison: University of Wisconsin Press, 1964), 18.

24. Heinrichs, "Role of the Navy," 199, 207–8; Pelz, *Race to Pearl Harbor,* 80–82. See also William Leuchtenberg, *Franklin D. Roosevelt and the New Deal* (New York: Harper & Row, 1963), 214–15.

25. Pelz, *Race to Pearl Harbor,* 92–94.

26. Hornbeck Précis, "Russo-Japanese Conflict," February 2, 1934, and Bullitt to Roosevelt, February 5, 1934, PSF 42, Roosevelt Papers.

27. Working Draft, "Russo-Japan Conflict," February 2, 1934, PSF 42, Roosevelt Papers.

28. Memorandum of Hull, Hornbeck, Standley, et al. Meeting, September 26, 1934, PSF 42, Roosevelt Papers; Diary, no. 57, p. 2114, no. 54, Appendix, Notes on Frank Simonds Letter, n.p., and no. 59, Appendix, Grew to Hull, December 27, 1934, n.p., Grew Papers.

29. Asada, "Japanese Navy," 226–32, 238–40; Michael A. Barnhart, *Japan Prepares for Total War: The Search for Economic Security, 1919–1941* (Ithaca, NY: Cornell University Press, 1987), 34–39. Barnhart emphasizes that, in 1933–1934, total war officers—those who wanted to build up Japanese industry so that the empire could win a protracted war—were in the minority. Had the total war faction been in a dominant position, it would have forbidden the armed services from undertaking a crash rearmament program because such a rapid buildup made it impossible to focus on sustained development. As Barnhart notes, the total war officers believed that it was "better to produce more steel mills now for more bullets later than to squander the empire's resources on short-term, stop-gap efforts" (ibid., 37).

30. Pelz, *Race to Pearl Harbor,* 25–40.

31. Ibid.

32. Asada, "Japanese Navy," 240–42; Wheeler, "Isolated Japan," 176.

33. Nish, *Japanese Foreign Policy, 1869–1942,* 205; Borg, *Far Eastern Crisis,* 107–12; Crowley, "Military Foreign Policies," 61; *FRUS, 1934,* 1:249–50, Davis to Hull, June 14, 1934; ibid., 250–54, Memorandum of Davis, Hull, Roosevelt Conversation, June 14, 1934.

34. Borg, *Far Eastern Crisis,* 109–11; Hornbeck Précis, "Russo-Japanese Conflict," February 2, 1934, PSF 42, and "Manchuria Situation," May 5, 1933, PSF 26, Roosevelt Papers; *FRUS, 1935,* 3:829–37, Hornbeck Memorandum, January 3, 1935.

35. Henry Morgenthau Diary, no. 2, p. 301, Franklin D. Roosevelt Library;

John Morton Blum, *Roosevelt and Morgenthau* (Boston: Houghton Mifflin, 1970), chaps. 1–2 passim.

36. Allan Seymore Everest, *Morgenthau, the New Deal and Silver* (New York: King's Crown, 1950), 31–44.

37. Ibid., 45, 102–6; Blum, *Roosevelt and Morgenthau,* 93–94; Morgenthau Diary, no. 2, pp. 338–43.

38. Morgenthau Diary, no. 2, pp. 295–301.

39. Hull to Roosevelt, March 7, 1935, PSF 42, Roosevelt Papers; Morgenthau Diary, no. 3, pp. 253–55, 296–302.

40. For studies that portray Hull as a moderate, see Jonathan G. Utley, *Going to War with Japan, 1937–1941* (Knoxville: University of Tennessee Press, 1985); and Abraham Ben-Zvi, *The Illusion of Deterrence: The Roosevelt Presidency and the Origins of the Pacific War* (London: Westview, 1987).

41. Borg, *Far Eastern Crisis,* 128–29; Louis, *British Strategy,* 231.

42. Bradford A. Lee, *Britain and the Sino-Japanese War, 1937–1939* (Stanford, CA: Stanford University Press, 1973), 10–11; *FRUS, 1935,* 3:95–97, Bingham to Hull, March 28, 1935; Phillips to Roosevelt, March 2, 1935, PSF 26, Roosevelt Papers; Sir Frederick Leith-Ross, *Money Talks: Fifty Years of International Finance: The Autobiography of Sir Frederick Leith-Ross* (London: Hutchinson, 1968), 196–97.

43. W. N. Medlicott et al., eds., *Documents on British Foreign Policy, 1919–1939,* 2nd ser., vol. 20 (Edinburgh: HM Stationery Office, 1984), 596–97; Leith-Ross, *Money Talks,* 200–201.

44. Leith-Ross, *Money Talks,* 205–7; Morgenthau Diary, no. 10, p. 180, and no. 11, p. 17. See also Young, *China's Nation Building,* chap. 9 passim.

45. Everest, *Morgenthau, the New Deal and Silver,* 113–17; Blum, *Roosevelt and Morgenthau,* 104–7; White to Morgenthau, April 9, 1936, folder 3 A, box 1, White Papers. Another copy of White's study (in book 20 A of the Morgenthau Diary) lists George Haas, rather than Harry White, as the sender and/or author of the memorandum.

46. Buck to Morgenthau, June 27, 1936, box 48, Henry Morgenthau Papers, Franklin D. Roosevelt Library; Spagent to Morgenthau, September 28, 1936, PSF 79, Roosevelt Papers.

47. Crowley, *Quest for Autonomy,* 201–2, 214–17, 229–31.

48. *FRUS, 1936,* 4:719, Grew to Hull, February 26, 1936. For a brief survey of the February 26 Incident, see Mamoru Shigemitsu, *Japan and Her Destiny: My Struggle for Peace* (New York: E. P. Dutton, 1958), 104–5; Hane, *Modern Japan,* 264–65; and Crowley, *Quest for Autonomy,* 244–46.

49. Crowley, *Quest for Autonomy,* 282, 291–94; Najita, *Intellectual Foundations,* 133–36; Barnhart, *Japan and the World,* 110–11; Katsumi Usui, "Japanese Approaches to China in the 1930s: Two Alternatives," in Iriye and Cohen, eds., *Perspectives,* 104–5.

50. Borg, *Far Eastern Crisis,* 187–88; Crowley, *Quest for Autonomy,* 307–8, 316.

51. Best, *Britain, Japan, and Pearl Harbor,* 25–26. Best compellingly demon-

strates that the British government recognized that Tokyo sought to avoid an armed clash and that Chiang, who faced increasing pressure to resist the Japanese, had within his power the ability to either keep the peace or make war.

52. Michael A. Barnhart, "Japanese Intelligence before the Second World War: 'Best Case' Analysis," in *Knowing One's Enemies: Intelligence Assessment before the Two World Wars,* ed. Ernest R. May (Princeton, NJ: Princeton University Press, 1986), 432.

53. James B. Crowley, "A Reconsideration of the Marco Polo Bridge Incident," *Journal of Asian Studies* 22, no. 3 (May 1963): 281–83.

54. Ibid., 283–87; Barnhart, "Japanese Intelligence," 433.

55. Youli Sun, *China and the Origins of the Pacific War, 1931–1941* (New York: St. Martin's, 1993), 89–90; Crowley, "Reconsideration," 287–89; Best, *Britain, Japan, and Pearl Harbor,* 41–42; William L. O'Neill, *A Democracy at War: America's Fight at Home and Abroad in World War II* (Cambridge, MA: Harvard University Press, 1993), 60.

56. Blum, *Roosevelt and Morgenthau,* 219; LaFeber, *The Clash,* 184; Ickes, *Inside Struggle,* 186.

57. Henry C. Adams, "The Road to Pearl Harbor: A Reexamination of American Far Eastern Policy, July 1937–December 1941," *Journal of American History* 48, no. 1 (June 1971): 76; *FRUS, 1937,* 3:459–60, Bullitt to Hull, August 23, 1937; ibid., 531–32, Hornbeck Memorandum, September 17, 1937; ibid., 582–83, State Department to British Embassy, October 5, 1937; Borg, *Far Eastern Crisis,* 374–80; John McVickar Haight Jr., "Franklin D. Roosevelt and a Naval Quarantine of Japan," *Pacific Historical Review* 40, no. 2 (May 1971): 205; Dorothy Borg, "Notes on Roosevelt's 'Quarantine' Speech," *Political Science Quarterly* 72, no. 3 (September 1957): 405, 413–14.

58. Nicholas R. Clifford, "Britain, America, and the Far East, 1937–1940: A Failure in Cooperation," *Journal of British Studies* 3, no. 1 (November 1963): 142; Borg, *Far Eastern Crisis,* 405–7; "Brussels Conference Official Report," folder Brussels Conference Official Report, box 5, Norman Davis Papers, Library of Congress; British Delegation at Geneva to Eden, October 6, 1937, and Extract from Cabinet Conclusions 37, October 13, 1937, Public Record Office 371-21015 7898.

59. "Brussels Conference Official Report," folder Brussels Conference Official Report, box 5, Davis Papers; Borg, *Far Eastern Crisis,* 438; Crowley, *Quest for Autonomy,* 348.

60. Extract from Cabinet Conclusion 43, November 24, 1937, and Clive-MacDonald Telegram, November 22, 1937, FO 371-2108, Public Record Office, London; "Brussels Conference Official Report," folder Brussels Conference Official Report, box 5, Davis Papers.

61. Clifford, "Failure in Cooperation," 144; Haight, "Naval Quarantine," 209–11, 218–19; Hamilton Darby Perry, *The Panay Incident: Prelude to Pearl Harbor* (New York: Macmillan, 1969), 280–81; Aaron Shai, *Origins of War in the East: Britain, China and Japan, 1937–1939* (London: Croom Helm, 1976), 131–32.

62. Borg, *Far Eastern Crisis,* 473–74; Memorandum of Yoshida-Moffat Conversation, December 2, 1937, folder Brussels Conference: Conversations/Memoranda, box 5, Davis Papers. For the Nanking death toll, see Barnhart, *Japan and the World,* 114; and LaFeber, *The Clash,* 187. Barnhart places the death toll at 200,000, while LaFeber notes that Chinese sources put the figure at 300,000.

63. Crowley, *Quest for Autonomy,* 358–75. See also Ikuhiko Hata, "The Marco Polo Bridge Incident," in Morley, ed., *China Quagmire,* 280–86; and Bix, *Hirohito,* 343–45. Hata and Crowley differ most fundamentally in their analysis of the role played by the army and Foreign Minister Hirota. Crowley, e.g., argues that War Minister Sugiyama remained in favor of negotiations on the basis of the November terms, while Hata argues that only Navy Minister Yonai stood with the general staff. Crowley also argues that Hirota used the specter of field army dissatisfaction as a cat's paw to keep the moderates in line. Hata does not paint Hirota in a favorable light, but he does argue that opposition among middle-echelon officers was quite real.

4. Containment at High Tide

Second epigraph: Wayne S. Cole, "The Role of the United States Congress and Political Parties," in Borg and Okamoto, eds., *Pearl Harbor,* 310–11.

1. Secretary of War Stimson, firmly convinced of the power of American deterrence, believed that a 1919 cotton embargo was a phenomenal success. See Stimson Diary, no. 31, pp. 11–12. On sanctions having little effect on Japanese policy, see Nish, *Japanese Foreign Policy in the Interwar Period,* 145–48.

2. Michael Schaller has argued that, "as 1938 wore on, the outlines of a new policy appeared, one predicated on the maintenance of a pro-American China which might be a bulwark against Japan." Michael Schaller, *The U.S. Crusade in China, 1938–1945* (New York: Columbia University Press, 1979), 17. The idea of the Chinese "bulwark," however, dates back at least to 1933, as does the policy of American economic aid.

3. Morgenthau Diary, no. 78, p. 22. Everest puts the amount of silver purchased at sixty-two million ounces. Everest, *Morgenthau, the New Deal and Silver,* 118.

4. Everest, *Morgenthau, the New Deal and Silver,* 120–21 (see also 118, table 4, app.).

5. Morgenthau Diary, no. 142, pp. 341–42, and no. 143, p. 152.

6. Morgenthau Diary, no. 143, pp. 224–25. It is not clear whether Feis's suggestion came from the State Department or was a personal suggestion.

7. Morgenthau Diary, no. 143, p. 153, and no. 144, p. 279.

8. *FRUS, 1938,* 3:569–72, Hamilton Memorandum, November 13, 1938.

9. Ibid., 572–74, Hornbeck Memorandum, November 14, 1938; Schaller, *Crusade,* 25–26; *FRUS, 1938,* 3:569–72, Hamilton Memorandum, November 14, 1938. For some of the State Department's more technical and legal objections as well as day-to-day bargaining between State and Treasury, see Morgenthau Diary, no. 155, pp. 47–48, 68, 76, 116–19.

10. Robert Dallek, *Franklin D. Roosevelt and American Foreign Policy, 1932–1945* (New York: Oxford University Press, 1979), 78–80; Koo to Quo, August 8, 1938, folder Japan-Russia Conflict, 1938, box 26, Koo Papers; John W. Garver, *Chinese-Soviet Relations, 1937–1945: The Diplomacy of Chinese Nationalism* (New York: Oxford University Press, 1988), 18, 21–22.

11. Morgenthau Diary, no. 153, pp. 269–70, 303, 367. For opposition on the part of leading Treasury officers, see Morgenthau Diary, no. 146, pp. 272–73. The fact that Washington had little reason to fear rising Soviet influence in China is borne out as well in subsequent reports. Stimson, e.g., noted, in August 1940, that Nelson Johnson confirmed Soong's estimate concerning a lack of Soviet influence. Stimson Diary, no. 30, p. 82.

12. Garver, *Chinese-Soviet Relations,* 43–44.

13. Morgenthau Diary, no. 153, pp. 366–69, and no. 158, pp. 223–24; John Morton Blum, *From the Morgenthau Dairies,* vol. 1, *Years of Urgency, 1938–1941* (Boston: Houghton Mifflin, 1965), 58–63; Utley, *Going to War,* 46.

14. Morgenthau Diary, no. 142, pp. 369–85, and no. 232, p. 28. See also Blum, *Years of Urgency,* 125.

15. Morgenthau Diary, no. 144, p. 306. Tanker trucks were also important if China were to have any hope of making good on its tung oil deliveries. Such deliveries were a secondary consideration for Morgenthau, but it was nonetheless important to keep up appearances. Morgenthau Diary, no. 205, pp. 94–95, and no. 206, p. 79; McNutt to Roosevelt, September 29, 1939, folder China 1939–1940, box 2, OF 150, Roosevelt Papers; *Merriam-Webster's Geographic Dictionary,* 3rd ed. (Springfield, IL: Merriam-Webster, 2001), s.v. *Burma Road,* p. 188.

16. *FRUS, 1939,* 3:550–55, Memorandum by Hornbeck and the Division of Far Eastern Affairs, December 29, 1939; ibid., *1940,* 4:645–46, Memorandum of Hornbeck-Morgenthau Conversation, March 6, 1940; ibid., 651, Hornbeck to Morgenthau, April 11, 1940.

17. *FRUS, 1940,* 4:658–59, Hamilton to Hull, June 3, 1940; Blum, *Years of Urgency,* 361–62; Schaller, *Crusade,* 43.

18. Schaller, *Crusade,* 28, 37. On March 30, 1940, Wang Ching-wei, a longtime leader of the Kuomintang's left wing, established a Japanese-controlled regime to rival Chiang Kai-shek's. Long a popular figure in China, Wang first rose to prominence as a result of his attempt on the life of the Manchu prince regent in 1910. A close confidant of the revolutionary leader Sun Yat-sen, he fought Chiang unsuccessfully for over a decade to control the Nationalist Party following Sun's death in 1925. Not long after the outbreak of the Sino-Japanese War, Wang called for peace talks with Japan, and, at the end of 1938, he fled to French Indochina after losing out once again in his bid to control the Kuomintang. Chiang's agents failed to assassinate him in Hanoi in early 1939, and, in the aftermath of the failed attempt on his life, he sought refuge in Japanese-occupied China. Given his tremendous name recognition, his decision to form an anti-Chiang puppet regime represented a potentially severe blow to the Chinese resistance. For more on Wang, see Howard L. Boorman, "Wang

Ching-wei: China's Romantic Radical," *Political Science Quarterly* 79, no. 4 (December 1964): 504, 516–18.

19. Rear Admiral Sadatoshi Tomioka, "Japanese Monograph #146," in *War in Asia and the Pacific* (2 vols.), ed. Donald S. Detwiler and Charles B. Burdick (New York: Garland, 1980), 2:8–9; Ikuhiko Hata, "The Army's Move into Northern Indochina," in Morley, ed., *Fateful Choice,* 155.

20. Tomioka, "Japanese Monograph #146," 9.

21. Chihiro Hosoya, "The Tripartite Pact," in Morley, ed., *Deterrent Diplomacy,* 242–43; Nobutaka Ike, ed., *Japan's Decision for War: Records of the 1941 Policy Conferences* (Stanford, CA: Stanford University Press, 1967), 4–5, 13, Imperial Conference, September 19, 1940.

22. Ike, ed., *Japan's Decision for War,* 80–81, Imperial Conference, July 2, 1941.

23. Stimson Diary, no. 29, p. 49. As late as spring 1940, Harry Price, the creator of the American Committee for Non-Participation in Japanese Aggression, informed Hull that State Department policy was held in low esteem by his organization. Stimson Diary, no. 30, p. 180. Stimson too felt that on certain issues, such as an aviation gasoline embargo, the State Department was "getting a little bit weak." Morgenthau's disagreement with State extended back to the silver purchase days of 1934, and, after 1937, he too felt that Hull and his men were too cautious. In addition to his differences with Hull, Morgenthau seems to have held Sumner Welles in especially low regard. Morgenthau Diary, no. 307, pp. 66–67, 70–71. Abraham Ben-Zvi writes that, unlike hard-liners, including Stimson, who understood the world through a balance-of-power approach, Hull interpreted both Japan and American policy through a cautious, "humanistic-Universalist vision of the world." This approach dictated caution, Ben-Zvi argues, until the Japanese occupation of southern Indochina. Ben-Zvi, *Illusion of Deterrence,* 101–6. Utley gives an even more favorable account of Hull's Far Eastern policy. He argues that Hull's ability to subordinate "his feelings of righteous indignation at Japan's aggression to the less emotional criteria of national interest" led him to adopt a cautious, measured policy. Utley, *Going to War,* 9–10. See also *FRUS, 1939,* 3:540–43, Memorandum of Welles–Saint-Quentin Conversation, July 21, 1939; and ibid., 530–33, Jones Memorandum, April 20, 1939. Analyses by FE found that Japan could withstand an oil embargo and also circumvent American efforts by making purchases outside the Anglo-French-American-Dutch sphere. Likewise, while an iron ore embargo would be disastrous in the long term, it would not be felt immediately. Ibid., 537, Hackworth to Hull, May 26, 1939; ibid., 497–500, Grew to Hull, January 31, 1939.

24. Green Letter, July 1, 1938, and Hull to Roosevelt, December 13, 1938, folder Diplomatic Correspondence: Japan, 1938–1942, box 42, Roosevelt Papers.

25. Mira Wilkins, "The Role of U.S. Business," in Borg and Okamoto, eds., *Pearl Harbor,* 373; *FRUS, 1939,* 3:494–95, Memorandum of Conversation, Hamilton-Breck, January 27, 1939; ibid., 503–5, Memorandum of Conversation, Hornbeck, Arensberg, Ruslander, and Lang, February 6, 1939; ibid., 545–46, Memorandum of Conversation, Ballantine, Hamilton, and Hellman, September 18, 1939.

26. *FRUS, 1939,* 3:549, Green Memorandum, December 10, 1939; Morgenthau Diary, no. 290, p. 95.

27. Morgenthau Diary, no. 139, p. 36; White to Morgenthau, April 8, 1939, folder 15 B, box 6, White Papers.

28. White to Morgenthau, April 8, 1939, folder 15 B, box 6, White Papers.

29. Minority View of HR 5191, Report 283, pt. 2, *House Reports,* 76th Cong., 1st sess., vol. 2 (Washington, DC: US Government Printing Office, 1939); *Congressional Record,* 76th Cong., 1st sess., 1939, 84, pt. 5. The $100 million figure does not begin to reflect the huge sums spent on preclusive purchasing. By the end of April 1941, the Rubber Reserve Co. and the Metals Reserve Co., just two arms of preclusive purchasing, had commitments for over $800 million in purchases. For details, see S. Shepard Jones and Denys P. Myers, eds., *Documents on American Foreign Relations, July 1939–June 1940 and July–June 1941,* 2 vols. (Boston: World Peace Foundation, 1940), 2:737–38.

30. Jonathan Marshall, *To Have and Have Not: Southeast Asian Raw Materials and the Origins of the Pacific War* (Berkeley and Los Angeles: University of California Press, 1995), 34–35; Memorandum "Recommendation on 'Protective' Buying," November 19, 1940, and Notes, December 2, 1940, folder Research Material Memoirs (Unpublished), box 127, Herbert Feis Papers, Library of Congress. In connection with the view that inadequate funding was weakening preclusive purchasing, see Thomas Bill and W. Y. Elliott to Hull, March 20, 1939, folder June 1939, box 55, Feis Papers.

31. Memorandum of December 23, 1940, Meeting, "Progress of the United States Government Stock Pile Program," folder Research Material, Memoirs (Unpublished) 1940 Strategic Materials, box 55, Feis Papers.

32. Feis to Welles, March 21, 1941, folder The Latin American Program, and Feis to Welles, April 30, 1941, folder Tin, box 56, Feis Papers; Morgenthau Diary, no. 439, p. 38; *FRUS, 1941,* 6:458–59, Hull to Jenkins, May 1, 1941 (emphasis added).

33. Excerpts of Jones's Report to President and Congress, March 21, 1942, and Rio Embassy to State Department, January 17, 1942, folder 1940 Preemptive Buying Program Begins, box 55, Feis Papers; Morgenthau Diary, no. 438, p. 39.

34. Morgenthau Diary, no. 439, p. 38, and no. 454, p. 153; Herbert Feis, *The Road to Pearl Harbor: The Coming of the War between Japan and America* (New York: Atheneum, 1962), 234.

35. Morgenthau Diary, no. 232, p. 28, no. 229, pp. 10–11, and no. 248, p. 10. Part of the problem in restricting molybdenum came from the availability to Japan of nickel imports. Climax Molybdenum noted that an embargo on its product would not be effective unless nickel, and to a lesser extent tungsten, exports were also cut off. By early spring 1940, Canada had ended nickel exports to Japan. See Morgenthau Diary, no. 229, p. 103, Max Schott to Morgenthau, December 14, 1939.

36. Stimson Diary, no. 29, p. 49.

37. Keith D. McFarland, *Harry H. Woodring: A Political Biography of FDR's Controversial Secretary of War* (Lawrence: University Press of Kansas, 1975), 210.

38. Dallek, *Roosevelt,* 232; Stimson Diary, no. 31, pp. 1, 11–12.

39. Stimson Letter to the *New York Times,* January 11, 1940, folder China 1939–1940, box 2, OF 150, Roosevelt Papers.

40. Ibid.

41. Morgenthau Diary, no. 284, p. 201.

42. Ibid. For a slightly different account of the evening, see Stimson Diary, no. 30, pp. 22–23.

43. Morgenthau Diary, no. 284, pp. 201–2, 209–10.

44. Stimson Diary, no. 30, pp. 39, 50, 67; Feis, *Pearl Harbor,* 91–92; Daniel Yergin, *The Prize: The Epic Quest for Oil, Money and Power,* new ed. (New York: Free Press, 2008), 296. Yergin notes that, in the five months following the decision to suspend shipments of high octane fuel, Tokyo purchased 550 percent more petroleum at eighty-six octane or below than in the first half of 1940.

45. Feis, *Pearl Harbor,* 88; *FRUS, 1940,* 4:588–89, Hornbeck to Welles, July 24, 1940.

46. *FRUS, Japan, 1931–1941,* 2:222–23, White House Press Release, September 26, 1940; ibid., 232–33, Proclamation #2449, December 10, 1940; ibid., 233–35, Executive Order 8607, December 10, 1940. For details of further export restriction, including enumerated articles, see ibid., 238–60 passim.

47. Ike, ed., *Japan's Decision for War,* 36–39, Record of the 25th Liaison Conference, May 22, 1941; ibid., 47–51, Records of the 29th Liaison Conference, June 11, 1941. Matsuoka certainly believed that the United States and Britain were responsible for Batavia's consistent rejection of Japanese demands. In addition to his arguments during the Twenty-fifth Liaison Conference (Ike, ed., *Japan's Decision for War,* 37–38), see Shinjiro Nagaoka, "Economic Demands on the Dutch East Indies," in Morley, ed., *Fateful Choice,* 152. As early as May 1940, well in advance of American export licensing, Tokyo sought to secure Dutch agreement for increased shipments of key East Indies raw materials, including oil, scrap iron, nickel, molybdenum, etc. For details, see ibid., 138.

48. Barnhart, *Japan Prepares,* 208–9; Jun Tsunoda, "The Navy's Role in the Southern Strategy," in Morley, ed., *Fateful Choice,* 264, 291, 293.

49. For a record of the July 2 imperial conference prepared for the army high command, see Ike, ed., *Japan's Decision for War,* 77–90. A substantial body of secondary literature argues that the Nazi-Soviet War emboldened or even explains Japan's decision to move south. See, e.g., Thomas A. Bailey, *A Diplomatic History of the American People,* 7th ed. (New York: Appleton-Century-Crofts, 1964), 734. On their face, these studies suffer from a number of fundamental flaws. Initially, the argument that, because the Soviet threat was neutralized, Japan felt free to move south after June 22 ignores certain facts. If this were the case, Japan would have felt free to move south in April, after concluding the Neutrality Pact with Moscow. April would have been the preferred time as well in that German pressure against England had not yet declined and it appeared quite possible that England might be invaded, starved into submission by the U-boat blockade, or even decisively defeated in the Middle East. Second,

given that the movement into southern French Indochina did not require large-scale troop deployments, Tokyo could have undertaken the move no matter how powerful a force the Soviets deployed in Siberia. After all, Japan absorbed northern French Indochina without a neutrality pact or a German-Soviet war. Moreover, in July 1941, Japan did not possess superiority over Soviet Far Eastern forces. Nor for that matter did numbers favor Tokyo in December 1941. On a second level, those who argue that June 22 in some way explains Japan's move south ignore the fact that the issues that contributed to the absorption of southern French Indochina—namely, settling the China Incident, securing raw materials, and preparing forward bases to strike the American-British-Dutch coalition—existed well before June 22. It seems quite clear that the Konoe cabinet would have approved the operation against southern French Indochina in the absence of a German-Soviet war.

50. Beale, *Roosevelt,* 328–31; Stimson, *Far Eastern Crisis,* 138; Diary, no. 58, p. 2150, Grew Papers.

51. Hornbeck to Hull, September 8, 1937, folder Japanese-Chinese Hostilities, September 1937, box 83, Hornbeck Papers; Davis to Welles, July 30, 1937, Welles to Roosevelt, July 30, 1937, and Welles to Davis, August 6, 1937, folder Welles, Sumner 1933–1941, box 63, Davis Papers.

52. Hadley Cantril, ed., *Public Opinion, 1935–1946,* prepared by Mildred Strunk (Princeton, NJ: Princeton University Press, 1951), 939 (polls 1, 2, 5); *New York Times,* December 30, 1937, 1; Cole, "Role," 310–11.

53. For cabinet discussions concerning the Japanese economy, see Ickes, *Inside Struggle,* 51.

54. Heinrichs, "Role of the Navy," 215, 218; *New York Times,* February 1, 1938, 6, March 8, 1939, 1, and June 19, 1940, 13; Jones and Myers, eds., *Documents,* 2:761; *Wall Street Journal,* May 16, 1940, 1.

55. Strong to Marshall, March 2, 1940, WPD 4192-3, National Archives and Records Administration, Washington, DC, and College Park, MD; Strong to Marshall, August 21, 1939, WPD 4192; Stimson Diary, no. 32, p. 34; Edward S. Miller, *War Plan Orange: The U.S. Strategy to Defeat Japan, 1897–1945* (Annapolis, MD: US Naval Institute Press, 1991), 60–61; Ross, *American War Plans,* 179.

56. Mark Skinner Watson, *The History of the War Department: Chief of Staff: Prewar Plans and Preparations,* vol. 6 of *The History of the War Department* (Washington, DC: Historical Division, Department of the Army, 1950), 419–24; Weigley, "Role," 181.

57. Elmer Belmont Potter, *Nimitz* (Annapolis, MD: US Naval Institute Press, 1976), 4.

58. Stimson Diary, no. 32, p. 34; Lionel Wigmore, *The Japanese Thrust,* vol. 4, ser. 1 (Army) of *Australia in the War of 1939–1945* (Adelaide: Griffin, 1957), 77; Paul Hasluck, *The Government and the People, 1939–1941,* vol. 1, ser. 4 (Civil) of *Australia in the War of 1939–1945* (Adelaide: Advertiser Printing Office, 1952), 350; "Data for War Department Strategic Estimate of the Situation," enclosure in Gerow to Marshall, July 16, 1941, WPD 4510.

59. For information on the growing strength of the general staff and the weakening of navy moderates, see Asada, "Japanese Navy," 248–51. Asada also notes that Oikawa "carefully coupled his consent to the Tripartite alliance with an insistence that the navy be given special consideration in the allocation of material" (ibid., 249). Tomioka's conclusions concerning navy support for the Axis Pact were based on the results of a roundtable discussion held in 1946 among Admirals Yoshida, Toyoda, Kondo, Sawamoto, and Inoue and some twenty other ranking members of the Navy Ministry and Navy General Staff. For details, see Tomioka, "Japanese Monograph #146," 27, 31–34. For the clearest explanation of the link between navy support for the Axis Pact and increased funding, see Matome Ugaki, *Fading Victory: The Diary of Admiral Matome Ugaki,* trans. Masataka Chihaya (Pittsburgh, PA: University of Pittsburgh Press, 1991), 5–6.

60. Asada, "Japanese Navy," 244, 251; Tsunoda, "Navy's Role," 246–52. Tsunoda seems to downplay the relation between the China Incident and the southern advance. Tomioka's postwar analysis of the "Outline," however, notes that settling "the China Incident as early as possible" and the "destruction of Chiang-aid activities by third powers" were major goals. Tomioka, "Japanese Monograph #146," 16. Tsunoda notes that, having "acknowledged the possibility of waging war against the United States," the Navy "hoped the army would cooperate in providing the materials, manpower, and industrial capacity necessary to strengthen the naval arm." Tsunoda, "Navy's Role," 252.

61. Asada, "Japanese Navy," 233–34. Admiral Sadatoshi Tomioka, whose monograph is used extensively in this section, was a central member of the First Committee. Tsunoda, "Leaning toward War," in Morley, ed., *Final Confrontation,* 106–10. For Yamamoto's opposition to Nagano, see Agawa, *Reluctant Admiral,* 213.

62. Tsunoda, "Leaning toward War," 110–11. For the edited and translated text of Ishikawa's position paper, see Morley, ed., *Final Confrontation,* 354–63 (app. 4).

63. Tsunoda, "Leaning toward War," 161. It is unclear what effect the First Committee had on Nagano's thinking. Ishikawa clearly believed that, as late as June 5, Nagano favored continuing negotiations with the United States. Tsunoda contends, however, that, since April, Nagano believed that war with the West was inevitable. On July 12, Nagano supported Matsuoka when the foreign minister called for ending the Hull-Nomura talks, and, just over a week later, he argued that, if Japan were to win the war, hostilities could not be delayed much longer. See ibid., 110–11; and Morley, ed., *Final Confrontation,* 354–63 (app. 4). For details, see Ike, ed., *Japan's Decision for War,* 103–7, Records of the 40th Liaison Conference, July 21, 1941.

64. Donald J. Friedman, *The Road from Isolation: The Campaign of the American Committee for Non-Participation in Japanese Aggression, 1938–1941* (Cambridge, MA: Harvard University Press, 1970), 2, 5, 7–8, 87; Herzberg, *Broken Bond,* 228–29.

65. Friedman, *The Road from Isolation,* 8, 31–32.

66. Waldo H. Heinrichs Jr., "Franklin D. Roosevelt and the Risks of War, 1939–1941," in Iriye and Cohen, eds., *Perspectives,* 149; *FRUS, 1940,* 3:78, Lothian to FDR, July 8, 1940; ibid., 79, Welles to Lothian, July 29, 1940; ibid., 2:52–53, Brit-

ish Embassy to State Department, July 3, 1940; John Baylis, *Anglo-American Relations since 1939: The Enduring Alliance* (Manchester: Manchester University Press, 1997), 18.

67. *FRUS, 1941,* 1:741–42, Memorandum of Henderson-Oumansky Conversation, April 18, 1941; ibid., 4:991–92, Langdon Memorandum, June 23, 1941. In the summer of 1938, a border clash between Soviet and Japanese troops led to nearly two weeks of heavy fighting in which the Kwantung Army fared very poorly. Ten months later, in the spring of 1939, Japanese forces advanced from Manchuria into a portion of Outer Mongolia protected by Soviet forces. Outnumbered nearly two to one at Nomonhan, Japanese forces were again badly beaten by the Red Army. For details, see Margaret E. Wagner, Linda Barrett Osborne, Susan Reyburn, and Staff of the Library of Congress, *The Library of Congress World War II Companion,* ed. and with an introduction by David M. Kennedy (New York: Simon & Schuster, 2007), 418–20.

5. Sinners in the Hands of an Angry Department

Epigraphs: Jonathan Edwards, "Sinners in the Hands of an Angry God" (1741), in *Jonathan Edwards: Basic Writings,* ed. Ola Elizabeth Winslow (New York: Signet/New American Library, 1966), 159; Stimson Diary, no. 35, p. 114.

1. Hata, "The Marco Polo Bridge Incident," 254–55; Peattie, *Confrontation with the West,* 294–301. Anthony Best notes that long before 1939 Washington should have recognized the possibility of mediation. Kazushige Ugakai's elevation to foreign minister in May 1938, e.g., offered a clear signal that the propeace faction was ascendant in Tokyo, in that Ugaki favored a negotiated peace. See Best, *Britain, Japan, and Pearl Harbor,* 56.

2. Confidential Report, "Problems of American Far Eastern Policy," December 3–4, 1938, box 19, Brooks Emeny Papers, Seeley Mudd Library; Johnson to Roosevelt, February 27, 1939, Diplomatic Correspondence, China, 1939–1940, PSF 27, Roosevelt Papers.

3. Bullitt to Roosevelt, August 28, 1939, Diplomatic Correspondence, China, 1939–1940, PSF 27, Roosevelt Papers; *FRUS, 1939,* 3:210–11, Bullitt to Hull, August 26, 1939. For a clear, if somewhat emotional, look at Bullitt's hatred of the Soviets, see Irwin F. Gellman, *Secret Affairs: Franklin Roosevelt, Cordell Hull and Sumner Welles* (Baltimore: Johns Hopkins University Press, 1995), 141; *Documents on German Foreign Policy,* ser. D (1937–1945), vol. 8, *The War Years: June 23–December 11, 1941* (Washington, DC: US Government Printing Office, 1954), 237–38, Ott to Weizsacker, October 7, 1939; *FRUS, 1939,* 3:213–14, Engert to Hull, August 28, 1939; ibid., 214–15, Lockhart to Hull, August 28, 1939; and ibid., 223–24, Dooman to Hull, September 1, 1939.

4. *FRUS, 1939,* 3:221–23, Bullitt to Hull, September 1, 1939; Waichiapu to London Embassy, August 2, 1938, folder Attempts at Mediation between China and Japan, 1933–1938, box 26, Koo Papers; *Documents on German Foreign Policy,* 220–22, Memorandum of Knoll-Ting Conversation, October 5, 1939.

5. Dooman Oral History, 105, 108. Dooman was perhaps not the best judge of Hornbeck's temperament regarding Japan. Nonetheless, he believed that Hornbeck "had two supreme passions": "One was a feeling of affection and sympathy for China. And the second was a pathological hatred of Japan and things Japanese."

6. *FRUS, 1939,* 3:211–12, Hornbeck Memorandum, August 26, 1939; ibid., 250–51, Hornbeck to Hull, September 16, 1939. Hornbeck's decision to forward a copy and to extensively paraphrase Yarnell's July 20, 1939, report, entitled "The Far Eastern Situation," is enlightening. Yarnell's report argued that Tokyo exercised no control over its armies in China and that the United States must be prepared to support China to the extent of intervening militarily against Japan. Hornbeck certainly knew Hull's opinion regarding proper American policy in the Far East, and, at a critical juncture, he felt that Yarnell's memorandum was appropriate reading for the secretary. His decision indicates that, rather than horrifying Hull, Hornbeck believed that Yarnell's analysis was, in many instances, consistent with the secretary's.

7. Paul Haggie, *Britannia at Bay: The Defense of the British Empire against Japan, 1931–1941* (Oxford: Clarendon, 1981), 164; Peter Lowe, "Great Britain's Assessment of Japan before the Outbreak of the Pacific War," in May, ed., *Knowing One's Enemies,* 463; *Documents on German Foreign Policy,* 243, Woermann to Weizsacker, October 8, 1941.

8. Hosoya, "The Tripartite Pact," 191–99; *FRUS, 1939,* 3:582–83, Dooman to Hull, September 25, 1939.

9. Grew, *Turbulent Era,* 2:1211–12.

10. Grew, *Ten Years,* 305; *FRUS, 1939,* 3:593–95, Grew to Hull, November 4, 1939; ibid., 597–99, Grew to Hull, November 21, 1939; ibid., 602–4, Grew to Hull, November 28, 1939.

11. *FRUS, 1939,* 3:604–13, Grew to Hull, December 1, 1939.

12. Ibid.

13. Ibid.

14. Grew, *Ten Years,* 309–12; *FRUS, 1939,* 3:619–20, Grew to Hull, December 18, 1939; ibid., 622, Grew to Hull, December 18, 1939; ibid., 624–25, Grew to Hull, December 20, 1939. Reopening the Yangtze as far as Nanking was a risky step for the Abe cabinet. Tokyo closed the river after Japanese warplanes sank several foreign ships, including the USS *Panay.* If, as the Japanese government claimed, the attack was unauthorized, then reopening the river in an effort to placate the United States increased the danger that Japanese forces might again attack American ships.

15. Hosoya, "The Tripartite Pact," 200–201.

16. Grew to Roosevelt, January 16, 1940, Letters, 1940, no. 2, Grew Papers; *FRUS, 1939,* 4:449–50, Dooman to Hull, September 12, 1939; ibid., *1940,* 4:957–59, Grew to Hull, January 15, 1940.

17. *FRUS, 1940,* 4:959–60, Ballantine to Hull, January 15, 1940; ibid., 960–61, Hornbeck Memorandum, January 16, 1940.

18. Grew, *Ten Years,* 312–13; Hosoya, "The Tripartite Pact," 203; Diary, no. 132, p. 4282, Grew Papers.

19. Grew to Roosevelt, December 14, 1940, Letters, 1940, no. 2, and Diary, no. 133, p. 4316, Grew Papers.

20. Diary, no. 136, p. 4405, and no. 137, p. 4431, Grew Papers.

21. Memorandum of Hull-Lothian Conversation, June 27, 1940, 711.94/1580, Record Group (RG) 59, National Archives and Records Administration.

22. Hull's Confidential Oral Statement, June 28, 1940, 711.94/1581, RG 59; Friedman, *The Road from Isolation,* 57.

23. Hull's Confidential Oral Statement, June 28, 1940, 711.94/1581, RG 59.

24. Congress approved the Selective Service Act in August, and the president activated the national guard in September. For details, see Watson, *History of the War Department,* 196.

25. Frederick W. Marks III, *Wind over Sand: The Diplomacy of Franklin Roosevelt* (Athens: University of Georgia Press, 1988), 85–86; Jean Edward Smith, *FDR* (New York: Random House, 2008), 445; Berle Memorandum, June 4, 1940, 711.94/1563, RG59; 711.94/1583, RG59.

26. 711.94/1570, RG69.

27. Ibid.; Grew-Craigie Conversation, May 31, 1940, Diary, no. 100, and Diary, no. 139, p. 4510, Grew Papers.

28. White to Morgenthau, April 8, 1939, folder 15 B, box 6, White Papers; Morton, *Strategy and Command,* 71–72; *FRUS, 1940,* 4:159–60, Memorandum of Hull-Lothian Conversation, September 30, 1940; Stimson Diary, no. 30, pp. 202–3.

29. John Costello, *The Pacific War, 1941–1945* (New York: Harper Perennial, 1982), 71; Sadao Asada, *From Mahan to Pearl Harbor: The Imperial Navy and the United States* (Annapolis, MD: US Naval Institute Press, 2006) 227; Nish, *Japanese Foreign Policy, 1869–1942,* 238; Doenecke and Stoler, *Roosevelt's Foreign Policies,* 45; Kazuo Yagami, *Konoe Fumimaro and the Failure of Peace in Japan, 1937–1941: A Critical Appraisal of the Three-Time Prime Minister* (Jefferson, NC: McFarland, 2006), 92–96.

30. Feis, *Pearl Harbor,* 102–3, 122; John W. Masland, "American Attitudes toward Japan," *Annals of the American Academy of Political Science,* May 1941, folder 8, box 81, Records of the Committee to Defend America by Aiding the Allies, Seeley Mudd Library.

31. Feis, *Pearl Harbor,* 106.

32. Hornbeck Memorandum, June 6, 1940, 711.94/1554, RG 59.

33. Tsunoda, "Confusion Arising from a Draft Understanding between Japan and the United States," 20–24; R. J. C. Butow, *The John Doe Associates: Backdoor Diplomacy for Peace* (Stanford, CA: Stanford University Press, 1974), 9.

34. Tsunoda, "Confusion Arising from a Draft Understanding," 19–20.

35. Butow, *John Doe,* 19. For details of the work of the John Doe Associates, see John H. Boyle, "The Drought-Walsh Mission to Japan," *Pacific Historical Review* 34, no. 2 (May 1965): 141–62; and Robert J. C. Butow, "The Hull-Nomura Conversations: A Fundamental Misconception," *American Historical Review* 65, no. 4 (July 1960): 822–36.

36. Stimson Diary, no. 32, pp. 11, 35; *FRUS, 1941,* 5:55, Navy Department to State, February 4, 1941; ibid., 61, British Embassy to State Department, February 7, 1941; ibid., 62–64, Grew to Hull, February 7, 1941; Butow, *John Doe,* 18; *FRUS, 1941,* 4:22–27, Hull to Roosevelt, February 5, 1941.

37. *FRUS, Japan, 1931–1941,* 2:387–89, Hull Memorandum, February 14, 1941.

38. Ibid., *1941,* 4:54, Walker to Roosevelt, February 28, 1941.

39. Ibid., 55, Hornbeck to Hull, March 1, 1941; ibid., 57–58, Hornbeck to Hull, March 4, 1941; ibid., 62–63, Hornbeck to Hull, March 7, 1941.

40. Walker to Hull, March 7, 1941, 711.94/2005-3/14, RG 59.

41. Hull Memorandum, March 8, 1941, 711.94/2005-9/14, RG 59; *FRUS, Japan, 1931–1941,* 2:389–96, Hull Memorandum, March 8, 1941; ibid., 397–98, Hull Memorandum, March 14, 1941. 711.94/1987, RG 59, contains a much fuller, detailed record of the March 8 Hull-Nomura meeting. On March 1, Hornbeck advised Hull that, if Tokyo really wished to have better relations with the United States, it "could give this Government concrete evidence . . . by itself nullifying . . . the Axis alliance and . . . desisting and abstaining from 'further political or military aggression in the Far East.'" For the text of Hornbeck's memorandum, see *FRUS, 1941,* 4:55, Hornbeck to Hull, March 1, 1941.

42. *FRUS, 1941,* 4:95–96, Walker to Hull, March 16, 1941; ibid., 97–107, Walker to Hull, March 17, 1941; ibid., 111–12, Walker to Hull, March 18, 1941; ibid., 119–20, Walker to Hull, April 4, 1941.

43. Ibid., 120–22, Hornbeck Memorandum, April 5, 1941; ibid., 123–26, Hornbeck Memorandum, April 7, 1941.

44. Ibid., 135–39, Far Eastern Division to Hull, April 10, 1941; Joseph Ballantine Oral History, 40, Butler Library. In March, Matsuoka set out to conclude a nonaggression pact with Moscow and shore up relations with Japan's Axis partners. Tokyo and Moscow concluded a neutrality pact on April 13. Matsuoka returned to Tokyo on April 21. For a brief discussion of this chapter of Matsuoka diplomacy, see Nish, *Japanese Foreign Policy, 1869–1942,* 240–43.

45. *FRUS, 1941,* 4:142–43, Hornbeck Memorandum, April 11, 1941; ibid., 147–48, Hamilton Memorandum, April 11, 1941. Hornbeck's April 11 analysis of Japanese duplicity was no flight of fancy but rather a reflection of his long-held belief in the inherently deceitful nature of Japanese diplomacy.

46. Ibid., 150–52, Far Eastern Affairs Division Memorandum, April 14, 1941.

47. Ibid., 148–50, Hornbeck to Hull, April 14, 1941; ibid., 152–53, Memorandum for Hull (unsigned but likely from Hornbeck), April 15, 1941. Hamilton and Ballantine prepared an additional draft response to the April 9 Japanese proposal. Like Hornbeck's earlier drafts, the new draft also contained terms for settling the China Incident that seem deliberately misleading. For specifics of the Hamilton-Ballantine draft, see ibid., 154–60, Hamilton/Ballantine Memorandum, April 16, 1941.

48. Ibid., 162, Hornbeck to Hull, April 18, 1941.

49. Ibid., *Japan, 1931–1941,* 2:406–10, Memorandum of Hull-Nomura Con-

versation, April 16, 1941; Peter Mauch, *Sailor Diplomat: Nomura Kichisaburo and the Japanese-American War* (Cambridge, MA: Harvard University Press, 2011), 161.

50. Dallek, *Roosevelt,* 260–61; *FRUS, 1941,* 1:129–31, Gunther to Hull, February 6, 1941; ibid., 133–34, Steinhardt to Hull, March 24, 1941; ibid., 4:186–87, Curie to Roosevelt, May 13, 1941; Grew to Hornbeck, May 26, 1941, Letters, 1941, no. 30, Grew Papers. In his letter, Grew enclosed a Foreign Office communication, apparently from Eden, that indicates both British suspicion at the highest levels of Japanese motives and the conviction that a continued firm policy would soon pay dividends.

51. Tsunoda, "Confusion Arising from a Draft Understanding," 74–81; *FRUS, Japan, 1931–1941,* 2:420–22, Japanese Draft Proposal, May 12, 1941; ibid., 423–25, Japanese Oral Explanation, May 12, 1941. Tsunoda also compellingly demonstrates that, like his American counterpart, Matsuoka saw little value in a Japanese-American accord. Rather, he hoped to deter the United States from entering the European War by insisting that Japan would honor the pact and fight on Germany's side.

52. *FRUS, 1941,* 4:184–86, Walker to Hull, May 8, 1941; ibid., 187–88, Grew to Hull, May 13, 1941; ibid., 188, Grew to Hull, May 14, 1941.

53. Ibid., 197–98, Memorandum of Hull-Lothian Conversation, May 16, 1941; ibid., 190–91, Hornbeck Memorandum, May 5/15 (?), 1941; Best, *Britain, Japan, and Pearl Harbor,* 168.

54. Robert A. Divine, *The Reluctant Belligerent: American Entry into World War II* (New York: John Wiley, 1967), 111–12. Tsunoda compellingly argues that Hull's insistence that Tokyo clarify its position on the Tripartite Pact was motivated by Roosevelt's April decision to expand American neutrality patrols. See Tsunoda, "Confusion Arising from a Draft Understanding," 97–98; *FRUS, Japan, 1931–1941,* 2:145–49, Grew to Hull, May 14, 1941. During early and mid-May, Hull discussed Matsuoka with Nomura on several occasions, apparently in an attempt to learn more regarding the foreign minister's intentions and power. See ibid., 425–26, Memorandum of Hull-Nomura Conversation, May 14, 1941; and Maxon, *Control of Japanese Foreign Policy,* 164–65.

55. Personal Notes, 1941, p. 5110, folder 55, Grew Papers.

56. Personal Notes, 1941, pp. 5100–5101, folder 55, box 1, Grew Papers; *FRUS, 1941,* 4:231–32, Grew to Hull, May 27, 1941. Peter Mauch reinforces Grew when he notes that, during April and early May, the armed forces were "prepared to seek Japanese-American rapprochement in line with the draft understanding." However, by late May, armed services enthusiasm was clearly waning. See Mauch, *Sailor Diplomat,* 166.

57. *FRUS, 1941,* 4:231–32.

58. *FRUS, Japan, 1931–1941,* 2:446–48, American Draft Proposal, May 31, 1941.

59. Ibid., 455–58, Memorandum of Conversation, Iwakura, Hamilton, et al., June 4, 1941.

60. Ibid., 465–67, Memorandum of Hull-Nomura Conversation, June 6, 1941;

ibid., 467–68, American Oral Statement to Nomura, June 6, 1941. On Matsuoka's power within the Konoe cabinet, see Peter Mauch, "Revisiting Nomura's Diplomacy: Ambassador Nomura's Role in the Japanese-American Negotiations, 1941," *Diplomatic History* 28, no. 2 (June 2004): 367–68. Mauch notes that an April 18 liaison conference agreed to negotiate with Washington on the basis of what it believed was an American proposal. On his return, however, Matsuoka reoriented Japanese policy back to its original pro-Axis position.

61. *FRUS, Japan, 1931–1941,* 2:425–26, Memorandum of Hull-Nomura Conversation, May 14, 1941; ibid., 427–28, Memorandum of Hull-Nomura Conversation, May 16, 1941; ibid., 440–43, Memorandum of Hull-Nomura Conversation, May 28, 1941; ibid., 454–55, Memorandum of Hull-Nomura Conversation, June 2, 1941.

62. *FRUS, 1941,* 4:263–64, Hornbeck to Hull, June 10, 1941; Ballantine Oral History, 41. On May 9, Ballantine penned a memorandum contending that, if the president requested China to approach Japan for peace talks, as the Japanese proposed in the draft understanding, it would "stamp Japan as the victor in the conflict and place Japan in a position of tactical advantage in negotiations with China." *FRUS, 1941,* 4:180–82, Ballantine Memorandum, May 9, 1941. See also Dooman Oral History, 105–6.

63. *FRUS, Japan, 1931–1941,* 2:471–72, Memorandum of Hull-Nomura Conversation, June 15, 1941.

64. Ibid., 483–84, Memorandum of Hull-Nomura Conversation, June 21, 1941; ibid., 485–86, Oral Statement, June 21, 1941.

65. Ibid., *1941,* 1:753, Hull to Steinhardt, June 9, 1941; ibid., 766–67, Memorandum, Division of European Affairs, June 21, 1941; Dallek, *Roosevelt,* 268; *FRUS, 1941,* 4:276–77, Hamilton Memorandum, June 23, 1941.

6. The Revolutionary Summer

Epigraphs: *FRUS, 1941,* 4:276–77, Hamilton Memorandum, June 23, 1941; Stimson Diary, no. 35, p. 67.

1. Shinjiro Nagaoka, "The Drive into Indochina and Thailand," in Morley, ed., *Fateful Choice,* 240.

2. In separate but related moves, the administration had also decided to extend aid to Thailand in order to bolster both Bangkok's resistance and Batavia's and had also ended all trade between the Philippines and Japan. For details, see Gary R. Hess, "The Emergence of U.S. Influence in Southeast Asia," in Iriye and Cohen, eds., *Perspectives,* 193. Washington had on June 20 also decided to require export licenses for all oil shipped from American ports. At the same time, the administration forbade the shipment of oil from Atlantic and Gulf ports except to the British Empire and Western Hemisphere. See Harold L. Ickes, *The Lowering Clouds, 1939–1941,* vol. 3 of *The Secret Diaries of Harold L. Ickes* (New York: Simon & Schuster, 1954), 547; and James H. Herzog, *Closing the Open Door: American-Japanese Diplomatic Negotiations, 1936–1941* (Annapolis, MD: US Naval Institute Press, 1973), 163.

3. Michael Smith, *The Emperor's Codes: The Breaking of Japan's Secret Ciphers* (New York: Arcade, 2000), 85, 87.

4. Warren F. Kimball, *Forged in War: Roosevelt, Churchill and the Second World War* (New York: William Morrow, 1997), 89; *FRUS, 1941,* 1:892–93, Welles to Steinhardt, July 4, 1941; ibid., 179–81, Steinhardt to Hull, July 9, 1941.

5. *FRUS, 1941,* 1:634–35, Steinhardt to Hull, August 5, 1941; ibid., 640–41, Steinhardt to Hull, August 17, 1941; ibid., 642–44, Steinhardt to Hull, August 23, 1941; Stimson Diary, no. 35, pp. 58, 67; Frank Costigliola, "Broken Circle: The Isolation of Franklin D. Roosevelt in World War II," *Diplomatic History* 32, no. 5 (November 2008): 698.

6. Miles to Marshall, September 5, 1941, WPD 4510.

7. Gerow to Marshall, July 7, 1941, WPD 4510.

8. *FRUS, 1941,* 4:276–77, Hamilton Memorandum, June 23, 1941; Ickes, *Lowering Clouds,* 557; Gerow to Marshall, July 16, 1941, WPD 4510; Gerow to Eisenhower, July 28, 1941, Leonard T. Gerow Papers, Virginia Military Institute, Lexington Virginia, http://www.vmi.edu/uploadedFiles/Archives/Manuscripts/00100Gerow/Gerow_Eisenhower.pdf.

9. Stimson Diary, no. 33, pp. 112–13; William L. Langer and Everett S. Gleason, *The Undeclared War, 1940–1941* (New York: Harper & Bros., 1953), 422; Divine, *Reluctant Belligerent,* 108.

10. Langer and Gleason, *Undeclared War,* chap. 14, esp. 419–51 passim.

11. Jun Tsunoda, "The Decision for War," in Morley, ed., *Final Confrontation,* 283–84; Marc Milner, "The Battle of the Atlantic," in *Decisive Campaigns of the Second World War,* ed. John Gooch (London: Frank Cass, 1990), 49.

12. Lucio Ceva, "The North African Campaign, 1940–1943: A Reconsideration," in Gooch, ed., *Decisive Campaigns,* 84–87; John Strawson, *The Battle for North Africa* (New York: Scribner's, 1969), 65–86; J. F. C. Fuller, *The Second World War* (New York: Da Capo, 1993), 108–10; John Keegan, *The Second World War* (New York: Penguin, 1989), 325–30.

13. Keegan, *The Second World War,* 325–30.

14. Memorandum of Conversation, Hull, Halifax, Casey, March 7, 1941, folder 214, box 58, Cordell Hull Papers, Library of Congress; *FRUS, 1941,* 3:855, Hull to MacMurray, June 15, 1941; ibid., 855–56, MacMurray to Hull, June 15, 1941; ibid., 867–68, MacMurray to Hull, June 21, 1941; ibid., 888–90, MacMurray to Hull, August 9, 1941; ibid., 909–10, MacMurray to Hull, October 15, 1941; Memorandum for Marshall entitled "Brief Periodic Estimate of World Situation," September 5, 1941, WPD 4510; MacMurray to Roosevelt, May 23, 1941, folder 4, box 60, MacMurray Papers; *FRUS, 1941,* 3:930–34, Graham Report, November 27, 1941. Folder 5, box 77, of the MacMurray Papers includes an October 2, 1941, memorandum for the ambassador's personal file noting that the British saw the Near Eastern Division Chief, Wallace Murray, as anti-Turkish.

15. Langer and Gleason, *Undeclared War,* 763–67.

16. Ibid. For Hull's views of Republican Spain, see Douglas Little, "Architects

of Appeasement: Franklin Roosevelt, the State Department and the Spanish Civil War," in *Appeasing Fascism: Articles from the Wayne State University Conference on Munich after 50 Years,* ed. Melvin Feinstein and Otto Small (Lanham, MD: Rowman & Littlefield, 1991), 73–75.

17. Gerow to Marshall, July 16, 1941, WPD 4510; Langer and Gleason, *Undeclared War,* 504–5.

18. Wigmore, *Japanese Thrust,* 58; David Reynolds, *The Creation of the Anglo-American Alliance, 1937–1941: A Study in Competitive Cooperation* (Chapel Hill: University of North Carolina Press, 1982), 223–24; May–September 1941 Strategic Estimate, WPD 4510; Notes on Plans for Destruction of Oil Properties in the Netherlands East Indies, May 1, 1941, and Miles to Bundy, Plans for Destruction of Oil Properties in Netherlands East Indies and British Borneo, May 22, 1941, WPD 4344.

19. Draft Agreement for ABD 2, August 1941, and Grunert to Asst. Chief of Staff, WPD, May 2, 1941, WPD 4402-18.

20. Draft Agreement for ABD 2, August 1941, WPD 4402-18.

21. Nagaoka, "Drive," 235; Robert J. C. Butow, *Tojo and the Coming of the War* (Princeton, NJ: Princeton University Press, 1961), 196–97.

22. Konoe argued that the move into southern Indochina was a "consolation prize" for those who wished to join in the German attack on the Soviet Union. Maxon, *Control of Japanese Foreign Policy,* 165–66.

23. Navy Department to Chief of Staff, July 5, 1941, WPD 4544. See also *FRUS, 1941,* 4:290, Hornbeck to Hamilton, July 5, 1941; ibid., 5:222–23, Grew to Hull, July 22, 1941; Personal Notes, 1941, folder 61, and Diary, no. 148, Grew Papers.

24. *FRUS, 1941,* 5:210, Grew to Hull, July 16, 1941. On Hornbeck's and Hamilton's opposition to preventative action, see ibid., 210 n. 90. See also *FRUS, Japan, 1931–1941,* 2:315–16, State Department Press Release, July 24, 1941; ibid., 527–30, Welles Memorandum, July 24, 1941; and *Pearl Harbor Attack: Hearings before the Joint Committee on the Investigation of the Pearl Harbor Attack,* 39 vols. (Washington, DC: US Government Printing Office, 1946), 12–14:1342, Miles to Marshall, July 17, 1941.

25. *Pearl Harbor Attack: Hearings,* 12–14:1342, Miles to Marshall, July 17, 1941; J. Garry Clifford and Robert H. Ferrell, "Roosevelt at the Rubicon—the Great Convoy Debate of 1941," in *The United States and the Second World War: New Perspectives on War, Diplomacy, and the Home Front,* ed. G. Kurt Piehler and Sidney Pash (New York: Fordham University Press, 2010), 14. Several studies argue that the Magic decryption of the July 2 imperial conference convinced Washington that Japan had decided to expand south against the ABD coalition. Evidence supporting this contention, however, remains thin. See esp. Barnhart, *Japan Prepares,* 226–27; and Roland H. Worth, *No Choice but War: The United States Embargo against Japan and the Eruption of War in the Pacific* (Jefferson, NC: McFarland, 1995), 55. On the other hand, there is considerable evidence indicating that senior US military and civilian officials did not believe that the occupation of southern Indochina was the precur-

sor to a major movement further south. The chief of naval operations, e.g., argued that, while war was imminent, Japan would strike north rather than south. The navy even hedged on this point, noting: "ATTACK MAY BE DEFERRED UNTIL AFTER COLLAPSE OF EUROPEAN RUSSIA." Navy to Marshall, July 3, 1941, WPD 4544. On July 11, the War Plans Division concluded that, while further expansion south was possible, the very "unanimity of opinion of various Japanese elements could scarcely have been achieved had they decided on aggression against the United States, the British Commonwealth, or the Netherlands East Indies." Director, WPD, to Chief of Naval Operations, July 11, 1941, WPD 4544-1.

26. Hamilton Memorandum, April 9, 1941, 694.119/361, RG59.

27. Ibid.

28. Ibid.

29. Hornbeck to Lamont, June 25, 1941, folder 32, vol. 209, Lamont Papers; Hornbeck to Welles, July 23, 1941 (all emphasis added), folder July 1941, box 463, Hornbeck Papers. For a discussion of Hornbeck's influence, see Marshall, *To Have and Have Not,* 72, 75–76.

30. For a recent, excellent look at the president's troubled personal life in the run-up to war, see Costigliola, "Broken Circle."

31. Like Morgenthau before him, Hornbeck played the Russian card. He seems to have had doubts that Russia would scale back aid to China. See Hiss Memorandum, June 25, 1941, folder China Assistance, 1939–1941, box 52, Hornbeck Papers; and Welles to Hopkins, July 7, 1941, WPD 4389-7.

32. Hiss Memorandum, June 25, 1941, folder China Assistance, 1939–1941, box 52, Hornbeck Papers.

33. Nagaoka, "Economic Demands," 152–53. Barnhart notes mounting anger over continued oil exports to Japan as well as the existence of several bills in Congress designed to limit exports. See Barnhart, *Japan Prepares,* 225.

34. Alan P. Dobson, *U.S. Economic Statecraft for Survival, 1933–1991: Of Sanctions, Embargoes and Economic Warfare* (New York: Routledge, 2002), 42; Memorandum of Welles-Nomura Conversation, July 18, 1941, folder 5, Japan 1938–1941, box 165, Sumner Welles Papers, Franklin D. Roosevelt Library.

35. *Far Eastern Survey* 10, no. 8 (May 1941): 87, Records of the Committee to Defend America by Aiding the Allies; Irvine H. Anderson, *The Standard-Vacuum Oil Company and United States East Asian Policy, 1933–1941* (Princeton, NJ: Princeton University Press, 1975), 159–68. In the weeks prior to the occupation of southern French Indochina, Britain too moved inexorably toward increased sanctions. On July 7, e.g., the cabinet approved a proposal by the foreign secretary to increase sanctions "even in the absence of further provocation by that country." See Nicholas Tarling, *Britain, Southeast Asia and the Onset of the Pacific War* (Cambridge: Cambridge University Press, 1996), 320.

36. For examples of historians who see the embargo emerging from the July 26 freeze and the subsequent guidelines, see Feis, *Pearl Harbor,* 242–43; Utley, *Going to War,* 153; and Barnhart, *Japan Prepares,* 229–31.

37. Green to Yost, June 10, 1941, folder To Princeton, 1941, box 37, Joseph Coy Green Papers, Seeley Mudd Library. Jonathan Utley, e.g., argues that the administration never intended for the freeze to become an embargo. He contends that Acheson released no Japanese funds either because he "believed his actions were in keeping with the spirit of the freeze" or because he and other "hawks believed they were doing the country a favor." Utley, *Going to War,* 155. Irvine Anderson argues that, although neither Hull nor Roosevelt wanted an embargo, one nonetheless evolved owing to "an unguided bureaucracy biased at the working level against liberality toward Japan" and "a bureaucratic tangle as various agencies, governments, and companies . . . attempted to discern the real intent of American policy." Anderson, *East Asian Policy,* 178–79.

38. Ickes, *Lowering Clouds,* 567; Feis, *Pearl Harbor,* 227–30. Feis notes on the following page: "The use of the word 'embargoes' . . . may have been intended or careless." While his point is well taken, the reader must remember that it was Welles, a career diplomat well versed in the subject of economic sanctions in general and Japan in particular, who delivered the president's message to Halifax. Had Roosevelt spoken directly to the British ambassador, perhaps the use of the word *embargo* could be construed differently. However, as it was Welles who passed on the message, it is clear that, as of July 10, the president was considering a complete embargo. Moreover, while Feis intimates that Roosevelt may not have meant *embargo* in the strict sense of the word, Welles makes no such assertion in his coverage of the meeting with Halifax. Sumner Welles, *Seven Decisions That Shaped History* (New York: Harper & Bros., 1950), 83. Anthony Best's coverage of the Welles-Halifax meeting has the undersecretary telling the ambassador that he had urged Roosevelt to pursue an embargo. Best, *Britain, Japan, and Pearl Harbor,* 163.

39. Ickes, *Lowering Clouds,* 583, 588; Dean Acheson, *Present at the Creation: My Years in the State Department* (New York: Norton, 1969), 24; Blum, *Years of Urgency,* 378–79; Clifford and Ferrell, "Roosevelt at the Rubicon," 27–28. There is a strong body of literature arguing that Roosevelt never intended the freeze to become an embargo. Robert Dallek, e.g., argues that, as of July 24, "Roosevelt still had no intention of closing off all oil to Japan" and that he "did not realize that a full embargo had been introduced until early September." Dallek, *Roosevelt,* 274–75.

40. Feis, *Pearl Harbor,* 229; Acheson, *Present at the Creation,* 24; Mrs. Hull to Norman Davis, [July 28, 1941], folder Cordell Hull, box 27, Davis Papers. Mrs. Hull's letter is not dated, but it was written on a Monday, which, given the content of the letter as well as that of her previous correspondence with Norman Davis, indicates that it was Monday, July 28.

41. Welles, *Seven Decisions,* 80–82; Barnhart, *Japan Prepares,* 229–30; Utley, *Going to War,* 153–54; Edward S. Miller, *Bankrupting the Enemy: The U.S. Financial Siege of Japan before Pearl Harbor* (Annapolis, MD: US Naval Institute Press, 2007), 174–76, 178. Welles clearly emerges as a moderate regarding the petroleum question. In addition to axing Acheson's embargo plan, the undersecretary also prevented Ickes from going forward on his plan to bring about "a cessation of, or even

a substantial reduction in, the amount of gasoline going to Japan." Ickes, *Lowering Clouds,* 583.

42. Acheson, *Present at the Creation,* 24; *FRUS, Japan, 1931–1941,* 2:537–39, Welles Memorandum, July 28, 1941.

43. Feis, *Pearl Harbor,* 246; Miller, *Bankrupting the Enemy,* 178, 198.

44. Utley, *Going to War,* 155; Miller, *Bankrupting the Enemy,* 207, 209, 211–12; Langer and Gleason, *Undeclared War,* 659.

45. Hamilton Memorandum, July 17, 1941, 711.94/2178-9/10, RG 59. See also *FRUS, 1941,* 4:325–26, Memorandum of Hamilton-Hull Conversation, July 17, 1941.

46. Miller, *Bankrupting the Enemy,* 86; Green to Yost, June 27, 1941, Green to Yost, June 10, 1941, J. M. Martinez to Hull, July 2, 1941, Green to Pierpont Moffat, January 27, 1941, and Green to Yost, June 27, 1941, folder To Princeton, 1941, box 37, Green Papers.

47. Feis, *Pearl Harbor,* 242–43; Langer and Gleason, *Undeclared War,* 655; State Department to American Embassy, Tokyo, August 22, 1941, 711.94/2248A, RG 59. See also the folder China-Assistance, 1939–1941 in box 52, Hornbeck Papers.

48. Langer and Gleason, *Undeclared War,* 655; Cole, "Role," 320.

49. Morton, *Strategy and Command,* 81–84; Joint Board 325-670, "Draft Proposal," December 1940, RG 225.

50. *FRUS, 1941,* 4:836–41, Turner to Stark, July 19, 1941; *Pearl Harbor Attack: Hearings,* 12–14:1344–45, Miles to Marshall, July 25, 1941. Turner's message reached the president. Miles's message was sent to Stimson. It is not known whether Stimson read the contents or passed them on to the president.

51. *Pearl Harbor Attack: Hearings,* 12–14:1346–47, Miles to Marshall, August 16, 1941.

52. Ibid., 1342–43, Miles to Marshall, July 17, 1941.

53. Feis, *Pearl Harbor,* 235, 245–46; Best, *Britain, Japan, and Pearl Harbor,* 130, 146, 162–63; Blum, *Years of Urgency,* 378.

7. Rollback

Epigraphs: Grew, *Turbulent Era,* 2:1262; Robert B. Jeans, *Terasaki Hidenari, Pearl Harbor, and Occupied Japan: A Bridge to Reality* (Lanham, MD: Lexington, 2009), 74.

1. Diary, pp. 200–201, folder Diary, box 1, Joseph Ballantine Papers, Hoover Institution on War, Revolution, and Peace, Stanford University, Stanford, CA; Langer and Gleason, *Undeclared War,* 659; Gerow to Stimson, October 8, 1941, WPD 3251-60.

2. Stimson Diary, no. 35, pp. 17–18; Hornbeck to Hull, September 13, 1941, folder Japan-U.S. Conversations, box 254, Hornbeck Papers; Diary, p. 198, folder Diary, box 1, Ballantine Papers. Ballantine's warning came during the spring Hull-Nomura talks. I see no indication, however, that his suspicions changed over time. Hornbeck to Hull, November 17, 1941, folder Japan-U.S. Conversations, box 254, Hornbeck Papers; Iguchi, *Demystifying Pearl Harbor,* 45.

3. *Pearl Harbor Attack: Hearings,* 12–14:1349–53, Miles to Marshall, September 5, 1941; Kimball, ed., *Alliance Emerging,* 250, Roosevelt to Churchill, October 15, 1941.

4. Ickes, *Lowering Clouds,* 557, 592; Hornbeck Memorandum, September 2, 1941, and Hornbeck Memorandum, September 13, 1941, folder Japan-U.S. Conversations, box 254, Hornbeck Papers.

5. Miles to Marshall, July 18, 1941, and War Department Strategic Estimate, October 1941, WPD 4510.

6. Notes on Plans for Destruction of Oil Properties in the Netherlands East Indies, May 1, 1941, Miles Memorandum, April 30, 1941, and Miles to Bundy, May 22, 1941, WPD 4344; War Department Strategic Estimate, October 1941, WPD 4510.

7. Larry I. Bland et al., eds., *The Papers of George Catlett Marshall,* vol. 2, *We Cannot Delay: July 1, 1939–December 6, 1941* (Baltimore: Johns Hopkins University Press, 1986), 414, Marshall to Grunert, February 8, 1941; William Manchester, *American Caesar: Douglas MacArthur, 1880–1964* (Boston: Little, Brown, 1978), 196; Michael S. Sherry, *The Rise of American Airpower: The Creation of Armageddon* (New Haven, CT: Yale University Press, 1989), 102; Manchester, *American Caesar,* 196; Bland et al., eds., *We Cannot Delay,* 599, Marshall to MacArthur, September 5, 1941; ibid., 599 n. 2, MacArthur to Marshall, September 7, 1941; Daniel F. Harrington, "A Careless Hope: American Airpower and Japan, 1941," *Pacific Historical Review* 48, no. 2 (May 1979): 223; Michael Schaller, "The Debacle in the Philippines," in *Pearl Harbor Revisited,* ed. Robert W. Love Jr. (New York: St. Martin's, 1995), 117–20; Brian McAllister Linn, *Guardians of Empire: The U.S. Army and the Pacific, 1902–1940* (Chapel Hill: University of North Carolina Press, 1997), 215–16.

8. Dower, *War without Mercy.* For an example of a positive American assessment of Japanese strength, see Memorandum for the Chief of Staff, September 5, 1941, WPD 4510. It is of course possible, but not likely, that, rather than reflecting real military thinking, positive studies were produced to secure greater funding or speed delivery of men and matériel.

9. Tsunoda, "Leaning toward War," 159–61; *Pearl Harbor Attack: Hearings,* 18–20:3999, Konoe Memoirs; War Department Strategic Estimate, October 1941, WPD 4510. In early August, both branches of the Japanese armed services were divided over going to war with America. Within the army, there was a growing conviction that war was inevitable. There was, however, little confidence that a war with the United States could be won. Within the navy, meanwhile, Nagano continued to push for an early decision, motivated as he was, even before July 26, by middle-echelon officers and his conviction that, since war was inevitable, Japan had to strike quickly. But, in his audience with the emperor on July 26, the admiral was forced to tell His Majesty that, in the event of war, he should expect neither a repeat of Tsushima Straits nor even eventual victory. For the army's glum assessment of its chances, see Tsunoda, "Leaning toward War," 163–64. For Nagano's admission to the emperor, see Butow, *Tojo,* 234.

10. Tsunoda, "Leaning toward War," 179–81. See also *Pearl Harbor Attack: Hearings,* 18–20:4000, Konoe Memoirs.

11. Theodore A. Wilson, *The First Summit: Roosevelt and Churchill at Placentia Bay, 1941* (Lawrence: University Press of Kansas, 1991), 32, 137, 207–8.

12. Utley, *Going to War,* 159; Stimson Diary, no. 36, p. 3; Gellman, *Secret Affairs,* 243. Hull's anger at Welles predates August 1941 and was something of an open secret. In this regard, see Nancy Harvison Hooker, ed., *The Moffat Papers: Selections from the Diplomatic Papers of Jay Pierrepont Moffat, 1919–1943* (Cambridge, MA: Harvard University Press, 1956), 332.

13. Stimson Diary, no. 35, p. 20; *FRUS, Japan, 1931–1941,* 2:550–51, Memorandum of Hull-Nomura Conversation, August 8, 1941.

14. Grew, *Ten Years,* 416–21; Grew to Hull, August 18, 1941, 711.94/2182, RG 59.

15. Stimson Diary, no. 36, p. 37. For an account of the August 16 and 17 meetings, see *FRUS, Japan, 1931–1941,* 2:553–54, Memorandum of Hull-Nomura Conversation, August 16, 1941; ibid., 554–55, Memorandum of Hull, Roosevelt, Nomura Conversation, August 17, 1941; ibid., 556–57, American Oral Statement, August 17, 1941; ibid., 557–59, American Statement, August 17, 1941.

16. *FRUS, Japan, 1931–1941,* 2:557–59, American Statement, August 17, 1941; Hornbeck to Hull, September 12, 1941, folder Japan-U.S. Conversations, box 254, Hornbeck Papers. The first paragraph of Hornbeck's memorandum reads as follows: "This gives support to the theory which you advanced . . . that if we could just 'let nature take its course' (with a little help on our part) the Germans would within three months or so 'not be speaking to the Japanese.'" It is not clear whether the reference "with a little help on our part" is Hornbeck's quote of Hull or his own thought. It is also not completely clear what was meant by "with a little help on our part." However, the Japanese Foreign Office had already speculated that American leaks regarding the ongoing talks were in part designed to weaken the Axis.

17. *FRUS, Japan, 1931–1941,* 2:571–72, Memorandum of Conversation, Roosevelt, Hull, Nomura, August 28, 1941; ibid., 572–73, Konoe Letter to Roosevelt, delivered August 28, 1941; ibid., 573–75, Statement of Japanese Government, delivered by Nomura August 28, 1941. Roosevelt made a startling statement in explaining his anger over Japanese protests regarding oil shipments to the Soviets. Hull recorded the president as saying "that under the oil quota allowed Japan by this government, Japan was in a position to have a number of tankers loaded with oil and transported to Japan if and when it so desired." This comment indicates one of two things. It is possible that the president was trying to ruffle Nomura's feathers, but this seems unlikely. Rather, it is possible that, as late as August 28, he did not know that the freeze had in fact become a de facto oil embargo.

18. Dallek, *Roosevelt,* 301–2; Hull, *Memoirs,* 2:1025.

19. *Pearl Harbor Attack: Hearings,* 15–17:2794–95, Nomura Telegram, August 28, 1941; *FRUS, Japan, 1931–1941,* 2:576–79, Memorandum of Hull-Nomura Conversation, August 28, 1941; ibid., 588–89, Hull Memorandum, September 3, 1941;

ibid., 589–91, American Oral Statement, September 3, 1941; ibid., 485–86, American Oral Statement, June 21, 1941.

20. "Oral History Interview: Columbia University 1973," folder Oral History Interview, box 1, Eugene Dooman Papers, Hoover Institution on War, Revolution and Peace. Dooman's memoirs are written in cursive script and suffer from water damage and, therefore, are at times virtually illegible. Every effort has been made to ensure that all quoted material is accurate. If a word is unclear and sufficiently important that it could materially affect Dooman's argument, it has been left out of this work. Maxon, *Control of Japanese Foreign Policy,* 170–71.

21. Dooman Oral History, 99. Dooman's draft memoirs assert that in an effort to derail the talks Hull telephoned Nomura and informed him that Konoe had accepted the Four Principles. Dooman notes that Tokyo had cabled Hull that only he and the president could be privy to such information in an effort to prevent any leaks reaching Japan. Dooman's account is at odds with Prince Konoe's own recollection of the meeting. According to his memoirs, he met secretly with Grew and Dooman "with the full cognizance of the Army, Navy and Foreign Ministers." *Pearl Harbor Attack: Hearings,* 18–20:4005, Konoe Memoirs. For Grew's cable regarding the meeting, see *FRUS, Japan, 1931–1941,* 2:604–6, Grew Memorandum, September 6, 1941.

22. "Oral History Interview," folder Oral History Interview, box 1, Dooman Papers; Dooman Oral History, 95.

23. Butow, *Tojo,* 260–61; Akira Iriye, *The Origins of the Second World War in Asia and the Pacific* (London: Longman, 1987), 157–59; Waldo H. Heinrichs Jr., *Threshold of War: Franklin D. Roosevelt and American Entry into World War II* (New York: Oxford University Press, 1988), 184; Bix, *Hirohito,* 403.

24. Bix, *Hirohito,* 404–5.

25. For Shigeharu Matsumoto's comments at the "Conference on Japanese-American Relations, 1931–1941," Lake Kawaguchi, Japan, July 14–18, 1969, see p. 109 of the unpublished proceedings compiled by Michael K. Blaker and Dale K. Anderson (copy in author's possession); Iguchi, *Demystifying Pearl Harbor,* 110; Jun Tsunoda, "On the So-Called Hull-Nomura Negotiations," in Conroy and Wray, eds., *Pearl Harbor Reexamined,* 93; Seishiro Sugihara, *Between Incompetence and Culpability: Assessing the Diplomacy of Japan's Foreign Ministry from Pearl Harbor to Potsdam,* trans. Norman Hu (Lanham, MD: University Press of America, 1997).

26. Hilary Conroy, "Ambassador Nomura and His 'John Doe Associates': Pre–Pearl Harbor Diplomacy Revisited," in Conroy and Wray, eds., *Pearl Harbor Reexamined,* 98, 102–3; Norman A. Graebner, "Nomura in Washington: Conversations in Lieu of Diplomacy," in ibid., 111–13; Sugihara, *Between Incompetence and Culpability,* 31, 36; Scott D. Sagan, "The Origins of the Pacific War," *Journal of Interdisciplinary History* 18, no. 4 (Spring 1988): 908–10.

27. *Pearl Harbor Attack: Hearings,* 12–14:1352, Miles to Marshall et al. (including Roosevelt and Hull), September 5, 1941; ibid., 18–20:4000, Konoe Memoirs; *FRUS, Japan, 1931–1941,* 2:604–6, Grew to Hull, September 6, 1941.

28. Tsunoda, "Leaning toward War," 193.

29. Grew to Hull, August 19, 1941, and Hornbeck to Hull, August 21, 1941, 711.94/2244-5/11, RG 59; *Pearl Harbor Attack: Hearings,* 15–17:2796, Nomura to Tokyo, August 28, 1941; ibid., 2797, Tokyo to Nomura, August 29, 1941; ibid., 2798–99, Tokyo to Nomura, August 29, 1941.

30. *Pearl Harbor Attack: Hearings,* 18–20:4085–87, Memorandum of Hull–Hu Shih Conversation, September 4, 1941; Iriye, *Origins,* 158–59; Christopher Thorne, *Allies of a Kind: The United States, Britain and the War against Japan, 1941–1945* (New York: Oxford University Press, 1978), 65; Grew to Hull, September 3, 1941, 711.94/223, RG 59; Jeans, *Occupied Japan,* 64. It is possible that Welles gave Hornbeck Grew's original message. But, because Hull and Hornbeck had worked closely together for years, it is far more likely that Hornbeck received the cable through the secretary. It should also be noted that, in addition to bearing the official stamps of Hull, Welles, and Hornbeck, Grew's strictly confidential report also displayed several other sets of distribution initials, including those of Maxwell Hamilton and perhaps Joseph Ballantine.

31. *FRUS, Japan, 1931–1941,* 2:565–67, Memorandum of Hull-Nomura Conversation, August 23, 1941; ibid., 568–69, Memorandum of Dooman-Terasaki Conversation, August 27, 1941.

32. Ibid., 569–70, Memorandum of Hull-Nomura Conversation, August 27, 1941; ibid., 583–85, Memorandum of Conversation, Hull, Ballantine, Nomura, Obata, September 1, 1941; ibid., 579–82, Memorandum of Grew-Terasaki Conversation, August 29, 1941.

33. *Pearl Harbor Attack: Hearings,* 18–20:3201. The army was not alone in opposing the Vladivostok route. In July, Stalin informed Harry Hopkins that he preferred that supplies arrive at one of Russia's Arctic ports. Heinrichs, *Threshold of War,* 156.

34. Ickes, *Lowering Clouds,* 635. In fairness to Hull, one major archival source indicates that the secretary may have opposed shipping oil via Vladivostok. See Fred L. Israel, *The War Diary of Breckenridge Long: Selections from the Years 1939–1944* (Lincoln: University of Nebraska Press, 1966), 211.

35. *FRUS, Japan, 1931–1941,* 2:588–89, Memorandum of Hull, Nomura, Roosevelt Conversation, September 3, 1941; ibid., 589–91, American Oral Statement, September 3, 1941; ibid., 591–92, President Roosevelt's Reply to Konoe Letter Handed to Nomura, September 3, 1941; ibid., 597–600, Nomura Statement Handed to Hull, September 4, 1941; ibid., 606–7, Memorandum of Hull, Nomura, Obata, Ballantine Conversation, September 6, 1941; ibid., Japanese Draft Proposal, Handed to Hull, September 6, 1941; ibid., 601–3, Grew to Hull, September 5, 1941.

36. Ibid., 610–13, American Statement, September 10, 1941; ibid., 613–14, Memorandum of Conversation, Hull, Ballantine, Nomura, Obata, September 10, 1941.

37. Ibid., 608–9, Japanese Draft Proposal Handed to Hull, September 6, 1941; ibid., 610–13, American Statement, September 10, 1941; ibid., 613–14, Memorandum of Conversation, Hull, Ballantine, Nomura, Obata, September 10, 1941; *Pearl Harbor Attack: Hearings,* 12–14:1357–59, Kroner to Marshall, October 2, 1941.

38. *Pearl Harbor Attack: Hearings,* 12–14:1352, Miles to Marshall, September 5, 1941; ibid., 1354, Miles to Marshall, September 5, 1941; Mayumi Itoh, *The Hatoyama Dynasty: Japanese Political Leadership through the Generations* (New York: Palgrave Macmillan, 2003), 67–68.

39. *FRUS, Japan, 1931–1941,* 2:631–33, Memorandum of Grew-Toyoda Conversation, September 22, 1941; ibid., 633, Text of Basic Terms of Peace with China, Handed to Grew, September 22, 1941; ibid., 636, Document Handed to Hull, September 23, 1941; ibid., 636, Document Handed to Ballantine, September 27, 1941; ibid., 637–40, Japanese Proposals Submitted to Grew, September 25, 1941.

40. Ibid., 645–50, Grew to Hull and Welles, September 29, 1941; Paraphrase of Embassy Telegram 1529 to Hull, September 29, 1941, Personal Notes, 1941, folder 20, Grew Papers.

41. *FRUS, Japan, 1931–1941,* 2:645–50, Grew to Hull and Welles, September 29, 1941.

42. Ibid.

43. Memoranda of September 5, 13, folder Japan-U.S. Conversations, box 254, Hornbeck Papers.

44. *FRUS, Japan, 1931–1941,* 2:656–61, Oral Statement, October 2, 1941.

45. Paul W. Schroeder, *The Axis Alliance and Japanese-American Relations, 1941* (Ithaca, NY: Cornell University Press, 1958), 181, 203. Schroeder and I agree that Washington abandoned both its cautious diplomacy and its limited aims during the second half of 1941 but differ as to the reason for this policy shift.

46. By this time London's thinking on a Sino-Japanese peace closely mirrored Washington's. See Thorne, *Allies of a Kind,* 66.

47. *FRUS, Japan, 1931–1941,* 2:662–63, Dooman Memorandum, October 7, 1941.

48. Ike, ed., *Japan's Decision for War,* 179–84, Records of the 57th and 58th Liaison Conferences, October 4, 9, 1941; Tsunoda, "Leaning toward War," 210–11.

49. Tsunoda, "Leaning toward War," 210–11.

50. *FRUS, Japan, 1931–1941,* 2:672–77, Memorandum of Conversation, Hamilton, Ballantine, Schmidt, Nomura, October 9, 1941.

51. Ibid., 680–86, Memorandum of Welles-Wakasugi Conversation, October 13, 1941.

52. *Pearl Harbor Attack: Hearings,* 18–20:4009, Konoe Memoirs; Tsunoda, "Leaning toward War," 214, 223; Kido, *Diary,* 310–11; Maxon, *Control of Japanese Foreign Policy,* 173–74.

53. Tsunoda, "Leaning toward War," 217; *Pearl Harbor Attack: Hearings,* 18–20:4010, Konoe Memoirs. Tsunoda maintains that Tojo had a far more accurate understanding of the American position than did Nomura, Toyoda, or Konoe. While the war minister probably did not understand that Washington had no intention of making an agreement and did not want to see the China Incident end, he nonetheless understood that withdrawing all Japanese forces from China would not lead to normalized Japanese-American relations. See Tsunoda, "Leaning toward

War," 220. In his postwar memoirs, Toshikazu Kase made the point that by October "negotiations were hopelessly muddled." Kase seems unaware or unwilling to openly state that Hull's repeated references to differences over China were a red herring. But he does accurately state: "Neither the foreign office nor the embassy in Washington understood the real issue clearly. They believed that the withdrawal of our armed forces from China constituted the main—and almost the sole—point of disagreement." Tohikazu Kase, *Journey to the Missouri,* ed. David Nelson Rowe (New Haven, CT: Yale University Press, 1950), 56.

54. *Pearl Harbor Attack: Hearings,* 12–14:1357–58, Kroner to Marshall, October 2, 1941.

55. Ibid., 18–20:4010, Konoe Memoirs; Ike, ed., *Japan's Decision for War,* 135, Records of the Imperial Conference, September 6, 1941; Kido, *Diary,* 312–13; Tsunoda, "Leaning toward War," 222, and "Decision for War," 231, 235.

56. *Pearl Harbor Attack: Hearings,* 18–20:4011, Konoe Memoirs; Kido, *Diary,* 313–14; Butow, *Tojo,* 286. Tsunoda offers a somewhat different interpretation of events. He notes, e.g., that Kido approved Konoe's meeting with Higashikuni and that Konoe telephoned Kido to explain the prince's position on forming a new cabinet. By the next day, however, Kido had changed his mind and opposed a Higashikuni cabinet. According to General Suzuki, Konoe decided to resign only after Kido came out against a Higashikuni cabinet. See Tsunoda, "Decision for War," 233–34.

57. Kido, *Diary,* 314–15; Butow, *Tojo,* 292–93; *Pearl Harbor Attack: Hearings,* 18–20:4011, Konoe Memoirs; Tsunoda, "Decision for War," 237–39.

8. All or Nothing

Epigraphs: Knox to Winant, November 10, 1941, box 4, folder General Correspondence, 1941, Frank Knox Papers, Library of Congress; Williams, *Tragedy of American Diplomacy,* 302.

1. Tsunoda, "Decision for War," 247; Butow, *Tojo,* 302–3.

2. Kase, *Journey to the Missouri,* 56–57; Butow, *Tojo,* 301, 304; Tsunoda, "Decision for War," 247–48, and "Hull-Nomura Negotiations," 89; Shigenori Togo, *The Cause of Japan,* trans. and ed. Togo Fumihiko and Ben Bruce Blakeney (New York: Simon & Schuster, 1956), 53–55.

3. Tsunoda, "Decision for War," 248–53; Kase, *Journey to the Missouri,* 56–57; Butow, *Tojo,* 301, 304.

4. Tsunoda, "Decision for War," 255–58.

5. Ibid., 259–61; Ike, ed., *Japan's Decision for War,* 201–4, Records of the 66th Liaison Conference, November 1, 1941; Tomioka, "Japanese Monograph #146," app. 7.

6. Tsunoda, "Decision for War," 254. See also Morley, ed., *Final Confrontation,* 368–69 (app. 9).

7. Ike, ed., *Japan's Decision for War,* 200, 210–11, Records of the 66th Liaison Conference, November 1, 1941; *International Military Tribunal for the Far East*

(Washington, DC: Library of Congress Photoduplication Service, 1974), 26082–83. The liaison committee–imperial conference draft differs slightly from the wording that Togo gave to those at the November 1 imperial conference. At this meeting the contents of plan B as submitted to the United States were as follows:

> 1. Both the Governments of Japan and the United States undertake not to make any armed advancement into any regions, excepting French Indo-China, in the Southeastern Asia and the Southern Pacific area.
> 2. The Governments of Japan and the United States shall cooperate with a view to securing the acquisition of those goods and commodities which the two countries need in the Netherlands East Indies.
> 3. The Governments of Japan and the United States mutually undertake to restore their commercial relations to those prevailing prior to the freezing of the assets. The Government of the United States shall supply Japan a required amount of oil.
> 4. The Government of the United States undertakes not to indulge in measures and actions prejudicial to the endeavors for the restoration of general peace between Japan and China.
> 5. The Japanese government undertakes to withdraw troops now stationed in French Indo-China upon either the restoration of peace between Japan and China or the establishment of an equitable peace in the Pacific area.
> 6. The Government of Japan declares that it is prepared to remove the Japanese troops now stationed in the southern part of French Indo-China to the northern part of the said territory upon the conclusion of the present agreement.

8. Ike, ed., *Japan's Decision for War,* 204–7, Records of 66th Liaison Conference, November 1, 1941; Tsunoda, "Decision for War," 261–63; Iguchi, *Demystifying Pearl Harbor,* 101–2. According to Yoshida, Shidehara determined that China remained the point of divergence between Washington and Tokyo. Accordingly, he hoped to discuss this issue with Great Britain. Yoshida noted that he agreed and "accordingly had repeated conversations with the British and American Ambassadors." It appears that from these meetings and Shidehara's understanding of why the negotiations had thus far failed came plan B. See Shigeru Yoshida, *The Yoshida Memoirs: The Story of Japan in Crisis,* trans. Kenichi Yoshida (London: Heinemann, 1961), 16–17.

9. J. Garry Clifford and Masako Rachel Okura, "The Desperate Diplomat: Saburo Kurusu and Japanese-American Relations in the Weeks before Pearl Harbor" (n.d., draft in author's possession), 4.

10. *Pearl Harbor Attack: Hearings,* 12–14:1359, Miles to Marshall, October 16, 1941; ibid., 1359–60, Miles to Marshall, October 17, 1941; ibid., 15–17, 1844, "Summary of the Far Eastern Situation," October 21, 1941; ibid., 2140, Lee to Miles, October 21, 1941; ibid., 18–20, 3200–3202, "G-2 Estimate of International (Japanese) Situation," October 25, 1941.

11. *FRUS, 1941,* 4:519, Langdon Memorandum, October 17, 1941; ibid.,

522–23, Hamilton Memorandum, October 18, 1941; ibid., 541–43, Grew to Hull, October 20, 1941. For background on Langdon's Foreign Service experience, see Xiaoyuan Liu, *A Partnership for Disorder: China, the United States, and Their Policies for the Disposition of the Postwar Japanese Empire, 1941–1945* (Cambridge: Cambridge University Press, 1996), 97.

12. *Pearl Harbor Attack: Hearings,* 18–20:3202, "G-2 Estimate of International (Japanese) Situation," October 25, 1941; ibid., 3196–99, "G-2 Estimate of International (Japanese) Situation," October 17, 1941; ibid., 15–17:2140, "Paraphrase of Code Telegram," October 21, 1941; *FRUS, 1941,* 4:544–52, Langdon Memorandum, October 25, 1941. The G-2 estimate for October 17 placed a simultaneous strike against the coalition as fifth out of five possible Japanese options.

13. Message from Chiang Kai-shek, October 30, 1941, folder China, General, box 63, and Memorandum for Chief of Staff, November 3, 1941, folder Japan, General, 1941, box 75, Hull Papers.

14. Joint Board Minutes, November 3, 1941, and Hornbeck Memorandum, October 31, 1941, folder Japan, General, 1941, box 75, Hull Papers.

15. Joint Board Minutes, November 3, 1941, folder Japan, General, 1941, box 75, Hull Papers.

16. Ibid.; Sherry, *American Airpower,* 102, 107; Stimson Diary, no. 35, pp. 62, 150.

17. Admiralty to B. A. D. Washington, November 5, 1941, and Commander L. R. McDowell USN to British Joint Staff Mission, Washington, DC, November 11, 1941, WPD 4402-18.

18. Marshall-Stark Memorandum for President Roosevelt, November 5, 1941, folder Japan, General, box 75, Hull Papers.

19. Ibid.

20. Joint Board Minutes, November 3, 1941, folder Japan, General, 1941, box 75, Hull Papers.

21. Marshall-Stark Memorandum for Roosevelt, November 5, 1941, folder Japan, General, 1941, box 75, and Joint Board Minutes, November 3, 1941, folder Japan, General, 1941, box 75, Hull Papers. The American Volunteer Group (AVG) formed in 1941 with President Roosevelt's approval and functioned as an American air force for China. Although ostensibly part of the Central Aircraft Manufacturing Corp., AVG fliers were American, and operating funds for the program came from Lend-Lease. Although the AVG flew P-40 fighters, Lauchlin Currie, the head of the US Economic Mission to China, prodded the Joint Board into approving a plan to transfer long-range bombers to the AVG in order to undertake firebomb raids against targets in the Japanese home islands. For an insightful examination of the AVG and its plans for bringing the war to Japan, see Schaller, *Crusade,* 65–85.

22. Forest C. Pogue, *George C. Marshall: Ordeal and Hope* (New York: Viking, 1965), 201–2; Bland et al., eds., *We Cannot Delay,* 676–78, Robert Sherwood to David W. Hulburd Jr., November 15, 1941. For Marshall's belief that the Philippines would be secure by December 15, see Bland et al., eds., *We Cannot Delay,* 679

n. 8. Four days later, the *New York Times* carried a story by its columnist Arthur Krock explaining how the US Army Air Corps would bomb Japanese targets from its bases in the Philippines. Krock had not attended Marshall's November 15 briefing with newsmen, but the historian Michael Sherry speculates that his story "must have been based on it." While Sherry may be right, Cordell Hull may also have been the source. The secretary often used a contact at the *Times* to leak information, and Krock's article, which includes the contention that either Hull or Roosevelt might have already informed Kurusu of plans to use Philippines-based B-17s against Japanese cities, strongly suggests that, if not the main source, Hull at least filled in gaps and provided his blessing. Stimson, who warned Hull about premature public disclosure of the B-17 deployments, also clearly suspected that the secretary was tempted to leak information. For more on Hull's possible role, see Sherry, *American Airpower,* 107, 112; Kimball, *Forged in War,* 95; and *New York Times,* November 19, 1941, 10.

23. Manchester, *American Caesar,* 194; Pogue, *Marshall,* 208–9; *Pearl Harbor Attack: Hearings,* 15–17:2214–15, Stark to Kimmel, October 17, 1941. For insights into Stark's personality, see Rear Admiral Edwin T. Layton, Captain Roger Pineau, and John Costello, *And I Was There: Pearl Harbor and Midway—Breaking the Secrets* (Annapolis, MD: US Naval Institute Press, 2006), 99.

24. Kimball, ed., *Alliance Emerging,* 266–67; Dallek, *Roosevelt,* 304–5; Pogue, *Marshall,* 195; Stimson Diary, no. 36, p. 6, and no. 35, pp. 150, 169; Bland et al., eds., *We Cannot Delay,* 676–78, Robert Sherwood to David W. Hulburd Jr., November 15, 1941; *New York Times,* November 19, 1941, 10.

25. Stimson Diary, no. 36, pp. 9–10.

26. Knox to Winant, November 10, 1941, folder General Correspondence, 1941, box 4, F. Knox Papers.

27. Ickes, *Lowering Clouds,* 649–50. See also Ben-Zvi, *Illusion of Deterrence,* 22–23; and Blum, *Roosevelt and Morgenthau,* 418–19.

28. Dallek, *Roosevelt,* 305; "An Approach to the Problem of Eliminating Tension with Japan and Insuring the Defeat of Germany," November 17, 1941, folder 16 A, box 6, White Papers.

29. "An Approach to the Problem of Eliminating Tension with Japan and Insuring the Defeat of Germany," November 17, 1941, folder 16 A, box 6, White Papers.

30. Ibid.

31. Ibid.

32. *Pearl Harbor Attack: Hearings,* 12–14:1097, Hamilton to Hull, November 19, 1941; ibid., 1106–7, Gerow to Hull, November 21, 1941; ibid., 1104–5, Stark to Hull, November 21, 1941.

33. Ibid., 1109, Roosevelt to Hull, n.d.; *FRUS, Japan, 1931–1941,* 2:755–56, Draft Proposal, November 20, 1941.

34. Hornbeck to Hull, November 17, 1941, and Hornbeck to Hull, November 19, 1941, folder Japan-U.S. Conversations, box 254, Hornbeck Papers; Diary, chaps. 7–11, folder Diary, box 1, Ballantine Papers.

35. Hull, *Memoirs,* 2:1062, 1067; Grew, *Turbulent Era,* 2:1378–1379.

36. Hull, *Memoirs,* 2:1056–57; Keiichiro Komatsu, *The Origins of the Pacific War and the Importance of "Magic"* (New York: St. Martin's, 1999), 453, Togo to Nomura Cable, November 5, 1941.

37. *Pearl Harbor Attack: Hearings,* 15–17:2141–42. Lee to War Department, November 21, 1941; ibid., 2142–43, "Summary of Estimate by J. I. C. of Japanese Intentions," November 22, 1941; Richard J. Aldrich, *Intelligence and the War against Japan: Britain, America, and the Politics of the Secret Service* (Cambridge: Cambridge University Press, 2000), 55–56, 59. See also Robert E. Sherwood, *Roosevelt and Hopkins: An Intimate History* (New York: Harper & Bros., 1948), 421–22. Sherwood quotes a third report that differs in wording but not meaning from the Pearl Harbor report. The upshot is that all British intelligence information pointed to Thailand. Ambassador Craigie seems to have been among a handful of Englishmen who anticipated that Japan would hit a target other than Siam. General Lee reported from London on November 9 Craigie's estimate "that the Netherlands East Indies provide the most likely spot at which the Japanese will strike next." According to Craigie, the fear of war with the United States would not deter Japan. For Lee's full report on Craigie's estimate, see ibid., 420.

38. Marshall-Stark Memorandum to Roosevelt, November 27, 1941, WPD 4544-13.

39. Far East Theater, #1, November 1941, WPD 4510; Marshall-Stark Memorandum to Roosevelt, November 5, 1941, WPD 4389-29.

40. *Pearl Harbor Attack: Hearings,* 15–17:2437–43, Hornbeck Memorandum, November 27, 1941.

41. *Institute of Pacific Relations* 91 (July 19, 1941), folder 12, box 4, William W. Lockwood Papers, Seeley Mudd Library.

42. Memorandum of Hull-Halifax Conversation, October 3, 1941, folder 214, box 58, Hull Papers; Hull, *Memoirs,* 2:1043; Stimson Diary, no. 35, pp. 24–25, and no. 36, p. 98; Tsunoda, "Decision for War," 283.

43. Stimson Diary, no. 36, p. 6; Ickes, *Lowering Clouds,* 655; Ben-Zvi, *Illusion of Deterrence,* 96.

44. Undated, unsigned letter, folder 16 A, box 6, White Papers. The authorship of this letter is in question. It reads like White's writing, but Harry White would not write directly to the president. John Morton Blum uses a letter that is similar in content but that reads far more like a Morgenthau letter than a White letter. It is possible that Morgenthau used parts of White's letter for the final draft that he never sent. See Blum, *Years of Urgency,* 389–91.

45. Ickes, *Lowering Clouds,* 655.

46. LaFeber, *The Clash,* 209; Ben-Zvi, *Illusion of Deterrence,* 96; State to American Embassy, Tokyo, September 11, 1941, 711.94/2281, RG 59; Cantril, ed., *Public Opinion,* 1173; Clifford and Ferrell, "Roosevelt at the Rubicon," 14. Even well-informed citizens privy to close relationships with leading government figures doubted Japan's ability or willingness to embark on an all-out, do-or-die, assault. Thomas Lamont, for one, confided to the Dutch minister shortly after the attack

on Pearl Harbor that, because Japan traditionally wanted to be on the winning side, he believed that Tokyo would have waited until the direction of the European War became clearer. See Lamont to Loudon, December 24, 1941, folder 44, vol. 115, Lamont Papers.

47. Justus D. Doenecke, *Storm on the Horizon: The Challenge to American Intervention, 1939–1941* (Lanham, MD: Rowman & Littlefield, 2000), 4.

48. Hornbeck Memorandum, May 9, 1933, PSF 26, Roosevelt Papers; Stimson Diary, no. 30, p. 203; Roger S. Green to John W. Masland, June 5, 1941, folder 8, box 8, Records of the Committee to Defend America by Aiding the Allies.

49. Beatrice Bishop Berle and Travis Beal Jacobs, eds., *Navigating the Rapids, 1918–1971: From the Papers of Adolph A. Berle* (New York: Harcourt Brace Jovanovich, 1973), 381; Gellman, *Secret Affairs,* 266–68.

50. The State Department produced several modus vivendi drafts. For a copy of the final draft, see *FRUS, 1941,* 4:661–64. See also ibid., *Japan, 1931–1941,* 2:762–64, Memorandum of Grew-Togo Conversation, November 24, 1941.

51. *FRUS, 1941,* 4:640, Hull Memorandum, November 22, 1941; Reynolds, *Anglo-American Alliance,* 242; Bix, *Hirohito,* 427; Norman Rose, *Churchill: The Unruly Giant* (New York: Free Press, 1994), 355. The coalition representatives were not the only foreign officials to learn that day of the American modus vivendi. When coalition diplomats informed their governments of the plan, Tokyo intercepted at least one of these transmissions and found the American proposal quite promising. Hull also learned on November 22 that Tokyo extended its deadline for concluding an agreement for an additional four days. See Komatsu, *Origins,* 313. Some historiography maintains that this decision was a sign of Japanese duplicity. Robert Sherwood, e.g., argued: "The Japanese task force sailed for Pearl Harbor on November 25, the day before the Hull outline was delivered in Washington, and four days before the absolute 'deadline' designated in the Togo message to Nomura. The dogs of war had been unleashed while the solemn and futile diplomatic exchanges continued." Other early postwar studies argue that, rather than interpret the new deadline as positive, Hull correctly viewed it in a negative light. Langer and Gleason, e.g., note that, because Togo's telegram warned that after November 29 "things are automatically going to happen," Washington necessarily understood this as the "victory of the war party over the moderates." Hull, they argue, "can scarcely be blamed if the impetus to achieve a settlement was blunted by a sense of futility and if subsequent moves were made in a fatalistic spirit." Initially, it must be noted that the deadline extension and the fleet's departure were hardly duplicitous. The November 1–2 liaison conference agreed that, once the fleet sailed, it could still be recalled up to the very last minute on November 30. Second, Hull's meeting with Nomura and Kurusu indicates that his position had not changed and that he was merely going through the motions. Sherwood, *Roosevelt and Hopkins,* 421; Langer and Gleason, *Undeclared War,* 884. For the record of the November 1–2 liaison conference, see Ike, ed., *Japan's Decision for War,* 199–208.

52. *FRUS, Japan, 1931–1941,* 2:757–62, Memorandum of Conversation, Hull,

Ballantine, Nomura, Kurusu, November 22, 1941; Iguchi, *Demystifying Pearl Harbor,* 114.

53. *FRUS, 1941,* 4:646–47, Memorandum of Conversation, Casey, Hu Shih, Halifax, Loudon (Dutch Minister), November 24, 1941; W. J. Hudson and H. J. W. Stokes, eds., *Documents on Australian Foreign Policy, 1937–1949,* vol. 5, *July 1941–June 1942* (Canberra: Australian Government Publishing Service, 1982), 224–27, Casey to Curtin and Evatt, November 24, 1941.

54. Stimson Diary, no. 36, pp. 48–49.

55. Iguchi, *Demystifying Pearl Harbor,* 117; Jeans, *Occupied Japan,* 112; Richard N. Current, "How Stimson Meant to 'Maneuver' the Japanese," *Mississippi Valley Historical Review* 40, no. 1 (June 1953): 73–74; Raymond A. Esthus, "President Roosevelt's Commitment to Britain to Intervene in a Pacific War," *Mississippi Valley Historical Review* 50, no. 1 (June 1963): 34.

56. Cantril, ed., *Public Opinion,* 783, 975.

57. Hudson and Stokes, eds., *Documents on Australian Foreign Policy,* 222–23, Evatt to Casey, November 25, 1941.

58. *FRUS, 1941,* 4:655–56, British Embassy to Department of State, November 25, 1941.

59. Ibid., 654, Quo-Tai-chi to Hu Shih, November 24, 1941; ibid., 652, Lattimore to Currie, November 25, 1941; ibid., 650, Memorandum of Hornbeck–Hu Shih Conversation, November 25, 1941; ibid., 652–54, Memorandum of Hull–Hu Shih Conversation, November 25, 1941.

60. Ibid., 665, Hull to Roosevelt, November 26, 1941; Stimson Diary, no. 36, p. 50.

61. Clifford and Okura, "Desperate Diplomat," 8; Hudson and Stokes, eds., *Documents on Australian Foreign Policy,* 230–31, Casey to Evatt, November 26, 1941; *FRUS, 1941,* 4:669, Memorandum of Hull-Loudon Conversation, November 27, 1941; ibid., 667, Memorandum of Welles-Halifax Conversation, November 27, 1941.

62. Memorandum of Hull-Halifax Conversation, November 29, 1941, folder 214, box 58, Hull Papers; *FRUS, 1941,* 4:669, Memorandum of Hull-Loudon Conversation, November 27, 1941; Komatsu, *Origins,* 319–20; Marshall, *To Have and Have Not,* 143–44, 155.

63. Blum, *Roosevelt and Morgenthau,* 417–18.

64. *FRUS, 1941,* 4:623–25, Hamilton to Hull, November 19, 1941.

65. Ibid., 627–30, Draft Document, November 21, 1941; ibid., 637–40, Draft Document, November 22, 1941.

66. Ibid., 645–46, Draft Document, November 24, 1941.

67. Ibid., 664–65, Draft Proposal, November 25, 1941.

68. Paraphrase of Embassy #1759, November 6, 1941, Personal Notes, 1941, folder 75, Grew Papers; *FRUS, 1941,* 4:522–23, Hamilton Memorandum, October 18, 1941; book 1, p. 105 (December 11, 1941), Krock Papers.

69. On December 2, Hamilton prepared a memorandum that examined the pros and cons of publicly releasing documents regarding the Hull-Nomura talks. Despite

Hull's denial that the proposal was an ultimatum, Hamilton noted that the press and public "would construe the documents as something in the nature of an ultimatum." *FRUS, 1941,* 4:709–10, Hamilton Memorandum, December 2, 1941. See also *International Military Tribunal for the Far East,* 26380.

70. *International Military Tribunal for the Far East,* 26055–56. Togo stated at the December 1 imperial conference that, when Nomura reported that Washington had made public details of the negotiations, it helped "confirm our opinion that the United States had by this time become determined on war with Japan."

Conclusion

Second epigraph: Hornbeck to Bullitt, July 12, 1940, box 42, Hornbeck Papers.

1. Ike, ed., *Japan's Decision for War,* 262–83, Record of Imperial Conference, December 1, 1941.

2. Stimson Diary, no. 36, pp. 53–54; Gerow to Marshall, November 27, 1941, and Marshall and Stark to President Roosevelt, November 27, 1941, WPD 4533-13.

3. Stimson Diary, no. 36, pp. 57–60, 65.

4. Berle and Jacobs, eds., *Navigating,* 379–80; Sherwood, *Roosevelt and Hopkins,* 383.

5. Jeans, *Occupied Japan,* 123. On the basis of *The War Diary of Breckenridge Long,* Roger Jeans argues that Hamilton and Ballantine "saw it [Magic] on a regular basis." If this was the case, one can assume that Hornbeck did also. Roberta Wohlstetter, *Pearl Harbor: Warning and Decision* (Stanford, CA: Stanford University Press, 1962), 264.

6. Clifford and Okura, "Desperate Diplomat," 21–22.

7. Spector, *Ruins of Empire,* 21.

Bibliography

Primary Sources

Collected Papers

Hamilton Fish Armstrong Papers. Seeley Mudd Library, Princeton University, Princeton, NJ.

Joseph Ballantine Papers. Hoover Institution on War, Revolution, and Peace, Stanford University, Stanford, CA.

William Jennings Bryan Papers. Library of Congress, Washington, DC.

Arthur Bullard Papers. Seeley Mudd Library, Princeton University, Princeton, NJ.

Norman Davis Papers. Library of Congress, Washington, DC.

Eugene Dooman Papers. Hoover Institution on War, Revolution, and Peace, Stanford University, Stanford, CA.

Brooks Emeny Papers. Seeley Mudd Library, Princeton University, Princeton, NJ.

Herbert Feis Papers. Library of Congress, Washington, DC.

James V. Forestall Papers. Seeley Mudd Library, Princeton University, Princeton, NJ.

Lindley Garrison Papers. Seeley Mudd Library, Princeton University, Princeton, NJ.

Leonard T. Gerow Papers. Virginia Military Institute, Lexington, VA.

Ulysses S. Grant Papers. Library of Congress, Washington, DC.

Joseph Coy Green Papers. Seeley Mudd Library, Princeton University, Princeton, NJ.

Joseph Grew Papers. Houghton Library, Harvard University, Cambridge, MA.

Lloyd C. Griscom Papers. Library of Congress, Washington, DC.

Richard Pearson Hobson Papers. Library of Congress, Washington, DC.

Stanley Hornbeck Papers. Hoover Institution on War, Revolution, and Peace, Stanford University, Stanford, CA.

Cordell Hull Papers. Library of Congress, Washington, DC.

Nelson Johnson Papers. Library of Congress, Washington, DC.

Frank Knox Papers. Library of Congress, Washington, DC.

Philander Knox Papers. Library of Congress, Washington, DC.

Wellington Koo Papers. Butler Library, Columbia University, New York.

Arthur Krock Papers. Seeley Mudd Library, Princeton University, Princeton, NJ.

Thomas Lamont Papers. Baker Library, Harvard University, Cambridge, MA.

Robert Lansing Papers. Seeley Mudd Library, Princeton University, Princeton, NJ.

William W. Lockwood Papers. Seeley Mudd Library, Princeton University, Princeton, NJ.

Breckenridge Long Papers. Library of Congress, Washington, DC.

John Van Antwerp MacMurray Papers. Seeley Mudd Library, Princeton University, Princeton, NJ.
George V. L. Meyer Papers. Library of Congress, Washington, DC.
Henry Morgenthau Papers. Franklin D. Roosevelt Library, Hyde Park, NY.
Roland Morris Papers. Seeley Mudd Library, Princeton University, Princeton, NJ.
Franklin D. Roosevelt Papers. Franklin D. Roosevelt Library, Hyde Park, NY.
Eli T. Sheppard Papers. Library of Congress, Washington, DC.
William Speiden Papers. Library of Congress, Washington, DC.
Sumner Welles Papers. Franklin D. Roosevelt Library, Hyde Park, NY.
Harry Dexter White Papers. Seeley Mudd Library, Princeton University, Princeton, NJ.

Institutional Records

Committee to Defend America by Aiding the Allies. Seeley Mudd Library, Princeton University, Princeton, NJ.
Council on Foreign Relations Meetings Records. Seeley Mudd Library, Princeton University, Princeton, NJ.
Council on Foreign Relations Records: Studies Department Series. Seeley Mudd Library, Princeton University, Princeton, NJ.

Government Archives

National Archives and Records Administration, Washington, DC, and College Park, MD: Record Group (RG) 59: General Records of the State Department; RG 80: General Records of the Department of the Navy; RG 165: Records of the War Department General and Special Staff; RG 225: Records of Joint Army and Navy Boards and Committees.
Public Record Office, London.

Diaries and Oral Histories

Joseph Ballantine Oral History. Butler Library, Columbia University, New York.
Eugene Dooman Oral History. Butler Library, Columbia University, New York.
Henry Morgenthau Diary. Franklin D. Roosevelt Library, Hyde Park, NY.
Henry Stimson Diary. Sterling Library, Yale University, New Haven, CT.

Secondary Sources

Acheson, Dean. *Present at the Creation: My Years in the State Department.* New York: Norton, 1969.
Adams, Henry C. "The Road to Pearl Harbor: A Reexamination of American Far Eastern Policy, July 1937–December 1941." *Journal of American History* 48, no. 1 (June 1971): 73–92.
Agawa, Hiroyuki. *The Reluctant Admiral: Yamamoto and the Imperial Navy.* Translated by John Bester. Tokyo: Kodansha International, 1969.
Aldrich, Richard J. *Intelligence and the War against Japan: Britain, America, and the Politics of the Secret Service.* Cambridge: Cambridge University Press, 2000.

Allen, G. C. *A Short Economic History of Japan.* London: George Allen & Unwin, 1946.

American Journal of International Law, vol. 4, no. 4, suppl., *Official Documents.* New York: Baker, Voorhis, 1910.

Anderson, Irvine H. *The Standard-Vacuum Oil Company and United States East Asian Policy, 1933–1941.* Princeton, NJ: Princeton University Press, 1975.

Andrade, Ernest, Jr. "The Cruiser Controversy in Naval Limitations Negotiations, 1922–1936." *Military Affairs* 48, no. 3 (July 1984): 113–20.

Appeal of the Chinese Government, Draft of the Report. Series of League of Nations Publications, 7, Political, no. 2. Geneva, 1933.

Asada, Sadao. *Culture Shock and Japanese-American Relations: Historical Essays.* Columbia: University of Missouri Press, 2007.

———. *From Mahan to Pearl Harbor: The Imperial Navy and the United States.* Annapolis, MD: US Naval Institute Press, 2007.

———. "The Japanese Navy and the United States." In Borg and Okamoto, eds., *Pearl Harbor as History,* 225–59.

———. "Japan's 'Special Interests' and the Washington Conference, 1921–1922." *American Historical Review* 67, no. 1 (October 1962): 62–70.

Bailey, Thomas A. *A Diplomatic History of the American People.* 7th ed. New York: Appleton-Century-Crofts, 1964.

———. "Japan's Protest against the Annexation of Hawaii." *Journal of Modern History* 3, no. 1 (March 1931): 46–61.

———. "The Lodge Corollary to the Monroe Doctrine." *Political Science Quarterly* 48, no. 2 (June 1933): 220–39.

———. "The Root-Takahira Agreement of 1908." *Pacific Historical Review* 9, no. 1 (1940): 19–35.

Balinska, Marta Alexandra. *For the Good of Humanity: Ludwik Rajchman, Medical Statesman.* Budapest: Central European University Press, 1995.

Bamba, Nobuya. *Japanese Diplomacy in a Dilemma: New Light on Japan's China Policy, 1924–1929.* Vancouver: University of British Columbia Press, 1972.

Barclay, Glen St. John. "Singapore Strategy: The Role of the United States in Imperial Defense." *Military Affairs* 39, no. 2 (April 1975): 54–59.

Barnhart, Michael A. *Japan and the World since 1868.* London: Edward Arnold, 1995.

———. *Japan Prepares for Total War: The Search for Economic Security, 1919–1941.* Ithaca, NY: Cornell University Press, 1987.

———. "Japanese Intelligence before the Second World War: 'Best Case' Analysis." In May, ed., *Knowing One's Enemies,* 425–55.

———. "Japan's Drive to Autarchy." In *Japan Examined: Perspectives on Modern Japanese History,* ed. Harry Wray and Hilary Conroy, 293–300. Honolulu: University of Hawaii Press, 1983.

Barrett, David P., and Lawrence N. Shyu, eds. *Chinese Collaboration with Japan, 1932–1945: The Limits of Accommodation.* Stanford, CA: Stanford University Press, 2001.

Bartlett, C. J. *The Global Conflict: The International Rivalry of the Great Powers, 1880–1970.* New York: Longman, 1984.

Baylis, John. *Anglo-American Relations since 1939: The Enduring Alliance.* Manchester: Manchester University Press, 1997.

Beale, Howard K. *Theodore Roosevelt and the Rise of America to World Power.* Baltimore: Johns Hopkins University Press, 1956.

Beard, Charles A. *President Roosevelt and the Coming of the War, 1941.* New Haven, CT: Yale University Press, 1948.

Beers, Burton F. *Vain Endeavor: Robert Lansing's Attempts to End the American-Japanese Rivalry.* Durham, NC: Duke University Press, 1962.

Ben-Zvi, Abraham. *The Illusion of Deterrence: The Roosevelt Presidency and the Origins of the Pacific War.* London: Westview, 1987.

Berle, Beatrice Bishop, and Travis Beal Jacobs, eds. *Navigating the Rapids, 1918–1971: From the Papers of Adolph A. Berle.* New York: Harcourt Brace Jovanovich, 1973.

Best, Anthony. *Britain, Japan, and Pearl Harbor: Avoiding War in East Asia, 1936–1941.* New York: Routledge, 1995.

Bix, Herbert P. *Hirohito and the Making of Modern Japan.* New York: Harper Perennial, 2000.

Bland, Larry I., et al., eds. *The Papers of George Catlett Marshall.* Vol. 2, *We Cannot Delay: July 1, 1939–December 6, 1941.* Baltimore: Johns Hopkins University Press, 1986.

Blum, John Morton. *From the Morgenthau Diaries.* Vol. 1, *Years of Urgency, 1938–1941.* Boston: Houghton Mifflin, 1965.

———. *Roosevelt and Morgenthau.* Boston: Houghton Mifflin, 1970.

Boorman, Howard L. "Wang Ching-wei: China's Romantic Radical." *Political Science Quarterly* 79, no. 4 (December 1964): 504–25.

Borg, Dorothy. *American Policy and the Chinese Revolution, 1925–1928.* New York: Macmillan, 1947.

———. "Notes on Roosevelt's 'Quarantine' Speech." *Political Science Quarterly* 72, no. 3 (September 1957): 405–33.

———. *The United States and the Far Eastern Crisis of 1933–1938: From the Manchurian Incident through the Initial Stages of the Undeclared Sino-Japanese War.* Cambridge, MA: Harvard University Press, 1964.

Borg, Dorothy, and Shumpei Okamoto, eds. *Pearl Harbor as History: Japanese-American Relations, 1931–1941.* New York: Columbia University Press, 1973.

Bose, Sudhindra. "A New Situation in the Orient." *Scientific Monthly* 6 (January–June 1918): 331–42.

Boyle, John H. "The Drought-Walsh Mission to Japan." *Pacific Historical Review* 34, no. 2 (May 1965): 141–62.

Buckley, Thomas H. *The United States and the Washington Conference, 1921–1922.* Knoxville: University of Tennessee Press, 1970.

Butow, Robert J. C. "The Hull-Nomura Conversations: A Fundamental Misconception." *American Historical Review* 65, no. 4 (July 1960): 822–36.

———. *The John Doe Associates: Backdoor Diplomacy for Peace.* Stanford, CA: Stanford University Press, 1974.

———. *Tojo and the Coming of the War.* Princeton, NJ: Princeton University Press, 1961.

Cantril, Hadley, ed. *Public Opinion, 1935–1946.* Prepared by Mildred Strunk. Princeton, NJ: Princeton University Press, 1951.

Ceva, Lucio. "The North African Campaign, 1940–1943: A Reconsideration." In Gooch, ed., *Decisive Campaigns of the Second World War,* 84–104.

Chang, Gordon H. "Whose 'Barbarism'? Whose 'Treachery'? Civilization in the Unknown United States–Korean War of 1871." *Journal of American History* 89, no. 4 (March 2003): 1331–65.

Chi, Madeline. *China Diplomacy, 1914–1918.* Cambridge, MA: Harvard University East Asia Center, 1970.

Clifford, J. Garry, and Robert H. Ferrell. "Roosevelt at the Rubicon—the Great Convoy Debate of 1941." In Piehler and Pash, eds., *The United States and the Second World War,* 10–37.

Clifford, J. Garry, and Masako Rachel Okura. "The Desperate Diplomat: Saburo Kurusu and Japanese-American Relations in the Weeks before Pearl Harbor." N.d. Draft in author's possession.

Clifford, Nicholas R. "Britain, America, and the Far East, 1937–1940: A Failure in Cooperation." *Journal of British Studies* 3, no. 1 (November 1963): 137–54.

Cho, Yukio. "Importing American Capital into Manchuria." In Borg and Okamoto, eds., *Pearl Harbor as History,* 377–410.

Chor, So Wai. "The Making of the Guomindang's Japan Policy, 1932–1937: The Roles of Chiang Kai-shek and Wang Jingwei." *Modern China* 28, no. 2 (April 2002): 213–52.

Cohen, Warren I. "American Leaders in East Asia, 1931–1938." In Iriye and Cohen, eds., *Perspectives,* 1–27.

———. "America's New Order for East Asia: The Four-Power Financial Consortium for China." In *Essays in the History of China and Chinese-American Relations,* ed. Warren I. Cohen and Kwan Wai So, 41–74. East Lansing: Michigan State University East Asian Studies Center, 1982.

———. *America's Response to China: A History of Sino-American Relations.* New York: Columbia University Press, 1990.

———. *The Chinese Connection: Roger S. Greene, Thomas W. Lamont, George Sokolsky and American–East Asian Relations.* New York: Columbia University Press, 1978.

———. *Empire without Tears: America's Foreign Relations, 1921–1933.* New York: Knopf, 1987.

Cole, Wayne S. "The Role of the United States Congress and Political Parties." In Borg and Okamoto, eds., *Pearl Harbor as History,* 303–20.

Conant, Charles A. *The United States in the Orient: The Nature of the Economic Problem.* 1900. Edited by Ralph Adams Brown. Reprint, Port Washington, NY: Kennikat, 1971.

Congressional Record, 76th Cong., 1st sess., 1939, 84, pt. 5.

Connaughton, R. M. *The War of the Rising Sun and the Tumbling Bear: A Military History of the Russo-Japanese War, 1904–1905.* London: Routledge, 1988.

Conroy, Hilary. "Ambassador Nomura and His 'John Doe Associates': Pre–Pearl Harbor Diplomacy Revisited." In Conroy and Wray, eds., *Pearl Harbor Reexamined,* 97–105.

Conroy, Hilary, and Harry Wray, eds. *Pearl Harbor Reexamined: Prologue to the Pacific War.* Honolulu: University of Hawaii Press, 1990.

Coox, Alvin D. "The Kwantung Army Dimension." In Duus, Myers, and Peattie, eds., *Informal Empire,* 395–428.

———. *Nomonhan: Japan against Russia, 1939.* Vol. 2. Stanford, CA: Stanford University Press, 1985.

Costello, John. *The Pacific War, 1941–1945.* New York: Harper Perennial, 1982.

Costigliola, Frank. "Broken Circle: The Isolation of Franklin D. Roosevelt in World War II." *Diplomatic History* 32, no. 5 (November 2008): 677–718.

Craigie, Sir Robert. *Behind the Japanese Mask.* London: Hutchinson, 1945.

Cronon, E. David. *The Cabinet Diaries of Josephus Daniels, 1913–1921.* Lincoln: University of Nebraska Press, 1963.

Crowley, James B. *Japan's Quest for Autonomy: National Security and Foreign Policy, 1930–1938.* Princeton, NJ: Princeton University Press, 1966.

———. "Military Foreign Policies." In Morley, ed., *Japan's Foreign Policy,* 3–117.

———. "A Reconsideration of the Marco Polo Bridge Incident." *Journal of Asian Studies* 22, no. 3 (May 1963): 277–91.

Current, Richard N. "How Stimson Meant to 'Maneuver' the Japanese." *Mississippi Valley Historical Review* 40, no. 1 (June 1953): 67–74.

———. *Secretary Stimson: A Study in Statecraft.* Hamden, CT: Archon, 1970.

Curry, Roy Watson. *Woodrow Wilson and Far Eastern Policy, 1913–1921.* New York: Bookman, 1957.

Dallek, Robert. *The American Style of Foreign Policy: Cultural Politics and Foreign Affairs.* New York: Oxford University Press, 1983.

———. *Franklin D. Roosevelt and American Foreign Policy, 1932–1945.* New York: Oxford University Press, 1979.

Dennett, Tyler. "American Choices in the Far East in 1882." *American Historical Review* 30, no. 1 (October 1924): 84–108.

———. *Roosevelt and the Russo-Japanese War.* Garden City, NY: Doubleday, Page, 1925.

Detwiler, Donald S., and Charles B. Burdick, eds. *War in Asia and the Pacific.* 15 vols. New York: Garland, 1980.

Dilks, David, ed. *The Diaries of Sir Alexander Cadogan, 1938–1945.* London: Cassell, 1971.

Dingman, Roger. "American Policy and Strategy in East Asia, 1898–1950: The Creation of a Commitment." In Dixon, ed., *The American Military and the Far East,* 20–45.

———. *Power in the Pacific: The Origins of Naval Arms Limitation, 1914–1922.* Chicago: University of Chicago Press, 1976.

Divine, Robert A. *The Reluctant Belligerent: American Entry into World War II.* New York: John Wiley, 1967.

Dixon, Joe C., ed. *The American Military and the Far East: Proceedings of the Ninth Military History Symposium, USAF Academy, 1–3 October, 1980.* Washington, DC: US Government Printing Office, 1980.

Dobson, Alan P. *U.S. Economic Statecraft for Survival, 1933–1991: Of Sanctions, Embargoes and Economic Warfare.* New York: Routledge, 2002.

Documents on German Foreign Policy. Ser. D (1937–1945), vol. 8, *The War Years: June 23–December 11, 1941.* Washington, DC: US Government Printing Office, 1954.

Doenecke, Justus D., comp. *The Diplomacy of Frustration: The Manchurian Crisis of 1931–1933 as Revealed in the Papers of Stanley K. Hornbeck.* Stanford, CA: Hoover Institution Press, 1981.

———. *Storm on the Horizon: The Challenge to American Intervention, 1939–1941.* Lanham, MD: Rowman & Littlefield, 2000.

Doenecke, Justus D., and Mark A. Stoler. *Debating Franklin D. Roosevelt's Foreign Policies, 1933–1945.* New York: Routledge, 2005.

Dower, John W. *Empire and Aftermath: Yoshida Shigeru and the Japanese Experience, 1878–1954.* Cambridge, MA: Harvard University Press, 1979.

———. *War without Mercy: Race and Power in the Pacific War.* New York: Pantheon, 1986.

Duus, Peter. "Zaikabo: Japanese Cotton Mills, 1895–1937." In Duus, Myers, and Peattie, eds., *Informal Empire,* 65–100.

Duus, Peter, Ramon H. Myers, and Mark R. Peattie, eds. *The Japanese Informal Empire in China, 1895–1937.* Princeton, NJ: Princeton University Press, 1989.

Endicott, Stephen Lyon. *Diplomacy and Enterprise: British China Policy, 1933–1937.* Manchester: Manchester University Press, 1975.

Esthus, Raymond A. "The Changing Concept of the Open Door, 1899–1910." *Mississippi Valley Historical Review* 46, no. 3 (December 1959): 435–54.

———. "President Roosevelt's Commitment to Britain to Intervene in a Pacific War." *Mississippi Valley Historical Review* 50, no. 1 (June 1963): 28–38.

———. "The Taft-Katsura Agreement—Reality or Myth?" *Journal of Modern History* 31, no. 1 (March 1959): 46–51.

———. *Theodore Roosevelt and Japan.* Seattle: University of Washington Press, 1966.

Evans, Donald C., and Mark R. Peattie. *Kaigun: Strategy, Tactics and Technology in the Imperial Japanese Navy, 1887–1941.* Annapolis, MD: US Naval Institute Press, 1997.

Everest, Allan Seymour. *Morgenthau, the New Deal and Silver.* New York: King's Crown, 1950.

Fanning, Richard W. *Peace and Disarmament: Naval Rivalry and Arms Control, 1922–1923.* Lexington: University Press of Kentucky, 1994.

Feinstein, Melvin, and Otto Small, eds. *Appeasing Fascism: Articles from the Wayne State Conference on Munich after 50 Years.* Lanham, MD: Rowman & Littlefield, 1991.

Feis, Herbert. *The Road to Pearl Harbor: The Coming of the War between Japan and the United States.* New York: Atheneum, 1962.

Ferrell, Robert H. *American Diplomacy in the Great Depression, 1929–1933.* New Haven, CT: Yale University Press, 1957.

Fifield, Russell H. "Disposal of the Carolines, Marshalls, and Marianas at the Paris Peace Conference." *American Historical Review* 51, no. 3 (April 1946): 472–79.

Fitzpatrick, Earnest Hugh. *The Coming Conflict of Nations; or, The Japanese-American War: A Narrative.* Springfield, IL: H. W. Rokker, 1909.

Flint, Roy K. "The United States Army on the Pacific Frontier, 1899–1939." In Dixon, ed., *The American Military and the Far East,* 139–59.

Friedman, Donald J. *The Road from Isolation: The Campaign of the American Committee for Non-Participation in Japanese Aggression, 1938–1941.* Cambridge, MA: Harvard University Press, 1970.

Fry, M. G. "The North Atlantic Triangle and the Abrogation of the Anglo-Japanese Alliance." *Journal of Modern History* 39, no. 1 (March 1967): 46–64.

Fujiwara, Akira. "The Role of the Japanese Army." In Borg and Okamoto, eds., *Pearl Harbor as History,* 189–95.

Fuller, J. F. C. *The Second World War.* New York: Da Capo, 1993.

Gardner, Lloyd C. *Economic Aspects of New Deal Diplomacy.* Madison: University of Wisconsin Press, 1964.

———. "The Role of the Commerce and Treasury Departments." In Borg and Okamoto, eds., *Pearl Harbor as History,* 267–85.

———. *Safe for Democracy: The Anglo-American Response to World Revolution, 1913–1919.* New York: Oxford University Press, 1984.

Garver, John W. "Chiang Kai-shek's Quest for Soviet Entry into the Sino-Japanese War." *Political Science Quarterly* 102, no. 2 (Summer 1987): 295–316.

———. *Chinese-Soviet Relations, 1937–1945: The Diplomacy of Chinese Nationalism.* New York: Oxford University Press, 1988.

Gellman, Irwin F. *Secret Affairs: Franklin Roosevelt, Cordell Hull and Sumner Welles.* Baltimore: Johns Hopkins University Press, 1995.

Glad, Betty. *Charles Evans Hughes and the Illusion of Innocence: A Study in American Diplomacy.* Urbana: University of Illinois Press, 1966.

Goldman, Emily O. *Sunken Treaties: Naval Arms Control between the Wars.* University Park: Penn State University Press, 1994.

Goldstein, Erik. "The Evolution of British Diplomatic Strategy for the Washington Conference." In *The Washington Conference, 1921–1922: Naval Rivalry, East Asian Stability and the Road to Pearl Harbor,* ed. Erik Goldstein and John H. Maurer, 4–34. New York: Routledge, 1994.

Goldstein, Erik, and John H. Maurer. *The Washington Conference, 1921–1922: Naval Rivalry, East Asian Stability and the Road to Pearl Harbor.* New York: Routledge, 1994.

Gooch, John, ed. *Decisive Campaigns of the Second World War.* London: Frank Cass, 1990.

Gowen, Robert Joseph. "Great Britain and the Twenty-one Demands of 1915:

Cooperation versus Effacement." *Journal of Modern History* 43, no. 1 (March 1971): 76–106.

Graebner, Norman A. "Nomura in Washington: Conversations in Lieu of Diplomacy." In Conroy and Wray, eds., *Pearl Harbor Reexamined,* 107–18.

Greene, Fred. "The Military View of American National Policy, 1904–1940." *American Historical Review* 66, no. 2 (January 1961): 354–77.

Grew, Joseph C. *Ten Years in Japan.* New York: Simon & Schuster, 1944.

———. *Turbulent Era: A Diplomatic Record of Forty Years.* 2 vols. London: Hammond & Hammond, 1953.

Griswold, A. Whitney. *The Far Eastern Policy of the United States.* New Haven, CT: Yale University Press, 1938.

Guins, George C. "The Siberian Intervention, 1918–1919." *Russian Review* 28, no. 4 (October 1969): 428–40.

Haggie, Paul. *Britannia at Bay: The Defence of the British Empire against Japan.* London: Clarendon, 1981.

Haight, John McVickar, Jr. "Franklin D. Roosevelt and a Naval Quarantine of Japan." *Pacific Historical Review* 40, no. 2 (May 1971): 203–26.

Hane, Mikiso. *Modern Japan: A Historical Survey.* Boulder, CO: Westview, 1992.

Harrington, Daniel F. "A Careless Hope: American Airpower and Japan, 1941." *Pacific Historical Review* 48, no. 2 (May 1979): 217–39.

Harrington, Fred Harvey. *God, Mammon and the Japanese: Dr. Horace N. Allen and Korean-American Relations, 1894–1905.* Madison: University of Wisconsin Press, 1944.

Harrison, Richard A. "A Neutralization Plan for the Pacific: Roosevelt and Anglo-American Cooperation, 1934–1937." *Pacific Historical Review* 47, no. 1 (February 1988): 47–72.

Hart, Albert Bushnell. *The Monroe Doctrine: An Interpretation.* Boston: Little, Brown, 1916.

Hasluck, Paul. *The Government and the People, 1939–1941.* Vol. 1, ser. 4 (Civil) of *Australia in the War of 1939–1945.* Adelaide: Advertiser Printing Office, 1952.

Hata, Ikuhiko. "The Army's Move into Northern Indochina." In Morley, ed., *Fateful Choice,* 155–208.

———. "Continental Expansion, 1905–1941." Translated by Alvin D. Coox. In *The Cambridge History of Japan,* vol. 6, *The Twentieth Century,* ed. Peter Duus, 271–314. London: Cambridge University Press, 1988.

———. "The Marco Polo Bridge Incident." In Morley, ed., *China Quagmire,* 233–86.

Hawkins, H. B. "Review of Thomas Millard's *America and the Far Eastern Question.*" *Political Science Quarterly* 25, no. 3 (September 1910): 538–40.

Hawks, Francis L., comp. *Commodore Perry and the Opening of Japan: Narrative of the Expedition to the China Seas and Japan, 1852–1854.* 1856. Reprint, Gloucestershire: Nonsuch, 2005.

Heinrichs, Waldo H., Jr. *American Ambassador Joseph C. Grew and the Development of the United States Diplomatic Tradition.* Boston: Little, Brown, 1966.

———. "Franklin D. Roosevelt and the Risk of War, 1939–1941." In Iriye and Cohen, eds., *Perspectives,* 147–78.

———. "The Role of the United States Navy." In Borg and Okamoto, eds., *Pearl Harbor as History,* 197–223.

———. *Threshold of War: Franklin D. Roosevelt and American Entry into World War II.* New York: Oxford University Press, 1988.

Herzberg, James R. *A Broken Bond: American Economic Policies toward Japan, 1931–1941.* New York: Garland, 1988.

Herzog, James H. *Closing the Open Door: Japanese-American Diplomatic Negotiations, 1936–1941.* Annapolis, MD: US Naval Institute Press, 1973.

Hess, Gary R. "The Emergence of U.S. Influence in Southeast Asia." In Iriye and Cohen, eds., *Perspectives,* 179–222.

———. *The United States' Emergence as a Southeast Asian Power, 1940–1950.* New York: Columbia University Press, 1987.

Hixson, John A. "The Army-Navy Joint Board." In *Historical Dictionary of the US Army,* ed. Jerold E. Brown, 255. Westport, CT: Greenwood, 2000.

Hooker, Nancy Harvison, ed. *The Moffat Papers: Selections from the Diplomatic Papers of Jay Pierrepont Moffat, 1919–1943.* Cambridge, MA: Harvard University Press, 1956.

Hoover, Herbert Clark. *The Memoirs of Herbert Hoover.* Vol. 2, *The Cabinet and the Presidency, 1920–1933.* New York: Macmillan, 1952.

Hornbeck, Stanley K. *Contemporary Politics in the Far East.* New York: D. Appleton, 1916.

Hosoya, Chihiro, "Characteristics of the Foreign Policy Decision-Making System in Japan." *World Politics* 26, no. 3 (April 1974): 353–69.

———. "The Japanese-Soviet Neutrality Pact." In Morley, ed., *Fateful Choice,* 13–143.

———. "Miscalculation in Deterrent Policy: Japanese-U.S. Relations, 1938–1941." *Journal of Peace Research* 2 (1968): 79–115.

———. "Policies toward Russia." In Morley, ed., *Japan's Foreign Policy,* 344–406.

———. "The Role of Japan's Foreign Ministry and Its Embassy in Washington." In Borg and Okamoto, eds., *Pearl Harbor as History,* 107–26.

———. "The Tripartite Pact." In Morley, ed., *Deterrent Diplomacy,* 191–257.

Hu, Shizhang. *Stanley K. Hornbeck and the Open Door Policy, 1919–1937.* Westport, CT: Greenwood, 1995.

Hudson, Geoffrey. "The Far East at the End of the First World War." *Journal of Contemporary History* 4, no. 2 (April 1969): 165–79.

Hudson, W. J., and H. J. W. Stokes, eds. *Documents on Australian Foreign Policy, 1937–1949.* Vol. 5, *July 1941–June 1942.* Canberra: Australian Government Publishing Service, 1982.

Hull, Cordell. *The Memoirs of Cordell Hull.* 2 vols. London: Hodder & Stoughton, 1948.

Humphreys, Leonard A. *The Way of the Heavenly Sword: The Japanese Army in the 1920s.* Stanford, CA: Stanford University Press, 1995.

Ickes, Harold L. *The Inside Struggle, 1936–1939*. Vol. 2 of *The Secret Diary of Harold L. Ickes*. New York: Simon & Schuster, 1954.

———. *The Lowering Clouds, 1939–1941*. Vol. 3 of *The Secret Diary of Harold L. Ickes*. New York: Simon & Schuster, 1954.

Iguchi, Takeo. *Demystifying Pearl Harbor: A New Perspective from Japan*. Translated by David Noble. Tokyo: International House of Japan, 2010.

Ike, Nobutaka, ed. *Japan's Decision for War: Records of the 1941 Policy Conference*. Stanford, CA: Stanford University Press, 1967.

Ikei, Masaru. "Examples of Mismanagement in U.S. Policy toward Japan before World War II." In Conroy and Wray, eds., *Pearl Harbor Reexamined*, 47–50.

Imai, Seiichi. "Cabinet, Emperor and Senior Statesman." In Borg and Okamoto, eds., *Pearl Harbor as History*, 53–79.

International Military Tribunal for the Far East. Washington, DC: Library of Congress Photoduplication Service, 1974.

Iriye, Akira. *Across the Pacific: An Inner History of American–East Asian Relations*. New York: Harcourt, 1967.

———. *After Imperialism: The Search for a New Order in the Far East, 1921–1931*. Cambridge, MA: Harvard University Press, 1965.

———. "Chang Hsueh-liang and the Japanese." *Journal of Asian Studies* 20, no. 1 (November 1960): 33–43.

———. *The Globalizing of America, 1913–1945*. Vol. 3 of *The Cambridge History of American Foreign Relations*. New York: Cambridge University Press, 1993.

———. "Japan's Drive to Great Power Status." In Jansen, ed., *The Emergence of Meiji Japan*, 268–330.

———, ed. *Mutual Images: Essays in Japanese-American Relations*. Cambridge, MA: Harvard University Press, 1975.

———. *The Origins of the Second World War in Asia and the Pacific*. London: Longman, 1987.

———. *Pacific Estrangement: Japanese and American Expansion, 1897–1911*. Cambridge, MA: Harvard University Press, 1972.

———. "Policies toward the United States." In Morley, ed., *Japan's Foreign Policy*, 407–59.

Iriye, Akira, and Warren Cohen, eds. *American, Chinese and Japanese Perspectives on Wartime Asia, 1931–1939*. Wilmington, DE: Scholarly Resources, 1990.

Israel, Fred L. *The War Diary of Breckenridge Long: Selections from the Years 1939–1944*. Lincoln: University of Nebraska Press, 1966.

Itoh, Mayumi. *The Hatoyama Dynasty: Japanese Political Leadership through the Generations*. New York: Palgrave Macmillan, 2003.

Jansen, Marius B., ed. *The Emergence of Meiji Japan*. New York: Cambridge University Press, 1995.

———. "The Meiji Restoration." In Jansen, ed., *The Emergence of Meiji Japan*, 144–202.

———. "Modernization and Foreign Policy." In Ward, ed., *Political Development in Modern Japan*, 149–88.

Jeans, Roger B. *Terasaki Hidenari, Pearl Harbor, and Occupied Japan: A Bridge to Reality.* Lanham, MD: Lexington, 2009.

Johnson, Robert David. *The Peace Progressives and American Foreign Relations.* Cambridge, MA: Harvard University Press, 1995.

Jones, Shepard, and Denys P. Myers, eds. *Documents on American Foreign Relations, July 1939–June 1940.* Vol. 2. Boston: World Peace Foundation, 1941.

———, eds. *Documents on American Foreign Relations, July 1940–June 1941.* Vol. 3. Boston: World Peace Foundation, 1942.

Jordan, Donald A. *China's Trial by Fire: The Shanghai War of 1932.* Ann Arbor: University of Michigan Press, 2001.

Kajima, Morinosuke. *The Diplomacy of Japan, 1894–1922.* 3 vols. Tokyo: Kajima Institute of International Peace, 1978.

Kase, Toshikazu. *Journey to the Missouri.* Edited by David Nelson Rowe. New Haven, CT: Yale University Press, 1950.

Kawakami, K. K. "The Far Eastern Triangle." *Foreign Affairs* 18, no. 4 (July 1940): 632–45.

Keegan, John. *The Second World War.* New York: Penguin, 1989.

Kennan, George F. *American Diplomacy, 1900–1950.* Chicago: University of Chicago Press, 1951.

Kido, Koichi. *The Diary of Marquis Kido Koichi, 1931–1945.* Frederick, MD: University Publications of America, 1984.

Kimball, Warren F., ed. *Alliance Emerging.* Vol. 1 of *Churchill and Roosevelt: The Complete Correspondence.* Princeton, NJ: Princeton University Press, 1984.

———. *Forged in War: Roosevelt, Churchill and the Second World War.* New York: William Morrow, 1997.

Kobayashi, Tatsuo. "The London Naval Treaty, 1930." In Morley, ed., *Japan Erupts,* 11–117.

Komatsu, Keiichiro. *The Origins of the Pacific War and the Importance of "Magic."* New York: St. Martin's, 1999.

Kosaka, Tamura. "The Taisho Era: The Immigration Act and World War One." In *Japan-American Diplomatic Relations in the Meiji-Taisho Era,* ed. Kamikawa Hikomatsu, trans. Michiko Kimura, 294–454. Tokyo: Pan-Pacific Press, 1958.

LaFeber, Walter. *The American Age: U.S. Foreign Policy at Home and Abroad, 1750 to the Present.* 2 vols. in 1. New York: Norton, 1994.

———. *The Clash: A History of U.S.-Japan Relations throughout History.* New York: Norton, 1997.

———. *The New Empire: An Interpretation of American Expansion, 1860–1898.* Ithaca, NY: Cornell University Press, 1963.

Langer, William L., and Everett S. Gleason. *The Undeclared War, 1940–1941.* New York: Harper & Bros., 1953.

Lansing, Robert. *War Memoirs of Robert Lansing.* Indianapolis: Bobbs-Merrill, 1935.

Lasch, Christopher. "American Intervention in Siberia: A Reinterpretation." *Political Science Quarterly* 77, no. 2 (June 1962): 205–23.

Layton, Rear Admiral Edwin T., Captain Roger Pineau, and John Costello. *And I Was There: Pearl Harbor and Midway—Breaking the Secrets*. Annapolis, MD: US Naval Institute Press, 2006.

Lea, Homer. *The Valor of Ignorance*. New York: Harper & Bros., 1909.

Lee, Bradford A. *Britain and the Sino-Japanese War, 1937–1939*. Stanford, CA: Stanford University Press, 1973.

Leinwand, Gerald. *1927: The High Tide of the Twenties*. New York: Basic, 2002.

Leith-Ross, Sir Frederick. *Money Talks: Fifty Years of International Finance: The Autobiography of Sir Frederick Leith-Ross*. London: Hutchinson, 1968.

Leuchtenberg, William E. *Franklin D. Roosevelt and the New Deal*. New York: Harper & Row, 1963.

Link, Arthur S., ed. *The Papers of Woodrow Wilson*. 69 vols. Princeton, NJ: Princeton University Press, 1966–1994.

———. *Wilson: The Struggle for Neutrality, 1914–1915*. Princeton, NJ: Princeton University Press, 1960.

———. *Woodrow Wilson: Revolution, War and Peace*. Arlington Heights, IL: AHM, 1979.

Linn, Brian McAllister. *Guardians of Empire: The U.S. Army and the Pacific, 1902–1940*. Chapel Hill: University of North Carolina Press, 1997.

Little, Douglas. "Architects of Appeasement: Franklin Roosevelt, the State Department and the Spanish Civil War." In Feinstein and Small, eds., *Appeasing Fascism*, 73–88.

Liu, Xiaoyuan. *A Partnership for Disorder: China, the United States, and Their Policies for the Disposition of the Postwar Japanese Empire*. Cambridge: Cambridge University Press, 1996.

Louis, Wm. Roger. *British Strategy in the Far East, 1919–1939*. Oxford: Clarendon, 1971.

Love, Robert W., Jr., ed. *Pearl Harbor Revisited*. New York: St. Martin's, 1995.

Lowe, Peter. "Great Britain's Assessment of Japan before the Outbreak of the Pacific War." In May, ed., *Knowing One's Enemies*, 456–75.

Lowenthal, Mark M. *Leadership and Indecision: American War Planning and Policy Process, 1937–1942*. 2 vols. New York: Garland, 1988.

Maddox, Robert James. *William E. Borah and American Foreign Policy*. Baton Rouge: Louisiana State University Press, 1969.

The "Magic" Background of Pearl Harbor. 5 vols. in 8. Washington, DC: US Government Printing Office, 1977.

Maki, John M. *Conflict and Tension in the Far East: Key Documents, 1894–1960*. Seattle: University of Washington Press, 1961.

Malozemoff, Andrew. *Russian Far Eastern Policy, 1881–1904, with Special Emphasis on the Causes of the Russo-Japanese War*. Berkeley: University of California Press, 1958.

Manchester, William. *American Caesar: Douglas MacArthur, 1880–1964*. Boston: Little, Brown, 1978.

Marks, Frederick W., III. *Wind over Sand: The Diplomacy of Franklin Roosevelt.* Athens: University of Georgia Press, 1988.

Marshall, Jonathan. *To Have and Have Not: Southeast Asian Raw Materials and the Origins of the Pacific War.* Berkeley and Los Angeles: University of California Press, 1995.

Mauch, Peter. "Revisiting Nomura's Diplomacy: Ambassador Nomura's Role in the Japanese-American Negotiations, 1941." *Diplomatic History* 28, no. 3 (June 2004): 353–83.

———. *Sailor Diplomat: Nomura Kichisaburo and the Japanese-American War.* Cambridge, MA: Harvard University Press, 2011.

Maxon, Yale Candee. *Control of Japanese Foreign Policy: A Study of Civil-Military Rivalry, 1930–1945.* 1957. Reprint, Westport, CT: Greenwood, 1973.

May, Ernest R., ed. *Knowing One's Enemies: Intelligence Assessment before the Two World Wars.* Princeton, NJ: Princeton University Press, 1986.

May, Ernest R., and Charles E. Thompson, eds. *American–East Asian Relations: A Survey.* Cambridge, MA: Harvard University Press, 1972.

McDougal, Walter A. *Promised Land, Crusader State.* Boston: Mariner, 1997.

McFarland, Keith D. *Harry H. Woodring: A Political Biography of FDR's Controversial Secretary of War.* Lawrence: University Press of Kansas, 1975.

McLain, James L. *Japan: A Modern History.* New York: Norton, 2002.

Mead, Walter Russell. *Special Providence: American Foreign Policy and How It Changed the World.* New York: Routledge, 2002.

Medlicott, W. N., et al., eds. *Documents on British Foreign Policy, 1919–1939.* 2nd ser., vol. 20. London: HM Stationery Office, 1984.

Mehnert, Ute. "German Weltpolitik and the American Two-Front Dilemma: The 'Japanese Peril' in German-American Relations, 1904–1917." *Journal of American History* 82, no. 4 (March 1996): 1452–77.

Merriam-Webster's Geographic Dictionary. Springfield, IL: Merriam-Webster, 2001.

Merrill, Henry F. "Present Conditions in China." *Political Science Quarterly* 36, no. 4 (December 1921): 642–62.

Miller, Edward S. *Bankrupting the Enemy: The U.S. Financial Siege of Japan before Pearl Harbor.* Annapolis, MD: US Naval Institute Press, 2007.

———. *War Plan Orange: The U.S. Strategy to Defeat Japan, 1897–1945.* Annapolis, MD: US Naval Institute Press, 1991.

Milner, Marc. "The Battle of the Atlantic." In Gooch, ed., *Decisive Campaigns of the Second World War,* 45–66.

Minger, Ralph Edwin. *William Howard Taft and United States Foreign Policy: The Apprenticeship Years, 1900–1908.* Urbana: University of Illinois Press, 1975.

Minority View of HR 5191. Report 283, pt. 2. *House Reports,* 76th Cong., 1st sess., vol. 2. Washington, DC: US Government Printing Office, 1939.

Mizoguchi, Toshiyuki, "Sino-Japanese Trade." In Duus, Myers, and Peattie, eds., *Informal Empire,* 10–30.

Morison, Elting E., ed. *The Letters of Theodore Roosevelt.* 8 vols. Cambridge, MA: Harvard University Press, 1951–1954.

Morley, James William, ed. *The China Quagmire: Japan's Expansion on the Asian Continent: Selected Translations from Taiheiyo senso e no michi: kaisen gaiko shi.* Translated by James William Morley. New York: Columbia University Press, 1983.

———, ed. *Deterrent Diplomacy: Japan, Germany, and the USSR, 1935–1940: Selected Translations from Taiheiyo senso e no michi: kaisen gaiko shi.* Translated by James William Morley, Alvin D. Coox, and Hans Baerwald. New York: Columbia University Press, 1976.

———, ed. *The Fateful Choice: Japan's Advance into Southeast Asia, 1939–1941: Selected Translations from Taiheiyo senso e no michi: kaisen gaiko shi.* Translated by Peter A. Berton and Robert A. Scalapino. New York: Columbia University Press, 1980.

———, ed. *Japan Erupts: The London Naval Conference and the Manchurian Incident, 1928–1932: Selected Translations from Taiheiyo senso e no michi: kaisen gaiko shi.* Translated by Arthur E. Tiedemann, Marius B. Jansen, and Akira Iriye. New York: Columbia University Press, 1984.

———, ed. *Japan's Foreign Policy, 1868–1941: A Research Guide.* New York: Columbia University Press, 1974.

———, ed. *The Final Confrontation: Selected Translations from Taiheiyo senso e no michi: kaisen gaiko shi.* Translated by David A. Titus. New York: Columbia University Press, 1994.

Morton, Louis. *Strategy and Command: The First Two Years.* Vol. 10 of *The War in the Pacific.* Washington, DC: Office of the Chief of Military History, Department of the Army, 1962.

Myers, Ramon H. "South Manchurian Railway Company." In Duus, Myers, and Peattie, eds., *Informal Empire,* 101–32.

Nagaoka, Shinjiro. "The Drive into Southern Indochina and Thailand." In Morley, ed., *Fateful Choice,* 204–40.

———. "Economic Demands on the Dutch East Indies." In Morley, ed., *Fateful Choice,* 125–53.

Najita, Tetsuo. *The Intellectual Foundations of Modern Japanese Politics.* Chicago: University of Chicago Press, 1974.

Neu, Charles E. "1906–1913." In May and Thompson, eds., *American–East Asian Relations,* 155–72.

———. *An Uncertain Friendship: Theodore Roosevelt and Japan, 1906–1909.* Cambridge, MA: Harvard University Press, 1967.

Neumann, William L. *America Encounters Japan: From Perry to Pearl Harbor.* Baltimore: Johns Hopkins University Press, 1963.

Nish, Ian. *Japanese Foreign Policy, 1869–1942: Kasumigaseki to Miyakezaka.* London: Routledge & Kegan Paul, 1977.

———. *Japanese Foreign Policy in the Interwar Period.* Westport, CT: Praeger, 2002.

———. *The Origins of the Russo-Japanese War.* New York: Longman, 1985.

Nomura, Kichisaburo. "In Memory of Washington." Translated by General Headquarters Far East Command, Military Intelligence Section, General Staff, January 1950. In Detwiler and Burdick, eds., *War in Asia and the Pacific,* vol. 2. Only individual documents in *War in Asia and the Pacific* are continuously paginated, each document beginning with p. 1.

Ogata, Sadako N. *Defiance in Manchuria: The Making of Japanese Foreign Policy, 1931–1932.* Berkeley: University of California Press, 1964.

Ohata, Tokushiro. "The Anti-Comintern Pact, 1935–1939." In Morley, ed., *Deterrent Diplomacy,* 9–111.

Oka, Yoshitake. *Konoe Fumimaro: A Political Biography.* Translated by Shumpei Okamoto and Patricia Murray. Tokyo: University of Tokyo Press, 1983.

O'Neill, William L. *A Democracy at War: America's Fight at Home and Abroad in World War II.* Cambridge, MA: Harvard University Press, 1993.

Ong, Chit Chung. *Operation Matador: Britain's War Plans against the Japanese 1918–1941.* Singapore: Times Academic, 1997.

Ostrower, Gary B. *Collective Insecurity: The United States and the League of Nations during the Early Thirties.* Lewisburg, PA: Bucknell University Press, 1979.

Pearl Harbor Attack: Hearings before the Joint Committee on the Investigation of the Pearl Harbor Attack. 39 vols. Washington, DC: US Government Printing Office, 1946.

Peattie, Mark R. *Ishiwara Kanji and Japan's Confrontation with the West.* Princeton, NJ: Princeton University Press, 1975.

Pelz, Stephen E. *Race to Pearl Harbor: The Failure of the Second London Naval Conference and the Onset of World War II.* Cambridge, MA: Harvard University Press, 1974.

Perry, Hamilton Darby. *The Panay Incident: Prelude to Pearl Harbor.* New York: Macmillan, 1969.

Piehler, G. Kurt, and Sidney Pash, eds. *The United States and the Second World War: New Perspectives on War, Diplomacy, and the Home Front.* New York: Fordham University Press, 2010.

Pogue, Forest C. *George C. Marshall: Ordeal and Hope.* New York: Viking, 1965.

Potter, Elmer Belmont. *Nimitz.* Annapolis, MD: US Naval Institute Press, 1976.

Pugach, Noel H. "American Friendship for China and the Shantung Question at the Washington Conference." *Journal of American History* 64, no. 1 (June 1977): 67–86.

———. *Paul S. Reinsch: Open Door Diplomat in Action.* Millwood, NY: KTO, 1979.

Rappaport, Armin. *Henry L. Stimson and Japan, 1931–1933.* Chicago: University of Chicago Press, 1963.

Rea, George Bronson. "Closing the Open Door." *North American Review* 203, no. 726 (May 1916): 690–99.

Reed, James. *The Missionary Mind and American East Asian Policy, 1911–1915.* Cambridge, MA: Harvard University Press, 1983.

Rees, David. *Harry Dexter White: A Study in Paradox.* New York: Coward, McCann & Geoghegan, 1973.

Reinsch, Paul S. *An American Diplomat in China.* Garden City, NY: Doubleday, Page, 1922.

———. "Diplomatic Affairs and International Law, 1909." *American Political Science Review* 4, no. 1 (February 1910): 16–51.

Reischauer, Edwin O. *My Life between Japan and America.* New York: Harper & Row, 1986.

Reynolds, David. *The Creation of the Anglo-American Alliance, 1937–1941: A Study in Competitive Cooperation.* Chapel Hill: University of North Carolina Press, 1982.

Roberts, J. A. G. *A Concise History of China.* Cambridge, MA: Harvard University Press, 1999.

Rose, Norman. *Churchill: The Unruly Giant.* New York: Free Press, 1994.

Ross, Stephen T. *American War Plans, 1890–1939.* New York: Routledge, 2004.

Roth, Andrew. *Japan Strikes South.* New York: American Council, Institute of Pacific Relations, 1941.

Safford, Jeffery J. "Experiment in Containment: The United States Steel Embargo and Japan, 1917–1918." *Pacific Historical Review* 39, no. 4 (November 1970): 439–48.

Sagan, Scott D. "The Origins of the Pacific War." *Journal of Interdisciplinary History* 18, no. 4 (Spring 1988): 893–922.

Schaller, Michael. "The Debacle in the Philippines." In Love, ed., *Pearl Harbor Revisited,* 111–30.

———. *The United States and China in the Twentieth Century.* New York: Oxford University Press, 1990.

———. *The U.S. Crusade in China, 1938–1945.* New York: Columbia University Press, 1979.

Schirokauer, Conrad. *A Brief History of Chinese and Japanese Civilization.* New York: Harcourt, 1978.

Scholes, Walter V., and Marie V. Scholes. *The Foreign Policies of the Taft Administration.* Columbia: University of Missouri Press, 1970.

Schratz, Paul R. "The Orient and U.S. Naval Strategy." In Dixon, ed., *The American Military and the Far East,* 127–38.

Schroeder, Paul W. *The Axis Alliance and Japanese-American Relations, 1941.* Ithaca, NY: Cornell University Press, 1958.

Schwantes, Robert. "America and Japan." In May and Thompson, eds., *American–East Asian Relations,* 97–128.

Seki, Hiroharu. "The Manchurian Incident." In Morley, ed., *Japan Erupts,* 139–230.

Shai, Aaron. *Origins of the War in the East: Britain, China, and Japan, 1937–1939.* London: Croom Helm, 1976.

Shaw, Yu-ming. *An American Missionary in China: John Leighton Stuart and Chinese-American Relations.* Cambridge, MA: Harvard University Press, 1992.

Sherry, Michael S. *The Rise of American Airpower: The Creation of Armageddon.* New Haven, CT: Yale University Press, 1989.

Sherwood, Robert E. *Roosevelt and Hopkins: An Intimate History.* New York: Harper & Bros., 1948.

Shigemitsu, Mamoru. *Japan and Her Destiny: My Struggle for Peace.* New York: E. P. Dutton, 1958.

Shimada, Toshihiko. "Extension of Hostilities." In Morley, ed., *Japan Erupts,* 241–335.

Shimazu, Naoka. *Japan, Race and Equality: The Racial Equality Proposal of 1919*. New York: Routledge, 1998.

Sklar, Martin. *The Corporate Reconstruction of American Capitalism, 1890–1916*. New York: Cambridge University Press, 1988.

Smith, Jean Edward. *FDR*. New York: Random House, 2008.

Smith, Michael. *The Emperor's Codes: The Breaking of Japan's Secret Ciphers*. New York: Arcade, 2000.

Spector, Ronald H. *In the Ruins of Empire: The Japanese Surrender and the Battle for Postwar Asia*. New York: Random House, 2008.

Sternsher, Bernard. "The Stimson Doctrine: F.D.R. versus Moley and Tugwell." *Pacific Historical Review* 31, no. 3 (August 1962): 281–89.

Stillson, Albert C. "Military Policy without Political Guidance: Theodore Roosevelt's Navy." *Military Affairs* 25, no. 1 (Spring 1961): 18–31.

Stimson, Henry L. *The Far Eastern Crisis: Recollections and Observations*. New York: Harper & Bros., 1936.

Stimson, Henry L., and McGeorge Bundy. *On Active Service in Peace and War*. New York: Harper & Bros., 1947.

Stoler, Mark A. "From Continentalism to Globalism: General Stanley D. Embick, the Joint Strategic Survey Committee, and the Military View of American National Policy during the Second World War." *Diplomatic History* 6, no. 3 (Summer 1982): 303–21.

Strawson, John. *The Battle for North Africa*. New York: Scribner's, 1969.

Sugihara, Seishiro. *Between Incompetence and Culpability: Assessing the Diplomacy of Japan's Foreign Ministry from Pearl Harbor to Potsdam*. Translated by Norman Hu. Lanham, MD: University Press of America, 1997.

Sun, Youli. *China and the Origins of the Pacific War, 1931–1941*. New York: St. Martin's, 1993.

Takeuchi, Tatsuji. *War and Diplomacy in the Japanese Empire*. New York: Doubleday, Doran, 1935.

Tarling, Nicholas. *Britain, Southeast Asia and the Onset of the Pacific War*. New York: Cambridge University Press, 1996.

Thompson, Robert Smith. *A Time for War*. New York: Prentice-Hall, 1991.

Thorne, Christopher. *Allies of a Kind: The United States, Britain and the War against Japan, 1941–1945*. New York: Oxford University Press, 1978.

———. *The Limits of Foreign Policy: The West, the League and the Far Eastern Crisis of 1931–1933*. London: Hamish Hamilton, 1972.

Tilchin, William N. *Theodore Roosevelt and the British Empire: A Study in Presidential Statecraft*. New York: St. Martin's, 1997.

Togo, Shigenori. *The Cause of Japan*. Translated and edited by Fumihiko Togo and Ben Bruce Blakeney. New York: Simon & Schuster, 1956.

Tomioka, Rear Admiral Sadatoshi. "Japanese Monograph #146." In Detwiler and Burdick, eds., *War in Asia and the Pacific*, vol. 2. Only individual documents in *War in Asia and the Pacific* are continuously paginated, each document beginning with p. 1.

Tsunoda, Jun. "Confusion Arising from a Draft Understanding between Japan and the United States." In Morley, ed., *Final Confrontation,* 1–105.

———. "The Decision for War." In Morley, ed., *Final Confrontation,* 230–348.

———. "Leaning toward War." In Morley, ed., *Final Confrontation,* 106–229.

———. "The Navy's Role in the Southern Strategy." In Morley, ed., *Fateful Choice,* 241–95.

———. "On the So-Called Hull-Nomura Negotiations." In Conroy and Wray, eds., *Pearl Harbor Reexamined,* 89–95.

Ugaki, Matome. *Fading Victory: The Diary of Admiral Matome Ugaki.* Translated by Masataka Chihaya. Pittsburgh, PA: University of Pittsburgh Press, 1991.

Unterberger, Betty Miller. *America's Siberian Expedition, 1918–1920: A Study of National Policy.* Durham, NC: Duke University Press, 1956.

US Department of State. *Papers Relating to the Foreign Relations of the United States, 1888–1890,* 1 vol.; *1894,* app. 1, 1 vol.; *1895,* 2 vols.; *1908,* 1 vol.; *1910,* 1 vol.; *1915,* 1 vol. plus suppl.; *1919, Paris Peace Conference,* 11 vols.; *1920,* 3 vols.; *1922,* 2 vols.; *1923,* 2 vols.; *1925,* 2 vols.; *1926,* 2 vols.; *1927,* 3 vols.; *1928,* 3 vols.; *1930,* 3 vols.; *1931,* 3 vols.; *Japan, 1931–1941,* 2 vols.; *1933,* 5 vols.; *1934,* 5 vols.; *1935,* 4 vols.; *1936,* 5 vols.; *1937,* 5 vols.; *1938,* 5 vols.; *1939,* 5 vols.; *1940,* 5 vols.; *1941,* 7 vols.; *FRUS, 1946, Paris Peace Conference,* 2 vols. Washington, DC: US Government Printing Office, 1861–.

Usui, Katsumi. "Japanese Approaches to China in the 1930s: Two Alternatives." In Iriye and Cohen, eds., *Perspectives,* 93–116.

———. "The Role of the Foreign Ministry." In Borg and Okamoto, eds., *Pearl Harbor as History,* 127–48.

Utley, Freda. *Japan's Feet of Clay.* New York: Norton, 1937.

Utley, Jonathan G. *Going to War with Japan, 1937–1941.* Knoxville: University of Tennessee Press, 1985.

Varg, Paul A. *Open Door Diplomat: The Life of W. W. Rockhill.* Urbana: University of Illinois Press, 1952.

Vevier, Charles. *The United States and China, 1906–1913: A Study of Finance and Diplomacy.* New Brunswick, NJ: Rutgers University Press, 1955.

Vinson, John Chalmers. *The Parchment Peace: The United States Senate and the Washington Conference, 1921–1922.* Athens: University of Georgia Press, 1955.

Wagner, Margaret E., Linda Barrett Osborne, Susan Reyburn, and Staff of the Library of Congress. *The Library of Congress World War II Companion.* Edited and with an introduction by David M. Kennedy. New York: Simon & Schuster, 2007.

Waldron, Arthur, ed. *How the Peace Was Lost: The 1935 Memorandum "Developments Affecting American Policy in the Far East."* Prepared for the State Department by Ambassador John Van Antwerp MacMurray. Stanford, CA: Hoover Institution Press, 1992.

Wang, Ke-wen. "Wang Jingwei and the Policy Origins of the 'Peace Movement,' 1932–1937." In Barrett and Shuy, eds., *Chinese Collaboration with Japan,* 21–37.

Ward, Robert E., ed. *Political Development in Modern Japan.* Princeton, NJ: Princeton University Press, 1968.

Watson, Mark Skinner. *The History of the War Department: Chief of Staff: Prewar Plans and Preparations*. Vol. 6 of *The History of the War Department*. Washington, DC: Historical Division, Department of the Army, 1950.

Weigley, Russell F. "The Role of the War Department and the Army." In Borg and Okamoto, eds., *Pearl Harbor as History*, 165–88.

Weland, James. "Misguided Intelligence: Japanese Military Intelligence Officers in the Manchurian Incident, September 1931." *Journal of Military History* 58, no. 3 (July 1994): 445–60.

Welles, Sumner. *Seven Decisions That Shaped History*. New York: Harper & Bros., 1950.

Wheeler, Gerald E. "Isolated Japan: Anglo-American Diplomatic Co-Operation, 1927–1936." *Pacific Historical Review* 30, no. 1 (May 1961): 165–78.

———. "The United States Navy and the Japanese 'Enemy,' 1919–1931." *Military Affairs* 21, no. 2 (Summer 1957): 61–74.

White, John Albert. *The Diplomacy of the Russo-Japanese War*. Princeton, NJ: Princeton University Press, 1964.

Wigmore, Lionel. *The Japanese Thrust*. Vol. 4, ser. 1 (Army) of *Australia in the War of 1939–1945*. Adelaide: Griffin, 1957.

Wilbur, Ray Lyman, and Arthur Mastick Hyde. *The Hoover Policies*. New York: Scribner's, 1937.

Wilkins, Mira. "The Role of U.S. Business." In Borg and Okamoto, eds., *Pearl Harbor as History*, 341–76.

Williams, William Appleman. *The Tragedy of American Diplomacy*. New ed. New York: Norton, 1988.

Wilson, Theodore A. *The First Summit: Roosevelt and Churchill at Placentia Bay, 1941*. Lawrence: University Press of Kansas, 1991.

Wohlstetter, Roberta. *Pearl Harbor: Warning and Decision*. Stanford, CA: Stanford University Press, 1962.

Worth, Roland H. *No Choice but War: The United States Embargo against Japan and the Eruption of War in the Pacific*. Jefferson, NC: McFarland, 1995.

Wray, Harry. "Japanese-American Relations and Perceptions, 1900–1940." In Conroy and Wray, eds., *Pearl Harbor Reexamined*, 1–15.

Wright, Quincy. "American View of Far Eastern Problems." *International Affairs* 14, no. 1 (January–February 1935): 69–88.

Yagami, Kazuo. *Konoe Fumimaro and the Failure of Peace in Japan, 1937–1941: A Critical Appraisal of the Three-Time Prime Minister*. Jefferson, NC: McFarland, 2006.

Yamamura, Katsuro. "The Role of the Finance Ministry." In Borg and Okamoto, eds., *Pearl Harbor as History*, 127–48.

Yergin, Daniel. *The Prize: The Epic Quest for Oil, Money and Power*. New ed. New York: Free Press, 2008.

Yoshida, Shigeru. *The Yoshida Memoirs: The Story of Japan in Crisis*. Translated by Kenichi Yoshida. London: Heinemann, 1961.

Yoshihashi, Takehiko. *Conspiracy at Mukden: The Rise of the Japanese Military*. New Haven, CT: Yale University Press, 1963.

Young, Arthur Nichols. *China's Nation Building, 1927–1937: The Financial and Economic Record.* Stanford, CA: Hoover Institution Press, 1971.

Yui, David Z. T. "China and the Pacific Relations during 1925–1927." *News Bulletin of the Institute of Pacific Relations,* August 1927, 13–17.

Index

ABD coalition, 134, 137, 141, 163, 177–78, 197, 217; modus vivendi, 243
Abe, Nobuyuki, 145, 147; reopens Yangtze, 149–50, 288n14
Acheson, Dean, 184–88, 238
Adams, Henry, 10
Afrika Korps. *See* North African campaign
Allen, Horace, 10
Alston, Beilby, 45
Amau, Eiji. *See* Amau declaration
Amau declaration, 89–90, 102
American Committee for Non-Participation in Japanese Aggression, 140, 282n23
American Council of the Institute of Pacific Relations, 144
American-Japanese relations, postwar, 255
American Volunteer Group, 305n21
Anglo-Japanese Alliance, 10, 22, 62; and the Washington Conference, 49, 51, 53–55, 270
Anglo-Soviet Alliance, 190
Aoki, Shuzo, 19
Arita, Hachiro, 153
Army Air Corps, 135
Army-Navy Joint Board, 20, 31, 136; November 3 meeting, 225; Rainbow war plans, 155
Army War Plans Division, 136–37, 173–74
Asada, Sadao, 56, 58, 128, 286n59
Asama Maru incident, 151
assets freeze, 124, 139, 143, 171, 186, 296n37; disrupting the Axis, 190; leads to war, 183; military opinion of, 188–90; Morgenthau proposes, 109; southern French Indochina, 179
Atlantic, Battle of the, 174, 235
Atlantic Conference, 199
Australia, 42, 53, 108, 177; supports modus vivendi, 242
Axis Alliance, xiv–xv, 119–20, 126, 128, 146–47, 150–52, 154–57, 164, 171, 175, 183; issue in US-Japanese negotiations, 159, 161, 163, 165–68, 208–9, 211, 219–20, 290n4, 291n54; Japanese decision to join, 121–22, 141–42, 286n59; United States seeks to disrupt, 111, 113, 130, 251; White memorandum redrafts, 247
Azores, 173, 176

Balfour, Arthur, 52, 55
Ballantine, Joseph, 151, 162, 194, 254; Hull-Nomura-Kurusu talks, 232; Hull-Nomura talks, 165–67; influence on Hull, 195; negotiations on preliminary agreement, 208, 213
Barnhart, Michael, xvi
Batavia talks. *See* Dutch East Indies
Bell, Daniel, 185
Ben-Zvi, Abraham, 282n23
Berle, Adolph, 154, 238
Best, Anthony, xvi, 287n1
Bethlehem Steel Corporation, 61
Biddle, James, 1
Bingham, Robert, 89
Bishop, Max, 167
Bix, Herbert, 58, 203–4, 240
Bolivia, 127
Borah, William, 50, 63; Borah letter, 79; recognition of Soviet Union, 83
Bose, Sudhindra, 38
Boxer Rebellion, 66
Brazil, 127–28, 173
Breckinridge, Clifton, 10
Bristol, Mark, 60

Brussels Conference, 106, 108–9, 111, 114–15, 140
Bryan, J. Ingram, 31
Bryan, William Jennings, 31, 39
Buck, J. Lossing, 104, 118
Buckley, Thomas, 56
Bullitt, William, 117, 172; naval buildup, 96, 101, 111; negotiated end to Sino-Japanese War, 144–46
Burma, 137
Burma Road, 119, 121, 131, 252; Chiang fears assault on, 222–23
Butow, Robert J. C., 203

California, 21, 43, 135–36; anti-Japanese legislation, 17, 31, 34, 36, 59
Canada, 53, 128
Canary Islands, 173, 176
Casey, Richard, 152; modus vivendi, 241–43
Castle, William, 76
Chamberlin, Neville, 108–9
Chang, Hsueh-liang, 69–70, 73, 106
Chang, Tso-lin, 61, 68, 73, 272n40
Chankufeng, Battle of, 141, 287n67
Chengchiatun incident, 35
cherry-picking intelligence, 254
Chiang, Kai-shek, 64, 66–70, 119; Far Eastern Crisis, 75, 78, 106; Marco Polo Bridge Incident, 106–7; modus vivendi, 243; negotiated end to Sino-Japanese War, 145
Chicago Tribune, 237
China, xi, xiv, 5, 10, 70, 280n2; Amau declaration, 89–90; American economic aid, 87–88, 114–20, 171; American perceptions of, 60–61, 65–66, 68; Anglo-American-Japanese cooperation in, 59, 63–65; antiforeignism, 50, 62; army, 106; boycotts, 61, 66; civil war, 44, 50; currency reform, 99–104; dollar diplomacy, 31; Far Eastern Crisis, 74–84; First Sino-Japanese War, 5–7, 9, 22; foreign ministry, 145; image in United States, xv, 6, 65; importance to Japan, 47, 62; importance to United States, xiv, 47; Japanese commercial dominance in, xii, 44; Japanese expansion in, 51, 106; Japan's special interests in, 56, 58; joint Sino-Japanese defense of border, 40; Lansing-Ishii Agreement, 37–39; League of Nation's Development Committee, 88; Manchu reforms, 29; Marco Polo Bridge Incident, 106–7; missionary activity in, 29; multinational banking consortium, 31, 43–46, 55; nationalism, 50, 61–62, 69, 94; Nine Power Treaty, 55; Northern Expedition, 64, 66–67, 69; Open Door, xii, 8–9, 13–17, 24, 34; relations with Russia, 10; Chinese Revolution, 27–28, 30, 32, 50; Second Sino-Japanese War, 86, 106–11, 145–46; Shantung question, 57; Sian Incident, 106; Sun Yat-sen, 32; Taft's sympathy for, 24; treaty revision, 62–65, 70; Twenty-one Demands, 32–35, 38, 42, 92; warlord period, 50, 61; Washington Conference (1921–1922), 49–50, 58; Willard Straight's railroad plan, 25; World War I, 32, 35–36
China Incident. *See* Sino-Japanese War, Second
Chinchow-Aigun Railway, 25–26
Chinese Eastern Railway, 25
Chinese Nationalist Party. *See* Kuomintang
Christmas Memorandum, 64–65
Churchill, Winston, 169, 177–78, 233, 244; assets freeze, 190; Atlantic Conference, 199
Clark, J. Rueben, 55
Clayton, Will, 126
Clifford, John Garry, 180, 237
Cohen, Warren, 56, 79, 268

Cole, Wayne S., 189
Commerce Department, 123–24
commercial nondiscrimination: Konoe-Roosevelt summit, 202, 208–9, 211; Plan A, 219; Plan B clarifying notes, 220
Committee to Defend America by Aiding the Allies, 238
commodity credit (1933), 87–89
Conant, Charles A., 10, 24
Congress, 20, 30, 71, 82, 99, 100, 115, 119, 163, 174, 179; assets freeze, 189; containment, 117, 122–23, 125–26, 129, 132, 135–36, 146, 150, 153, 157, 171, 193; disarmament, 51; isolationists, 86, 94, 114, 125; naval buildup, 94–95; Versailles Treaty, 42
Conroy, Hilary, 204
containment: balance of power, 14; cautious version of, 223, 227–28; creation of, xiii; deterrence and, 14, 22, 77, 81, 85, 136, 140; diplomatic engagement, 16–17, 92, 112, 142–44, 217, 251; economic sanctions, 85; failure of, 212, 251, 256; goals and objectives change, xiv–xv, 179, 251; international support for, 140–41; Japanese moderates, 27, 41, 49; method changes, xiv; militarized, 20; public support, 123, 155–56, 237; policy abandoned, xv, 191; Russian program fails, xii; Second Sino-Japanese War, 110–11; successful containment and postwar Asia, 255–56; success of, xv, 86, 106, 141, 157, 165, 178, 193, 197, 208, 210, 232, 234; Taft, 13–14, 23–24; Theodore Roosevelt, 13–14, 16–17, 20; universalism, 113; Washington Conference, 49, 60; Wilson, 13–14; World War I, 32
Coolidge, Calvin, 143
Co-Prosperity Sphere, 18, 113, 121
Craigie, Robert, 152, 254, 307n37; approves of Plan B, 220
Cripps, Stafford, 172
Crowley, James, 109, 280n63
Curtiss-Wright, 89

Dallek, Robert, 201
Davis, Norman, 108, 134
Dawes, Charles, 76–77
deterrence, 22, 110–12, 116, 129–30, 143, 146, 196, 228; economic, 35, 52, 77, 82, 219; military, xii, 7, 13, 14, 20, 30–31, 81, 96–99, 134, 137, 219, 227; Russian, 11
Division of Controls. *See* Green, Joseph C.
Doenecke, Justus, 83
Dooman, Eugene, 85, 145, 150, 167, 288n5, 300n21; Hull's opposition to Konoe-Roosevelt summit, 202, 205
Dower, John, xvi, 197
Drought, James M., 157, 164
Dun, Edwin, 7
Dutch East Indies, 133, 136–37, 139, 177–79; assets freeze, 190–91; Batavia talks, 134, 168, 182, 284n47; destruction of oil wells, 131, 177, 194, 196, 234; Plan B, 220

economic sanctions, 112, 128–33, 171, 197, 282n23, 283n35, 284n44; steel embargo (1917), 35–36, 133; Far Eastern Crisis, 76–77, 82. *See also* assets freeze; preclusive purchasing
Einstein, Louis, 26
embargoes. *See* assets freeze; economic sanctions
enigma cipher, 174–75
Evatt, H. V., 242
Everest, Allen, 101, 280n3
export control. *See* economic sanctions
Export Control Act, 123
Export Control Division, 183
Export-Import Bank, 120, 125

Far Eastern Crisis, xiv, 74–84, 92, 110, 276

February 26 Incident, 105
Feis, Herbert, 115, 126–27, 132, 280n6
Ferrell, Robert, 180, 237
Fillmore, Millard, 1
Fitzpatrick, E. H., 21
Fleisher, Wilfrid, 206
Foreign Funds Control Committee. *See* assets freeze
Fourteen Points. *See* Versailles Conference
France: Brussels Conference, 109; defeat (1940), 120, 122, 128, 140, 152–53, 175; Knox railroad plan, 26, 50, 76, 120; Manchukuo, 80; South Manchuria, 19; Washington Conference, 55; World War I, 32, 43, 50; World War II, 111
Frankfurter, Felix, 252
French Indochina; xv, 128, 139, 177; Japan occupies northern French Indochina, 120, 171; Japan occupies southern French Indochina, 121, 133–34, 171, 178, 286n60, 294, 295n25; Plan B provides for Japanese evacuation from, 220
French West Africa, 173

Gardner, Lloyd C., 25
Garner, John Nance, 108
Garver, John W., 117
General Board: Anglo-Japanese Alliance, 11, 53; London Conference, 95; view of Japan, 83
"General Outline of a Solution for the Manchurian Problem," 72
German-American naval war, 200
Germany, 21, 26, 54; negotiated end to Sino-Japanese War, 147; relations with Japan, 80. *See also* Axis Alliance; Nazi-Soviet War
Gerow, Leonard T., 173–74, 194, 223; modus vivendi, 231; White memorandum, 231
Glad, Betty, 56
Glynn, James, 2
Graebner, Norman, 204
Grant, Frederick Dent, 21
Grant, Ulysses S., 3
Graziani, Rodolfo. *See* North African campaign
Great Britain, 19, 26, 71, 120, 173; Admiralty, 224; Amau declaration, 89; American destroyers to, 140; appeasement of Japan, 90–91, 102–3, 131, 152; assets freeze, 179, 184, 188, 190; backs firm policy against Japan, 152, 163, 291n50; Brussels Conference, 109; China, 25–26, 32, 61–66, 85, 102, 114, 137; doubts Japan will fight ABD, 222, 233, 307n37; Far Eastern Crisis, 76, 78–79; Hull-Nomura-Kurusu talks, 240–41, 243–44; Knox railroad plan, 26; negotiated end to Sino-Japanese War, 107, 147; Open Door, 8, 11, 24, 35; overestimates military power, 224; reaction to Tojo, 221; sanctions, 140, 190, 295n35; South Manchuria, 19, 33; steel embargo (1917), 36; threat to Hawaii, 7; Twenty-one Demands, 34; Washington Conference, 51–52, 56–58; White peace plan, 229–30; World War I, 43; World War II, Europe, 152, 158, 163, 171–75, 177–78, 181, 196, 234–35, 284
Greater East Asian Co-Prosperity Sphere, 18, 113, 121
Great Depression, 71
Great White Fleet, xiii, 112, 134, 143
Green, Joseph C., 187–88
Greene, Roger. *See* Committee to Defend America by Aiding the Allies
Gresham, Walter, 5
Grew, Joseph: Amau declaration, 89; effect of German victories on Japan, 152; failure of American containment, 193; Far Eastern Crisis, 74, 78, 82, 84; goodwill

visits, 91–92; Hull-Nomura-Kurusu talks, 249; Hull-Nomura talks, 163–66, 291; inability to influence Washington, 254; Konoe-Roosevelt summit, 200, 205–6, 208, 210–11; London Naval Conference, 96–97, 99; military deterrence, 96, 134; negotiations for a new commercial treaty, 148–51, 154–55; occupation of southern Indochina, 179; sanctions, 122, 147–49, 152; Tojo's appointment, 222
Griscom, Lloyd, 18
Griswold, A. Whitney, 19
Grunert, George, 136, 197
Guam, 8, 42
Guthrie, George, 31

Hackworth, Green H., 77
Halifax, Earl of, 234–35; concern over Hull-Nomura talks, 164; modus vivendi, 241, 243–44
Hamaguchi, Osayuki, 70, 72
Hamilton, Maxwell: Chinese commodity credit, 116–17; Chinese loans, 119–20; Hull-Nomura-Kurusu talks, 249, 309, 310n69; Hull-Nomura talks, 162, 166, 169, 290n47; Hull Note, 309, 310n69; John Doe Associates, 159; "Magic" decryption system, 310; moral embargo, 124; Nazi-Soviet War, 171, 173–74; negotiations on preliminary agreement, 213; opposes assets freeze, 180–81, 187–88; southern French Indochina, 179; supports economic sanctions, 116; Tojo's appointment, 222, 249; White memorandum and redrafts, 231, 244–49
Hara, Kei, 41–43
Hara, Yoshimichi, 121, 151; reaction to Hull note, 251
Harding, Warren G., 49, 51
Harriman, E. H., 18
Harriman, W. Averell, 126
Hart, Albert Bushnell, 38
Hata, Ikuhiko, 280n63
Hay, John: Open Door Notes, 8–9
Hayashi, Senjuro, 105–6
Hayashi, Tadasu, 19, 262
Hawaii, 31, 42, 47, 117; 1897 crisis, 7–8; US fleet stationed at, 77, 81–82, 132, 134, 136–37, 156
Heinrichs, Waldo, 203
Higashikuni, 216
Hippisley, Alfred E., 8
Hiranuma, Kiichiro, 147
Hirohito, 75, 105, 165; Konoe-Roosevelt summit, 198–99; orders Tojo to form government, 217; "wipe the slate clean" injunction, 218
Hirota, Koki, 89, 91, 93, 98, 105, 280n63
Hiss, Alger: advocates assets freeze, 182
Hobson, Richard Henry, 28–29
Hoover, Herbert, 55, 71; Far Eastern Crisis, 74, 76, 81–82, 96
Hopkins, Harry, 171, 173, 252
Horinouchi, Kensuke, 150
Hornbeck, Stanley K., 68, 88, 112, 117, 237, 252, 288n6; aid for China, 119; Amau declaration, 89; Brussels Conference, 109; Chinese nationalism threatens Open Door, 62; comprehensive statement of American principles, 244; deterrence, 96, 116, 253–54; diplomatic agreement with Japan, general, 142–43, 151, 156, 164, 212, 265; Japanese military capabilities, 159, 181, 195, 223–24, 235; Far Eastern Crisis, 75–77, 82–83; Hull-Nomura-Kurusu talks, 232, 244; Hull-Nomura talks, 160–62, 164–65, 167, 292n62; importance of the Open Door, 34; influence on Hull, 195; Japanese goodwill visits, 91–92; John Doe Associates,

Hornbeck, Stanley K. *(cont.)* 157, 159–61; Konoe-Roosevelt summit, 194–95, 211; London naval talks, 99; MacMurray review of American Far Eastern Diplomacy, 93–94; "Magic" decryption system, 253, 310n5; moral embargo, 124; navy expansion, 134; negative view of Japan, 85, 111, 145–46, 254, 265n33, 290n45; negotiated end to Sino-Japanese War, 144, 146; Nine Power Treaty, 55; Price Committee, 140; reaction to Pearl Harbor, 253; Russia card, 295; Shantung question, 57; Sino-Japanese relations, 86–87, 91–92; southern French Indochina, 179; support for sanctions, 111, 116, 132, 183; supports Soviet Union against Japan, 96; underestimates chance of war, 181, 234, 253; Versailles Conference, 42; vision of a new Japan, 251, 255; White plan, 231; Yonai, 151

Hoshino, Naokoi, 121

Ho-Umezu agreement, 107

House Military Affairs Committee, 125

Howard, Frank, 124

Hu, Shi, 120, 243

Hughes, Charles Evans, 41; Washington Conference, 50–58

Hughes, William, 90

Hull, Cordell, 57, 88, 102, 109, 115, 117, 142, 154, 160, 178, 194, 223, 252; antipathy toward Japan, 108; assets freeze, 185–88; Axis Alliance, 155; China and modus vivendi, 244; commodity credit, 116–17; discounts Japanese military capability, 235; four principles, 153, 162, 219; Franco's Spain, 176–77; health, 238; historians view of, 102, 282n23; Hull Note, 244, 249, 252, 255; improved relations with Japan, 92–93; Konoe-Roosevelt summit, 199–202; Kurusu, 232; leaks B-17 deployment, 306n22; London Naval Conference, 98–99; Lothian proposal, 152–53; maneuvers to oust Matsuoka, 166–68; modus vivendi proposals, 235, 238–44; negotiated end to Second Sino-Japanese War, 144, 209, 287n1; opposes new commercial treaty, 150–51; Pearl Harbor attack, 252; Pearl Harbor Congressional Committee, 249; sanctions against Japan, 122–23, 129, 131; preclusive purchasing, 126; Vladivostok-bound tankers, 206–8, 301n34. *See also* Hull-Nomura-Kurusu talks; Hull-Nomura talks

Hull, Rose Francis Whitney, 185–86

Hull-Nomura-Kurusu talks, 232, 240–41, 243–44, 249

Hull-Nomura talks, 157–69, 200–202, 291n56, 292n60

Iberian Peninsula. *See* Spain

Iceland, 173

Ickes, Harold, 85, 108, 130; assets freeze, 185; Japanese military capabilities, 195, 228; modus vivendi, 235–36; Nazi-Soviet War, 174

Iguchi, Takeo, 204, 242

immigration controversies, 7, 17, 22–23, 29, 31, 47, 59, 83, 143

Imperial Japanese Army: Axis Alliance, 138; control faction, 105–6, 144; general staff, 67–68, 107, 110, 144, 218–19; imperial way faction, 105; northern French Indochina, 120–21, 171, 179; southern French Indochina, 133–34, 178; total war faction, 277n29; victory in Pacific War, 298n9; war plans, 20, 43

Imperial Japanese Navy: Axis Alliance, 137; first committee, 138–39,

286n63; fleet faction, 51, 81, 97–98; general staff, 71–72, 97, 286n59; ministry, 97–98, 103, 138; southern French Indochina, 133–34, 178; treaty faction, 51, 81, 97
Ingersoll, Royal, 223–24
Inner Mongolia, 33–35, 37, 45–46
Inoue, Junnosuke, 46, 71
International Banking Consortium for China, 31, 42–46, 55
interventionists, xiv, 125, 235
Inukai, Tsuyoshi, 75–76, 79, 98
Iran, 175
Iraq, 175, 256
Iriye, Akira, 203
Ishii, Akiko, 205
Ishii, Kikujiro. *See* Lansing-Ishii Agreement
Ishikawa, Shingo, 138
Ishiwara, Kanji, 72, 74, 107
isolationists, xiv, 21, 76, 106, 114, 117, 125, 129, 135
Issekikai, 73
Italy, 109
Ito, Hirobumi, 9, 23
Iwakura, Hideo, 160, 166

Japan: cabinet planning board, 198; efforts to improve relations with United States, 91–92; expansion as part of national character, 194; foreign ministry, 67; loans to China, 44; Meiji modernization, 4; Monroe Doctrine for Asia, 37–38; popular perception of the United States, 47, 206–8; pro-Anglo-American policy, 22–23; postwar, 255; ultranationalists, 73; war plans, 20, 43; war ministry, 75, 144
Japanese-American War, 20–21, 27
Japanism. *See* Japan: ultranationalists
Jeans, Roger B., 242
John Doe Associates, 157, 200. *See also* Frank Walker
Johnson, Hiram, 135
Johnson, Nelson T., 63, 70, 119, 144
Jones, Jesse, 126

Kahn, Julius, 43
Kanagawa Treaty, 2–3
Kanaya, Hanza, 75
Kaneko, Kentaro, 15
Kan'in, 121
Kase, Tohikazu, 303n53
Kato, Kanji, 71, 97–98
Kato, Komei, 32
Kato, Tomosaburo, 51, 97
Katsura, Taro, xi–xii, 17
Kawada, Isao, 121
Kaya, Okinori, 219
Kellogg, Frank, 62–65; Kellogg-Briand Pact, 21, 77
Kennedy, J. Russell, 31
Kido, Koichi, 75, 216, 303n55
Kimball, Warren F., xvi
King, Ernest, 136
Kita, Ikki, 73, 105
Knox, Frank, 111, 136, 174, 217; doubts Japan will attack United States, 228
Knox, Philander, 24, 28, 31, 34, 44, 46, 55, 60, 81; railroad plan, 25–26; Treaty of Commerce and Navigation, 28–29
Kobayashi, Seizo, 139
Komura, Jutaro, 17, 23, 26
Konoe, Fumimaro, 91, 120, 157–59, 165, 190, 194–95; Axis Alliance, 121, 156, 160, 164–66, 193; Japanese expansion, 100, 133, 178; resignation, 215–16, 303n56; terms for China, 107, 110; three principles, 163; withdraws recognition from Chiang, 110. *See also* Konoe-Roosevelt summit
Konoe cabinet, 120–21
Konoe-Roosevelt summit, 198–203; Hull leaks information on, 205–6, 301n30; likely outcome of, 203–5; negotiations on preliminary agreement, 208–9, 211, 213–14

Koo, Wellington, 75, 80, 117
Korea, 5–6, 15; Japanese annexation of, 27, 265; origins of Russo-Japanese War, 11; Taft-Katsura, 17
Korean-American relations, 5
Krock, Arthur, 84, 227, 249
Kroner, Hayes, 209, 215
Kung, H. H., 101
Kuomintang, 40, 50, 60, 62, 69; declining control in north China, 104–5; treaty revision, 62–65, 70
Kurusu, Saburo, 221, 227, 231, 240, 254, 306n22
Kwantung Army, 27, 58–59, 73; Far Eastern Crisis, 74

Ladybird, HMS, 109
Lamont, Thomas, 43–46, 53, 268, 307, 308n46
Lampson, Miles, 49, 65
Lansdowne, Marquis of, 262n28, 265n33
Langdon, William, 222
Lansing, Robert, 32, 34–36, 40–43, 142
Lansing-Ishii Agreement, xiii, 37–39, 45, 51, 56, 58, 62, 89, 92–93, 143
Lassiter, William, 76
Lattimore, Owen, 243
Lea, Homer, 21
League of Nations, 42–43, 50; Far Eastern Crisis, 74, 76, 79–80; Chinese infrastructure development committee, 88
Leahy, William D., 135
Lebanon, 175
Lee, Raymond E., 232
Leith-Ross, Frederick, 103
Lend-Lease, 127, 141, 163, 175
likin, 62
Lippmann, Walter, 76, 154
Lockwood, William W., 234
Lodge, Henry Cabot, 265. *See also* Lodge Corollary to the Monroe Doctrine
Lodge Corollary to the Monroe Doctrine, 27–28
London Naval Conference (1935), 95–99; Japanese Navy Ministry opposition to, 98; State Department opposition to Japanese cruiser parity, 96
London Naval Treaty, 58, 71, 143
Long, Breckenridge, 35, 42, 45
Lothian, Lord, 131, 152, 156, 164
Loudon, Alexander, 241–43
Lowell, A. Lawrence, 82
Lytton Commission, 79, 81

MacArthur, Douglas, 136, 197
MacArthur, R. S., 6
MacDonald, Ramsay, 79
MacMurray, John Van Antwerp, 49, 59, 69; Christmas Memorandum, 64–65; international banking consortium for China, 45; review of American Far Eastern Diplomacy, 93–94; Shanghai Incident, 61; Shantung question, 57; treaty revision, 61–64; Tsinan Incident, 68; Turkey, 175–76
MacVeagh, Charles, 60
"Magic" decryption system, 179, 184, 200, 205, 214, 239
Malaya, 137
Malta, 175
Manchuria, 22, 25, 37, 59, 93, 95, 273; American loans to, 60, 68; importance to Japan, 17–18, 27, 56, 67, 70–71, 273; importance to the United States, 18, 56; international banking consortium for China, 45–46; Japan reinforces, 190; Sino-Japanese joint defense of, 40; Taft-Katsura, 17; Twenty-one Demands, 33–35. *See also* Open Door; Far Eastern Crisis
Manchukuo, xiv, 50, 76, 79, 93, 146
Marco Polo Bridge Incident, 82, 106–7, 183
Marshall, George C., 252; Burma Road, 223; Marshall-Stark

memorandum (November 5), 224–27; November 15 interview, 226; Philippine reinforcements, 136–37, 197
Masland, John W., 156
Matsudaira, Tsuneo, 71, 76
Matsumoto, Shigeharu, 204
Matsuoka, Yosuke, 79, 121, 157, 160–61, 163–64, 166, 172, 284n47, 291n51
May 30 Incident. *See* Shanghai Incident
McCormick, Medill, 43
McKinley, William, 8
Meiji, 218
Meiji Restoration, 3; impact on American-Japanese relations, 4–7
Metals Reserve Company, 120, 128
Mexico, 265. *See also* Lodge Corollary to the Monroe Doctrine
Meyer, George V. L., 16
Miles, Sherman, 189–90, 196, 209; Tojo's appointment, 222
Millard, Thomas, 43, 78
Miller, Hunter, 77
Min, 10
Minami, Jiro, 72, 74
Minseito Party, 69–72
missionaries: impact on American-Japanese relations, 4, 6, 28–29
Mitsubishi 96 bomber, 97
modus vivendi proposals, 235, 238–44
Moley, Raymond, 84
Monroe Doctrine for China, 37–38, 113, 183
moral embargo, 123–24, 128, 132, 146, 150
Morgenthau, Henry, 108, 124; Chinese currency reform, 99–104; Chinese silver purchase, 114–15, 280n3; commodity credits, 115–19, 281n15; Hull-Nomura-Kurusu talks, 244; preclusive purchasing, 125; rejects modus vivendi, 228, 236, 307n44; Russian card, 117–18; supports oil embargo, 131
Morley, James William, xvi
Morris, Roland, 45
Morrison, USS, 1
Mukden Incident, 73, 77, 81, 107, 183, 273n52
Mutsu, Munemitsu, 17

Nagano, Osami, 138–39, 198; advocates early start to hostilities, 218–19, 286n63, 298n9; rejects Plan B, 220
Nanking, fall of (1938), 110
Nanking Incident, 66, 280n62
National Defense Act, 132, 156
National Origins Act, 59, 140
Navy, US, 77, 122, 223; expansion of, 82, 94–95, 134–36; reinforcement of Philippines, 136; strength on eve of war, 223–24, 226, 228; undeclared German-American naval war, 200; World War I buildup, 51. *See also* General Board; Knox, Frank
Nazi-Soviet Pact, 145, 147
Nazi-Soviet War, 134, 210, 235, 255; assets freeze, 182; Japanese foreign and military policy, 169, 173–74, 180–82, 190, 198, 222, 284, 285n49; limits use of German military elsewhere, 172–73, 177; US foreign policy, xv, 172, 198, 217; United States sees as imminent, 163, 168–69, 172
Netherlands, 125; assets freeze, 184; modus vivendi, 241, 243
New York Commercial Advertiser, 9
New York Daily News, 237
New York Times, 3, 7, 8, 10, 130, 237
New Zealand, 53
Nikolaevsky incident, 41
Nine Power Treaty. *See* Washington Conference
Nomonhan, Battle of, 141, 145, 147, 287n67
Nomura, Kichisaburo, 87, 147–50, 157–60, 162–64, 166–67, 179, 186, 250, 254; Konoe-Roosevelt summit, 199, 201–2, 204, 206–7, 209, 213–14. *See also* Hull-Nomura talks

Norris, George, 63, 135
North African campaign, 175, 235, 255
Northern Expedition, 64, 66–67

occupied Japan, 255
Oda, Nobunaga, 1
O'Brien, Thomas, 19
Ohl, J. K., 26
Oikawa, Koshiro, 138, 198–99, 214, 224
oil embargo. *See* assets freeze
oil exports, 182–83
Okada, Kikiusaburo, 133–34
Okuma, Shigenobu, 35
Oliphant, Herman, 124
O'Malley, Owen, 64
Open Door notes. *See* Open Door policy
Open Door policy, xvi, 11, 13, 20, 22, 29–30, 36, 183; Amau declaration, 89; Chinese threat to, 62; first Open Door note, 8–9; German threat to, 16; integral part of US foreign policy, xii–xv, 13–14, 23, 32, 34, 60, 85, 113; interpretations of, xii, 51, 57, 60, 81; Japanese support for, xiii, 9–11, 262; Japanese threat to, xii, 12–14, 33, 104; Manchuria, 18–20, 46, 263; Nine Power Treaty, 56; Russia threat to, xii, 11, 63; Russo-Japanese War, 16; second Open Door note, 9; World War I, 32; Oshima, Hiroshi, 172
Ott, Eugene, 147, 150
Oumansky, Constantine, 141

Pacific War, xv–xvi, 11, 21, 254; impact on postwar Japan, 255–56
Panama Canal, 76, 182
Panay, USS, 109, 183, 288n14
Pearl Harbor, xv–xvi, 20, 22, 58, 137, 252; US fleet deployed to, 132, 136, 156; Japanese fleet departs for, 308n51
Pearson, Drew, 188
Peck, Willys, 75, 101
Peking Tariff Conference, 63–64
Perry, Mathew, 1–3
Philadelphia Inquirer, 237
Philippines, 8, 19–21, 24, 31, 128, 179, 252; British plan to base capital ship force in, 224; reinforcement of, 136–37, 139, 156, 177, 196–97, 224, 227
Philippine Scouts, 136
Philips, William, 102–3
Pittman, Key, 140
Placentia Bay. *See* Atlantic Conference
Plan A, 219
Plan B, 219–21, 304nn7–8; compared to American draft modus vivendi, 239–40; Hull rejects, 239; Nomura and Kurusu present, 231
Popham, Robert Brooke, 177
Port Arthur, Battle of, 16
Porter resolution, 65
Portsmouth Treaty, xiii, 14–16, 26
Preble, USS, 1
preclusive purchasing, 124–28, 146, 171, 283nn29–30
Price, Frank and Harry. *See* American Committee for Non-Participation in Japanese Aggression
Price Committee. *See* American Committee for Non-Participation in Japanese Aggression
public opinion, 141, 146–47, 153, 156, 171, 178–79; assets freeze, 188–89; Axis Alliance, 155–56; export restrictions, 184; interventionist foreign policy, 238, 242; Japan, 4–7, 47, 112; Japanese military capability, 236; modus vivendi, 237; naval expansion, 135, 140
Purvis, Arthur, 118, 131

Quarantine Speech (Roosevelt), 108
Quezon, Manuel, 136
Quo, Tai-chi, 117

race, xi, xvi, 113, 197
Raeder, Eric, 174

Rajchman, Ludwig, 88, 276n7
Rea, George Bronson, 13
Reading, Lord, 40
Reconstruction Finance Corporation, 125
Red Army, 147, 172–73, 181, 190, 196, 211, 235
Reed, David, 71
Reed, James, xvi, 29
Reinsch, Paul, 33–35
Reventlow, Graf von, 21
Richardson, James O., 137
Rockhill, William W., 8, 18, 26
Rodgers, William L., 55
rollback, 179, 183, 251–53
Rommel, Erwin. *See* North African campaign
Roosevelt, Franklin D., xiv, xvi, 85, 104, 109, 115, 125, 131, 136, 155, 174, 178, 195, 232; aircraft production, 136; assets freeze, 184–85, 188, 296nn38–39; cabinet support, 228; containment policy evaluated, 112; deploys fleet to Pearl Harbor, 132, 136; dismisses Japanese military capability, 147–48; European war, 238–39; John Doe Associates, 157; Konoe-Roosevelt summit, 201; maneuvering Japan into firing first shot, 241–42; modus vivendi proposals, 227, 231, 236, 238, 242; naval expansion, 94–95; negative views of Japan, 83–84; Pearl Harbor attack, 253; Pearl Harbor conspiracy dismissed, xvi; promises Halifax support, 242; proposes Indochina neutralization, 179; tung oil credit, 118
Roosevelt, Theodore, 142; Anglo-Japanese Alliance, 11; Boxer Rebellion, 9; containment policy, xiii, 13–23; perception of Japan, 14–15, 23; reaction to Taft's Far Eastern diplomacy, 26
Root, Elihu, 15, 52, 56, 76; Root Resolution, 270; Root-Takahira Agreement, xiii, 19–20, 22, 51, 56, 58, 92–93, 143
Royal Navy: Battle of the Atlantic, 174; World War I expansion, 51
Rubber Reserve Company, 127
Russia, 19, 21, 26, 50; civil war, 30; revolution, 30, 40
Russo-Japanese Alliance (1910), 27
Russo-Japanese Alliance (1916), 35, 40
Russo-Japanese War, 11–12, 15, 253; Japanese goals, 262n28; impact on US-Japanese relations, xii, 12, 14–16, 20; origins of, xi–xii, 11, 253

Sagan, Scott D., 204
Saionji, Kimmochi, 24, 27, 32
Saito, Hiroshi, 93
Saito, Makino, 84
Saito, Makoto, 93, 105
Sakhalin, 49
San Francisco Examiner, 90
Sato, Naotoke, 106
Sato, Kenryo, 254
Sayre, Francis, 153–54
Schroeder, Paul, 212
Schwellenbach, Lewis, 140
Seiyukai Party, 66–67
Sekigahara, Battle of, 1
Selective Service Act, 153, 289n24
Shanghai: Far Eastern Crisis, 77–79
Shanghai Incident, 61
Shantung, 32–37, 42, 49, 51, 57
Shaw, Leslie, 27
Sherman, John, 7
Shidehara, Kijuro, 46, 61, 66, 70–71, 74; coauthor of Plan B, 220, 304n8
Shigemitsu, Mamaoru, 70
Shigeru, Yoshida: coauthor of Plan B, 220
Shimada, Shigetaro, 218
Shiratori, Toshio, 91
Showa Restoration, 105
Sian Incident, 106
Siberian intervention, 40–41, 57

Sill, John M. B., 5
Silver Purchase Act, 100
Simon, John, 76, 89–90
Singapore, 137, 152, 163, 177, 179; protected by Philippine-based airpower, 224
Sino-Japanese War, First, 5–7, 9, 22, 253
Sino-Japanese War, Second, xiv, 141; Axis and French Indochina, 121–22; German mediation, 109; Japanese peace terms, 110, 209; origins of, 278, 279n51; and US-Japanese negotiations, 162, 165–67, 208, 211
Soong, T. V., 80, 88; Hull-Nomura-Kurusu talks, 244
Southeast Asia, postwar, 256
South Manchuria Railway, 22, 25, 27, 33, 45, 70, 73–74
Soviet-Japanese Neutrality Pact, 121, 141, 290n45
Soviet Union, 54, 70; collapse of, 256; five-year plans, 70, 72; influence in China, 281n11; relations with United States, 83, 86, 110, 141; relations with Japan, 80, 106, 141. *See also* Nazi-Soviet War
Spain, 172, 176–77
Spanish-American War, 7; impact on American-Japanese relations, 8
Spring-Rice, Cecil, 15
Standard Oil, 60, 124
Stark, Harold, 137, 174, 189, 223–24, 252; discounts likelihood of Japanese attack, 226–27; White memorandum, 231. *See also* Marshall-Stark memorandum
State Department, Division of Far Eastern Affairs (FE), 88, 102; comprehensive statement of American principles, 244; John Doe Associates, 160; opposition to improved American-Japanese relations, 93; support for the Soviet Union over Japan, 96; White memorandum redrafts, 244–49
Steinhardt, Laurence, 172–73
Stimson, Henry, 70–71, 129, 131, 194; assets freeze, 185; Axis Alliance, 155–57, 237–38; Borah letter, 79; cabinet, 228; convoys, 174; deterrence, 81–82, 129–30, 134, 141, 145, 254, 280n1; discounts likelihood of Japanese attack, 242, 251–52; economic sanctions, 132, 141, 186, 282; Far Eastern Crisis, 74–79, 81–83; Hull and B-17 leak, 306n22; Japanese duplicity, 194; Konoe-Roosevelt summit, 194, 200; last-minute compromise, 251–52; maneuvering Japan into firing first shot, 241; modus vivendi proposals, 227, 235, 241–42; navy caution, 226; Nazi-Soviet War, 173; opposes mediation for Sino-Japanese War, 130; Pearl Harbor attack, 252–53; Philippine reinforcements, 136–37, 224, 227; sanctions, 130; Soviet influence in China, 281; state department, 282n23; Stimson Doctrine, 77–78; tung oil credit, 118; war with Japan inevitable, 83
Straight, Willard, 22, 24–26
Strategic Materials Agreement, 128
Strong, George, 136
Stuart, John Leighton, 29, 63
Suez Canal, 172–73, 175
Sugihara, Seishiro, 204
Sugiyama, Gen, 121, 199, 280n63; opposes Plan B, 220
Suzuki, Teiichi, 215, 219
Syria, 175
Sze, Alfred, 86, 103

Taft, William Howard, 31, 34, 44, 60, 110, 129; containment policy, 13–14, 23–30; Japanese immigration to United States, 17; sympathy for China, 24
Taft-Katsura agreement, 17, 22, 24, 27, 58, 143, 265

Takahira, Kogoro. *See* Root, Elihu: Root-Takahira agreement
Takahashi, Korekiyo, 52, 105
Taketomi, Toshihiko, 88
Tanaka, Giichi, 41, 66–67, 69–70
Tanaka, Kunishige, 56
Tangku Truce, 80
Terasaki, Hidenari, 193
Terauchi, Masatake, 37
Thailand, 128, 139, 178, 252
Togo, Heihachiro, xii, 218
Togo, Shigenori, 218–21; extends deadline, 240; reaction to Hull Note, 250–51, 310n70
Tojo, Hideki, 198–99, 214, 216, 302, 303n54; American reaction, 221–22; forms cabinet, 217–18; modus vivendi, 240, 254, 308n51; reaction to Hull note, 251, 254
Tokugawa, Iyesato, 91
Tokugawa Japan: collapse, 3; isolation policy, 1–2
Tomioka, Sadatoshi, 286nn59–61
Toyoda, Teijiro, 198
Trautmann, Oscar, 109
Treasury Department: and Far Eastern Diplomacy, 104. *See also* Morgenthau, Henry
Treaty of Commerce and Navigation (1911), 29–30, 122–23, 129, 146, 150–51, 156
Treaty of Kanagawa, 2
Treaty of Shimonoseki, 6
Tripartite Pact. *See* Axis Alliance
Triple Entente, 26
Triple Intervention, 6, 10
Tsinan Incident, 68
Tsukada, Ko: opposes Plan B, 220
Tsunoda, Jun, 204, 286n60, n63
Tsushima Straits, Battle of, 16, 218
Tuan, Ch'i-jui, 61
Tugwell, Rexford, 84
Turkey, 128, 175–76
Turner, Richmond Kelly, 189
Twenty-one Demands, 32–35, 38, 42, 92

Uchida, Yasuya, 68–69
United States Maritime Commission. *See* oil exports
Universal Trading Corporation, 118
Ushiba, Tomohiko, 212
Utley, Jonathan, 282n23

Versailles Conference, 41, 42, 43, 47, 50, 57
Vevier, Charles, 25
Vichy France, 175
Vinson-Trammell Acts, 82, 95, 97, 135–36, 146, 150, 153, 255; impact on Japanese Navy, 137–39, 214

Wakasugi, Kaname, 166, 213–14
Wakatsuki, Reijiro, 66, 74–75, 79
Walden, George, 183
Walker, Frank, 157; delivers purported Japanese terms, 158–60
Walsh, James E., 157
Wang, Chiang-wei, 120, 146, 160, 209, 230, 281, 282n18
Wang, C. T., 70
Wang, Wempu, 272
War Department: Japanese capabilities and intentions, 196; Nazi-Soviet War, 172–73; strategic estimates, 195–96
war scares, 17, 20–21, 47, 79, 92, 191
War Trade Board, 35–36
war warning, 252
Washington Conference (1921–1922), 49–50, 58–60, 84, 92, 94, 110, 143; and Anglo-Japanese Alliance, 53–55; Four Power Pact, 54; Naval Treaty, 51–53, 79; Nine Power Treaty, 55, 78, 89, 146, 247, 270; postconference cruiser race, 53, 71; Shantung Treaty, 57
Washington Treaty System. *See* Washington Conference
Watanabe, Kazan, 105
Webb-Heney Alien Land Act, 31
Weddell, Alexander, 176
Wedemeyer, Albert C., 256

Welles, Sumner, 118, 223, 296, 297n41; assets freeze, 185–88; Konoe-Roosevelt summit, 213–14; naval expansion, 134–35; sanctions, 131
Wellesley, Victor, 89
Wheeler, Burton K., 63, 189
White, Harry Dexter, 104, 125, 128, 131–32, 155; memorandum, 228–31; memorandum redrafts, 244–49
Wilhelm II, 15
Williams, E. T., 34–35, 39, 42–43, 57
Williams, John, 99
Williams, William Appleman, xvi, 217
Wilmington News, 237
Wilson, Woodrow: containment policy of, xiii, 13–14, 30–46, 143; Fourteen Points, 41; Siberian Intervention, 40–41
Woodin, William, 100
Woodring, Henry, 129
World War I, 30, 32, 43
World War II. *See* Atlantic, Battle of; North African campaign; Nazi-Soviet War
Wray, Harry, 56

Yamagata, Aritomo, xii, 41
Yamamoto, Gonnohyoe, xi–xii
Yamato class battleship, 97
Yap Island, 51
Yarnell, Harry, 146, 288n6
Yasukuni Shrine, 218
Yergin, Daniel, 284n44
Yonai, Mitsumasa, 131, 150–51, 280n63
Yoshizawa, Kenkichi, 61, 65
Yost, Charles W., 187
Yuan, Shikai, 29, 50

Studies in Conflict, Diplomacy, and Peace

Series Editors

George C. Herring, Andrew L. Johns, and Kathryn C. Statler

This series focuses on key moments of conflict, diplomacy, and peace from the eighteenth century to the present to explore their wider significance in the development of U.S. foreign relations. The series editors welcome new research in the form of original monographs, interpretive studies, biographies, and anthologies from historians, political scientists, journalists, and policymakers. A primary goal of the series is to examine the United States' engagement with the world, its evolving role in the international arena, and the ways in which the state, nonstate actors, individuals, and ideas have shaped and continue to influence history, both at home and abroad.

Books in the Series

The Gulf: The Bush Presidencies and the Middle East
Michael F. Cairo

Nothing Less Than War: A New History of America's Entry into World War I
Justus D. Doenecke

The Currents of War: A New History of American-Japanese Relations, 1899–1941
Sidney Pash